THE HARVARD CLASSICS

The Five-Foot Shelf of Books

Virgil's Æneid

TRANSLATED BY JOHN DRYDEN

With Introductions and Notes
Volume 13

THE HARVARD CLASSICS
EDITED BY CHARLES W. ELIOT, LL.D.

P. F. Collier & Son Corporation
NEW YORK

Copyright, 1937
By P. F. Collier & Son Corporation

Copyright, 1909
By P. F. Collier & Son

MANUFACTURED IN U. S. A.

CONTENTS

	PAGE
Dedication	5
The First Book of the Æneis	73
The Second Book of the Æneis	100
The Third Book of the Æneis	128
The Fourth Book of the Æneis	152
The Fifth Book of the Æneis	178
The Sixth Book of the Æneis	207
The Seventh Book of the Æneis	239
The Eighth Book of the Æneis	268
The Ninth Book of the Æneis	293
The Tenth Book of the Æneis	321
The Eleventh Book of the Æneis	355
The Twelfth Book of the Æneis	389
Postscript to the Reader	424

INTRODUCTORY NOTE

Publius Vergilius Maro, the friend of Augustus and the great representative poet of the first age of the Roman Empire, was a man of humble origin. Born Oct. 15, B. C. 70, the son of a small farmer near Mantua in Northern Italy, he was educated at Cremona, Milan, and Rome. Probably as a result of the turmoil of the Civil Wars, Virgil seems to have returned to his native district, where he was engaged for some time in writing his "Eclogues." Though he was never a soldier, and though there is no evidence of his having taken any part in politics, he suffered severely from the results of the wars. His father's farm lay within the territory which was confiscated by the Triumvirs for the purpose of bestowing grants of land upon their soldiers, and Virgil succeeded in having it restored only through the personal intervention of Octavianus, the future emperor. But a change of governors deprived him of protection, and he was forced to desert his heritage in peril of death, escaping only by swimming the river Mincio. The rest of his life was spent farther south, in Rome, Naples, Sicily, and elsewhere. As he gained reputation he became the possessor of a large fortune, bestowed upon him by the generosity of friends and patrons, the most distinguished of whom, apart from Augustus, was Mæcenas, the center of the literary society of the day. The "Eclogues" had been finished in B. C. 37, and in B. C. 30 he published his great poem on farming, the "Georgics." It is characteristic of his laborious method of composition that this work of little more than 2,000 lines occupied him for seven years.

The completion of the "Georgics" established Virgil's position as the chief poet of his time; and at this momentous date, when, the Civil Wars over, the victorious Augustus was laying the foundations of imperial government, the poem which was to be the supreme expression of the national life was begun. At the end of eleven years Virgil had written the whole of the "Æneid," and planned to devote three more to its final revision. But this revision was never accomplished, for returning from Athens with Augustus in B. C. 19, he was seized with illness and died on September 21. He was buried at Naples, where his tomb was long a place of religious pilgrimage.

The modern appreciation of the "Iliad" and the "Odyssey" has tended to carry with it a depreciation of the "Æneid," the spirit of which appeals less forcibly to the taste of our time. But it is foolish to lose sight of the splendor of a poet who, for nearly two thousand years, has been one of the most powerful factors in European culture. "The concurrent testimony of the most refined minds of all times," says one of the finest of his critics, "marks him out as one of the greatest masters of the language which touches the heart or moves the manlier sensibilities, who has ever lived. A mature and mellow truth of sentiment, a conformity to the deeper experiences of life in every age, a fine humanity as well as a generous elevation of feeling, and some magical charm of music in his words, have enabled them to serve many minds in many ages as a symbol of some swelling thought or overmastering emotion, the force and meaning of which they could scarcely define to themselves."

The subtler elements of the exquisite style of Virgil no translator can ever hope to reproduce; but Dryden was a master of English versification, and the content of Virgil's epic is here rendered in vigorous and nervous couplets. "Despite many revolutions of public taste," says Professor Noyes, Dryden's latest editor, "Dryden's Virgil still remains practically without a rival as the standard translation of the greatest Roman poet; the only one that, like two or three versions of Homer, has become an English classic."

Dryden's "Dedication" is an excellent example of his prose style, and gives an interesting view of the method and standpoint of the greatest of English seventeenth century critics.

TO THE
MOST HONORABLE
JOHN, LORD MARQUIS OF NORMANBY
EARL OF MULGRAVE, &C.

AND KNIGHT OF THE MOST NOBLE ORDER OF THE GARTER

A HEROIC poem, truly such, is undoubtedly the greatest work which the soul of man is capable to perform. The design of it is to form the mind to heroic virtue by example. 'Tis convey'd in verse, that it may delight, while it instructs: the action of it is always one, entire, and great. The least and most trivial episodes, or underactions, which are interwoven in it, are parts either necessary or convenient to carry on the main design; either so necessary, that, without them, the poem must be imperfect, or so convenient, that no others can be imagin'd more suitable to the place in which they are. There is nothing to be left void in a firm building; even the cavities ought not to be fill'd with rubbish, (which is of a perishable kind, destructive to the strength,) but with brick or stone, tho' of less pieces, yet of the same nature, and fitted to the crannies. Even the least portions of them must be of the epic kind: all things must be grave, majestical, and sublime; nothing of a foreign nature, like the trifling *novels* which Ariosto and others have inserted in their poems; by which the reader is misled into another sort of pleasure, opposite to that which is design'd in an epic poem. One raises the soul, and hardens it to virtue; the other softens it again, and unbends it into vice. One conduces to the poet's aim, the completing of his work, which he is driving on, laboring and hast'ning in every line; the other slackens his pace, diverts him from his way, and locks him up, like a knight-errant, in an enchanted castle, when he should be pursuing his first adventure. Statius, as Bossu has well observ'd, was ambitious of trying his strength with his master Virgil, as Virgil had before tried his with

Homer. The Grecian gave the two Romans an example, in the games which were celebrated at the funerals of Patroclus. Virgil imitated the invention of Homer, but chang'd the sports. But both the Greek and Latin poet took their occasions from the subject; tho' to confess the truth, they were both ornamental, or at best convenient parts of it, rather than of necessity arising from it. Statius, who, thro' his whole poem, is noted for want of conduct and judgment, instead of staying, as he might have done, for the death of Capaneus, Hippomedon, Tydeus, or some other of his seven champions, (who are heroes all alike), or more properly for the tragical end of the two brothers, whose exequies the next successor had leisure to perform when the siege was rais'd, and in the interval betwixt the poet's first action and his second, went out of his way, as it were on prepense malice, to commit a fault. For he took his opportunity to kill a royal infant by the means of a serpent (that author of all evil), to make way for those funeral honors which he intended for him. Now if this innocent had been of any relation to his *Thebais;* if he had either farther'd or hinder'd the taking of the town; the poet might have found some sorry excuse at least, for detaining the reader from the promis'd siege. On these terms, this Capaneus of a poet ingag'd his two immortal predecessors; and his success was answerable to his enterprise.

If this economy must be observ'd in the minutest parts of an epic poem, which, to a common reader, seem to be detach'd from the body, and almost independent of it; what soul, tho' sent into the world with great advantages of nature, cultivated with the liberal arts and sciences, conversant with histories of the dead, and enrich'd with observations of the living, can be sufficient to inform the whole body of so great a work? I touch here but transiently, without any strict method, on some few of those many rules of imitating nature which Aristotle drew from Homer's *Iliads* and *Odysses,* and which he fitted to the drama; furnishing himself also with observations from the practice of the theater when it flourish'd under Æschylus, Euripides, and Sophocles: for the original of the stage was from the epic poem. Narration, doubtless, preceded acting, and gave laws to it; what at first was told artfully, was, in process of time, represented gracefully to the sight and hearing. Those episodes of Homer

DEDICATION OF THE ÆNEIS

which were proper for the stage, the poets amplified each into an action; out of his limbs they form'd their bodies; what he had contracted, they enlarg'd; out of one Hercules were made infinite of pigmies, yet all endued with human souls; for from him, their great creator, they have each of them the *divinæ particulam auræ*. They flow'd from him at first, and are at last resolv'd into him. Nor were they only animated by him, but their measure and symmetry was owing to him. His one, entire, and great action was copied by them according to the proportions of the drama. If he finish'd his orb within the year, it suffic'd to teach them, that their action being less, and being also less diversified with incidents, their orb, of consequence, must be circumscrib'd in a less compass, which they reduc'd within the limits either of a natural or an artificial day; so that, as he taught them to amplify what he had shorten'd, by the same rule, applied the contrary way, he taught them to shorten what he had amplified. Tragedy is the miniature of human life; an epic poem is the draught at length. Here, my Lord, I must contract also; for, before I was aware, I was almost running into a long digression, to prove that there is no such absolute necessity that the time of a stage action should so strictly be confin'd to twenty-four hours as never to exceed them, for which Aristotle contends, and the Grecian stage has practic'd. Some longer space, on some occasions, I think, may be allow'd, especially for the English theater, which requires more variety of incidents than the French. Corneille himself, after long practice, was inclin'd to think that the time allotted by the ancients was too short to raise and finish a great action: and better a mechanic rule were stretch'd or broken, than a great beauty were omitted. To raise, and afterwards to calm the passions, to purge the souls from pride, by the examples of human miseries, which befall the greatest; in few words, to expel arrogance, and introduce compassion, are the great effects of tragedy; great, I must confess, if they were altogether as true as they are pompous. But are habits to be introduc'd at three hours' warning? Are radical diseases so suddenly remov'd? A mountebank may promise such a cure, but a skilful physician will not undertake it. An epic poem is not in so much haste; it works leisurely; the changes which it makes are slow; but the cure is likely to be more perfect. The effects of tragedy, as I said, are too violent to be lasting. If it be answer'd that, for this reason, tragedies are often to be seen, and the dose to be repeated, this is tacitly to confess that there is more virtue in one heroic poem than in many tragedies. A man is humbled one day, and his pride returns the next. Chymical medicines are observ'd to relieve oft'ner than to cure; for 'tis the nature of spirits to make swift impressions, but not deep. Galenical decoctions, to which I may properly compare an epic poem, have more of body in them; they work by their substance and their weight. It is one reason of Aristotle's to prove that tragedy is the more noble, because it turns in a shorter compass; the whole action being circumscrib'd within the space of four-and-twenty hours. He might prove as well that a mushroom is to be preferr'd before a peach, because it shoots up in the compass of a night. A chariot may be driven round the pillar in less space than a large machine, because the bulk is not so great. Is the Moon a more noble planet than Saturn, because she makes her revolution in less than thirty days, and he in little less than thirty years? Both their orbs are in proportion to their several magnitudes; and consequently the quickness or slowness of their motion, and the time of their circumvolutions, is no argument of the greater or less perfection. And, besides, what virtue is there in a tragedy which is not contain'd in an epic poem, where pride is humbled, virtue rewarded, and vice punish'd; and those more amply treated than the narrowness of the drama can admit? The shining quality of an epic hero, his magnanimity, his constancy, his patience, his piety, or whatever characteristical virtue his poet gives him, raises first our admiration. We are naturally prone to imitate what we admire; and frequent acts produce a habit. If the hero's chief quality be vicious, as, for example, the choler and obstinate desire of vengeance in Achilles, yet the moral is instructive: and, besides, we are inform'd in the very proposition of the *Iliads* that this anger was pernicious; that it brought a thousand ills on the Grecian camp. The courage of Achilles is propos'd to imitation, not his pride and disobedience to his general, nor his brutal cruelty to his dead enemy, nor the selling his body to his father. We abhor these actions while we read them; and what we abhor we never imitate. The poet only shews them, like rocks or quicksands, to be shunn'd.

By this example the critics have concluded that it is not necessary the manners of the hero should be virtuous. They are poetically good, if they are of a piece: tho', where a character of perfect virtue is set before us, 'tis more lovely; for there the whole hero is to be imitated. This is the Æneas of our author; this is that idea of perfection in an epic poem which painters and statuaries have only in their minds, and which no hands are able to express. These are the beauties of a god in a human body. When the picture of Achilles is drawn in tragedy, he is taken with those warts, and moles, and hard features, by those who represent him on the stage, or he is no more Achilles; for his creator, Homer, has so describ'd him. Yet even thus he appears a perfect hero, tho' an imperfect character of virtue. Horace paints him after Homer, and delivers him to be copied on the stage with all those imperfections. Therefore, they are either not faults in a heroic poem, or faults common to the drama. After all, on the whole merits of the cause, it must be acknowledg'd that the epic poem is more for the manners, and tragedy for the passions. The passions, as I have said, are violent; and acute distempers require medicines of a strong and speedy operation. Ill habits of the mind are like chronical diseases, to be corrected by degrees, and cur'd by alteratives; wherein, tho' purges are sometimes necessary, yet diet, good air, and moderate exercise have the greatest part. The matter being thus stated, it will appear that both sorts of poetry are of use for their proper ends. The stage is more active; the epic poem works at greater leisure, yet is active too, when need requires; for dialogue is imitated by the drama from the more active parts of it. One puts off a fit, like the *quinquina,* and relieves us only for a time; the other roots out the distemper, and gives a healthful habit. The sun enlightens and cheers us, dispels fogs, and warms the ground with his daily beams; but the corn is sow'd, increases, is ripen'd, and is reap'd for use in process of time, and in its proper season. I proceed from the greatness of the action to the dignity of the actors; I mean to the persons employ'd in both poems. There likewise tragedy will be seen to borrow from the epopee; and that which borrows is always of less dignity, because it has not of its own. A subject, 'tis true, may lend to his sovereign; but the act of borrowing makes the king inferior, because he wants, and the subject supplies. And suppose the persons of the drama wholly fabulous, or of the poet's invention, yet heroic poetry gave him the examples of that invention, because it was first, and Homer the common father of the stage. I know not of any one advantage which tragedy can boast above heroic poetry, but that it is represented to the view, as well as read, and instructs in the closet, as well as on the theater. This is an uncontended excellence, and a chief branch of its prerogative; yet I may be allow'd to say, without partiality, that herein the actors share the poet's praise. Your Lordship knows some modern tragedies which are beautiful on the stage, and yet I am confident you would not read them. Tryphon the stationer complains they are seldom ask'd for in his shop. The poet who flourish'd in the scene is damn'd in the *ruelle;* nay more, he is not esteem'd a good poet by those who see and hear his extravagances with delight. They are a sort of stately fustian, and lofty childishness. Nothing but nature can give a sincere pleasure; where that is not imitated, 'tis grotesque painting; the fine woman ends in a fish's tail.

I might also add that many things which not only please, but are real beauties in the reading, would appear absurd upon the stage; and those not only the *speciosa miracula,* as Horace calls them, of transformations, of Scylla, Antiphates, and the Læstrygons, which cannot be represented even in operas; but the prowess of Achilles or Æneas would appear ridiculous in our dwarf heroes of the theater. We can believe they routed armies, in Homer or in Virgil; but *ne Hercules contra duos* in the drama. I forbear to instance in many things which the stage cannot, or ought not to represent; for I have said already more than I intended on this subject, and should fear it might be turn'd against me, that I plead for the preëminence of epic poetry because I have taken some pains in translating Virgil, if this were the first time that I had deliver'd my opinion in this dispute. But I have more than once already maintain'd the rights of my two masters against their rivals of the scene, even while I wrote tragedies myself, and had no thoughts of this present undertaking. I submit my opinion to your judgment, who are better qualified than any man I know to decide this controversy. You come, my Lord, instructed in the cause, and needed not that I should open it. Your *Essay of Poetry,* which was publish'd without a name, and of which I was not honor'd with the confidence, I read over and over with much delight, and as much instruction, and, without flattering you, or making myself more moral than I am, not without some envy. I was loth to be inform'd how an epic poem should be written, or how a tragedy should be contriv'd and manag'd, in better verse, and with more judgment, than I could teach others. A native of Parnassus, and bred up in the studies of its fundamental laws, may receive new lights from his contemporaries; but 'tis a grudging kind of praise which he gives his benefactors. He is more oblig'd than he is willing to acknowledge; there is a tincture of malice in his commendations; for where I own I am taught, I confess my want of knowledge. A judge upon the bench may, out of good nature, or at least interest, encourage the pleadings of a puny counselor; but he does not willingly commend his brother sergeant at the bar, especially when he controls his law, and exposes that ignorance which is made sacred by his place. I gave the unknown author his due commendation, I must confess; but who can answer for me and for the rest of the poets who heard me read the poem, whether we should not have been better pleas'd to have seen our own names at the bottom of the title-page? Perhaps we commended it the more, that we might seem to be above the censure. We are naturally displeas'd with an unknown critic, as the ladies are with the lampooner, because we are bitten in the dark, and know not where to fasten our revenge. But great excellencies will work their way thro' all sorts of opposition. I applauded rather out of decency than affection; and was ambitious, as some yet can witness, to be acquainted with a man with whom I had the honor to converse, and that almost daily, for so many years together. Heaven knows if I have heartily forgiven you this deceit. You extorted a praise which I should willingly have given, had I known you. Nothing had been more easy than to commend a patron of a long standing. The world would join with me, if the *encomiums* were just; and, if unjust, would excuse a grateful flatterer. But to come anonymous upon me, and force me to commend you against my interest, was not altogether so fair, give me leave to say, as it was politic; for by concealing your quality, you might clearly understand how your work succeeded, and that the general approbation was given to your merit, not your titles. Thus, like Apelles, you stood unseen behind your own Venus, and receiv'd the praises of the passing multitude; the work was commended, not the author; and I doubt not this was one of the most pleasing adventures of your life.

I have detain'd your Lordship longer than I intended in this dispute of preference betwixt the epic poem and the drama, and yet have not formally answer'd any of the arguments which are brought by Aristotle on the other side, and set in the fairest light by Dacier. But I suppose, without looking on the book, I may have touch'd on some of the objections; for, in this address to your Lordship, I design not a treatise of heroic poetry, but write in a loose epistolary way, somewhat tending to that subject, after the example of Horace, in his First Epistle of the Second Book, to Augustus Cæsar, and of that to the Pisos, which we call his *Art of Poetry;* in both of which he observes no method that I can trace, whatever Scaliger the Father or Heinsius may have seen or rather think they had seen. I have taken up, laid down, and resum'd as often as I pleas'd, the same subject; and this loose proceeding I shall use thro' all this prefatory dedication. Yet all this while I have been sailing with some side wind or other toward the point I propos'd in the beginning, the greatness and excellency of an heroic poem, with some of the difficulties which attend that work. The comparison, therefore, which I made betwixt the epopee and the tragedy was not altogether a digression; for 'tis concluded on all hands that they are both the masterpieces of human wit.

In the mean time, I may be bold to draw this corollary from what has been already said, that the file of heroic poets is very short; all are not such who have assum'd that lofty title in ancient or modern ages, or have been so esteem'd by their partial and ignorant admirers.

There have been but one great *Ilias,* and one *Æneis,* in so many ages. The next, but the next with a long interval betwixt, was the *Jerusalem:* I mean not so much in distance of time, as in excellency. After these three are enter'd, some Lord Chamberlain should be appointed, some critic of authority should be set before the door, to keep out a crowd of little poets, who press for admission, and are not of quality. Mævius would be deaf'ning your Lordship's ears with his

> Fortunam Priami cantabo, et nobile bellum—

mere fustian, as Horace would tell you from behind, without pressing forward, and more smoke than fire. Pulci, Boiardo, and Ariosto would cry out: "Make room for the Italian poets, the descendants of Virgil in a right line." Father Le Moine, with his *Saint Louis;* and Scudéry with his *Alaric:* "for a godly king and a Gothic conqueror;" and Chapelain would take it ill that his *Maid* should be refus'd a place with Helen and Lavinia. Spenser has a better plea for his *Fairy Queen,* had his action been finish'd, or had been one; and Milton, if the Devil had not been his hero, instead of Adam; if the giant had not foil'd the knight, and driven him out of his stronghold, to wander thro' the world with his lady errant; and if there had not been more machining persons than human in his poem. After these, the rest of our English poets shall not be mention'd. I have that honor for them which I ought to have; but, if they are worthies, they are not to be rank'd amongst the three whom I have nam'd, and who are establish'd in their reputation.

Before I quitted the comparison betwixt epic poetry and tragedy, I should have acquainted my judge with one advantage of the former over the latter, which I now casually remember out of the preface of Segrais before his translation of the *Æneis,* or out of Bossu, no matter which. The style of the heroic poem is, and ought to be, more lofty than that of the drama. The critic is certainly in the right, for the reason already urg'd; the work of tragedy is on the passions, and in dialogue; both of them abhor strong metaphors, in which the epopee delights. A poet cannot speak too plainly on the stage; for *volat irrevocabile verbum;* the sense is lost, if it be not taken flying; but what we read alone, we have leisure to digest. There an author may beautify his sense by the boldness of his expression, which if we understand not fully at the first, we may dwell upon it till we find the secret force and excellence. That which cures the manners by alterative physic, as I said before, must proceed by insensible degrees; but that which purges the passions must do its business all at once, or wholly fail of its effect, at least in the present operation, and without repeated doses. We must beat the iron while 'tis hot, but we may polish it at leisure. Thus, my Lord, you pay the fine of my forgetfulness; and yet the merits of both causes are where they were, and undecided, till you declare whether it be more for the benefit of mankind to have their manners in general corrected, or their pride and hard-heartedness remov'd.

I must now come closer to my present business, and not think of making more invasive wars abroad, when, like Hannibal, I am call'd back to the defense of my own country. Virgil is attack'd by many enemies; he has a whole confederacy against him; and I must endeavor to defend him as well as I am able. But their principal objections being against his moral, the duration or length of time taken up in the action of the poem, and what they have to urge against the manners of his hero, I shall omit the rest as mere cavils of grammarians; at the worst, but casual slips of a great man's pen, or inconsiderable faults of an admirable poem, which the author had not leisure to review before his death. Macrobius has answer'd what the ancients could urge against him; and some things I have lately read in Tanneguy le Fèvre, Valois, and another whom I name not, which are scarce worth answering. They begin with the moral of his poem, which I have elsewhere confess'd, and still must own, not to be so noble as that of Homer. But let both be fairly stated; and, without contradicting my first opinion, I can shew that Virgil's was as useful to the Romans of his age, as Homer's was to the Grecians of his, in what time soever he may be suppos'd to have liv'd and flourish'd. Homer's moral was to urge the necessity of union, and of a good understanding betwixt confederate states and princes engag'd in a war with a mighty monarch; as also of discipline in an army, and obedience in the several chiefs to the supreme commander of the joint forces. To inculcate this, he sets forth the ruinous effects of discord in the camp of those allies, occasion'd by the quarrel betwixt the general and one of the next in office under him. Agamemnon gives the provocation, and Achilles resents the injury. Both parties are faulty in the quarrel, and accordingly they are both punish'd; the aggressor is forc'd to sue for peace to his inferior on dishonorable conditions; the deserter refuses the satisfaction offer'd, and his obstinacy costs him his best friend. This works the natural effect of choler, and turns his rage against him by whom he was last affronted, and most sensibly. The greater anger expels the less; but his character is still preserv'd. In the mean time, the Grecian army receives loss on loss, and is half destroy'd by a pestilence into the bargain:

> Quicquid delirant reges, plectuntur Achivi.

As the poet, in the first part of the example, had shewn the bad effects of discord, so, after the reconcilement, he gives the good effects of unity; for Hector is slain, and then Troy must fall. By this 'tis probable that Homer liv'd when the Median monarchy was grown formidable to the Grecians, and that the joint endeavors of his countrymen were little enough to preserve their common freedom from an encroaching enemy. Such was his moral, which all critics have allow'd to be more noble than that of Virgil, tho' not adapted to the times in which the Roman poet liv'd. Had Virgil flourish'd in the age of Ennius, and address'd to Scipio, he had probably taken the same moral, or some other not unlike it. For then the Romans were in as much danger from the Carthaginian commonwealth as the Grecians were from the Assyrian or Median monarchy. But we are to consider him as writing his poem in a time when the old form of government was subverted, and a new one just establish'd by Octavius Cæsar, in effect by force of arms, but seemingly by the consent of the Roman people. The commonwealth had receiv'd a deadly wound in the former civil wars betwixt Marius and Sylla. The commons, while the first prevail'd, had almost shaken off the yoke of the nobility; and Marius and Cinna, like the captains of the mob, under the specious pretense of the public good, and of doing justice on the oppressors of their liberty, reveng'd themselves, without form of law, on their private enemies. Sylla, in his turn, proscrib'd the heads of the adverse party: he too had nothing but liberty and reformation in his mouth; for the cause of religion is but a modern motive to rebellion, invented by the Christian priesthood, refining on the heathen. Sylla, to be sure, meant no more good to the Roman people than Marius before him, whatever he declar'd; but sacrific'd the lives and took the estates of all his enemies, to gratify those who brought him into power. Such was the reformation of the government by both parties. The senate and the commons were the two bases on which it stood, and the two champions of either faction each destroy'd the foundations of the other side; so the fabric, of consequence, must fall betwixt them, and tyranny must be built upon their ruins. This comes of altering fundamental laws and constitutions; like him, who, being in good health, lodg'd himself in a physician's house, and was overpersuaded by his landlord to take physic, of which he died, for the benefit of his doctor. *Stavo ben;* (was written on his monument,) *ma, per star meglio, sto qui.*

After the death of those two usurpers, the commonwealth seem'd to recover, and held up its head for a little time. But it was all the while in a deep consumption, which is a flattering disease. Pompey, Crassus, and Cæsar had found the sweets of arbitrary power; and, each being a check to the other's growth, struck up a false friendship amongst themselves, and divided the government betwixt them, which none of them was able to assume alone. These were the public-spirited men of their age; that is, patriots for their own interest. The commonwealth look'd with a florid countenance in their management, spread in bulk, and all the while was wasting in the vitals. Not to trouble your Lordship with the repetition of what you know; after the death of Crassus, Pompey found himself outwitted by Cæsar, broke with him, overpower'd him in the senate, and caus'd many unjust decrees to pass against him. Cæsar, thus injur'd, and unable to resist the faction of the nobles, which was now uppermost, (for he was a Marian,) had recourse to arms; and his cause was just against Pompey, but not against his country, whose constitution ought to have been sacred to him, and never to have been violated on the account of any private wrong. But he prevail'd; and, Heav'n declaring for him, he became a providential monarch, under the title of perpetual dictator. He being murther'd by his own son whom I neither dare commend, nor can justly blame, (tho' Dante, in his *Inferno,* has put him and Cassius, and Judas Iscariot betwixt them, into the great devil's mouth,) the commonwealth popp'd up its head for the third time, under Brutus and Cassius, and then sunk for ever.

Thus the Roman people were grossly gull'd, twice or thrice over, and as often enslav'd in one century, and under the same pretense of reformation. At last the two battles of Philippi gave the decisive stroke against liberty; and, not long after, the commonwealth was turn'd into a monarchy by the conduct and good fortune of Augustus. 'Tis true that the despotic power could not have fallen into better hands than those of the first and second Cæsar. Your Lordship well knows what obligations Virgil had to the latter of them: he saw, beside, that the commonwealth was lost without resource; the heads of it destroy'd; the senate, new molded, grown degenerate, and either bought off, or thrusting their own necks into the yoke, out of fear of being forc'd. Yet I may safely affirm for our great author, (as men of good sense are generally honest,) that he was still of republican principles in heart.

   Secretisque piis, his dantem jura Catonem.

I think I need use no other argument to justify my opinion, than that of this one line, taken from the Eighth Book of the *Æneis*. If he had not well studied his patron's temper, it might have ruin'd him with another prince. But Augustus was not discontented, at least that we can find, that Cato was plac'd, by his own poet, in Elysium, and there giving laws to the holy souls who deserv'd to be separated from the vulgar sort of good spirits. For his conscience could not but whisper to the arbitrary monarch, that the kings of Rome were at first elective, and govern'd not without a senate; that Romulus was no hereditary prince; and tho', after his death, he receiv'd divine honors for the good he did on earth, yet he was but a god of their own making; that the last Tarquin was expell'd justly, for overt acts of tyranny and maladministration; for such are the conditions of an elective kingdom: and I meddle not with others, being, for my own opinion, of Montaigne's principles, that an honest man ought to be contented with that form of government, and with those fundamental constitutions of it, which he receiv'd from his ancestors, and under which himself was born; tho' at the same time he confess'd freely, that if he could have chosen his place of birth, it should have been at Venice; which, for many reasons, I dislike, and am better pleas'd to have been born an Englishman.

But, to return from my long rambling, I say that Virgil, having maturely weigh'd the condition of the times in which he liv'd; that an entire liberty was not to be retriev'd; that the present settlement had the prospect of a long continuance in the same family, or those adopted into it; that he held his paternal estate from the bounty of the conqueror, by whom he was likewise enrich'd, esteem'd, and cherish'd; that this conqueror, tho' of a bad kind, was the very best of it; that the arts of peace flourish'd under him; that all men might be happy, if they would be quiet; that, now he was in possession of the whole, yet he shar'd a great part of his authority with the senate; that he would be chosen into the ancient offices of the commonwealth, and rul'd by the power which he deriv'd from them, and prorogued his government from time to time, still, as it were, threat'ning to dismiss himself from public cares, which he exercis'd more for the common good than for any delight he took in greatness—these things, I say, being consider'd by the poet, he concluded it to be the interest of his country to be so govern'd; to infuse an awful respect into the people towards such a prince; by that respect to confirm their obedience to him, and by that obedience to make them happy. This was the moral of his divine poem; honest in the poet; honorable to the emperor, whom he derives from a divine extraction; and reflecting part of that honor on the Roman people, whom he derives also from the Trojans; and not only profitable, but necessary, to the present age, and likely to be such to their posterity. That it was the receiv'd opinion that the Romans were descended from the Trojans, and Julius Cæsar from Julius the son of Æneas, was enough for Virgil; tho' perhaps he thought not so himself, or that Æneas ever was in Italy; which Bochartus manifestly proves. And Homer, where he says that Jupiter hated the house of Priam, and was resolv'd to transfer the kingdom to the family of Æneas, yet mentions nothing of his leading a colony into a foreign country and settling there. But that the Romans valued themselves on their Trojan ancestry is so undoubted a truth that I need not prove it. Even the seals which we have remaining of Julius Cæsar, which we know to be antique, have the star of Venus over them, tho' they were all graven after his death, as a note that he was deified. I doubt not but it was one reason why Augustus should be so passionately concern'd for the preservation of the *Æneis,* which its author had condemn'd to be burnt, as an imperfect poem, by his last will and testament; was because it did him a real service, as well as an honor; that a work should not be lost where his divine original was celebrated in verse which had the character of immortality stamp'd upon it.

Neither were the great Roman families which flourish'd in his time less oblig'd by him than the emperor. Your Lordship knows with what address he makes mention of them, as captains of ships, or leaders in the war; and even some of Italian extraction are not forgotten. These are the single stars which are sprinkled thro' the *Æneis;* but there are whole constellations of them in the Fifth Book. And I could not but take notice, when I translated it, of some favorite families to which he gives the victory and awards the prizes, in the person of his hero, at the funeral games which were celebrated in honor of Anchises. I insist not on their names; but am pleas'd to find the Memmii amongst them, deriv'd from Mnestheus, because Lucretius dedicates to one of that family, a branch of which destroy'd Corinth. I likewise either found or form'd an image to myself of the contrary kind; that those who lost the prizes were such as had disoblig'd the poet, or were in disgrace with Augustus, or enemies to Mæcenas; and this was the poetical revenge he took. For *genus irritabile vatum,* as Horace says. When a poet is thoroughly provok'd, he will do himself justice, however dear it cost him; *animamque in vulnere ponit.* I think these are not bare imaginations of my own, tho' I find no trace of them in the commentators; but one poet may judge of another by himself. The vengeance we defer is not forgotten. I hinted before that the whole Roman people were oblig'd by Virgil, in deriving them from Troy; an ancestry which they affected. We and the French are of the same humor: they would be thought to descend from a son, I think, of Hector; and we would have our Britain both nam'd and planted by a descendant of Æneas. Spenser favors this opinion what he can. His Prince Arthur, or whoever he intends by him, is a Trojan. Thus the hero of Homer was a Grecian, of Virgil a Roman, of Tasso an Italian.

I have transgress'd my bounds, and gone farther than the moral led me. But, if your Lordship is not tir'd, I am safe enough.

Thus far, I think, my author is defended. But, as Augustus is still shadow'd in the person of Æneas, (of which I shall say more when I come to the manners which the poet gives his hero,) I must prepare that subject by shewing how dext'rously he manag'd both the prince and people, so as to displease neither, and to do good to both; which is the part of a wise and an honest man, and proves that it is possible for a courtier not to be a knave. I shall continue still to speak my thoughts like a free-born subject, as I am; tho' such things, perhaps, as no Dutch commentator could, and I am sure no Frenchman durst. I have already told your Lordship my opinion of Virgil, that he was no arbitrary man. Oblig'd he was to his master for his bounty; and he repays him with good counsel, how to behave himself in his new monarchy, so as to gain the affections of his subjects, and deserve to be call'd the father of his country. From this consideration it is that he chose, for the groundwork of his poem, one empire destroy'd, and another rais'd from the ruins of it. This was just the parallel. Æneas could not pretend to be Priam's heir in a lineal succession; for Anchises, the hero's father, was only of the second branch of the royal family; and Helenus, a son of Priam, was yet surviving, and might lawfully claim before him. It may be Virgil mentions him on that account. Neither has he forgotten Priamus, in the Fifth of his *Æneis,* the son of Polites, youngest son of Priam, who was slain by Pyrrhus, in the Second Book. Æneas had only married Creüsa, Priam's daughter, and by her could have no title while any of the male issue were remaining. In this case the poet gave him the next title, which is that of an elective king. The remaining Trojans chose him to lead them forth, and settle them in some foreign country. Ilioneus, in his speech to Dido, calls him expressly by the name of king. Our poet, who all this while had Augustus in his eye, had no desire he should seem to succeed by any right of inheritance deriv'd from Julius Cæsar, (such a title being but one degree remov'd from conquest,) for what was introduc'd by force, by force may be remov'd. 'Twas better for the people that they should give, than he should take; since that gift was indeed no more at bottom than a trust. Virgil gives us an example of this in the person of Mezentius: he govern'd arbitrarily; he was expell'd, and came to the deserv'd end of all tyrants. Our author shews us another sort of kingship, in the person of Latinus. He was descended from Saturn, and, as I remember, in the third degree. He is describ'd a just and gracious prince, solicitous for the welfare of his people, always consulting with his senate to promote the common good. We find him at the head of them, when he enters into the council hall, speaking first, but still demanding their advice, and steering by it, as far as the iniquity of the times would suffer him. And this is the proper character of a king by inheritance, who is born a father of his country. Æneas, tho' he married the heiress of the crown, yet claim'd no title to it during the life of his father-in-law. *Pater arma Latinus habeto,* &c., are Virgil's words. As for himself, he was contented to take care of his country gods, who were not those of Latium; wherein our divine author seems to relate to the after-practice of the Romans, which was to adopt the gods of those they conquer'd, or receiv'd as members of their commonwealth. Yet, withal, he plainly touches at the office of the high-priesthood, with which Augustus was invested, and which made his person more sacred and inviolable than even the tribunitial power. It was not therefore for nothing that the most judicious of all poets made that office vacant by the death of Panthus in the Second Book of the *Æneis,* for his hero to succeed in it, and consequently for Augustus to enjoy. I know not that any of the commentators have taken notice of that passage. If they have not, I am sure they ought; and if they have, I am not indebted to them for the observation. The words of Virgil are very plain:

      Sacra, suosque tibi commendat Troja penates.

As for Augustus, or his uncle Julius, claiming by descent from Æneas, that title is already out of doors. Æneas succeeded not, but was elected. Troy was foredoom'd to fall for ever:

Postquam res Asiæ Priamique evertere regnum
Immeritum visum superis.
                —Æneis, lib. iii, lin. 1.

Augustus, 'tis true, had once resolv'd to rebuild that city, and there to make the seat of empire; but Horace writes an ode on purpose to deter him from that thought, declaring the place to be accurst, and that the gods would as often destroy it as it should be rais'd. Hereupon the emperor laid aside a project so ungrateful to the Roman people. But by this, my Lord, we may conclude that he had still his pedigree in his head, and had an itch of being thought a divine king, if his poets had not given him better counsel.

I will pass by many less material objections, for want of room to answer them: what follows next is of great importance, if the critics can make out their charge; for 'tis level'd at the manners which our poet gives his hero, and which are the same which were eminently seen in his Augustus. Those manners were piety to the gods and a dutiful affection to his father, love to his relations, care of his people, courage and conduct in the wars, gratitude to those who had oblig'd him, and justice in general to mankind.

Piety, as your Lordship sees, takes place of all, as the chief part of his character; and the word in Latin is more full than it can possibly be express'd in any modern language; for there it comprehends not only devotion to the gods, but filial love and tender affection to relations of all sorts. As instances of this, the deities of Troy and his own Penates are made the companions of his flight: they appear to him in his voyage, and advise him; and at last he replaces them in Italy, their native country. For his father, he takes him on his back; he leads his little son; his wife follows him; but, losing his footsteps thro' fear or ignorance, he goes back into the midst of his enemies to find her, and leaves not his pursuit till her ghost appears, to forbid his farther search. I will say nothing of his duty to his father while he liv'd, his sorrows for his death, of the games instituted in honor of his memory, or seeking him, by his command, even after death, in the Elysian fields. I will not mention his tenderness for his son, which everywhere is visible—of his raising a tomb for Polydorus, the obsequies for Misenus, his pious remembrance of Deiphobus, the funerals of his nurse, his grief for Pallas, and his revenge taken on his murtherer, whom otherwise, by his natural compassion, he had forgiven: and then the poem had been left imperfect; for we could have had no certain prospect of his happiness, while the last obstacle to it was unremov'd. Of the other parts which compose his character, as a king or as a general, I need say nothing; the whole *Æneis* is one continued instance of some one or other of them; and where I find anything of them tax'd, it shall suffice me, as briefly as I can, to vindicate my divine master to your Lordship, and by you to the reader. But herein Segrais, in his admirable preface to his translation of the *Æneis,* as the author of the Dauphin's *Virgil* justly calls it, has prevented me. Him

I follow, and what I borrow from him, am ready to acknowledge to him. For, impartially speaking, the French are as much better critics than the English, as they are worse poets. Thus we generally allow that they better understand the management of a war than our islanders; but we know we are superior to them in the day of battle. They value themselves on their generals, we on our soldiers. But this is not the proper place to decide that question, if they make it one. I shall say perhaps as much of other nations and their poets, excepting only Tasso; and hope to make my assertion good, which is but doing justice to my country; part of which honor will reflect on your Lordship, whose thoughts are always just; your numbers harmonious, your words chosen, your expressions strong and manly, your verse flowing, and your turns as happy as they are easy. If you would set us more copies, your example would make all precepts needless. In the mean time, that little you have written is own'd, and that particularly by the poets, (who are a nation not over lavish of praise to their contemporaries,) as a principal ornament of our language; but the sweetest essences are always confin'd in the smallest glasses.

When I speak of your Lordship, 'tis never a digression, and therefore I need beg no pardon for it; but take up Segrais where I left him, and shall use him less often than I have occasion for him; for his preface is a perfect piece of criticism, full and clear, and digested into an exact method; mine is loose, and, as I intended it, epistolary. Yet I dwell on many things which he durst not touch; for 'tis dangerous to offend an arbitrary master, and every patron who has the power of Augustus has not his clemency. In short, my Lord, I would not translate him, because I would bring you somewhat of my own. His notes and observations on every book are of the same excellency; and, for the same reason, I omit the greater part.

He takes notice that Virgil is arraign'd for placing piety before valor, and making that piety the chief character of his hero. I have said already from Bossu, that a poet is not oblig'd to make his hero a virtuous man; therefore, neither Homer nor Tasso are to be blam'd for giving what predominant quality they pleas'd to their first character. But Virgil, who design'd to form a perfect prince, and would insinuate that Augustus, whom he calls Æneas in his poem, was truly such, found himself oblig'd to make him without blemish, thoroughly virtuous; and a thorough virtue both begins and ends in piety. Tasso, without question, observ'd this before me, and therefore split his hero in two; he gave Godfrey piety, and Rinaldo fortitude, for their chief qualities or manners. Homer, who had chosen another moral, makes both Agamemnon and Achilles vicious; for his design was to instruct in virtue by shewing the deformity of vice. I avoid repetition of that I have said above. What follows is translated literally from Segrais:

"Virgil had consider'd that the greatest virtues of Augustus consisted in the perfect art of governing his people; which caus'd him to reign for more than forty years in great felicity. He consider'd that his emperor was valiant, civil, popular, eloquent, politic, and religious; he has given all these qualities to Æneas. But, knowing that piety alone comprehends the whole duty of man towards the gods, towards his country, and towards his relations, he judg'd that this ought to be his first character, whom he would set for a pattern of perfection. In reality, they who believe that the praises which arise from valor are superior to those which proceed from any other virtues, have not consider'd (as they ought) that valor, destitute of other virtues, cannot render a man worthy of any true esteem. That quality, which signifies no more than an intrepid courage, may be separated from many others which are good, and accompanied with many which are ill. A man may be very valiant, and yet impious and vicious. But the same cannot be said of piety, which excludes all ill qualities, and comprehends even valor itself, with all other qualities which are good. Can we, for example, give the praise of valor to a man who should see his gods profan'd, and should want the courage to defend them? To a man who should abandon his father, or desert his king in his last necessity?"

Thus far Segrais, in giving the preference to piety before valor. I will now follow him, where he considers this valor, or intrepid courage, singly in itself; and this also Virgil gives to his Æneas, and that in a heroical degree.

Having first concluded that our poet did for the best in taking the first character of his hero from that essential virtue on which the rest depend, he proceeds to tell us that in the ten years' war of

Troy he was consider'd as the second champion of his country (allowing Hector the first place); and this, even by the confession of Homer, who took all occasions of setting up his own countrymen the Grecians, and of undervaluing the Trojan chiefs. But Virgil (whom Segrais forgot to cite) makes Diomede give him a higher character for strength and courage. His testimony is this, in the Eleventh Book:

>―― Stetimus tela aspera contra,
>Contulimusque manus: experto credite, quantus
>In clypeum assurgat quo turbine torqueat hastam.
>Si duo præterea tales Idæa tulisset
>Terra viros, ultro Inachias venisset ad urbes
>Dardanus, et versis lugeret Græcia fatis.
>Quicquid apud duræ cessatum est mœnia Trojæ,
>Hectoris Æneæque manu victoria Graium
>Hæsit, et in decumum vestigia retulit annum.
>Ambo animis, ambo insignes præstantibus armis:
>Hic pietate prior.―

I give not here my translation of these verses, (tho' I think I have not ill succeeded in them,) because your Lordship is so great a master of the original that I have no reason to desire you should see Virgil and me so near together. But you may please, my Lord, to take notice that the Latin author refines upon the Greek, and insinuates that Homer had done his hero wrong in giving the advantage of the duel to his own countryman; tho' Diomedes was manifestly the second champion of the Grecians; and Ulysses preferr'd him before Ajax, when he chose him for the companion of his nightly expedition; for he had a headpiece of his own, and wanted only the fortitude of another to bring him off with safety, and that he might compass his design with honor.

The French translator thus proceeds: "They who accuse Æneas for want of courage, either understand not Virgil, or have read him slightly; otherwise they would not raise an objection so easy to be answer'd." Hereupon he gives so many instances of the hero's valor, that to repeat them after him would tire your Lordship, and put me to the unnecessary trouble of transcribing the greatest part of the three last *Æneids*. In short, more could not be expected from an Amadis, a Sir Lancelot, or the whole Round Table, than he performs.

Proxima quæque metit gladio, is the perfect account of a knight-errant. "If it be replied," continues Segrais, "that it was not difficult for him to undertake and achieve such hardy enterprises, because he wore enchanted arms; that accusation, in the first place, must fall on Homer, ere it can reach Virgil." Achilles was as well provided with them as Æneas, tho' he was invulnerable without them. And Ariosto, the two Tassos (Bernardo and Torquato), even our own Spenser, in a word, all modern poets, have copied Homer as well as Virgil: he is neither the first nor last, but in the midst of them; and therefore is safe, if they are so. "Who knows," says Segrais, "but that his fated armor was only an allegorical defense, and signified no more than that he was under the peculiar protection of the gods? —born, as the astrologers will tell us out of Virgil, (who was well vers'd in the Chaldæan mysteries,) under the favorable influence of Jupiter, Venus, and the Sun." But I insist not on this, because I know you believe not in such an art; tho' not only Horace and Persius, but Augustus himself, thought otherwise. But, in defense of Virgil, I dare positively say that he has been more cautious in this particular than either his predecessor or his descendants; for Æneas was actually wounded in the Twelfth of the *Æneis,* tho' he had the same god-smith to forge his arms as had Achilles. It seems he was no warluck, as the Scots commonly call such men, who, they say, are iron-free, or lead-free. Yet, after this experiment that his arms were not impenetrable, when he was cur'd indeed by his mother's help, because he was that day to conclude the war by the death of Turnus, the poet durst not carry the miracle too far, and restore him wholly to his former vigor; he was still too weak to overtake his enemy; yet we see with what courage he attacks Turnus, when he faces and renews the combat. I need say no more; for Virgil defends himself without needing my assistance, and proves his hero truly to deserve that name. He was not then a second-rate champion, as they would have him who think fortitude the first virtue in a hero. But, being beaten from this hold, they will not yet allow him to be valiant, because he wept more often, as they think, than well becomes a man of courage.

In the first place, if tears are arguments of cowardice, what shall I say of Homer's hero? Shall Achilles pass for timorous because he wept, and wept on less occasions than Æneas? Herein Virgil must be granted to have excell'd his master. For once both heroes are describ'd lamenting their lost loves: Briseis was taken away by force from the Grecian; Creüsa was lost for ever to her husband. But Achilles went roaring along the salt sea-shore, and, like a booby, was complaining to his mother, when he should have reveng'd his injury by arms. Æneas took a nobler course; for, having secur'd his father and his son, he repeated all his former dangers to have found his wife, if she had been above ground. And here your Lordship may observe the address of Virgil; it was not for nothing that this passage was related with all these tender circumstances. Æneas told it; Dido heard it. That he had been so affectionate a husband was no ill argument to the coming dowager that he might prove as kind to her. Virgil has a thousand secret beauties, tho' I have not leisure to remark them.

Segrais, on this subject of a hero's shedding tears, observes that historians commend Alexander for weeping when he read the mighty actions of Achilles; and Julius Cæsar is likewise prais'd, when, out of the same noble envy, he wept at the victories of Alexander. But, if we observe more closely, we shall find that the tears of Æneas were always on a laudable occasion. Thus he weeps out of compassion and tenderness of nature, when, in the temple of Carthage, he beholds the pictures of his friends, who sacrific'd their lives in defense of their country. He deplores the lamentable end of his pilot Palinurus, the untimely death of young Pallas his confederate, and the rest, which I omit. Yet, even for these tears, his wretched critics dare condemn him. They make Æneas little better than a kind of St. Swithen hero, always raining. One of these censors is bold enough to argue him of cowardice, when, in the beginning of the First Book, he not only weeps, but trembles at an approaching storm:

> Extemplo Æneæ solvuntur frigore membra:
> Ingemit, et duplices tendens ad sidera palmas, &c.

But to this I have answer'd formerly, that his fear was not for himself, but for his people. And who can give a sovereign a better commendation, or recommend a hero more to the affection of the reader? They were threaten'd with a tempest, and he wept; he was promis'd Italy, and therefore he pray'd for the accomplishment of that promise. All this in the beginning of a storm; therefore he shew'd the more early piety, and the quicker sense of compassion. Thus much I have urg'd elsewhere in the defense of Virgil; and, since, I have been inform'd by Mr. Moyle, a young gentleman whom I can never sufficiently commend, that the ancients accounted drowning an accursed death; so that, if we grant him to have been afraid, he had just occasion for that fear, both in relation to himself and to his subjects. I think our adversaries can carry this argument no farther, unless they tell us that he ought to have had more confidence in the promise of the gods. But how was he assur'd that he had understood their oracles aright? Helenus might be mistaken; Phœbus might speak doubtfully; even his mother might flatter him that he might prosecute his voyage, which if it succeeded happily, he should be the founder of an empire. For that she herself was doubtful of his fortune is apparent by the address she made to Jupiter on his behalf; to which the god makes answer in these words:

> Parce metu, Cytherea: manent immota tuorum
> Fata tibi, &c.

notwithstanding which, the goddess, tho' comforted, was not assur'd; for even after this, thro' the course of the whole *Æneis,* she still apprehends the interest which Juno might make with Jupiter against her son. For it was a moot point in heaven, whether he could alter fate, or not. And indeed some passages in Virgil would make us suspect that he was of opinion Jupiter might defer fate, tho' he could not alter it. For in the latter end of the Tenth Book he introduces Juno begging for the life of Turnus, and flattering her husband with the power of changing destiny—*Tua, qui potes, orsa reflectas!* To which he graciously answers:

> Si mora præsentis lethi, tempusque caduco
> Oratur juveni, meque hoc ita ponere sentis,
> Tolle fuga Turnum, atque instantibus eripe fatis.
> Hactenus indulsisse vacat. Sin altior istis
> Sub precibus venia ulla latet, totumque moveri
> Mutarive putas bellum, spes pascis inaneis.

But that he could not alter those decrees, the King of Gods himself confesses, in the book above cited, when he comforts Hercules for the death of Pallas, who had invok'd his aid before he threw his lance at Turnus:

    —— Trojæ sub mœnibus altis
   Tot nati cecidere deum; quin occidit una
   Sarpedon, mea progenies. Etiam sua Turnum
   Fata manent, metasque dati pervenit ad ævi——

where he plainly acknowledges that he could not save his own son, or prevent the death which he foresaw. Of his power to defer the blow I once occasionally discours'd with that excellent person Sir Robert Howard, who is better conversant than any man that I know in the doctrine of the Stoics; and he set me right, from the concurrent testimony of philosophers and poets, that Jupiter could not retard the effects of fate, even for a moment. For, when I cited Virgil as favoring the contrary opinion in that verse,

    Tolle fuga Turnum, atque instantibus eripe fatis, &c.

he replied, and, I think, with exact judgment, that, when Jupiter gave Juno leave to withdraw Turnus from the present danger, it was because he certainly foreknew that his fatal hour was not come; that it was in destiny for Juno at that time to save him; and that himself obey'd destiny in giving her that leave.

I need say no more in justification of our hero's courage, and am much deceiv'd if he be ever attack'd on this side of his character again. But he is arraign'd with more shew of reason by the ladies, who will make a numerous party against him, for being false to love, in forsaking Dido. And I cannot much blame them; for, to say the truth, 'tis an ill precedent for their gallants to follow. Yet, if I can bring him off with flying colors, they may learn experience at her cost, and, for her sake, avoid a cave, as the worst shelter they can choose from a shower of rain, especially when they have a lover in their company.

In the first place, Segrais observes with much acuteness that they who blame Æneas for his insensibility of love when he left Carthage, contradict their former accusation of him for being always crying, compassionate, and effeminately sensible of those misfortunes which befell others. They give him two contrary characters; but Virgil makes him of a piece, always grateful, always tender-hearted. But they are impudent enough to discharge themselves of this blunder, by laying the contradiction at Virgil's door. He, they say, has shewn his hero with these inconsistent characters, acknowledging and ungrateful, compassionate and hard-hearted, but, at the bottom, fickle and self-interested; for Dido had not only receiv'd his weather-beaten troops before she saw him, and given them her protection, but had also offer'd them an equal share in her dominion:

> Vultus et his mecum pariter considere regnis?
> Urbem quam statuo, vestra est.

This was an obligement never to be forgotten; and the more to be consider'd, because antecedent to her love. That passion, 'tis true, produc'd the usual effects, of generosity, gallantry, and care to please; and thither we refer them. But when she had made all these advances, it was still in his power to have refus'd them; after the intrigue of the cave (call it marriage, or enjoyment only) he was no longer free to take or leave; he had accepted the favor, and was oblig'd to be constant, if he would be grateful.

My Lord, I have set this argument in the best light I can, that the ladies may not think I write booty; and perhaps it may happen to me, as it did to Doctor Cudworth, who has rais'd such strong objections against the being of a God, and Providence, that many think he has not answer'd them. You may please at least to hear the adverse party. Segrais pleads for Virgil, that no less than an absolute command from Jupiter could excuse this insensibility of the hero, and this abrupt departure, which looks so like extreme ingratitude. But, at the same time, he does wisely to remember you, that Virgil had made piety the first character of Æneas; and, this being allow'd, (as I am afraid it must,) he was oblig'd, antecedent to all other considerations, to search an asylum for his gods in Italy—for those very gods, I say, who had promis'd to his race the universal empire. Could a pious man dispense with the commands of Jupiter, to satisfy his passion, or (take it in the strongest sense) to comply with the obligations of his gratitude? Religion, 'tis true, must have moral honesty for its groundwork, or we shall be apt to suspect its truth; but an immediate revelation dispenses with all duties of morality. All casuists agree that theft is a breach of the moral law; yet, if I might

DEDICATION OF THE ÆNEIS

presume to mingle things sacred with profane, the Israelites only spoil'd the Egyptians, not robb'd them, because the propriety was transferr'd by a revelation to their lawgiver. I confess Dido was a very infidel in this point; for she would not believe, as Virgil makes her say, that ever Jupiter would send Mercury on such an immoral errand. But this needs no answer, at least no more than Virgil gives it:

> Fata obstant; placidasque viri deus obstruit aures.

This notwithstanding, as Segrais confesses, he might have shewn a little more sensibility when he left her; for that had been according to his character.

But let Virgil answer for himself. He still lov'd her, and struggled with his inclinations to obey the gods:

> —— Curam sub corde premebat,
> Multa gemens, magnoque animum labefactus amore.

Upon the whole matter, and humanly speaking, I doubt there was a fault somewhere; and Jupiter is better able to bear the blame than either Virgil or Æneas. The poet, it seems, had found it out, and therefore brings the deserting hero and the forsaken lady to meet together in the lower regions, where he excuses himself when 'tis too late; and accordingly she will take no satisfaction, nor so much as hear him. Now Segrais is forc'd to abandon his defense, and excuses his author by saying that the *Æneis* is an imperfect work, and that death prevented the divine poet from reviewing it; and for that reason he had condemn'd it to the fire; tho', at the same time, his two translators must acknowledge that the Sixth Book is the most correct of the whole *Æneis*. O, how convenient is a machine sometimes in a heroic poem! This of Mercury is plainly one; and Virgil was constrain'd to use it here, or the honesty of his hero would be ill defended. And the fair sex, however, if they had the deserter in their power, would certainly have shewn him no more mercy than the Bacchanals did Orpheus: for, if too much constancy may be a fault sometimes, then want of constancy, and ingratitude after the last favor, is a crime that never will be forgiven. But of machines, more in their proper place; where I shall shew with how much judgment they have been us'd by Virgil; and, in the mean time, pass to another article of his defense on the present subject; where, if I cannot clear the hero, I hope at least to bring off the poet; for here I must divide their causes. Let Æneas trust to his machine, which will only help to break his fall; but the address is incomparable. Plato, who borrow'd so much from Homer, and yet concluded for the banishment of all poets, would at least have rewarded Virgil before he sent him into exile. But I go farther, and say that he ought to be acquitted, and deserv'd, beside, the bounty of Augustus and the gratitude of the Roman people. If, after this, the ladies will stand out, let them remember that the jury is not all agreed; for Octavia was of his party, and was of the first quality in Rome; she was also present at the reading of the *Sixth Æneid,* and we know not that she condemn'd Æneas; but we are sure she presented the poet for his admirable elegy on her son Marcellus.

But let us consider the secret reasons which Virgil had for thus framing this noble episode, wherein the whole passion of love is more exactly describ'd than in any other poet. Love was the theme of his Fourth Book: and, tho' it is the shortest of the whole *Æneis,* yet there he has given its beginning, its progress, its traverses, and its conclusion; and had exhausted so entirely this subject, that he could resume it but very slightly in the eight ensuing books.

She was warm'd with the graceful appearance of the hero; she smother'd those sparkles out of decency; but conversation blew them up into a flame. Then she was forc'd to make a confident of her whom she best might trust, her own sister, who approves the passion, and thereby augments it; then succeeds her public owning it; and, after that, the consummation. Of Venus and Juno, Jupiter and Mercury, I say nothing, for they were all machining work; but, possession having cool'd his love, as it increas'd hers, she soon perceiv'd the change, or at least grew suspicious of a change; this suspicion soon turn'd to jealousy, and jealousy to rage; then she disdains and threatens, and again is humble, and intreats, and, nothing availing, despairs, curses, and at last becomes her own executioner. See here the whole process of that passion, to which nothing can be added. I dare go no farther, lest I should lose the connection of my discourse.

DEDICATION OF THE ÆNEIS

To love our native country, and to study its benefit and its glory, to be interested in its concerns, is natural to all men, and is indeed our common duty. A poet makes a farther step; for, endeavoring to do honor to it, 't is allowable in him even to be partial in its cause; for he is not tied to truth, or fetter'd by the laws of history. Homer and Tasso are justly prais'd for choosing their heroes out of Greece and Italy; Virgil indeed made his a Trojan; but it was to derive the Romans and his own Augustus from him. But all the three poets are manifestly partial to their heroes, in favor of their country; for Dares Phrygius reports of Hector that he was slain cowardly: Æneas, according to the best account, slew not Mezentius, but was slain by him; and the chronicles of Italy tell us little of that Rinaldo d'Este who conquers Jerusalem in Tasso. He might be a champion of the Church; but we know not that he was so much as present at the siege. To apply this to Virgil, he thought himself engag'd in honor to espouse the cause and quarrel of his country against Carthage. He knew he could not please the Romans better, or oblige them more to patronize his poem, than by disgracing the foundress of that city. He shews her ungrateful to the memory of her first husband, doting on a stranger; enjoy'd, and afterwards forsaken by him. This was the original, says he, of the immortal hatred betwixt the two rival nations. 'Tis true, he colors the falsehood of Æneas by an express command from Jupiter, to forsake the queen who had oblig'd him; but he knew the Romans were to be his readers, and them he brib'd, perhaps at the expense of his hero's honesty; but he gain'd his cause, however, as pleading before corrupt judges. They were content to see their founder false to love, for still he had the advantage of the amour: it was their enemy whom he forsook, and she might have forsaken him, if he had not got the start of her: she had already forgotten her vows to her Sichæus; and *varium et mutabile semper femina* is the sharpest satire, in the fewest words, that ever was made on womankind; for both the adjectives are neuter, and *animal* must be understood, to make them grammar. Virgil does well to put those words into the mouth of Mercury. *If a god had not spoken them, neither durst he have written them, nor I translated them.* Yet the deity was forc'd to come twice on the same errand; and the second time, as much a hero as Æneas was, he frighted him. It seems he fear'd not Jupiter so much as Dido; for your Lordship may observe that, as much intent as he was upon his voyage, yet he still delay'd it, till the messenger was oblig'd to tell him plainly, that, if he weigh'd not anchor in the night, the queen would be with him in the morning. *Notumque furens quid femina possit*—she was injur'd; she was revengeful; she was powerful. The poet had likewise before hinted that her people were naturally perfidious; for he gives their character in their queen, and makes a proverb of *Punica fides,* many ages before it was invented.

Thus I hope, my Lord, that I have made good my promise, and justified the poet, whatever becomes of the false knight. And sure a poet is as much privileg'd to lie as an ambassador, for the honor and interests of his country; at least as Sir Henry Wotton has defin'd.

This naturally leads me to the defense of the famous anachronism, in making Æneas and Dido contemporaries; for 'tis certain that the hero liv'd almost two hundred years before the building of Carthage. One who imitates Bocaline says that Virgil was accus'd before Apollo for this error. The god soon found that he was not able to defend his favorite by reason, for the case was clear: he therefore gave this middle sentence, that anything might be allow'd to his son Virgil, on the account of his other merits; that, being a monarch, he had a dispensing power, and pardon'd him. But, that this special act of grace might never be drawn into example, or pleaded by his puny successors in justification of their ignorance, he decreed for the future, no poet should presume to make a lady die for love two hundred years before her birth. To moralize this story, Virgil is the Apollo who has this dispensing power. His great judgment made the laws of poetry; but he never made himself a slave to them: chronology, at best, is but a cobweb law, and he broke thro' it with his weight. They who will imitate him wisely must choose, as he did, an obscure and a remote *æra,* where they may invent at pleasure, and not be easily contradicted. Neither he, nor the Romans, had ever read the Bible, by which only his false computation of times can be made out against him. This Segrais says in his defense, and proves it from his learned friend Bochartus, whose letter on this subject he has printed at the end of the *Fourth Æneid,* to which I refer your Lordship and the reader. Yet the credit of Virgil was so great that he made this fable of his own invention pass for an authentic history, or at least as credible as anything in Homer. Ovid takes it up after him, even in the same age, and makes an ancient heroine of Virgil's new-created Dido; dictates a letter for her, just before her death, to the ingrateful fugitive; and, very unluckily for himself, is for measuring a sword with a man so much superior in force to him, on the same subject. I think I may be judge of this, because I have translated both. The famous author of the *Art of Love* has nothing of his own; he borrows all from a greater master in his own profession and, which is worse, improves nothing which he finds. Nature fails him; and, being forc'd to his old shift, he has recourse to witticism. This passes indeed with his soft admirers, and gives him the preference to Virgil in their esteem. But let them like for themselves, and not prescribe to others; for our author needs not their admiration.

The motives that induc'd Virgil to coin this fable I have shew'd already; and have also begun to shew that he might make this anachronism by superseding the mechanic rules of poetry, for the same reason that a monarch may dispense with or suspend his own laws, when he finds it necessary so to do, especially if those laws are not altogether fundamental. Nothing is to be call'd a fault in poetry, says Aristotle, but what is against the art; therefore a man may be an admirable poet without being an exact chronologer. Shall we dare, continues Segrais, to condemn Virgil for having made a fiction against the order of time, when we commend Ovid and other poets who have made many of their fictions against the order of nature? For what else are the splendid miracles of the *Metamorphoses*? Yet these are beautiful as they are related, and have also deep learning and instructive mythologies couch'd under them; but to give, as Virgil does in this episode, the original cause of the long wars betwixt Rome and Carthage, to draw truth out of fiction after so probable a manner, with so much beauty, and so much for the honor of his country, was proper only to the divine wit of Maro; and Tasso, in one of his discourses, admires him for this particularly. 'Tis not lawful, indeed, to contradict a point of history which is known to all the world, as, for example, to make Hannibal and Scipio contemporaries with Alexander; but, in the dark recesses of antiquity, a great poet may and ought to feign such things as he finds not there, if they can be brought to embellish that subject which he treats. On the other side, the pains and diligence of ill poets is but thrown away when they want the genius to invent and feign agreeably. But if the fictions be delightful; (which they always are, if they be natural); if they be of a piece; if the beginning, the middle, and the end be in their due places, and artfully united to each other, such works can never fail of their deserv'd success. And such is Virgil's episode of Dido and Æneas; where the sourest critic must acknowledge that, if he had depriv'd his *Æneis* of so great an ornament because he found no traces of it in antiquity, he had avoided their unjust censure, but had wanted one of the greatest beauties of his poem. I shall say more of this in the next article of their charge against him, which is want of invention. In the mean time I may affirm, in honor of this episode, that it is not only now esteem'd the most pleasing entertainment of the *Æneis,* but was so accounted in his own age, and before it was mellow'd into that reputation which time has given it; for which I need produce no other testimony than that of Ovid, his contemporary:

> Nec pars ulla magis legitur de corpore toto,
> Quam non legitimo fœdere junctus amor.

Where, by the way, you may observe, my Lord, that Ovid, in those words, *non legitimo fœdere junctus amor,* will by no means allow it to be a lawful marriage betwixt Dido and Æneas. He was in banishment when he wrote those verses, which I cite from his letter to Augustus: "You, sir," saith he, "have sent me into exile for writing my *Art of Love,* and my wanton *Elegies;* yet your own poet was happy in your good graces, tho' he brought Dido and Æneas into a cave, and left them there not over honestly together. May I be so bold to ask your Majesty, is it a greater fault to teach the art of unlawful love, than to shew it in the action?" But was Ovid, the court poet, so bad a courtier as to find no other plea to excuse himself than by a plain accusation of his master? Virgil confess'd it was a lawful marriage betwixt the lovers, that Juno, the goddess of matrimony, had ratified it by her presence; for it was her business to bring matters to that issue. That the ceremonies were short, we may believe; for Dido was not only amorous, but a widow. Mercury himself, tho' employ'd on a quite contrary errand, yet owns it a marriage by an *innuendo: pulchramque uxorius urben Exstrusis.* He calls Æneas not only a husband, but upbraids him for being a fond husband, as the word *uxorius* implies. Now mark a little, if your Lordship pleases, why Virgil is so much concern'd to make this marriage (for he seems to be the father of the bride himself, and to give her to the bridegroom): it was to make away for the divorce which he intended afterwards; for he was a finer flatterer than Ovid, and I more than conjecture that he had in his eye the divorce which not long before had pass'd betwixt the emperor and Scribonia. He drew this dimple in the cheek of Æneas, to prove Augustus of the same family, by so remarkable a feature in the same place. Thus, as we say in our homespun English proverb, *he kill'd two birds with one stone;* pleas'd the emperor, by giving him the resemblance of his ancestor, and gave him such a resemblance as was not scandalous in that age. For to leave one wife, and take another, was but a matter of gallantry at that time of day among the Romans. *Neque hæc in fœdera veni* is the very excuse which Æneas makes, when he leaves his lady: "I made no such bargain with you at our marriage, to live always drudging on at Carthage: my business was Italy and I never made a secret of it. If I took my pleasure, had not you your share of it? I leave you free, at my departure, to comfort yourself with the next stranger who happens to be shipwreck'd on your coast. Be as kind a hostess as you have been to me, and you can never fail of another husband. In the mean time, I call the gods to witness that I leave your shore unwillingly; for tho' Juno made the marriage, yet Jupiter commands me to forsake you." This is the effect of what he saith, when it is dishonor'd out of Latin verse into English prose. If the poet argued not aright, we must pardon him for a poor blind heathen, who knew no better morals.

I have detain'd your Lordship longer than I intended on this objection, which would indeed weigh something in a spiritual court but I am not to defend our poet there. The next, I think, is but a cavil, tho' the cry is great against him, and hath continued from the time of Macrobius to this present age. I hinted it before. They lay no less than want of invention to his charge—a capital crime,

I must acknowledge; for a poet is a maker, as the word signifies; and who cannot make, that is, invent, hath his name for nothing. That which makes this accusation look so strange at the first sight, is, that he has borrow'd so many things from Homer, Apollonius Rhodius, and others who preceded him. But in the first place, if invention is to be taken in so strict a sense, that the matter of a poem must be wholly new, and that in all its parts, then Scaliger hath made out, saith Segrais, that the history of Troy was no more the invention of Homer than of Virgil. There was not an old woman, or almost a child, but had it in their mouths, before the Greek poet or his friends digested it into this admirable order in which we read it. At this rate, as Solomon hath told us, there is nothing new beneath the sun. Who then can pass for an inventor, if Homer, as well as Virgil, must be depriv'd of that glory? Is Versailles the less a new building, because the architect of that palace hath imitated others which were built before it? Walls, doors and windows, apartments, offices, rooms of convenience and magnificence, are in all great houses. So descriptions, figures, fables, and the rest, must be in all heroic poems; they are the common materials of poetry, furnish'd from the magazine of nature; every poet hath as much right to them as every man hath to air or water. *Quid prohibetis aquas? Usus communis aquarum est.* But the argument of the work, that is to say, its principal action, the economy and disposition of it; these are the things which distinguish copies from originals. The poet who borrows nothing from others is yet to be born; he and the Jews' Messias will come together. There are parts of the *Æneis* which resemble some parts both of the *Ilias* and of the *Odysses;* as, for example, Æneas descended into hell, and Ulysses had been there before him; Æneas lov'd Dido, and Ulysses lov'd Calypso: in few words, Virgil hath imitated Homer's *Odysses* in his first six books, and in his six last the *Ilias*. But from hence can we infer that the two poets write the same history? Is there no invention in some other parts of Virgil's *Æneis?* The disposition of so many various matters, is not that his own? From what book of Homer had Virgil his episode of Nisus and Euryalus, of Mezentius and Lausus? From whence did he borrow his design of bringing Æneas into Italy? of establishing the Roman empire on the foundations of a Trojan colony? to say nothing of the honor he did his patron, not only in his descent from Venus, but in making him so like him in his best features, that the goddess might have mistaken Augustus for her son. He had indeed the story from common fame, as Homer had his from the Egyptian priestess. *Æneadum genetrix* was no more unknown to Lucretius than to him. But Lucretius taught him not to form his hero, to give him piety or valor for his manners, and both in so eminent a degree, that, having done what was possible for man, to save his king and country, his mother was forc'd to appear to him, and restrain his fury, which hurried him to death in their revenge. But the poet made his piety more successful; he brought off his father and his son; and his gods witness'd to his devotion, by putting themselves under his protection, to be replac'd by him in their promis'd Italy. Neither the invention nor the conduct of this great action were owing to Homer or any other poet. 'Tis one thing to copy, and another thing to imitate from nature. The copier is that servile imitator, to whom Horace gives no better a name than that of animal; he will not so much as allow him to be a man. Raphael imitated nature; they who copy one of Raphael's pieces imitate but him, for his work is their original. They translate him, as I do Virgil; and fall as short of him, as I of Virgil. There is a kind of invention in the imitation of Raphael; for, tho' the thing was in nature, yet the idea of it was his own. Ulysses travel'd; so did Æneas: but neither of them were the first travelers; for Cain went into the land of Nod before they were born, and neither of the poets ever heard of such a man. If Ulysses had been kill'd at Troy, yet Æneas must have gone to sea, or he could never have arriv'd in Italy. But the designs of the two poets were as different as the courses of their heroes; one went home, and the other sought a home. To return to my first similitude: suppose Apelles and Raphael had each of them painted a burning Troy, might not the modern painter have succeeded as well as the ancient, tho' neither of them had seen the town on fire? for the draughts of both were taken from the ideas which they had of nature. Cities had been burnt before either of them were in being. But, to close the simile as I began it, they would not have design'd it after the same manner: Apelles would have distinguish'd Pyrrhus from the rest of all the Grecians, and shew'd him forcing his entrance into Priam's palace; there he had set him in the fairest light, and given him the chief place of all his figures; because he was a Grecian, and he would do honor to his country. Raphael, who was an Italian, and descended from the Trojans, would have made Æneas the hero of his piece; and perhaps not with his father on his back, his son in one hand, his bundle of gods in the other, and his wife following; for an act of piety is not half so graceful in a picture as an act of courage: he would rather have drawn him killing Androgeos, or some other, hand to hand; and the blaze of the fires should have darted full upon his face, to make him conspicuous amongst his Trojans. This, I think, is a just comparison betwixt the two poets, in the conduct of their several designs. Virgil cannot be said to copy Homer; the Grecian had only the advantage of writing first. If it be urg'd that I have granted a resemblance in some parts, yet therein Virgil has excell'd him. For what are the tears of Calypso for being left, to the fury and death of Dido? Where is there the whole process of her passion and all its violent effects to be found, in the languishing *episode* of the *Odysses?* If this be to copy, let the critics shew us the same disposition, features, or coloring, in their original. The like may be said of the descent to hell, which was not of Homer's invention neither; he had it from the story of Orpheus and Eurydice. But to what end did Ulysses make that journey? Æneas undertook it by the express commandment of his father's ghost: there he was to shew him all the succeeding heroes of his race, and, next to Romulus (mark, if you please, the address of Virgil,) his own patron, Augustus Cæsar. Anchises was likewise to instruct him how to manage the Italian war, and how to conclude it with his honor; that is, in other words, to lay the foundations of that empire which Augustus was to govern. This is the noble invention of our author; but it hath been copied by so many signpost daubers, that now 't is grown fulsome, rather by their want of skill than by the commonness.

In the last place, I may safely grant that, by reading Homer, Virgil was taught to imitate his invention; that is, to imitate like him; which is no more than if a painter studied Raphael, that he might learn to design after his manner. And thus I might imitate Virgil, if I were capable of writing an heroic poem, and yet the invention be my own; but I should endeavor to avoid a servile copying. I would not give the same story under other names, with the same characters, in the same order, and with the same sequel; for every common reader to find me out at the first sight for a plagiary, and cry: "This I read before in Virgil, in a better language, and in better verse. This is like Merry Andrew on the low rope, copying lubberly the same tricks which his master is so dext'rously performing on the high."

I will trouble your Lordship but with one objection more, which I know not whether I found in Le Fèvre, or Valois; but I am sure I have read it in another French critic, whom I will not name, because I think it is not much for his reputation. Virgil, in the heat of action—suppose, for example, in describing the fury of his hero in a battle, when he is endeavoring to raise our concernments to the highest pitch—turns short on the sudden into some similitude, which diverts, say they, your attention from the main subject, and misspends it on some trivial image. He pours cold water into the caldron, when his business is to make it boil.

This accusation is general against all who would be thought heroic poets; but I think it touches Virgil less than any. He is too great a master of his art, to make a blot which may so easily be hit. Similitudes, as I have said, are not for tragedy, which is all violent, and where the passions are in a perpetual ferment; for there they deaden where they should animate; they are not of the nature of dialogue, unless in comedy: a metaphor is almost all the stage can suffer, which is a kind of similitude comprehended in a word. But this figure has a contrary effect in heroic poetry; there 'tis employ'd to raise the admiration, which is its proper business; and admiration is not of so violent a nature as fear or hope, compassion or horror, or any concernment we can have for such a person on the stage. Not but I confess that similitudes and descriptions, when drawn into an unreasonable length, must needs nauseate the reader. Once, I remember, and but once, Virgil makes a similitude of fourteen lines; and his description of Fame is about the same number. He is blam'd for both; and I doubt not but he would have contracted them, had he liv'd to have review'd his work; but faults are no precedents. This I have observ'd of his similitudes in general, that they are not plac'd, as our unobserving critics tell us, in the heat of any action, but commonly in its declining. When he has warm'd us in his description as much as possibly he can, then, lest that warmth should languish, he renews it by some apt similitude, which illustrates his subject, and yet palls not his audience. I need give your Lordship but one example of this kind, and leave the rest to your observation, when next you review the whole *Æneis* in the original, unblemish'd by my rude translation. 'Tis in the First Book, where the poet describes Neptune composing the ocean, on which Æolus had rais'd a tempest without his permission. He had already chidden the rebellious winds for obeying the commands of their usurping master; he had warn'd them from the seas; he had beaten down the billows with his mace, dispell'd the clouds, restor'd the sunshine, while Triton and Cymothoe were heaving the ships from off the quicksands, before the poet would offer at a similitude for illustration:

>   Ac, veluti magno in populo cum sæpe coorta est
>   Seditio, sævitque animis ignobile vulgus,
>   Jamque faces et saxa volant; furor arma ministrat;
>   Tum, pietate gravem ac meritis si forte virum quem
>   Conspexere, silent, arrectisque auribus adstant;
>   Ille regit dictis animos, et pectora mulcet:
>   Sic cunctus pelagi cecidit fragor, æquora postquam
>   Prospiciens genitor cœloque invectus aperto
>   Flectit equos, curruque volans dat lora secundo.

This is the first similitude which Virgil makes in this poem, and one of the longest in the whole; for which reason I the rather cite it. While the storm was in its fury, any allusion had been improper; for the poet could have compar'd it to nothing more impetuous than itself; consequently he could have made no illustration. If he could have illustrated, it had been an ambitious ornament out of season, and would have diverted our concernment: *nunc non erat hisce locus;* and therefore he deferr'd it to its proper place.

These are the criticisms of most moment which have been made against the *Æneis* by the ancients or moderns. As for the particular exceptions against this or that passage, Macrobius and Pontanus have answer'd them already. If I desir'd to appear more learned than I am, it had been as easy for me to have taken their objections

DEDICATION OF THE ÆNEIS

and solutions, as it is for a country parson to take the expositions of the fathers out of Junius and Tremellius, or not to have nam'd the authors from whence I had them; for so Ruæus, otherwise a most judicious commentator on Virgil's works, has us'd Pontanus, his greatest benefactor; of whom he is very silent; and I do not remember that he once cites him.

What follows next is no objection; for that implies a fault: and it had been none in Virgil, if he had extended the time of his action beyond a year. At least Aristotle has set no precise limits to it. Homer's, we know, was within two months: Tasso, I am sure, exceeds not a summer; and, if I examin'd him, perhaps he might be reduc'd into a much less compass. Bossu leaves it doubtful whether Virgil's action were within the year, or took up some months beyond it. Indeed, the whole dispute is of no more concernment to the common reader, than it is to a plowman, whether February this year had 28 or 29 days in it. But, for the satisfaction of the more curious, of which number I am sure your Lordship is one, I will translate what I think convenient out of Segrais, whom perhaps you have not read; for he has made it highly probable that the action of the *Æneis* began in the spring, and was not extended beyond the autumn. And we have known campaigns that have begun sooner and have ended later.

Ronsard, and the rest whom Segrais names, who are of opinion that the action of this poem takes up almost a year and half, ground their calculations thus. Anchises died in Sicily at the end of winter, or beginning of the spring. Æneas, immediately after the interment of his father, puts to sea for Italy. He is surpris'd by the tempest describ'd in the beginning of the First Book; and there it is that the scene of the poem opens, and where the action must commence. He is driven by this storm on the coasts of Afric; he stays at Carthage all that summer, and almost all the winter following, sets sail again for Italy just before the beginning of the spring, meets with contrary winds, and makes Sicily the second time. This part of the action completes the year. Then he celebrates the anniversary of his father's funerals, and shortly after arrives at Cumes; and from thence his time is taken up in his first treaty with Latinus, the overture of the war, the siege of his camp by Turnus, his going for succors to relieve it, his return, the raising of the siege by the first battle, the twelve days' truce, the second battle, the assault of Laurentum, and the single fight with Turnus; all which, they say, cannot take up less than four or five months more; by which account we cannot suppose the entire action to be contain'd in a much less compass than a year and half.

Segrais reckons another way; and his computation is not condemn'd by the learned Ruæus, who compil'd and publish'd the commentaries on our poet which we call the Dauphin's *Virgil*.

He allows the time of year when Anchises died to be in the latter end of winter, or the beginning of the spring: he acknowledges that, when Æneas is first seen at sea afterwards, and is driven by the tempest on the coast of Afric, is the time when the action is naturally to begin: he confesses, farther, that Æneas left Carthage in the latter end of winter; for Dido tells him in express terms, as an argument for his longer stay:

> Quinetiam hiberno moliris sidere classem.

But, whereas Ronsard's followers suppose that when Æneas had buried his father, he set sail immediately for Italy, (tho' the tempest drove him on the coast of Carthage,) Segrais will by no means allow that supposition, but thinks it much more probable that he remain'd in Sicily till the midst of July, or the beginning of August; at which time he places the first appearance of his hero on the sea, and there opens the action of the poem. From which beginning to the death of Turnus, which concludes the action, there need not be suppos'd above ten months of intermediate time: for, arriving at Carthage in the latter end of summer, staying there the winter following, departing thence in the very beginning of the spring, making a short abode in Sicily the second time, landing in Italy, and making the war, may be reasonably judg'd the business but of ten months. To this the Ronsardians reply, that, having been for seven years before in quest of Italy, and having no more to do in Sicily than to inter his father—after that office was perform'd, what remain'd for him, but, without delay, to pursue his first adventure? To which Segrais answers, that the obsequies of his father, according to the rites of the Greeks and Romans, would detain him for many days; that a longer time must be taken up in the refitting of his ships after so tedious a voyage, and in refreshing his weather-beaten soldiers on a friendly coast. These indeed are but suppositions on both sides; yet those of Segrais seem better grounded. For the feast of Dido, when she entertain'd Æneas first, has the appearance of a summer's night, which seems already almost ended when he begins his story; therefore the love was made in autumn: the hunting follow'd properly, when the heats of that scorching country were declining; the winter was pass'd in jollity, as the season and their love requir'd; and he left her in the latter end of winter, as is already prov'd. This opinion is fortified by the arrival of Æneas at the mouth of Tiber, which marks the season of the spring; that season being perfectly describ'd by the singing of the birds, saluting the dawn, and by the beauty of the place, which the poet seems to have painted expressly in the *Seventh Æneid:*

> Aurora in roseis fulgebat lutea bigis,
> Cum venti posuere; variæ circumque supraque
> Assuetæ ripis volucres et fluminis alveo
> Æthera mulcebant cantu.——

The remainder of the action requir'd but three months more: for, when Æneas went for succor to the Tuscans, he found their army in a readiness to march, and wanting only a commander; so that, according to this calculation, the *Æneis* takes not up above a year complete, and may be comprehended in less compass.

This, amongst other circumstances treated more at large by Segrais, agrees with the rising of Orion, which caus'd the tempest describ'd in the beginning of the First Book. By some passages in the *Pastorals,* but more particularly in the *Georgics,* our poet is found to be an exact astronomer, according to the knowledge of that age. Now Ilioneus (whom Virgil twice employs in embassies, as the best speaker of the Trojans) attributes that tempest to Orion, in his speech to Dido:

> Cum subito assurgens fluctu nimbosus Orion.

He must mean either the *heliacal* or *achronical* rising of that sign. The *heliacal* rising of a constellation is when it comes from under the rays of the sun and begins to appear before daylight. The *achronical* rising, on the contrary, is when it appears at the close of day, and in opposition of the sun's diurnal course.

The *heliacal* rising of Orion is at present computed to be about the sixth of July; and about that time it is that he either causes or presages tempests on the seas.

Segrais has observ'd farther, that, when Anna counsels Dido to stay Æneas during the winter, she speaks also of Orion:

> Dum pelago desævit hiems, et aquosus Orion.

If therefore Ilioneus, according to our supposition, understand the *heliacal* rising of Orion, Anna must mean the *achronical,* which the different epithets given to that constellation seem to manifest. Ilioneus calls him *nimbosus;* Anna, *aquosus.* He is tempestuous in the summer, when he rises *heliacally,* and rainy in the winter, when he rises *achronically.* Your Lordship will pardon me for the frequent repetition of these cant words, which I could not avoid in this abbreviation of Segrais, who, I think, deserves no little commendation in this new criticism.

I have yet a word or two to say of Virgil's machines, from my own observation of them. He has imitated those of Homer, but not copied them. It was establish'd long before this time, in the Roman religion as well as in the Greek, that there were gods; and both nations, for the most part, worship'd the same deities; as did also the Trojans, from whom the Romans, I suppose, would rather be thought to derive the rites of their religion than from the Grecians; because they thought themselves descended from them. Each of those gods had his proper office, and the chief of them their particular attendants. Thus Jupiter had in propriety Ganymede and Mercury, and Juno had Iris. It was not for Virgil then to create new ministers; he must take what he found in his religion. It cannot therefore be said that he borrow'd them from Homer, any more than Apollo, Diana, and the rest, whom he uses as he finds occasion for them, as the Grecian poet did; but he invents the occasions for which he uses them. Venus, after the destruction of Troy, had gain'd Neptune entirely to her party; therefore we find him busy in the beginning of the *Æneis,* to calm the tempest rais'd by Æolus, and afterwards conducting the Trojan fleet to Cumes in safety, with the loss only of their pilot, for whom he bargains. I name those two examples amongst a hundred which I omit, to prove that Virgil, generally speaking, employ'd his machines in performing those things which might possibly have been done without them. What more frequent than a storm at sea, upon the rising of Orion? What wonder, if, amongst so many ships, there should one be overset, which was commanded by Orontes, tho' half the winds had not been there which Æolus employ'd? Might not Palinurus, without a miracle, fall asleep, and drop into the sea, having been overwearied with watching, and secure of a quiet passage, by his observation of the skies? At least Æneas, who knew nothing of the machine of Somnus, takes it plainly in this sense:

> O nimium cœlo et pelago confise sereno
> Nudus in ignota, Palinure, jacebis arena.

But machines sometimes are specious things, to amuse the reader and give a color of probability to things otherwise incredible. And, besides, it sooth'd the vanity of the Romans, to find the gods so visibly concern'd in all the actions of their predecessors. We, who are better taught by our religion, yet own every wonderful accident which befalls us for the best, to be brought to pass by some special providence of Almighty God, and by the care of guardian angels; and from hence I might infer that no heroic poem can be writ on the Epicurean principles; which I could easily demonstrate, if there were need to prove it, or I had leisure.

When Venus opens the eyes of her son Æneas, to behold the gods who combated against Troy in that fatal night when it was surpris'd, we share the pleasure of that glorious vision (which Tasso has not ill copied in the sacking of Jerusalem). But the Greeks had done their business, tho' neither Neptune, Juno, or Pallas had given them their divine assistance. The most crude machine which Virgil uses is in the episode of Camilla, where Opis, by the command of her mistress, kills Aruns. The next is in the *Twelfth Æneid,* where Venus cures her son Æneas. But in the last of these the poet was driven to a necessity; for Turnus was to be slain that very day; and Æneas, wounded as he was, could not have engag'd him in single combat, unless his hurt had been miraculously heal'd. And the poet had consider'd that the *dittany* which she brought from Crete could not have wrought so speedy an effect, without the juice of *ambrosia*, which she mingled with it. After all, that his machine might not seem too violent, we see the hero limping after Turnus. The wound was skinn'd, but the strength of his thigh was not restor'd. But what reason had our author to wound Æneas at so critical a time? And how came the cuisses to be worse temper'd than the rest of his armor, which was all wrought by Vulcan and his journeymen? These difficulties are not easily to be solv'd, without confessing that Virgil had not life enough to correct his work; tho' he had review'd it, and found those errors which he resolv'd to mend: but, being prevented by death, and not willing to leave an imperfect work behind him, he ordain'd, by his last testament, that his *Æneis* should be burn'd. As for the death of Aruns, who was shot by a goddess, the machine was not altogether so outrageous as the wounding Mars and Venus by the sword of Diomede. Two divinities, one would have thought, might have pleaded their prerogative of impassibility, or at least not have been wounded by any mortal hand; beside that the ἰχωρ which they shed was so very like our common blood, that it was not to be distinguish'd from it, but only by the name and color. As for what Horace says in his *Art of Poetry*, that no machines are to be us'd, unless on some extraordinary occasion:

Nec deus intersit, nisi dignus vindice nodus—

that rule is to be applied to the theater, of which he is then speaking; and means no more than this, that, when the knot of the play is to be untied, and no other way is left for making the discovery; then, and not otherwise, let a god descend upon a rope, and clear the business to the audience. But this has no relation to the machines which are us'd in an epic poem.

In the last place, for the *Dira,* or flying pest, which, flapping on the shield of Turnus, and fluttering about his head, dishearten'd him in the duel, and presag'd to him his approaching death, I might have plac'd it more properly amongst the objections; for the critics who lay want of courage to the charge of Virgil's hero quote this passage as a main proof of their assertion. They say our author had not only secur'd him before the duel, but also, in the beginning of it, had given him the advantage in impenetrable arms, and in his sword; for that of Turnus was not his own, which was forg'd by Vulcan for his father, but a weapon which he had snatch'd in haste, and by mistake, belonging to his charioteer Metiscus; that, after all this, Jupiter, who was partial to the Trojan, and distrustful of the event, tho' he had hung the balance, and given it a jog of his hand to weigh down Turnus, thought convenient to give the Fates a collateral security, by sending the screech owl to discourage him: for which they quote these words of Virgil:

> ——— Non me tua turbida virtus
> Terret, ait: dii me terrent, et Jupiter hostis.

In answer to which, I say that this machine is one of those which the poet uses only for ornament, and not out of necessity. Nothing can be more beautiful or more poetical than his description of the three *Diræ,* or the setting of the balance which our Milton has borrow'd from him, but employ'd to a different end: for, first, he makes God Almighty set the scale for St. Gabriel and Satan, when he knew no combat was to follow; then he makes the good angel's scale descend, and the Devil's mount, quite contrary to Virgil, if I have translated the three verses according to my author's sense:

> Jupiter ipse duas æquato examine lances
> Sustinet; et fata imponit diversa duorum;
> Quem damnet labor, et quo vergat pondere letum.

For I have taken these words, *quem damnet labor,* in the sense which Virgil gives them in another place—*damnabis tu quoque votis* —to signify a prosperous event. Yet I dare not condemn so great a genius as Milton: for I am much mistaken if he alludes not to the text in Daniel, where Belshazzar was put into the balance and found too light. This is digression; and I return to my subject. I said above that these two machines of the balance and the *Dira* were only ornamental, and that the success of the duel had been the same without them. For, when Æneas and Turnus stood fronting each other before the altar, Turnus look'd dejected, and his color faded in his face, as if he desponded of the victory before the fight; and not only he, but all his party, when the strength of the two champions was judg'd by the proportion of their limbs, concluded it was *impar pugna,* and that their chief was overmatch'd: whereupon Juturna (who was of the same opinion) took this opportunity to break the treaty and renew the war. Juno herself had plainly told the nymph beforehand that her brother was to fight

> Imparibus fatis, nec diis viribus æquis;

so that there was no need of an apparition to fright Turnus: he had the presage within himself of his impending destiny. The *Dira* only serv'd to confirm him in his first opinion, that it was his destiny to die in the ensuing combat; and in this sense are those words of Virgil to be taken:

> ——Non me tua turbida virtus
> Terret, ait: dii me terrent, et Jupiter hostis.

I doubt not but the adverb *solum* is to be understood: "'Tis not your valor *only* that gives me this concernment; but I find also, by this portent, that Jupiter is my enemy." For Turnus fled before, when his first sword was broken, till his sister supplied him with a better; which indeed he could not use, because Æneas kept him at a distance with his spear. I wonder Ruæus saw not this, where he charges his author so unjustly, for giving Turnus a second sword to no purpose. How could he fasten a blow, or make a thrust, when he was not suffer'd to approach? Besides, the chief errand of the *Dira* was to warn Juturna from the field, for she could have brought the chariot again, when she saw her brother worsted in the duel. I might farther add, that Æneas was so eager of the fight that he left the city, now almost in his possession, to decide his quarrel with Turnus by the sword; whereas Turnus had manifestly declin'd the combat, and suffer'd his sister to convey him as far from the reach of his enemy as she could. I say, not only suffer'd her, but consented to it; for 'tis plain he knew her, by these words:

> O soror, et dudum agnovi, cum prima per artem
> Fœdera turbasti, teque hæc in bella dedisti;
> Et nunc nequicquam fallis dea.—

I have dwelt so long on this subject, that I must contract what I have to say in reference to my translation, unless I would swell my preface into a volume, and make it formidable to your Lordship, when you see so many pages yet behind. And indeed what I have already written, either in justification or praise of Virgil, is against myself, for presuming to copy, in my coarse English, the thoughts and beautiful expressions of this inimitable poet, who flourish'd in an age when his language was brought to its last perfection, for which it was particularly owing to him and Horace. I will give your Lordship my opinion, that those two friends had consulted each other's judgment, wherein they should endeavor to excel; and they seem to have pitch'd on propriety of thought, elegance of words, and harmony of numbers. Acording to this model, Horace writ his *Odes* and *Epodes:* for his *Satires* and *Epistles,* being intended wholly for instruction, requir'd another style:

Ornari res ipsa negat, contenta doceri—

and therefore, as he himself professes, are *sermoni propiora,* nearer prose than verse. But Virgil, who never attempted the lyric verse, is everywhere elegant, sweet, and flowing in his hexameters. His words are not only chosen, but the places in which he ranks them for the sound; he who removes them from the station wherein their master sets them, spoils the harmony. What he says of the Sibyl's prophecies may be as properly applied to every word of his: they must be read in order as they lie; the least breath discomposes them; and somewhat of their divinity is lost. I cannot boast that I have been thus exact in my verses; but I have endeavor'd to follow the example of my master, and am the first Englishman, perhaps, who made it his design to copy him in his numbers, his choice of words, and his placing them for the sweetness of the sound. On this last consideration I have shunn'd the *cæsura* as much as possibly I could: for, wherever that is us'd, it gives a roughness to the verse; of which we can have little need in a language which is overstock'd with consonants. Such is not the Latin, where the vowels and consonants are mix'd in proportion to each other; yet Virgil judg'd the vowels to have somewhat of an over-balance, and therefore tempers their sweetness with *cæsuras.* Such difference there is in tongues, that the same figure which roughens one, gives majesty to another; and that was it which Virgil studied in his verses. Ovid uses it but rarely; and hence it is that his versification cannot so properly be call'd sweet, as luscious. The Italians are forc'd upon it once or twice in every line, because they have a redundancy of vowels in their language. Their metal is so soft that it will not coin without alloy to harden it. On the other side, for the reason already nam'd,'tis all we can do to give sufficient sweetness to our language: we must not only choose our words for elegance, but for sound; to perform which, a mastery in the language is requir'd; the poet must have a magazine of words, and have the art to manage his few vowels to the best advantage, that they may go the farther. He must also know the nature of the vowels—which are more sonorous, and which more soft and sweet—and so dispose them as his present occasions require: all which, and a thousand secrets of versification beside, he may learn from Virgil, if he will take him for his guide. If he be above Virgil, and is resolv'd to follow his own *verve,* (as the French call it,) the proverb will fall heavily upon him: "Who teaches himself, has a fool for his master."

Virgil employ'd eleven years upon his *Æneis;* yet he left it, as he thought himself, imperfect. Which when I seriously consider, I wish that, instead of three years, which I have spent in the translation of his works, I had four years more allow'd me to correct my errors, that I might make my version somewhat more tolerable than it is: for a poet cannot have too great a reverence for his readers, if he expects his labors should survive him. Yet I will neither plead my age nor sickness, in excuse of the faults which I have made: that I wanted time, is all I have to say; for some of my subscribers grew so clamorous that I could no longer defer the publication. I hope, from the candor of your Lordship, and your often experienc'd goodness to me, that, if the faults are not too many, you will make allowances with Horace:

> Si plura nitent in carmine, non ego paucis
> Offendar maculis, quas aut incuria fudit,
> Aut humana parum cavit natura.

You may please also to observe, that there is not, to the best of my remembrance, one vowel gaping on another for want of a *cæsura,* in this whole poem; but, where a vowel ends a word, the next begins either with a consonant, or what is its equivalent; for our *W* and *H* aspirate, and our diphthongs, are plainly such. The greatest latitude I take is in the letter *Y,* when it concludes a word and the first syllable of the next begins with a vowel. Neither need I have call'd this a latitude, which is only an explanation of this general rule, that no vowel can be cut off before another when we cannot sink the pronunciation of it; as *he, she, me, I, &c.* Virgil thinks it sometimes a beauty to imitate the license of the Greeks, and leave two vowels opening on each other, as in that verse of the *Third Pastoral:*

> Et succus pecori, et lac subducitur agnis.

But, *nobis non licet esse tam disertis,* at least if we study to refine our numbers. I have long had by me the materials of an English *prosodia,* containing all the mechanical rules of versification, wherein I have treated with some exactness of the feet, the quantities, and the pauses. The French and Italians know nothing of the two first; at least their best poets have not practic'd them. As for the pauses, Malherbe first brought them into France, within this last century; and we see how they adorn their *Alexandrins.* But, as Virgil propounds a riddle, which he leaves unsolv'd:

> Dic quibus in terris, inscripti nomina regum
> Nascantur flores; et Phyllida solus habeto;

so I will give your Lordship another, and leave the exposition of it to your acute judgment. I am sure there are few who make verses have observ'd the sweetness of these two lines in *Cooper's Hill:*

> Tho' deep, yet clear; tho' gentle, yet not dull;
> Strong without rage; without o'erflowing, full.

And there are yet fewer who can find the reason of that sweetness. I have given it to some of my friends in conversation, and they have allow'd the criticism to be just. But, since the evil of false quantities is difficult to be cur'd in any modern language; since the French and the Italians, as well as we, are yet ignorant what feet are to be us'd in heroic poetry; since I have not strictly observ'd those rules myself which I can teach others; since I pretend to no dictatorship among my fellow poets; since, if I should instruct some of them to make well-running verses, they want genius to give them strength as well as sweetness; and, above all, since your Lordship has advis'd me not to publish that little which I know, I look on your counsel as your command, which I shall observe inviolably, till you shall please to revoke it, and leave me at liberty to make my thoughts public. In the mean time, that I may arrogate nothing to myself, I must acknowledge that Virgil in Latin, and Spenser in English, have been my masters. Spenser has also given me the boldness to make use sometimes of his *Alexandrin* line, which we call, tho' improperly, the Pindaric, because Mr. Cowley has often employ'd it in his *Odes*. It adds a certain majesty to the verse, when 'tis us'd with judgment, and stops the sense from overflowing into another line. Formerly the French, like us and the Italians, had but five feet, or ten syllables, in their heroic verse; but since Ronsard's time, as I suppose, they found their tongue too weak to support their epic poetry without the addition of another foot. That indeed has given it somewhat of the run and measure of a *trimeter;* but it runs with more activity than strength: their language is not strung with sinews, like our English. It has the nimbleness of a greyhound, but not the bulk and body of a mastiff. Our men and our verses overbear them by their weight; and *pondere, non numero,* is the British motto. The French have set up purity for the standard of their language; and a masculine vigor is that of ours. Like their tongue is the genius of their poets, light and trifling in comparison of the English; more proper for sonnets, madrigals, and elegies, than heroic poetry. The turn on thoughts and words is their chief talent, but the epic poem is too stately to receive those little ornaments. The painters draw their nymphs in thin and airy habits; but the weight of gold and of embroideries is reserv'd for queens and goddesses. Virgil is never frequent in those turns, like Ovid, but much more sparing of them in his *Æneis* than in his *Pastorals* and *Georgics*.

> Ignoscenda quidem, scirent si ignoscere manes.

That turn is beautiful indeed; but he employs it in the story of Orpheus and Eurydice, not in his great poem. I have us'd that license in his *Æneis* sometimes, but I own it as my fault. 'Twas given to those who understand no better. 'Tis like Ovid's

> Semivirumque bovem, semibovemque virum.

The poet found it before his critics, but it was a darling sin, which he would not be persuaded to reform. The want of genius, of which I have accus'd the French, is laid to their charge by one of their own great authors, tho' I have forgotten his name, and where I read it. If rewards could make good poets, their great master has not been wanting on his part in his bountiful encouragements; for he is wise enough to imitate Augustus, if he had a Maro. The triumvir and proscriber had descended to us in a more hideous form than they now appear, if the emperor had not taken care to make friends of him and Horace. I confess the banishment of Ovid was a blot in his escutcheon: yet he was only banish'd; and who knows but his crime was capital, and then his exile was a favor? Ariosto, who, with all his faults, must be acknowledg'd a great poet, has put these words into the mouth of an evangelist; but whether they will pass for gospel now, I cannot tell:

> Non fu si santo ni benigno Augusto,
> Come la tuba di Virgilio suona.
> L' haver havuto in poesia buon gusto,
> La proscrittione iniqua gli perdona.

But heroic poetry is not of the growth of France, as it might be of England, if it were cultivated. Spenser wanted only to have read the rules of Bossu; for no man was ever born with a greater genius, or had more knowledge to support it. But the performance of the French is not equal to their skill; and hitherto we have wanted skill to perform better. Segrais, whose preface is so wonderfully good, yet is wholly destitute of elevation, tho' his version is much better than that of the two brothers, or any of the rest who have attempted Virgil. Hannibal Caro is a great name amongst the Italians; yet his translation of the *Æneis* is most scandalously mean, tho' he has taken the advantage of writing in blank verse, and freed himself from the shackles of modern rhyme, (if it be modern; for Le Clerc has told us lately, and I believe has made it out, that David's Psalms were written in as errant rhyme as they are translated.) Now, if a Muse cannot run when she is unfetter'd, 'tis a sign she has but little speed. I will not make a digression here, tho' I am strangely tempted to it; but will only say, that he who can write well in rhyme, may write better in blank verse. Rhyme is certainly a constraint even to the best poets, and those who make it with most ease; tho' perhaps I have as little reason to complain that hardship as any man, excepting Quarles and Withers. What it adds to sweetness, it takes away from sense; and he who loses the least by it may be call'd a gainer. It often makes us swerve from an author's meaning; as, if a mark be set up for an archer at a great distance, let him aim as exactly as he can, the least wind will take his arrow, and divert it from the white. I return to our Italian translator of the *Æneis*. He is a foot-poet, he lackeys by the side of Virgil at the best, but never mounts behind him. Doctor Morelli, who is no mean critic in our poetry, and therefore may be presum'd to be a better in his own language, has confirm'd me in this opinion by his judgment, and thinks, withal, that he has often mistaken his master's sense. I would say so, if I durst, but am afraid I have committed the same fault more often, and more grossly; for I have forsaken Ruæus (whom generally I follow) in many places, and made expositions of my own in some, quite contrary to him. Of which I will give but two examples, because they are so near each other, in the *Tenth Æneid:*

—— Sorti pater æquus utrique.

Pallas says it to Turnus, just before they fight. Ruæus thinks that the word *pater* is to be referr'd to Evander, the father of Pallas. But how could he imagine that it was the same thing to Evander, if his son were slain, or if he overcame? The poet certainly intended Jupiter, the common father of mankind; who, as Pallas hop'd, would stand an impartial spectator of the combat, and not be more favorable to Turnus than to him. The second is not long after it, and both before the duel is begun. They are the words of Jupiter, who comforts Hercules for the death of Pallas, which was immediately to ensue, and which Hercules could not hinder, (tho' the young hero had address'd his prayers to him for his assistance,) because the gods cannot control destiny.—The verse follows:

Sic ait; atque oculos Rutulorum rejicit arvis,

which the same Ruæus thus construes: Jupiter, after he had said this, immediately turns his eyes to the Rutulian fields, and beholds the duel. I have given this place another exposition, that he turn'd his eyes from the field of combat, that he might not behold a sight so unpleasing to him. The word *rejicit,* I know, will admit of both senses; but Jupiter having confess'd that he could not alter fate, and being griev'd he could not, in consideration of Hercules, it seems to me that he should avert his eyes, rather than take pleasure in the spectacle. But of this I am not so confident as the other, tho' I think I have follow'd Virgil's sense.

What I have said, tho' it has the face of arrogance, yet is intended for the honor of my country; and therefore I will boldly own that this English translation has more of Virgil's spirit in it than either the French or the Italian. Some of our countrymen have translated episodes and other parts of Virgil with great success; as particularly your Lordship, whose version of *Orpheus and Eurydice* is eminently good. Amongst the dead authors, the *Silenus* of my Lord Roscommon cannot be too much commended. I say nothing of Sir John Denham, Mr. Waller, and Mr. Cowley; 'tis the utmost of my ambition to be thought their equal, or not to be much inferior to them, and some others of the living. But 'tis one thing to take pains on a fragment, and translate it perfectly; and another thing to have the weight of a whole author on my shoulders. They who believe the burthen light, let them attempt the *Fourth, Sixth* or *Eighth Pastoral;* the *First* or *Fourth Georgic;* and, amongst the *Æneids,* the *Fourth,* the *Fifth,* the *Seventh,* the *Ninth,* the *Tenth,* the *Eleventh,* or the *Twelfth;* for in these I think I have succeeded best.

Long before I undertook this work, I was no stranger to the original. I had also studied Virgil's design, his disposition of it, his manners, his judicious management of the figures, the sober retrenchments of his sense, which always leaves somewhat to gratify our imagination, on which it may enlarge at pleasure; but, above all, the elegance of his expressions, and the harmony of his numbers. For, as I have said in a former dissertation, the words are in poetry what the colors are in painting. If the design be good, and the draught be true, the coloring is the first beauty that strikes the eye. Spenser and Milton are the nearest, in English, to Virgil and Horace in the Latin; and I have endeavor'd to form my style by imitating their masters. I will farther own to you, my Lord, that my chief ambition is to please those readers who have discernment enough to prefer Virgil before any other poet in the Latin tongue. Such spirits as he desir'd to please, such would I choose for my judges, and would stand or fall by them alone. Segrais has distinguish'd the readers of poetry, according to their capacity of judging, into three classes; (he might have said the same of writers too, if he had pleas'd.) In the lowest form he places those whom he calls *les petits esprits;* such things as are our upper-gallery audience in a playhouse, who like nothing but the husk and rind of wit; prefer a quibble, a conceit, an epigram, before solid sense and elegant expression; these are mob readers. If Virgil and Martial stood for Parliament-men, we know already who would carry it. But, tho' they make the greatest appearance in the field, and cry the loudest, the best on't is, they are but a sort of French Huguenots, or Dutch boors, brought over in herds, but not naturaliz'd; who have not land of two pounds *per annum* in Parnassus, and therefore are not privileg'd to poll. Their authors are of the same level, fit to represent them on a mountebank's stage, or to be masters of the ceremonies in a bear garden. Yet these are they who have the most admirers. But it often happens, to their mortification, that, as their readers improve their stock of sense, (as they may by reading better books, and by conversation with men of judgment,) they soon forsake them; and when the torrent from the mountains falls no more, the swelling writer is reduc'd into his shallow bed, like the Mançanares at Madrid, with scarce water to moisten his own pebbles. There are a middle sort of readers, (as we hold there is a middle state of souls,) such as have a farther insight than the former, yet have not the capacity of judging right; for I speak not of those who are brib'd by a party, and know better, if they were not corrupted; but I mean a company of warm young men, who are not yet arriv'd so far as to discern the difference betwixt fustian, or ostentatious sentences, and the true sublime. These are above liking Martial, or Owen's *Epigrams,* but they would certainly set Virgil below Statius or Lucan. I need not say their poets are of the same paste with their admirers. They affect greatness in all they write; but 'tis a bladder'd greatness, like that of the vain man whom Seneca describes; an ill habit of body, full of humors, and swell'd with dropsy. Even these too desert

DEDICATION OF THE ÆNEIS

their authors, as their judgment ripens. The young gentlemen themselves are commonly misled by their *pædagogue* at school, their tutor at the university, or their governor in their travels. And many of those three sorts are the most positive blockheads in the world. How many of those flatulent writers have I known who have sunk in their reputation after seven or eight editions of their works! for indeed they are poets only for young men. They had great success at their first appearance; but, not being of God, as a wit said formerly, they could not stand.

I have already nam'd two sorts of judges; but Virgil wrote for neither of them: and, by his example, I am not ambitious of pleasing the lowest or the middle form of readers.

He chose to please the most judicious, souls of the highest rank and truest understanding. These are few in number; but whoever is so happy as to gain their approbation can never lose it, because they never give it blindly. Then they have a certain *magnetism* in their judgment, which attracts others to their sense. Every day they gain some new proselyte, and in time become the Church. For this reason, a well-weigh'd judicious poem, which at its first appearance gains no more upon the world than to be just receiv'd, and rather not blam'd than much applauded, insinuates itself by insensible degrees into the liking of the reader: the more he studies it, the more it grows upon him; every time he takes it up, he discovers some new graces in it. And whereas poems which are produc'd by the vigor of imagination only, have a gloss upon them at the first which time wears off, the works of judgment are like the diamond; the more they are polish'd, the more luster they receive. Such is the difference betwixt Virgil's *Æneis* and Marini's *Adone*. And, if I may be allow'd to change the metaphor, I would say that Virgil is like the Fame which he describes:

> Mobilitate viget, viresque acquirit eundo.

Such a sort of reputation is my aim, tho' in a far inferior degree, according to my motto in the title-page: *Sequiturque patrem non passibus æquis:* and therefore I appeal to the highest court of judicature, like that of the peers, of which your Lordship is so great an ornament.

Without this ambition which I own, of desiring to please the *judices natos,* I could never have been able to have done anything at this age, when the fire of poetry is commonly extinguish'd in other men. Yet Virgil has given me the example of Entellus for my encouragement: when he was well heated, the younger champion could not stand before him. And we find the elder contended not for the gift, but for the honor: *nec dona moror.* For Dampier has inform'd us, in his *Voyages,* that the air of the country which produces gold is never wholesome.

I had long since consider'd that the way to please the best judges is not to translate a poet literally, and Virgil least of any other. For, his peculiar beauty lying in the choice of words, I am excluded from it by the narrow compass of our heroic verse, unless I would make use of monosyllables only, and those clogg'd with consonants, which are the dead weight of our mother tongue. 'Tis possible, I confess, tho' it rarely happens, that a verse of monosyllables may sound harmoniously; and some examples of it I have seen. My first line of the *Æneis* is not harsh:

Arms, and the man I sing, who, forc'd by fate, &c.

But a much better instance may be given from the last line of Manilius, made English by our learned and judicious Mr. Creech:

Nor could the world have borne so fierce a flame—

where the many liquid consonants are plac'd so artfully that they give a pleasing sound to the words, tho' they are all of one syllable.

'Tis true, I have been sometimes forc'd upon it in other places of this work; but I never did it out of choice: I was either in haste, or Virgil gave me no occasion for the ornament of words; for it seldom happens but a monosyllable line turns verse to prose; and even that prose is rugged and unharmonious. Philarchus, I remember, taxes Balzac for placing twenty monosyllables in file, without one dissyllable betwixt them. The way I have taken is not so strait as metaphrase, nor so loose as paraphrase: some things too I have omitted, and sometimes have added of my own. Yet the omissions, I hope, are but of circumstances, and such as would have no grace in English; and the additions, I also hope, are easily deduc'd from Virgil's sense. They will seem (at least I have the vanity to think so) not stuck into him, but growing out of him. He studies brevity more than any other poet; but he had the advantage of a language wherein much may be comprehended in a little space. We, and all the modern tongues, have more articles and pronouns, besides signs of tenses and cases, and other barbarities on which our speech is built by the faults of our forefathers. The Romans founded theirs upon the Greek: and the Greeks, we know, were laboring many hundred years upon their language before they brought it to perfection. They rejected all those signs, and cut off as many articles as they could spare; comprehending in one word what we are constrain'd to express in two; which is one reason why we cannot write so concisely as they have done. The word *pater,* for example, signifies not only *a* father, but *your* father, *my* father, *his* or *her* father, all included in a word.

This inconvenience is common to all modern tongues; and this alone constrains us to employ more words than the ancients needed. But having before observ'd that Virgil endeavors to be short, and at the same time elegant, I pursue the excellence and forsake the brevity. For there he is like ambergris, a rich perfume, but of so close and glutinous a body that it must be open'd with inferior scents of musk or civet, or the sweetness will not be drawn out into another language.

On the whole matter, I thought fit to steer betwixt the two extremes of paraphrase and literal translation; to keep as near my author as I could, without losing all his graces, the most eminent of which are in the beauty of his words; and those words, I must add, are always figurative. Such of these as would retain their elegance in our tongue, I have endeavor'd to graff on it; but most of them are of necessity to be lost, because they will not shine in any way but their own. Virgil has sometimes two of them in a line; but the scantiness of our heroic verse is not capable of receiving more than one; and that too must expiate for many others which have none. Such is the difference of the languages, or such my want of skill in choosing words. Yet I may presume to say, and I hope with as much reason as the French translator, that, taking all the materials of this divine author, I have endeavor'd to make Virgil speak such English as he would himself have spoken, if he had been born in England, and in this present age. I acknowledge, with Segrais, that I have not succeeded in this attempt according to my desire; yet I shall not be wholly without praise, if in some sort I may be allow'd to have copied the clearness, the purity, the easiness, and the magnificence of his style. But I shall have occasion to speak farther on this subject before I end the preface.

When I mention'd the Pindaric line, I should have added that I take another license in my verses; for I frequently make use of triplet rhymes, and for the same reason, because they bound the sense. And therefore I generally join these two licenses together, and make the last verse of the triplet a Pindaric: for, besides the majesty which it gives, it confines the sense within the barriers of three lines, which would languish if it were lengthen'd into four. Spenser is my example for both these privileges of English verses; and Chapman has follow'd him in his translation of Homer. Mr. Cowley has given in to them after both; and all succeeding writers after him. I regard them now as the *Magna Charta* of heroic poetry, and am too much an Englishman to lose what my ancestors have gain'd for me. Let the French and Italians value themselves on their regularity; strength and elevation are our standard. I said before, and I repeat it, that the affected purity of the French has unsinew'd their heroic verse. The language of an epic poem is almost wholly figurative; yet they are so fearful of a metaphor, that no example of Virgil can encourage them to be bold with safety. Sure they might warm themselves by that sprightly blaze, without approaching it so close as to singe their wings; they may come as near it as their master. Not that I would discourage that purity of diction in which he excels all other poets. But he knows how far to extend his franchises, and advances to the verge, without venturing a foot beyond it. On the other side, without being injurious to the memory of our English Pindar, I will presume to say that his metaphors are sometimes too violent, and his language is not always pure. But at the same time I must excuse him; for, thro' the iniquity of the times, he was forc'd to travel, at an age when, instead of learning foreign languages, he should have studied the beauties of his mother tongue, which, like all other speeches, is to be cultivated early, or we shall never write it with any kind of elegance. Thus by gaining abroad he lost at home; like the painter in the *Arcadia,* who, going to see a skirmish, had his arms lopp'd off, and return'd, says Sir Philip Sidney, well instructed how to draw a battle, but without a hand to perform his work.

There is another thing in which I have presum'd to deviate from him and Spenser. They both make hemistichs (or half verses) breaking off in the middle of a line. I confess there are not many such in the *Fairy Queen;* and even those few might be occasion'd by his unhappy choice of so long a stanza. Mr. Cowley had found out that no kind of staff is proper for a heroic poem, as being all too lyrical; yet, tho' he wrote in couplets, where rhyme is freer from constraint, he frequently affects half verses; of which we find not one in Homer, and I think not in any of the Greek poets, or the Latin, excepting only Virgil; and there is no question but he thought he had Virgil's authority for that license. But I am confident our poet never meant to leave him, or any other, such a precedent; and I ground my opinion on these two reasons. First, we find no example of a hemistich in any of his *Pastorals* or *Georgics;* for he had given the last finishing strokes to both these poems; but his *Æneis* he left so uncorrect, at least so short of that perfection at which he aim'd, that we know how hard a sentence he pass'd upon it. And, in the second place, I reasonably presume that he intended to have fill'd up all those hemistichs, because in one of them we find the sense imperfect:

> Quem tibi jam Troja—

which some foolish grammarian has ended for him with a half line of nonsense:

> ——peperit fumante Creusa:

for Ascanius must have been born some years before the burning of that city; which I need not prove. On the other side, we find also that he himself fill'd up one line in the *Sixth Æneid,* the enthusiasm seizing him while he was reading to Augustus:

> Misenum Æolidem, quo non præstantior alter
> Ære ciere viros—

to which he added, in that transport, *Martemque accendere cantu:* and never was any line more nobly finish'd; for the reasons which I have given in the *Book of Painting*. On these considerations I have shunn'd hemistichs; not being willing to imitate Virgil to a fault, like Alexander's courtiers, who affected to hold their necks awry, because he could not help it. I am confident your Lordship is by this time of my opinion, and that you will look on those half lines hereafter as the imperfect products of a hasty Muse; like the frogs and serpents in the Nile; part of them kindled into life, and part a lump of unform'd, unanimated mud.

I am sensible that many of my whole verses are as imperfect as those halves, for want of time to digest them better; but give me leave to make the excuse of Boccace, who, when he was upbraided that some of his novels had not the spirit of the rest, return'd this answer, that Charlemagne, who made the paladins, was never able to raise an army of them. The leaders may be heroes, but the multitude must consist of common men.

I am also bound to tell your Lordship, in my own defense, that, from the beginning of the *First Georgic* to the end of the last *Æneid*, I found the difficulty of translation growing on me in every succeeding book: for Virgil, above all poets, had a stock, which I may call almost inexhaustible, of figurative, elegant, and sounding words. I, who inherit but a small portion of his genius, and write in a language so much inferior to the Latin, have found it very painful to vary phrases, when the same sense returns upon me. Even he himself, whether out of necessity or choice, has often express'd the same thing in the same words, and often repeated two or three whole verses which he had us'd before. Words are not so easily coin'd as money; and yet we see that the credit not only of banks, but of exchequers, cracks, when little comes in and much goes out. Virgil call'd upon me in every line for some new word, and I paid so long, that I was almost bankrupt; so that the latter end must needs be more burdensome than the beginning or the middle; and, consequently, the *Twelfth Æneid* cost me double the time of the *First* and *Second*. What had become of me, if Virgil had tax'd me with another book? I had certainly been reduc'd to pay the public in hammer'd money, for want of mill'd; that is, in the same old words which I had us'd before; and the receivers must have been forc'd to have taken anything, where there was so little to be had.

Besides this difficulty (with which I have struggled, and made a shift to pass it over) there is one remaining, which is insuperable to all translators. We are bound to our author's sense, tho' with the latitudes already mention'd; for I think it not so sacred, as that one *iota* must not be added or diminish'd, on pain of an *anathema*. But slaves we are, and labor on another's man plantation; we dress the vineyard, but the wine is the owner's: if the soil be sometimes barren, then we are sure of being scourg'd; if it be fruitful, and our care succeeds, we are not thank'd; for the proud reader will only say the poor drudge has done his duty. But this is nothing to what follows; for, being oblig'd to make his sense intelligible, we are forc'd to untune our own verses, that we may give his meaning to the reader. He who invents is master of his thoughts and words; he can turn and vary them as he pleases, till he renders them harmonious. But the wretched translator has no such privilege; for, being tied to the thoughts, he must make what music he can in the expression; and for this reason it cannot always be so sweet as that of the original. There is a beauty of sound, as Segrais has observ'd, in some Latin words, which is wholly lost in any modern language. He instances in that *mollis amaracus,* on which Venus lays Cupid, in the *First Æneid*. If I should translate it *sweet marjoram,* as the word signifies, the reader would think I had mistaken Virgil: for those village words, as I may call them, give us a mean idea of the thing; but the sound of the Latin is so much more pleasing, by the just mixture of the vowels with the consonants, that it raises our fancies to conceive somewhat more noble than a common herb, and to spread roses under him, and strew lilies over him; a bed not unworthy the grandson of the goddess.

If I cannot copy his harmonious numbers, how shall I imitate his noble flights, where his thoughts and words are equally sublime?

> Quem quisquis studet æmulari,
> . . . . . . cæratis ope Dædalea
> Nititur pennis, vitreo daturus
> Nomina ponto.

What modern language, or what poet, can express the majestic beauty of this one verse, amongst a thousand others?

> Aude, hospes, contemnere opes, et te quoque dignum
> Finge deo.——

For my part, I am lost in the admiration of it: I contemn the world when I think on it, and myself when I translate it.

Lay by Virgil, I beseech your Lordship, and all my better sort of judges, when you take up my version; and it will appear a passable beauty when the original Muse is absent. But, like Spenser's false Florimel made of snow, it melts and vanishes when the true one comes in sight. I will not excuse, but justify myself for one pretended crime, with which I am liable to be charg'd by false critics, not only in this translation, but in many of my original poems—that I Latinize too much. 'Tis true that, when I find an English word significant and sounding, I neither borrow from the Latin or any other language; but, when I want at home, I must seek abroad.

If sounding words are not of our growth and manufacture, who shall hinder me to import them from a foreign country? I carry not out the treasure of the nation, which is never to return; but what I bring from Italy, I spend in England: here it remains, and here it circulates; for, if the coin be good, it will pass from one hand to another. I trade both with the living and the dead, for the enrichment of our native language. We have enough in England to supply our necessity; but, if we will have things of magnificence and splendor, we must get them by commerce. Poetry requires ornament; and that is not to be had from our old Teuton monosyllables: therefore, if I find any elegant word in a classic author, I propose it to be naturaliz'd, by using it myself; and, if the public approves of it, the bill passes. But every man cannot distinguish betwixt pedantry and poetry: every man, therefore, is not fit to innovate. Upon the whole matter, a poet must first be certain that the word he would introduce is beautiful in the Latin; and is to consider, in the next place, whether it will agree with the English idiom. After this, he ought to take the opinion of judicious friends, such as are learned in both languages; and, lastly, since no man is infallible, let him use this license very sparingly; for, if too many foreign words are pour'd in upon us, it looks as if they were design'd not to assist the natives, but to conquer them.

I am now drawing towards a conclusion, and suspect your Lordship is very glad of it. But permit me first to own what helps I have had in this undertaking. The late Earl of Lauderdale sent me over his new translation of the *Æneis,* which he had ended before I ingag'd in the same design. Neither did I then intend it; but, some proposals being afterwards made me by my bookseller, I desir'd his Lordship's leave that I might accept them, which he freely granted; and I have his letter to shew for that permission. He resolv'd to have printed his work; which he might have done two years before I could publish mine; and had perform'd it, if death had not prevented him. But having his manuscript in my hands, I consulted it as often as I doubted of my author's sense; for no man understood Virgil better than that learned nobleman. His friends, I hear, have yet another and more correct copy of that translation by them, which had they pleas'd to have given the public, the judges must have been convinc'd that I have not flatter'd him. Besides this help, which was not inconsiderable, Mr. Congreve has done me the favor to review the *Æneis,* and compare my version with the original. I shall never be asham'd to own that this excellent young man has shew'd me many faults, which I have endeavor'd to correct. 'Tis true, he might have easily found more, and then my translation had been more perfect.

Two other worthy friends of mine, who desire to have their names conceal'd, seeing me straiten'd in my time, took pity on me, and gave me the *Life of Virgil,* the two *Prefaces* to the *Pastorals* and the *Georgics,* and all the arguments in prose to the whole translation; which, perhaps, has caus'd a report that the two first poems are not mine. If it had been true that I had taken their verses for my own, I might have gloried in their aid; and, like Terence, have farther'd the opinion that Scipio and Lælius join'd with me. But the same style being continued thro' the whole, and the same laws of versification observ'd, are proofs sufficient that this is one man's work; and your Lordship is too well acquainted with my manner to doubt that any part of it is another's.

That your Lordship may see I was in earnest when I promis'd to hasten to an end, I will not give the reasons why I writ not always in the proper terms of navigation, land service, or in the cant of any profession. I will only say that Virgil has avoided those proprieties, because he writ not to mariners, soldiers, astronomers, gard'ners, peasants, &c., but to all in general, and in particular to men and ladies of the first quality, who have been better bred than to be too nicely knowing in the terms. In such cases, 'tis enough for a poet to write so plainly, that he may be understood by his readers; to avoid impropriety, and not affect to be thought learn'd in all things.

I have omitted the four preliminary lines of the *First Æneid,* because I think them inferior to any four others in the whole poem, and consequently believe they are not Virgil's. There is too great a gap betwixt the adjective *vicina* in the second line, and the substantive *arva* in the latter end of the third, which keeps his meaning in obscurity too long, and is contrary to the clearness of his style.

> Ut quamvis avidis

is too ambitious an ornament to be his; and

> Gratum opus agricolis

are all words unnecessary, and independent of what he said before.

> Horrentia Martis arma

is worse than any of the rest. *Horrentia* is such a flat epithet as Tully would have given us in his verses. 'Tis a mere filler, to stop a vacancy in the hexameter, and connect the preface to the work of Virgil. Our author seems to sound a charge, and begins like the clangor of a trumpet:

> Arma virumque cano, Trojæ qui primus ab oris—

scarce a word without an *r,* and the vowels for the greater part sonorous. The prefacer began with *Ille ego,* which he was constrain'd to patch up in the fourth line with *at nunc,* to make the sense cohere; and if both those words are not notorious botches, I am much deceiv'd, tho' the French translator thinks otherwise. For my own part, I am rather of the opinion that they were added by Tucca and Varius, than retrench'd.

I know it may be answer'd by such as think Virgil the author of the four lines, that he asserts his title to the *Æneis* in the beginning of this work, as he did to the two former in the last lines of the *Fourth Georgic.* I will not reply otherwise to this than by desiring them to compare these four lines with the four others, which we

DEDICATION OF THE ÆNEIS

know are his, because no poet but he alone could write them. If they cannot distinguish creeping from flying, let them lay down Virgil, and take up Ovid *de Ponto* in his stead. My master needed not the assistance of that preliminary poet to prove his claim. His own majestic mien discovers him to be the king, amidst a thousand courtiers. It was a superfluous office; and therefore I would not set those verses in the front of Virgil, but have rejected them to my own preface.

> I, who before, with shepherds in the groves,
> Sung to my oaten pipe their rural loves,
> And, issuing thence, compell'd the neighb'ring field
> A plenteous crop of rising corn to yield,
> Manur'd the glebe, and stock'd the fruitful plain,
> (A poem grateful to the greedy swain) &c.

If there be not a tolerable line in all these six, the prefacer gave me no occasion to write better. This is a just apology in this place, but I have done great wrong to Virgil in the whole translation. Want of time, the inferiority of our language, the inconvenience of rhyme, and all the other excuses I have made, may alleviate my fault, but cannot justify the boldness of my undertaking. What avails it me to acknowledge freely that I have not been able to do him right in any line? For even my own confession makes against me; and it will always be return'd upon me: "Why then did you attempt it?" To which no other answer can be made, than that I have done him less injury than any of his former libelers.

What they call'd his picture had been drawn at length, so many times, by the daubers of almost all nations, and still so unlike him, that I snatch'd up the pencil with disdain, being satisfied beforehand that I could make some small resemblance of him, tho' I must be content with a worse likeness. A *Sixth Pastoral,* a *Pharmaceutria,* a single *Orpheus,* and some other features, have been exactly taken; but those holiday authors writ for pleasure, and only shew'd us what they could have done, if they would have taken pains to perform the whole.

Be pleas'd, my Lord, to accept with your wonted goodness this unworthy present which I make you. I have taken off one trouble from you, of defending it, by acknowledging its imperfections; and, tho' some part of them are cover'd in the verse, (as Erichthonius rode always in a chariot, to hide his lameness,) such of them as cannot be conceal'd, you will please to connive at, tho', in the strictness of your judgment, you cannot pardon. If Homer was allow'd to nod sometimes in so long a work, it will be no wonder if I often fall asleep. You took my *Aureng-Zebe* into your protection, with all his faults; and I hope here cannot be so many, because I translate an author who gives me such examples of correctness. What my jury may be, I know not; but 'tis good for a criminal to plead before a favorable judge. If I had said partial, would your Lordship have forgiven me? Or will you give me leave to acquaint the world that I have many times been oblig'd to your bounty since the Revolution? Tho' I never was reduc'd to beg a charity, nor ever had the impudence to ask one, either of your Lordship, or your noble kinsman the Earl of Dorset, much less of any other; yet, when I least expected it, you have both remember'd me. So inherent it is in your family not to forget an old servant. It looks rather like ingratitude on my part, that, where I have been so often oblig'd, I have appear'd so seldom to return my thanks, and where I was also so sure of being well receiv'd. Somewhat of laziness was in the case, and somewhat too of modesty, but nothing of disrespect or of unthankfulness. I will not say that your Lordship has encourag'd me to this presumption, lest, if my labors meet with no success in public, I may expose your judgment to be censur'd. As for my own enemies, I shall never think them worth an answer; and, if your Lordship has any, they will not dare to arraign you for want of knowledge in this art, till they can produce somewhat better of their own than your *Essay on Poetry*. 'Twas on this consideration that I have drawn out my preface to so great a length. Had I not address'd to a poet, and a critic of the first magnitude, I had myself been tax'd for want of judgment, and sham'd my patron for want of understanding. But neither will you, my Lord, so soon be tir'd as any other, because the discourse is on your art; neither will the learned reader think it tedious, because it is *ad clerum*. At least, when he begins to be weary, the church doors are open. That I may pursue the allegory with a short prayer after a long sermon:

May you live happily and long, for the service of your country, the encouragement of good letters, and the ornament of poetry; which cannot be wish'd more earnestly by any man, than by

>Your Lordship's most humble,
>Most oblig'd, and most obedient Servant,
>JOHN DRYDEN.

THE FIRST BOOK OF THE ÆNEIS

THE ARGUMENT.—The Trojans, after a seven years' voyage, set sail for Italy, but are overtaken by a dreadful storm, which Æolus raises at Juno's request. The tempest sinks one, and scatters the rest. Neptune drives off the Winds, and calms the sea. Æneas, with his own ship, and six more, arrives safe at an African port. Venus complains to Jupiter of her son's misfortunes. Jupiter comforts her, and sends Mercury to procure him a kind reception among the Carthaginians. Æneas, going out to discover the country, meets his mother in the shape of an huntress, who conveys him in a cloud to Carthage, where he sees his friends whom he thought lost, and receives a kind entertainment from the queen. Dido, by a device of Venus, begins to have a passion for him, and, after some discourse with him, desires the history of his adventures since the siege of Troy, which is the subject of the two following books.

ARMS, and the man I sing, who, forc'd by fate,
    And haughty Juno's unrelenting hate,
    Expell'd and exil'd, left the Trojan shore.
Long labors, both by sea and land, he bore,
And in the doubtful war, before he won
The Latian realm, and built the destin'd town;
His banish'd gods restor'd to rites divine,
And settled sure succession in his line,
From whence the race of Alban fathers come,
And the long glories of majestic Rome.
    O Muse! the causes and the crimes relate;
What goddess was provok'd, and whence her hate;
For what offense the Queen of Heav'n began
To persecute so brave, so just a man;
Involv'd his anxious life in endless cares,
Expos'd to wants, and hurried into wars!
Can heav'nly minds such high resentment show,
Or exercise their spite in human woe?
    Against the Tiber's mouth, but far away,
An ancient town was seated on the sea;
A Tyrian colony; the people made
Stout for the war, and studious of their trade:
Carthage the name; belov'd by Juno more
Than her own Argos, or the Samian shore.

Here stood her chariot; here, if Heav'n were kind,
The seat of awful empire she design'd.
Yet she had heard an ancient rumor fly,
(Long cited by the people of the sky,)
That times to come should see the Trojan race
Her Carthage ruin, and her tow'rs deface;
Nor thus confin'd, the yoke of sov'reign sway
Should on the necks of all the nations lay.
She ponder'd this, and fear'd it was in fate;
Nor could forget the war she wag'd of late
For conqu'ring Greece against the Trojan state.
Besides, long causes working in her mind,
And secret seeds of envy, lay behind;
Deep graven in her heart the doom remain'd
Of partial Paris, and her form disdain'd;
The grace bestow'd on ravish'd Ganymed,
Electra's glories, and her injur'd bed.
Each was a cause alone; and all combin'd
To kindle vengeance in her haughty mind.
For this, far distant from the Latian coast
She drove the remnants of the Trojan host;
And sev'n long years th' unhappy wand'ring train
Were toss'd by storms, and scatter'd thro' the main.
Such time, such toil, requir'd the Roman name,
Such length of labor for so vast a frame.

Now scarce the Trojan fleet, with sails and oars,
Had left behind the fair Sicilian shores,
Ent'ring with cheerful shouts the wat'ry reign,
And plowing frothy furrows in the main;
When, lab'ring still with endless discontent,
The Queen of Heav'n did thus her fury vent:

"Then am I vanquish'd? must I yield?" said she,
"And must the Trojans reign in Italy?
So Fate will have it, and Jove adds his force;
Nor can my pow'r divert their happy course.
Could angry Pallas, with revengeful spleen,
The Grecian navy burn, and drown the men?
She, for the fault of one offending foe,
The bolts of Jove himself presum'd to throw:
With whirlwinds from beneath she toss'd the ship,

And bare expos'd the bosom of the deep;
Then, as an eagle gripes the trembling game,
The wretch, yet hissing with her father's flame,
She strongly seiz'd, and with a burning wound
Transfix'd, and naked, on a rock she bound.
But I, who walk in awful state above,
The majesty of heav'n, the sister wife of Jove,
For length of years my fruitless force employ
Against the thin remains of ruin'd Troy!
What nations now to Juno's pow'r will pray,
Or off'rings on my slighted altars lay?"

  Thus rag'd the goddess; and, with fury fraught,
The restless regions of the storms she sought,
Where, in a spacious cave of living stone,
The tyrant Æolus, from his airy throne,
With pow'r imperial curbs the struggling winds,
And sounding tempests in dark prisons binds.
This way and that th' impatient captives tend,
And, pressing for release, the mountains rend.
High in his hall th' undaunted monarch stands,
And shakes his scepter, and their rage commands;
Which did he not, their unresisted sway
Would sweep the world before them in their way;
Earth, air, and seas thro' empty space would roll,
And heav'n would fly before the driving soul.
In fear of this, the Father of the Gods
Confin'd their fury to those dark abodes,
And lock'd 'em safe within, oppress'd with mountain
    loads;
Impos'd a king, with arbitrary sway,
To loose their fetters, or their force allay.
To whom the suppliant queen her pray'rs address'd,
And thus the tenor of her suit express'd:
"O Æolus! for to thee the King of Heav'n
The pow'r of tempests and of winds has giv'n;
Thy force alone their fury can restrain,
And smooth the waves, or swell the troubled main—
A race of wand'ring slaves, abhorr'd by me,
With prosp'rous passage cut the Tuscan sea;
To fruitful Italy their course they steer,

And for their vanquish'd gods design new temples there
Raise all thy winds; with night involve the skies;
Sink or disperse my fatal enemies.
Twice sev'n, the charming daughters of the main,
Around my person wait, and bear my train:
Succeed my wish, and second my design;
The fairest, Deiopeia, shall be thine,
And make thee father of a happy line."

 To this the god: " 'Tis yours, O queen, to will
The work which duty binds me to fulfil.
These airy kingdoms, and this wide command,
Are all the presents of your bounteous hand:
Yours is my sov'reign's grace; and, as your guest,
I sit with gods at their celestial feast;
Raise tempests at your pleasure, or subdue;
Dispose of empire, which I hold from you."

 He said, and hurl'd against the mountain side
His quiv'ring spear, and all the god applied.
The raging winds rush thro' the hollow wound,
And dance aloft in air, and skim along the ground;
Then, settling on the sea, the surges sweep,
Raise liquid mountains, and disclose the deep.
South, East, and West with mix'd confusion roar,
And roll the foaming billows to the shore.
The cables crack; the sailors' fearful cries
Ascend; and sable night involves the skies;
And heav'n itself is ravish'd from their eyes.
Loud peals of thunder from the poles ensue;
Then flashing fires the transient light renew;
The face of things a frightful image bears,
And present death in various forms appears.
Struck with unusual fright, the Trojan chief,
With lifted hands and eyes, invokes relief;
And, "Thrice and four times happy those," he cried,
"That under Ilian walls before their parents died!
Tydides, bravest of the Grecian train!
Why could not I by that strong arm be slain,
And lie by noble Hector on the plain,
Or great Sarpedon, in those bloody fields
Where Simoïs rolls the bodies and the shields

Of heroes, whose dismember'd hands yet bear
The dart aloft, and clench the pointed spear!"

   Thus while the pious prince his fate bewails,
Fierce Boreas drove against his flying sails,
And rent the sheets; the raging billows rise,
And mount the tossing vessel to the skies:
Nor can the shiv'ring oars sustain the blow;
The galley gives her side, and turns her prow;
While those astern, descending down the steep,
Thro' gaping waves behold the boiling deep.
Three ships were hurried by the southern blast,
And on the secret shelves with fury cast.
Those hidden rocks th' Ausonian sailors knew:
They call'd them Altars, when they rose in view,
And show'd their spacious backs above the flood.
Three more fierce Eurus, in his angry mood,
Dash'd on the shallows of the moving sand,
And in mid ocean left them moor'd aland.
Orontes' bark, that bore the Lycian crew,
(A horrid sight!) ev'n in the hero's view,
From stem to stern by waves was overborne:
The trembling pilot, from his rudder torn,
Was headlong hurl'd; thrice round the ship was toss'd,
Then bulg'd at once, and in the deep was lost;
And here and there above the waves were seen
Arms, pictures, precious goods, and floating men.
The stoutest vessel to the storm gave way,
And suck'd thro' loosen'd planks the rushing sea.
Ilioneus was her chief: Alethes old,
Achates faithful, Abas young and bold,
Endur'd not less; their ships, with gaping seams,
Admit the deluge of the briny streams.

   Meantime imperial Neptune heard the sound
Of raging billows breaking on the ground.
Displeas'd, and fearing for his wat'ry reign,
He rear'd his awful head above the main,
Serene in majesty; then roll'd his eyes
Around the space of earth, and seas, and skies.
He saw the Trojan fleet dispers'd, distress'd,
By stormy winds and wintry heav'n oppress'd.

Full well the god his sister's envy knew,
And what her aims and what her arts pursue.
He summon'd Eurus and the western blast,
And first an angry glance on both he cast;
Then thus rebuk'd: "Audacious winds! from whence
This bold attempt, this rebel insolence?
Is it for you to ravage seas and land,
Unauthoriz'd by my supreme command?
To raise such mountains on the troubled main?
Whom I—but first 'tis fit the billows to restrain;
And then you shall be taught obedience to my reign.
Hence! to your lord my royal mandate bear—
The realms of ocean and the fields of air
Are mine, not his. By fatal lot to me
The liquid empire fell, and trident of the sea.
His pow'r to hollow caverns is confin'd:
There let him reign, the jailer of the wind,
With hoarse commands his breathing subjects call,
And boast and bluster in his empty hall."
He spoke; and, while he spoke, he smooth'd the sea,
Dispell'd the darkness, and restor'd the day.
Cymothoe, Triton, and the sea-green train
Of beauteous nymphs, the daughters of the main,
Clear from the rocks the vessels with their hands:
The god himself with ready trident stands,
And opes the deep, and spreads the moving sands;
Then heaves them off the shoals. Where'er he guides
His finny coursers and in triumph rides,
The waves unruffle and the sea subsides.
As, when in tumults rise th' ignoble crowd,
Mad are their motions, and their tongues are loud;
And stones and brands in rattling volleys fly,
And all the rustic arms that fury can supply:
If then some grave and pious man appear,
They hush their noise, and lend a list'ning ear;
He soothes with sober words their angry mood,
And quenches their innate desire of blood:
So, when the Father of the Flood appears,
And o'er the seas his sov'reign trident rears,
Their fury falls: he skims the liquid plains,

High on his chariot, and, with loosen'd reins,
Majestic moves along, and awful peace maintains.
The weary Trojans ply their shatter'd oars
To nearest land, and make the Libyan shores.

 Within a long recess there lies a bay:
An island shades it from the rolling sea,
And forms a port secure for ships to ride;
Broke by the jutting land, on either side,
In double streams the briny waters glide.
Betwixt two rows of rocks a sylvan scene
Appears above, and groves for ever green:
A grot is form'd beneath, with mossy seats,
To rest the Nereids, and exclude the heats.
Down thro' the crannies of the living walls
The crystal streams descend in murm'ring falls:
No haulsers need to bind the vessels here,
Nor bearded anchors; for no storms they fear.
Sev'n ships within this happy harbor meet,
The thin remainders of the scatter'd fleet.
The Trojans, worn with toils, and spent with woes,
Leap on the welcome land, and seek their wish'd repose.

 First, good Achates, with repeated strokes
Of clashing flints, their hidden fire provokes:
Short flame succeeds; a bed of wither'd leaves
The dying sparkles in their fall receives:
Caught into life, in fiery fumes they rise,
And, fed with stronger food, invade the skies.
The Trojans, dropping wet, or stand around
The cheerful blaze, or lie along the ground:
Some dry their corn, infected with the brine,
Then grind with marbles, and prepare to dine.
Æneas climbs the mountain's airy brow,
And takes a prospect of the seas below,
If Capys thence, or Antheus he could spy,
Or see the streamers of Caïcus fly.
No vessels were in view; but, on the plain,
Three beamy stags command a lordly train
Of branching heads: the more ignoble throng
Attend their stately steps, and slowly graze along.
He stood; and, while secure they fed below,

He took the quiver and the trusty bow
Achates us'd to bear: the leaders first
He laid along, and then the vulgar pierc'd;
Nor ceas'd his arrows, till the shady plain
Sev'n mighty bodies with their blood distain.
For the sev'n ships he made an equal share,
And to the port return'd, triumphant from the war.
The jars of gen'rous wine (Acestes' gift,
When his Trinacrian shores the navy left)
He set abroach, and for the feast prepar'd,
In equal portions with the ven'son shar'd.
Thus while he dealt it round, the pious chief
With cheerful words allay'd the common grief:
"Endure, and conquer! Jove will soon dispose
To future good our past and present woes.
With me, the rocks of Scylla you have tried;
Th' inhuman Cyclops and his den defied.
What greater ills hereafter can you bear?
Resume your courage and dismiss your care,
An hour will come, with pleasure to relate
Your sorrows past, as benefits of Fate.
Thro' various hazards and events, we move
To Latium and the realms foredoom'd by Jove.
Call'd to the seat (the promise of the skies)
Where Trojan kingdoms once again may rise,
Endure the hardships of your present state;
Live, and reserve yourselves for better fate."

   These words he spoke, but spoke not from his heart;
His outward smiles conceal'd his inward smart.
The jolly crew, unmindful of the past,
The quarry share, their plenteous dinner haste.
Some strip the skin; some portion out the spoil;
The limbs, yet trembling, in the caldrons boil;
Some on the fire the reeking entrails broil.
Stretch'd on the grassy turf, at ease they dine,
Restore their strength with meat, and cheer their souls
    with wine.
Their hunger thus appeas'd, their care attends
The doubtful fortune of their absent friends:
Alternate hopes and fears their minds possess,

THE FIRST BOOK OF THE ÆNEIS

Whether to deem 'em dead, or in distress.
Above the rest, Æneas mourns the fate
Of brave Orontes, and th' uncertain state
Of Gyas, Lycus, and of Amycus.
The day, but not their sorrows, ended thus.

When, from aloft, almighty Jove surveys
Earth, air, and shores, and navigable seas,
At length on Libyan realms he fix'd his eyes—
Whom, pond'ring thus on human miseries,
When Venus saw, she with a lowly look,
Not free from tears, her heav'nly sire bespoke:

"O King of Gods and Men! whose awful hand
Disperses thunder on the seas and land,
Disposing all with absolute command;
How could my pious son thy pow'r incense?
Or what, alas! is vanish'd Troy's offense?
Our hope of Italy not only lost,
On various seas by various tempests toss'd,
But shut from ev'ry shore, and barr'd from ev'ry coast.
You promis'd once, a progeny divine
Of Romans, rising from the Trojan line,
In after times should hold the world in awe,
And to the land and ocean give the law.
How is your doom revers'd, which eas'd my care
When Troy was ruin'd in that cruel war?
Then fates to fates I could oppose; but now,
When Fortune still pursues her former blow,
What can I hope? What worse can still succeed?
What end of labors has your will decreed?
Antenor, from the midst of Grecian hosts,
Could pass secure, and pierce th' Illyrian coasts,
Where, rolling down the steep, Timavus raves
And thro' nine channels disembogues his waves.
At length he founded Padua's happy seat,
And gave his Trojans a secure retreat;
There fix'd their arms, and there renew'd their name,
And there in quiet rules, and crown'd with fame.
But we, descended from your sacred line,
Entitled to your heav'n and rites divine,
Are banish'd earth; and, for the wrath of one,

Remov'd from Latium and the promis'd throne.
Are these our scepters? these our due rewards?
And is it thus that Jove his plighted faith regards?"
 To whom the Father of th' immortal race,
Smiling with that serene indulgent face,
With which he drives the clouds and clears the skies,
First gave a holy kiss; then thus replies:
 "Daughter, dismiss thy fears; to thy desire
The fates of thine are fix'd, and stand entire.
Thou shalt behold thy wish'd Lavinian walls;
And, ripe for heav'n, when fate Æneas calls,
Then shalt thou bear him up, sublime, to me:
No councils have revers'd my firm decree.
And, lest new fears disturb thy happy state,
Know, I have search'd the mystic rolls of Fate:
Thy son (nor is th' appointed season far)
In Italy shall wage successful war,
Shall tame fierce nations in the bloody field,
And sov'reign laws impose, and cities build,
Till, after ev'ry foe subdued, the sun
Thrice thro' the signs his annual race shall run:
This is his time prefix'd. Ascanius then,
Now call'd Iülus, shall begin his reign.
He thirty rolling years the crown shall wear,
Then from Lavinium shall the seat transfer,
And, with hard labor, Alba Longa build.
The throne with his succession shall be fill'd
Three hundred circuits more: then shall be seen
Ilia the fair, a priestess and a queen,
Who, full of Mars, in time, with kindly throes,
Shall at a birth two goodly boys disclose.
The royal babes a tawny wolf shall drain:
Then Romulus his grandsire's throne shall gain,
Of martial tow'rs the founder shall become,
The people Romans call, the city Rome.
To them no bounds of empire I assign,
Nor term of years to their immortal line.
Ev'n haughty Juno, who, with endless broils,
Earth, seas, and heav'n, and Jove himself turmoils;
At length aton'd, her friendly pow'r shall join,

To cherish and advance the Trojan line.
The subject world shall Rome's dominion own,
And, prostrate, shall adore the nation of the gown.
An age is ripening in revolving fate
When Troy shall overturn the Grecian state,
And sweet revenge her conqu'ring sons shall call,
To crush the people that conspir'd her fall.
Then Cæsar from the Julian stock shall rise,
Whose empire ocean, and whose fame the skies
Alone shall bound; whom, fraught with eastern spoils,
Our heav'n, the just reward of human toils,
Securely shall repay with rites divine;
And incense shall ascend before his sacred shrine.
Then dire debate and impious war shall cease,
And the stern age be soften'd into peace:
Then banish'd Faith shall once again return,
And Vestal fires in hallow'd temples burn;
And Remus with Quirinus shall sustain
The righteous laws, and fraud and force restrain.
Janus himself before his fane shall wait,
And keep the dreadful issues of his gate,
With bolts and iron bars: within remains
Imprison'd Fury, bound in brazen chains;
High on a trophy rais'd, of useless arms,
He sits, and threats the world with vain alarms."
 He said, and sent Cyllenius with command
To free the ports, and ope the Punic land
To Trojan guests; lest, ignorant of fate,
The queen might force them from her town and state.
Down from the steep of heav'n Cyllenius flies,
And cleaves with all his wings the yielding skies.
Soon on the Libyan shore descends the god,
Performs his message, and displays his rod:
The surly murmurs of the people cease;
And, as the fates requir'd, they give the peace:
The queen herself suspends the rigid laws,
The Trojans pities, and protects their cause.
 Meantime, in shades of night Æneas lies:
Care seiz'd his soul, and sleep forsook his eyes.
But, when the sun restor'd the cheerful day,

He rose, the coast and country to survey,
Anxious and eager to discover more.
It look'd a wild uncultivated shore;
But, whether humankind, or beasts alone
Possess'd the new-found region, was unknown.
Beneath a ledge of rocks his fleet he hides:
Tall trees surround the mountain's shady sides;
The bending brow above a safe retreat provides.
Arm'd with two pointed darts, he leaves his friends,
And true Achates on his steps attends.
Lo! in the deep recesses of the wood,
Before his eyes his goddess mother stood:
A huntress in her habit and her mien;
Her dress a maid, her air confess'd a queen.
Bare were her knees, and knots her garments bind;
Loose was her hair, and wanton'd in the wind;
Her hand sustain'd a bow; her quiver hung behind.
She seem'd a virgin of the Spartan blood:
With such array Harpalyce bestrode
Her Thracian courser and outstripp'd the rapid flood.
"Ho, strangers! have you lately seen," she said,
"One of my sisters, like myself array'd,
Who cross'd the lawn, or in the forest stray'd?
A painted quiver at her back she bore;
Varied with spots, a lynx's hide she wore;
And at full cry pursued the tusky boar."
   Thus Venus: thus her son replied again:
"None of your sisters have we heard or seen,
O virgin! or what other name you bear
Above that style—O more than mortal fair!
Your voice and mien celestial birth betray!
If, as you seem, the sister of the day,
Or one at least of chaste Diana's train,
Let not an humble suppliant sue in vain;
But tell a stranger, long in tempests toss'd,
What earth we tread, and who commands the coast?
Then on your name shall wretched mortals call,
And offer'd victims at your altars fall."
"I dare not," she replied, "assume the name
Of goddess, or celestial honors claim:

For Tyrian virgins bows and quivers bear,
And purple buskins o'er their ankles wear.
Know, gentle youth, in Libyan lands you are—
A people rude in peace, and rough in war.
The rising city, which from far you see,
Is Carthage, and a Tyrian colony.
Phœnician Dido rules the growing state,
Who fled from Tyre, to shun her brother's hate.
Great were her wrongs, her story full of fate;
Which I will sum in short. Sichæus, known
For wealth, and brother to the Punic throne,
Possess'd fair Dido's bed; and either heart
At once was wounded with an equal dart.
Her father gave her, yet a spotless maid;
Pygmalion then the Tyrian scepter sway'd:
One who contemn'd divine and human laws.
Then strife ensued, and cursed gold the cause.
The monarch, blinded with desire of wealth,
With steel invades his brother's life by stealth;
Before the sacred altar made him bleed,
And long from her conceal'd the cruel deed.
Some tale, some new pretense, he daily coin'd,
To soothe his sister, and delude her mind.
At length, in dead of night, the ghost appears
Of her unhappy lord: the specter stares,
And, with erected eyes, his bloody bosom bares.
The cruel altars and his fate he tells,
And the dire secret of his house reveals,
Then warns the widow, with her household gods,
To seek a refuge in remote abodes.
Last, to support her in so long a way,
He shows her where his hidden treasure lay.
Admonish'd thus, and seiz'd with mortal fright,
The queen provides companions of her flight:
They meet, and all combine to leave the state,
Who hate the tyrant, or who fear his hate.
They seize a fleet, which ready rigg'd they find;
Nor is Pygmalion's treasure left behind.
The vessels, heavy laden, put to sea
With prosp'rous winds; a woman leads the way.

I know not, if by stress of weather driv'n,
Or was their fatal course dispos'd by Heav'n;
At last they landed, where from far your eyes
May view the turrets of new Carthage rise;
There bought a space of ground, which (Byrsa call'd,
From the bull's hide) they first inclos'd, and wall'd.
But whence are you? what country claims your birth?
What seek you, strangers, on our Libyan earth?"

To whom, with sorrow streaming from his eyes,
And deeply sighing, thus her son replies:
"Could you with patience hear, or I relate,
O nymph, the tedious annals of our fate!
Thro' such a train of woes if I should run,
The day would sooner than the tale be done!
From ancient Troy, by force expell'd, we came—
If you by chance have heard the Trojan name.
On various seas by various tempests toss'd,
At length we landed on your Libyan coast.
The good Æneas am I call'd—a name,
While Fortune favor'd, not unknown to fame.
My household gods, companions of my woes,
With pious care I rescued from our foes.
To fruitful Italy my course was bent;
And from the King of Heav'n is my descent.
With twice ten sail I cross'd the Phrygian sea;
Fate and my mother goddess led my way.
Scarce sev'n, the thin remainders of my fleet,
From storms preserv'd, within your harbor meet.
Myself distress'd, an exile, and unknown,
Debarr'd from Europe, and from Asia thrown,
In Libyan desarts wander thus alone."

His tender parent could no longer bear;
But, interposing, sought to soothe his care.
"Whoe'er you are—not unbelov'd by Heav'n,
Since on our friendly shore your ships are driv'n—
Have courage: to the gods permit the rest,
And to the queen expose your just request.
Now take this earnest of success, for more:
Your scatter'd fleet is join'd upon the shore;
The winds are chang'd, your friends from danger free;

THE FIRST BOOK OF THE ÆNEIS

Or I renounce my skill in augury.
Twelve swans behold in beauteous order move,
And stoop with closing pinions from above;
Whom late the bird of Jove had driv'n along,
And thro' the clouds pursued the scatt'ring throng:
Now, all united in a goodly team,
They skim the ground, and seek the quiet stream.
As they, with joy returning, clap their wings,
And ride the circuit of the skies in rings;
Not otherwise your ships, and ev'ry friend,
Already hold the port, or with swift sails descend.
No more advice is needful; but pursue
The path before you, and the town in view."

Thus having said, she turn'd, and made appear
Her neck refulgent, and dishevel'd hair,
Which, flowing from her shoulders, reach'd the ground.
And widely spread ambrosial scents around:
In length of train descends her sweeping gown;
And, by her graceful walk, the Queen of Love is known.
The prince pursued the parting deity
With words like these: "Ah! whither do you fly?
Unkind and cruel! to deceive your son
In borrow'd shapes, and his embrace to shun;
Never to bless my sight, but thus unknown;
And still to speak in accents not your own."
Against the goddess these complaints he made,
But took the path, and her commands obey'd.
They march, obscure; for Venus kindly shrouds
With mists their persons, and involves in clouds,
That, thus unseen, their passage none might stay,
Or force to tell the causes of their way.
This part perform'd, the goddess flies sublime
To visit Paphos and her native clime;
Where garlands, ever green and ever fair,
With vows are offer'd, and with solemn pray'r:
A hundred altars in her temple smoke;
A thousand bleeding hearts her pow'r invoke.

They climb the next ascent, and, looking down,
Now at a nearer distance view the town.
The prince with wonder sees the stately tow'rs,

Which late were huts and shepherds' homely bow'rs,
The gates and streets; and hears, from ev'ry part,
The noise and busy concourse of the mart.
The toiling Tyrians on each other call
To ply their labor: some extend the wall;
Some build the citadel; the brawny throng
Or dig, or push unwieldy stones along.
Some for their dwellings choose a spot of ground,
Which, first design'd, with ditches they surround.
Some laws ordain; and some attend the choice
Of holy senates, and elect by voice.
Here some design a mole, while others there
Lay deep foundations for a theater;
From marble quarries mighty columns hew,
For ornaments of scenes, and future view.
Such is their toil, and such their busy pains,
As exercise the bees in flow'ry plains,
When winter past, and summer scarce begun,
Invites them forth to labor in the sun;
Some lead their youth abroad, while some condense
Their liquid store, and some in cells dispense;
Some at the gate stand ready to receive
The golden burthen, and their friends relieve;
All with united force, combine to drive
The lazy drones from the laborious hive:
With envy stung, they view each other's deeds;
The fragrant work with diligence proceeds.
"Thrice happy you, whose walls already rise!"
Æneas said, and view'd, with lifted eyes,
Their lofty tow'rs; then, ent'ring at the gate,
Conceal'd in clouds (prodigious to relate)
He mix'd, unmark'd, among the busy throng,
Borne by the tide, and pass'd unseen along.

Full in the center of the town there stood,
Thick set with trees, a venerable wood.
The Tyrians, landing near this holy ground,
And digging here, a prosp'rous omen found:
From under earth a courser's head they drew.
Their growth and future fortune to foreshew.
This fated sign their foundress Juno gave,

THE FIRST BOOK OF THE ÆNEIS

Of a soil fruitful, and a people brave.
Sidonian Dido here with solemn state
Did Juno's temple build, and consecrate,
Enrich'd with gifts, and with a golden shrine;
But more the goddess made the place divine.
On brazen steps the marble threshold rose,
And brazen plates the cedar beams inclose:
The rafters are with brazen cov'rings crown'd;
The lofty doors on brazen hinges sound.
What first Æneas in this place beheld,
Reviv'd his courage, and his fear expell'd.
For while, expecting there the queen, he rais'd
His wond'ring eyes, and round the temple gaz'd,
Admir'd the fortune of the rising town,
The striving artists, and their arts' renown;
He saw, in order painted on the wall,
Whatever did unhappy Troy befall:
The wars that fame around the world had blown,
All to the life, and ev'ry leader known.
There Agamemnon, Priam here, he spies,
And fierce Achilles, who both kings defies.
He stopp'd, and weeping said: "O friend! ev'n here
The monuments of Trojan woes appear!
Our known disasters fill ev'n foreign lands:
See there, where old unhappy Priam stands!
Ev'n the mute walls relate the warrior's fame,
And Trojan griefs the Tyrians' pity claim."
He said (his tears a ready passage find),
Devouring what he saw so well design'd,
And with an empty picture fed his mind:
For there he saw the fainting Grecians yield,
And here the trembling Trojans quit the field,
Pursued by fierce Achilles thro' the plain,
On his high chariot driving o'er the slain.
The tents of Rhesus next his grief renew,
By their white sails betray'd to nightly view;
And wakeful Diomede, whose cruel sword
The sentries slew, nor spar'd their slumb'ring lord,
Then took the fiery steeds, ere yet the food
Of Troy they taste, or drink the Xanthian flood.

Elsewhere he saw where Troilus defied
Achilles, and unequal combat tried;
Then, where the boy disarm'd, with loosen'd reins,
Was by his horses hurried o'er the plains,
Hung by the neck and hair, and dragg'd around:
The hostile spear, yet sticking in his wound,
With tracks of blood inscrib'd the dusty ground.
Meantime the Trojan dames, oppress'd with woe,
To Pallas' fane in long procession go,
In hopes to reconcile their heav'nly foe.
They weep, they beat their breasts, they rend their hair,
And rich embroider'd vests for presents bear;
But the stern goddess stands unmov'd with pray'r.
Thrice round the Trojan walls Achilles drew
The corpse of Hector, whom in fight he slew.
Here Priam sues; and there, for sums of gold,
The lifeless body of his son is sold.
So sad an object, and so well express'd,
Drew sighs and groans from the griev'd hero's breast,
To see the figure of his lifeless friend,
And his old sire his helpless hand extend.
Himself he saw amidst the Grecian train,
Mix'd in the bloody battle on the plain;
And swarthy Memnon in his arms he knew,
His pompous ensigns, and his Indian crew.
Penthisilea there, with haughty grace,
Leads to the wars an Amazonian race.
In their right hands a pointed dart they wield;
The left, for ward, sustains the lunar shield.
Athwart her breast a golden belt she throws,
Amidst the press alone provokes a thousand foes,
And dares her maiden arms to manly force oppose.

 Thus while the Trojan prince employs his eyes,
Fix'd on the walls with wonder and surprise,
The beauteous Dido, with a num'rous train
And pomp of guards, ascends the sacred fane.
Such on Eurotas' banks, or Cynthus' height,
Diana seems; and so she charms the sight,
When in the dance the graceful goddess leads
The choir of nymphs, and overtops their heads:

Known by her quiver, and her lofty mien,
She walks majestic, and she looks their queen;
Latona sees her shine above the rest,
And feeds with secret joy her silent breast.
Such Dido was; with such becoming state,
Amidst the crowd, she walks serenely great.
Their labor to her future sway she speeds,
And passing with a gracious glance proceeds;
Then mounts the throne, high plac'd before the shrine:
In crowds around, the swarming people join.
She takes petitions, and dispenses laws,
Hears and determines ev'ry private cause;
Their tasks in equal portions she divides,
And, where unequal, there by lots decides.
Another way by chance Æneas bends
His eyes, and unexpected sees his friends,
Antheus, Sergestus grave, Cloanthus strong,
And at their backs a mighty Trojan throng,
Whom late the tempest on the billows toss'd,
And widely scatter'd on another coast.
The prince, unseen, surpris'd with wonder stands,
And longs, with joyful haste, to join their hands;
But, doubtful of the wish'd event, he stays,
And from the hollow cloud his friends surveys,
Impatient till they told their present state,
And where they left their ships, and what their fate,
And why they came, and what was their request;
For these were sent, commission'd by the rest,
To sue for leave to land their sickly men,
And gain admission to the gracious queen.
Ent'ring, with cries they fill'd the holy fane;
Then thus, with lowly voice, Ilioneus began:
  "O queen! indulg'd by favor of the gods
To found an empire in these new abodes,
To build a town, with statutes to restrain
The wild inhabitants beneath thy reign,
We wretched Trojans, toss'd on ev'ry shore,
From sea to sea, thy clemency implore.
Forbid the fires our shipping to deface!
Receive th' unhappy fugitives to grace,

And spare the remnant of a pious race!
We come not with design of wasteful prey,
To drive the country, force the swains away:
Nor such our strength, nor such is our desire;
The vanquish'd dare not to such thoughts aspire.
A land there is, Hesperia nam'd of old;
The soil is fruitful, and the men are bold—
Th' Œnotrians held it once—by common fame
Now call'd Italia, from the leader's name.
To that sweet region was our voyage bent,
When winds and ev'ry warring element
Disturb'd our course, and, far from sight of land,
Cast our torn vessels on the moving sand:
The sea came on; the South, with mighty roar,
Dispers'd and dash'd the rest upon the rocky shore.
Those few you see escap'd the storm, and fear,
Unless you interpose, a shipwreck here.
What men, what monsters, what inhuman race,
What laws, what barb'rous customs of the place,
Shut up a desert shore to drowning men,
And drive us to the cruel seas again?
If our hard fortune no compassion draws,
Nor hospitable rights, nor human laws,
The gods are just, and will revenge our cause.
Æneas was our prince: a juster lord,
Or nobler warrior, never drew a sword;
Observant of the right, religious of his word.
If yet he lives, and draws this vital air,
Nor we, his friends, of safety shall despair;
Nor you, great queen, these offices repent,
Which he will equal, and perhaps augment.
We want not cities, nor Sicilian coasts,
Where King Acestes Trojan lineage boasts.
Permit our ships a shelter on your shores,
Refitted from your woods with planks and oars,
That, if our prince be safe, we may renew
Our destin'd course, and Italy pursue.
But if, O best of men, the Fates ordain
That thou art swallow'd in the Libyan main,
And if our young Iülus be no more,

Dismiss our navy from your friendly shore,
That we to good Acestes may return,
And with our friends our common losses mourn."
Thus spoke Ilioneus: the Trojan crew
With cries and clamors his request renew.

   The modest queen a while, with downcast eyes,
Ponder'd the speech; then briefly thus replies:
"Trojans, dismiss your fears; my cruel fate,
And doubts attending an unsettled state,
Force me to guard my coast from foreign foes.
Who has not heard the story of your woes,
The name and fortune of your native place,
The fame and valor of the Phrygian race?
We Tyrians are not so devoid of sense,
Nor so remote from Phœbus' influence.
Whether to Latian shores your course is bent,
Or, driv'n by tempests from your first intent,
You seek the good Acestes' government,
Your men shall be receiv'd, your fleet repair'd,
And sail, with ships of convoy for your guard:
Or, would you stay, and join your friendly pow'rs
To raise and to defend the Tyrian tow'rs,
My wealth, my city, and myself are yours.
And would to Heav'n, the storm, you felt, would bring
On Carthaginian coasts your wand'ring king.
My people shall, by my command, explore
The ports and creeks of ev'ry winding shore,
And towns, and wilds, and shady woods, in quest
Of so renown'd and so desir'd a guest."

   Rais'd in his mind the Trojan hero stood,
And long'd to break from out his ambient cloud:
Achates found it, and thus urg'd his way:
"From whence, O goddess-born, this long delay?
What more can you desire, your welcome sure,
Your fleet in safety, and your friends secure?
One only wants; and him we saw in vain
Oppose the storm, and swallow'd in the main.
Orontes in his fate our forfeit paid;
The rest agrees with what your mother said."
Scarce had he spoken, when the cloud gave way,

The mists flew upward and dissolv'd in day.

   The Trojan chief appear'd in open sight,
August in visage, and serenely bright.
His mother goddess, with her hands divine,
Had form'd his curling locks, and made his temples shine,
And giv'n his rolling eyes a sparkling grace,
And breath'd a youthful vigor on his face;
Like polish'd iv'ry, beauteous to behold,
Or Parian marble, when enchas'd in gold:
Thus radiant from the circling cloud he broke,
And thus with manly modesty he spoke:
   "He whom you seek am I; by tempests toss'd,
And sav'd from shipwreck on your Libyan coast;
Presenting, gracious queen, before your throne,
A prince that owes his life to you alone.
Fair majesty, the refuge and redress
Of those whom fate pursues, and wants oppress,
You, who your pious offices employ
To save the relics of abandon'd Troy;
Receive the shipwreck'd on your friendly shore,
With hospitable rites relieve the poor;
Associate in your town a wand'ring train,
And strangers in your palace entertain:
What thanks can wretched fugitives return,
Who, scatter'd thro' the world, in exile mourn?
The gods, if gods to goodness are inclin'd;
If acts of mercy touch their heav'nly mind,
And, more than all the gods, your gen'rous heart,
Conscious of worth, requite its own desert!
In you this age is happy, and this earth,
And parents more than mortal gave you birth.
While rolling rivers into seas shall run,
And round the space of heav'n the radiant sun;
While trees the mountain tops with shades supply,
Your honor, name, and praise shall never die.
Whate'er abode my fortune has assign'd,
Your image shall be present in my mind."
Thus having said, he turn'd with pious haste,
And joyful his expecting friends embrac'd:
With his right hand Ilioneus was grac'd,

THE FIRST BOOK OF THE ÆNEIS

Serestus with his left; then to his breast
Cloanthus and the noble Gyas press'd;
And so by turns descended to the rest.
  The Tyrian queen stood fix'd upon his face,
Pleas'd with his motions, ravish'd with his grace;
Admir'd his fortunes, more admir'd the man;
Then recollected stood, and thus began:
"What fate, O goddess-born; what angry pow'rs
Have cast you shipwrack'd on our barren shores?
Are you the great Æneas, known to fame,
Who from celestial seed your lineage claim?
  The same Æneas whom fair Venus bore
To fam'd Anchises on th' Idæan shore?
It calls into my mind, tho' then a child,
When Teucer came, from Salamis exil'd,
And sought my father's aid, to be restor'd:
My father Belus then with fire and sword
Invaded Cyprus, made the region bare,
And, conqu'ring, finish'd the successful war.
From him the Trojan siege I understood,
The Grecian chiefs, and your illustrious blood.
Your foe himself the Dardan valor prais'd,
And his own ancestry from Trojans rais'd.
Enter, my noble guest, and you shall find,
It not a costly welcome, yet a kind:
For I myself, like you, have been distress'd,
Till Heav'n afforded me this place of rest;
Like you, an alien in a land unknown,
I learn to pity woes so like my own."
She said, and to the palace led her guest;
Then offer'd incense, and proclaim'd a feast.
Nor yet less careful for her absent friends,
Twice ten fat oxen to the ships she sends;
Besides a hundred boars, a hundred lambs,
With bleating cries, attend their milky dams;
And jars of gen'rous wine and spacious bowls
She gives, to cheer the sailors' drooping souls.
Now purple hangings clothe the palace walls,
And sumptuous feasts are made in splendid halls:
On Tyrian carpets, richly wrought, they dine;

With loads of massy plate the sideboards shine,
And antique vases, all of gold emboss'd
(The gold itself inferior to the cost),
Of curious work, where on the sides were seen
The fights and figures of illustrious men,
From their first founder to the present queen.

   The good Æneas, whose paternal care
Iülus' absence could no longer bear,
Dispatch'd Achates to the ships in haste,
To give a glad relation of the past,
And, fraught with precious gifts, to bring the boy,
Snatch'd from the ruins of unhappy Troy:
A robe of tissue, stiff with golden wire;
An upper vest, once Helen's rich attire,
From Argos by the fam'd adultress brought,
With golden flow'rs and winding foliage wrought,
Her mother Leda's present, when she came
To ruin Troy and set the world on flame;
The scepter Priam's eldest daughter bore,
Her orient necklace, and the crown she wore;
Of double texture, glorious to behold,
One order set with gems, and one with gold.
Instructed thus, the wise Achates goes,
And in his diligence his duty shows.

   But Venus, anxious for her son's affairs,
New counsels tries, and new designs prepares:
That Cupid should assume the shape and face
Of sweet Ascanius, and the sprightly grace;
Should bring the presents, in her nephew's stead,
And in Eliza's veins the gentle poison shed:
For much she fear'd the Tyrians, double-tongued,
And knew the town to Juno's care belong'd.
These thoughts by night her golden slumbers broke,
And thus alarm'd, to winged Love she spoke:
"My son, my strength, whose mighty pow'r alone
Controls the Thund'rer on his awful throne,
To thee thy much-afflicted mother flies,
And on thy succor and thy faith relies.
Thou know'st, my son, how Jove's revengeful wife,
By force and fraud, attempts thy brother's life;
And often hast thou mourn'd with me his pains.

THE FIRST BOOK OF THE ÆNEIS

Him Dido now with blandishment detains;
But I suspect the town where Juno reigns.
For this 't is needful to prevent her art,
And fire with love the proud Phœnician's heart:
A love so violent, so strong, so sure,
As neither age can change, nor art can cure.
How this may be perform'd, now take my mind:
Ascanius by his father is design'd
To come, with presents laden, from the port,
To gratify the queen, and gain the court.
I mean to plunge the boy in pleasing sleep,
And, ravish'd, in Idalian bow'rs to keep,
Or high Cythera, that the sweet deceit
May pass unseen, and none prevent the cheat.
Take thou his form and shape. I beg the grace
But only for a night's revolving space:
Thyself a boy, assume a boy's dissembled face;
That when, amidst the fervor of the feast,
The Tyrian hugs and fonds thee on her breast,
And with sweet kisses in her arms constrains,
Thou may'st infuse thy venom in her veins."
The God of Love obeys, and sets aside
His bow and quiver, and his plumy pride;
He walks Iülus in his mother's sight,
And in the sweet resemblance takes delight.

The goddess then to young Ascanius flies,
And in a pleasing slumber seals his eyes:
Lull'd in her lap, amidst a train of Loves,
She gently bears him to her blissful groves,
Then with a wreath of myrtle crowns his head,
And softly lays him on a flow'ry bed.
Cupid meantime assum'd his form and face,
Foll'wing Achates with a shorter pace,
And brought the gifts. The queen already sate
Amidst the Trojan lords, in shining state,
High on a golden bed: her princely guest
Was next her side; in order sate the rest.
Then canisters with bread are heap'd on high;
Th' attendants water for their hands supply,
And, having wash'd, with silken towels dry.
Next fifty handmaids in long order bore

The censers, and with fumes the gods adore:
Then youths, and virgins twice as many, join
To place the dishes, and to serve the wine.
The Tyrian train, admitted to the feast,
Approach, and on the painted couches rest.
All on the Trojan gifts with wonder gaze,
But view the beauteous boy with more amaze,
His rosy-color'd cheeks, his radiant eyes,
His motions, voice, and shape, and all the god's disguise;
Nor pass unprais'd the vest and veil divine,
Which wand'ring foliage and rich flow'rs entwine.
But, far above the rest, the royal dame,
(Already doom'd to love's disastrous flame,)
With eyes insatiate, and tumultuous joy,
Beholds the presents, and admires the boy.
The guileful god about the hero long,
With children's play, and false embraces, hung;
Then sought the queen: she took him to her arms
With greedy pleasure, and devour'd his charms.
Unhappy Dido little thought what guest,
How dire a god, she drew so near her breast;
But he, not mindless of his mother's pray'r,
Works in the pliant bosom of the fair,
And molds her heart anew, and blots her former care.
The dead is to the living love resign'd;
And all Æneas enters in her mind.

   Now, when the rage of hunger was appeas'd,
The meat remov'd, and ev'ry guest was pleas'd,
The golden bowls with sparkling wine are crown'd,
And thro' the palace cheerful cries resound.
From gilded roofs depending lamps display
Nocturnal beams, that emulate the day.
A golden bowl, that shone with gems divine,
The queen commanded to be crown'd with wine:
The bowl that Belus us'd, and all the Tyrian line.
Then, silence thro' the hall proclaim'd, she spoke:
"O hospitable Jove! we thus invoke,
With solemn rites, thy sacred name and pow'r;
Bless to both nations this auspicious hour!
So may the Trojan and the Tyrian line
In lasting concord from this day combine.

Thou, Bacchus, god of joys and friendly cheer,
And gracious Juno, both be present here!
And you, my lords of Tyre, your vows address
To Heav'n with mine, to ratify the peace."
The goblet then she took, with nectar crown'd
(Sprinkling the first libations on the ground,)
And rais'd it to her mouth with sober grace;
Then, sipping, offer'd to the next in place.
'Twas Bitias whom she call'd, a thirsty soul;
He took the challenge, and embrac'd the bowl,
With pleasure swill'd the gold, nor ceas'd to draw,
Till he the bottom of the brimmer saw.
The goblet goes around: Iopas brought
His golden lyre, and sung what ancient Atlas taught:
The various labors of the wand'ring moon,
And whence proceed th' eclipses of the sun;
Th' original of men and beasts; and whence
The rains arise, and fires their warmth dispense,
And fix'd and erring stars dispose their influence;
What shakes the solid earth; what cause delays
The summer nights and shortens winter days.
With peals of shouts the Tyrians praise the song:
Those peals are echo'd by the Trojan throng.
Th' unhappy queen with talk prolong'd the night,
And drank large draughts of love with vast delight;
Of Priam much enquir'd, of Hector more;
Then ask'd what arms the swarthy Memnon wore,
What troops he landed on the Trojan shore;
The steeds of Diomede varied the discourse,
And fierce Achilles, with his matchless force;
At length, as Fate and her ill stars requir'd,
To hear the series of the war desir'd.
"Relate at large, my godlike guest," she said,
"The Grecian stratagems, the town betray'd:
The fatal issue of so long a war,
Your flight, your wand'rings, and your woes, declare;
For, since on ev'ry sea, on ev'ry coast,
Your men have been distress'd, your navy toss'd,
Sev'n times the sun has either tropic view'd,
The winter banish'd, and the spring renew'd."

THE SECOND BOOK
OF THE ÆNEIS

THE ARGUMENT.—Æneas relates how the city of Troy was taken, after a ten years' siege, by the treachery of Sinon, and the stratagem of a wooden horse. He declares the fix'd resolution he had taken not to survive the ruins of his country, and the various adventures he met with in the defense of it. At last, having been before advis'd by Hector's ghost, and now by the appearance of his mother Venus, he is prevail'd upon to leave the town, and settle his household gods in another country. In order to do this, he carries off his father on his shoulders, and leads his little son by the hand, his wife following him behind. When he comes to the place appointed for the general rendezvouze, he finds a great confluence of people, but misses his wife whose ghost afterwards appears to him, and tells him the land which was design'd for him.

ALL were attentive to the godlike man,
When from his lofty couch he thus began:
"Great queen, what you command me to relate
Renews the sad remembrance of our fate:
An empire from its old foundations rent,
And ev'ry woe the Trojans underwent;
A peopled city made a desart place;
All that I saw, and part of which I was:
Not ev'n the hardest of our foes could hear,
Nor stern Ulysses tell without a tear.
And now the latter watch of wasting night,
And setting stars, to kindly rest invite;
But, since you take such int'rest in our woe,
And Troy's disastrous end desire to know,
I will restrain my tears, and briefly tell
What in our last and fatal night befell.
"By destiny compell'd, and in despair,
The Greeks grew weary of the tedious war,
And by Minerva's aid a fabric rear'd,
Which like a steed of monstrous height appear'd:
The sides were plank'd with pine; they feign'd it made
For their return, and this the vow they paid.
Thus they pretend, but in the hollow side
Selected numbers of their soldiers hide:

With inward arms the dire machine they load,
And iron bowels stuff the dark abode.
In sight of Troy lies Tenedos, an isle
(While Fortune did on Priam's empire smile)
Renown'd for wealth; but, since, a faithless bay,
Where ships expos'd to wind and weather lay.
There was their fleet conceal'd. We thought, for Greece
Their sails were hoisted, and our fears release.
The Trojans, coop'd within their walls so long,
Unbar their gates, and issue in a throng,
Like swarming bees, and with delight survey
The camp deserted, where the Grecians lay:
The quarters of the sev'ral chiefs they show'd;
Here Phœnix, here Achilles, made abode;
Here join'd the battles; there the navy rode.
Part on the pile their wond'ring eyes employ:
The pile by Pallas rais'd to ruin Troy.
Thymœtes first ('t is doubtful whether hir'd,
Or so the Trojan destiny requir'd)
Mov'd that the ramparts might be broken down,
To lodge the monster fabric in the town.
But Capys, and the rest of sounder mind,
The fatal present to the flames designed,
Or to the wat'ry deep; at least to bore
The hollow sides, and hidden frauds explore.
The giddy vulgar, as their fancies guide,
With noise say nothing, and in parts divide.
Laocoon, follow'd by a num'rous crowd,
Ran from the fort, and cried, from far, aloud:
'O wretched countrymen! what fury reigns?
What more than madness has possess'd your brains?
Think you the Grecians from your coasts are gone?
And are Ulysses' arts no better known?
This hollow fabric either must inclose,
Within its blind recess, our secret foes;
Or 'tis an engine rais'd above the town,
T' o'erlook the walls, and then to batter down.
Somewhat is sure design'd, by fraud or force:
Trust not their presents, nor admit the horse.'
Thus having said, against the steed he threw

His forceful spear, which, hissing as it flew,
Pierc'd thro' the yielding planks of jointed wood,
And trembling in the hollow belly stood.
The sides, transpierc'd, return a rattling sound,
And groans of Greeks inclos'd come issuing thro' the wound.
And, had not Heav'n the fall of Troy design'd,
Or had not men been fated to be blind,
Enough was said and done t' inspire a better mind.
Then had our lances pierc'd the treach'rous wood,
And Ilian tow'rs and Priam's empire stood.
Meantime, with shouts, the Trojan shepherds bring
A captive Greek, in bands, before the king;
Taken to take; who made himself their prey,
T' impose on their belief, and Troy betray;
Fix'd on his aim, and obstinately bent
To die undaunted, or to circumvent.
About the captive, tides of Trojans flow;
All press to see, and some insult the foe.
Now hear how well the Greeks their wiles disguis'd;
Behold a nation in a man compris'd.
Trembling the miscreant stood, unarm'd and bound;
He star'd, and roll'd his haggard eyes around,
Then said: 'Alas! what earth remains, what sea
Is open to receive unhappy me?
What fate a wretched fugitive attends,
Scorn'd by my foes, abandon'd by my friends?'
He said, and sigh'd, and cast a rueful eye:
Our pity kindles, and our passions die.
We cheer the youth to make his own defense,
And freely tell us what he was, and whence:
What news he could impart, we long to know,
And what to credit from a captive foe.

"His fear at length dismiss'd, he said: 'Whate'er
My fate ordains, my words shall be sincere:
I neither can nor dare my birth disclaim;
Greece is my country, Sinon is my name.
Tho' plung'd by Fortune's pow'r in misery,
'Tis not in Fortune's pow'r to make me lie.
If any chance has hither brought the name
Of Palamedes, not unknown to fame,

Who suffer'd from the malice of the times,
Accus'd and sentenc'd for pretended crimes,
Because these fatal wars he would prevent;
Whose death the wretched Greeks too late lament—
Me, then a boy, my father, poor and bare
Of other means, committed to his care,
His kinsman and companion in the war.
While Fortune favor'd, while his arms support
The cause, and rul'd the counsels, of the court,
I made some figure there; nor was my name
Obscure, nor I without my share of fame.
But when Ulysses, with fallacious arts,
Had made impression in the people's hearts,
And forg'd a treason in my patron's name
(I speak of things too far divulg'd by fame),
My kinsman fell. Then I, without support,
In private mourn'd his loss, and left the court.
Mad as I was, I could not bear his fate
With silent grief, but loudly blam'd the state,
And curs'd the direful author of my woes.
'Twas told again; and hence my ruin rose.
I threaten'd, if indulgent Heav'n once more
Would land me safely on my native shore,
His death with double vengeance to restore.
This mov'd the murderer's hate; and soon ensued
Th' effects of malice from a man so proud.
Ambiguous rumors thro' the camp he spread,
And sought, by treason, my devoted head;
New crimes invented; left unturn'd no stone,
To make my guilt appear, and hide his own;
Till Calchas was by force and threat'ning wrought—
But why—why dwell I on that anxious thought?
If on my nation just revenge you seek,
And 'tis t' appear a foe, t' appear a Greek;
Already you my name and country know;
Assuage your thirst of blood, and strike the blow:
My death will both the kingly brothers please,
And set insatiate Ithacus at ease.'
This fair unfinish'd tale, these broken starts,
Rais'd expectations in our longing hearts:

Unknowing as we were in Grecian arts.
His former trembling once again renew'd,
With acted fear, the villain thus pursued:
 "'Long had the Grecians (tir'd with fruitless care,
And wearied with an unsuccessful war)
Resolv'd to raise the siege, and leave the town;
And, had the gods permitted, they had gone;
But oft the wintry seas and southern winds
Withstood their passage home, and chang'd their minds.
Portents and prodigies their souls amaz'd;
But most, when this stupendous pile was rais'd:
Then flaming meteors, hung in air, were seen,
And thunders rattled thro' a sky serene.
Dismay'd, and fearful of some dire event,
Eurypylus t' enquire their fate was sent.
He from the gods this dreadful answer brought:
"O Grecians, when the Trojan shores you sought,
Your passage with a virgin's blood was bought:
So must your safe return be bought again,
And Grecian blood once more atone the main."
The spreading rumor round the people ran;
All fear'd, and each believ'd himself the man.
Ulysses took th' advantage of their fright;
Call'd Calchas, and produc'd in open sight:
Then bade him name the wretch, ordain'd by fate
The public victim, to redeem the state.
Already some presag'd the dire event,
And saw what sacrifice Ulysses meant.
For twice five days the good old seer withstood
Th' intended treason, and was dumb to blood,
Till, tir'd, with endless clamors and pursuit
Of Ithacus, he stood no longer mute;
But, as it was agreed, pronounc'd that I
Was destin'd by the wrathful gods to die.
All prais'd the sentence, pleas'd the storm should fall
On one alone, whose fury threaten'd all.
The dismal day was come; the priests prepare
Their leaven'd cakes, and fillets for my hair.
I follow'd nature's laws, and must avow
I broke my bonds and fled the fatal blow.

Hid in a weedy lake all night I lay,
Secure of safety when they sail'd away.
But now what further hopes for me remain,
To see my friends, or native soil, again;
My tender infants, or my careful sire,
Whom they returning will to death require;
Will perpetrate on them their first design,
And take the forfeit of their heads for mine?
Which, O! if pity mortal minds can move,
If there be faith below, or gods above,
If innocence and truth can claim desert,
Ye Trojans, from an injur'd wretch avert.'
  "False tears true pity move; the king commands
To loose his fetters, and unbind his hands:
Then adds these friendly words: 'Dismiss thy fears;
Forget the Greeks; be mine as thou wert theirs.
But truly tell, was it for force or guile,
Or some religious end, you rais'd the pile?'
Thus said the king. He, full of fraudful arts,
This well-invented tale for truth imparts:
'Ye lamps of heav'n!' he said, and lifted high
His hands now free, 'thou venerable sky!
Inviolable pow'rs, ador'd with dread!
Ye fatal fillets, that once bound this head!
Ye sacred altars, from whose flames I fled!
Be all of you adjur'd; and grant I may,
Without a crime, th' ungrateful Greeks betray,
Reveal the secrets of the guilty state,
And justly punish whom I justly hate!
But you, O king, preserve the faith you gave,
If I, to save myself, your empire save.
The Grecian hopes, and all th' attempts they made,
Were only founded on Minerva's aid.
But from the time when impious Diomede,
And false Ulysses, that inventive head,
Her fatal image from the temple drew,
The sleeping guardians of the castle slew,
Her virgin statue with their bloody hands
Polluted, and profan'd her holy bands;
From thence the tide of fortune left their shore,

And ebb'd much faster than it flow'd before:
Their courage languish'd, as their hopes decay'd;
And Pallas, now averse, refus'd her aid.
Nor did the goddess doubtfully declare
Her alter'd mind and alienated care.
When first her fatal image touch'd the ground,
She sternly cast her glaring eyes around,
That sparkled as they roll'd, and seem'd to threat:
Her heav'nly limbs distill'd a briny sweat.
Thrice from the ground she leap'd, was seen to wield
Her brandish'd lance, and shake her horrid shield.
Then Calchas bade our host for flight prepare,
And hope no conquest from the tedious war,
Till first they sail'd for Greece; with pray'rs besought
Her injur'd pow'r, and better omens brought.
And now their navy plows the wat'ry main,
Yet soon expect it on your shores again,
With Pallas pleas'd; as Calchas did ordain.
But first, to reconcile the blue-ey'd maid
For her stol'n statue and her tow'r betray'd,
Warn'd by the seer, to her offended name
We rais'd and dedicate this wondrous frame,
So lofty, lest thro' your forbidden gates
It pass, and intercept our better fates:
For, once admitted there, our hopes are lost;
And Troy may then a new Palladium boast;
For so religion and the gods ordain,
That, if you violate with hands profane
Minerva's gift, your town in flames shall burn,
(Which omen, O ye gods, on Græcia turn!)
But if it climb, with your assisting hands,
The Trojan walls, and in the city stands;
Then Troy shall Argos and Mycenæ burn,
And the reverse of fate on us return.'

"With such deceits he gain'd their easy hearts,
Too prone to credit his perfidious arts.
What Diomede, nor Thetis' greater son,
A thousand ships, nor ten years' siege, had done—
False tears and fawning words the city won.

"A greater omen, and of worse portent,

THE SECOND BOOK OF THE ÆNEIS

Did our unwary minds with fear torment,
Concurring to produce the dire event.
Laocoon, Neptune's priest by lot that year,
With solemn pomp then sacrific'd a steer;
When, dreadful to behold, from sea we spied
Two serpents, rank'd abreast, the seas divide,
And smoothly sweep along the swelling tide.
Their flaming crests above the waves they show;
Their bellies seem to burn the seas below;
Their speckled tails advance to steer their course,
And on the sounding shore the flying billows force.
And now the strand, and now the plain they held;
Their ardent eyes with bloody streaks were fill'd;
Their nimble tongues they brandish'd as they came,
And lick'd their hissing jaws, that sputter'd flame.
We fled amaz'd; their destin'd way they take,
And to Laocoon and his children make;
And first around the tender boys they wind,
Then with their sharpen'd fangs their limbs and bodies grind.
The wretched father, running to their aid
With pious haste, but vain, they next invade;
Twice round his waist their winding volumes roll'd;
And twice about his gasping throat they fold.
The priest thus doubly chok'd, their crests divide,
And tow'ring o'er his head in triumph ride.
With both his hands he labors at the knots;
His holy fillets the blue venom blots;
His roaring fills the flitting air around.
Thus, when an ox receives a glancing wound,
He breaks his bands, the fatal altar flies,
And with loud bellowings breaks the yielding skies.
Their tasks perform'd, the serpents quit their prey,
And to the tow'r of Pallas make their way:
Couch'd at her feet, they lie protected there
By her large buckler and protended spear.
Amazement seizes all; the gen'ral cry
Proclaims Laocoon justly doom'd to die,
Whose hand the will of Pallas had withstood,
And dared to violate the sacred wood.
All vote t' admit the steed, that vows be paid

And incense offer'd to th' offended maid.
A spacious breach is made; the town lies bare;
Some hoisting-levers, some the wheels prepare
And fasten to the horse's feet; the rest
With cables haul along th' unwieldly beast.
Each on his fellow for assistance calls;
At length the fatal fabric mounts the walls,
Big with destruction. Boys with chaplets crown'd,
And choirs of virgins, sing and dance around.
Thus rais'd aloft, and then descending down,
It enters o'er our heads, and threats the town.
O sacred city, built by hands divine!
O valiant heroes of the Trojan line!
Four times he struck: as oft the clashing sound
Of arms was heard, and inward groans rebound.
Yet, mad with zeal, and blinded with our fate,
We haul along the horse in solemn state;
Then place the dire portent within the tow'r.
Cassandra cried, and curs'd th' unhappy hour;
Foretold our fate; but, by the god's decree,
All heard, and none believ'd the prophecy.
With branches we the fanes adorn, and waste,
In jollity, the day ordain'd to be the last.
Meantime the rapid heav'ns roll'd down the light,
And on the shaded ocean rush'd the night;
Our men, secure, nor guards nor sentries held,
But easy sleep their weary limbs compell'd.
The Grecians had embark'd their naval pow'rs
From Tenedos, and sought our well-known shores,
Safe under covert of the silent night,
And guided by th' imperial galley's light;
When Sinon, favor'd by the partial gods,
Unlock'd the horse, and op'd his dark abodes;
Restor'd to vital air our hidden foes,
Who joyful from their long confinement rose.
Tysander bold, and Sthenelus their guide,
And dire Ulysses down the cable slide:
Then Thoas, Athamas, and Pyrrhus haste;
Nor was the Podalirian hero last,
Nor injur'd Menelaüs, nor the fam'd

Epeüs, who the fatal engine fram'd.
A nameless crowd succeed; their forces join
T' invade the town, oppress'd with sleep and wine.
Those few they find awake first meet their fate;
Then to their fellows they unbar the gate.

" 'Twas in the dead of night, when sleep repairs
Our bodies worn with toils, our minds with cares,
When Hector's ghost before my sight appears:
A bloody shroud he seem'd, and bath'd in tears;
Such as he was, when, by Pelides slain,
Thessalian coursers dragg'd him o'er the plain.
Swoln were his feet, as when the thongs were thrust
Thro' the bor'd holes; his body black with dust;
Unlike that Hector who return'd from toils
Of war, triumphant, in Æacian spoils,
Or him who made the fainting Greeks retire,
And launch'd against their navy Phrygian fire.
His hair and beard stood stiffen'd with his gore;
And all the wounds he for his country bore
Now stream'd afresh, and with new purple ran.
I wept to see the visionary man,
And, while my trance continued, thus began:
'O light of Trojans, and support of Troy,
Thy father's champion, and thy country's joy!
O, long expected by thy friends! from whence
Art thou so late return'd for our defense?
Do we behold thee, wearied as we are
With length of labors, and with toils of war?
After so many fun'rals of thy own
Art thou restor'd to thy declining town?
But say, what wounds are these? What new disgrace
Deforms the manly features of thy face?'

"To this the specter no reply did frame,
But answer'd to the cause for which he came,
And, groaning from the bottom of his breast,
This warning in these mournful words express'd:
'O goddess-born! escape, by timely flight,
The flames and horrors of this fatal night.
The foes already have possess'd the wall;
Troy nods from high, and totters to her fall.

Enough is paid to Priam's royal name,
More than enough to duty and to fame.
If by a mortal hand my father's throne
Could be defended, 't was by mine alone.
Now Troy to thee commends her future state,
And gives her gods companions of thy fate:
From their assistance happier walls expect,
Which, wand'ring long, at last thou shalt erect.'
He said, and brought me, from their blest abodes,
The venerable statues of the gods,
With ancient Vesta from the sacred choir,
The wreaths and relics of th' immortal fire.
  "Now peals of shouts come thund'ring from afar,
Cries, threats, and loud laments, and mingled war:
The noise approaches, tho' our palace stood
Aloof from streets, encompass'd with a wood.
Louder, and yet more loud, I hear th' alarms
Of human cries distinct, and clashing arms.
Fear broke my slumbers; I no longer stay,
But mount the terrace, thence the town survey,
And hearken what the frightful sounds convey.
Thus, when a flood of fire by wind is borne,
Crackling it rolls, and mows the standing corn;
Or deluges, descending on the plains,
Sweep o'er the yellow year, destroy the pains
Of lab'ring oxen and the peasant's gains;
Unroot the forest oaks, and bear away
Flocks, folds, and trees, and undistinguish'd prey:
The shepherd climbs the cliff, and sees from far
The wasteful ravage of the wat'ry war.
Then Hector's faith was manifestly clear'd,
And Grecian frauds in open light appear'd.
The palace of Deïphobus ascends
In smoky flames, and catches on his friends.
Ucalegon burns next: the seas are bright
With splendor not their own, and shine with Trojan light.
New clamors and new clangors now arise,
The sound of trumpets mix'd with fighting cries.
With frenzy seiz'd, I run to meet th' alarms,
Resolv'd on death, resolv'd to die in arms,

But first to gather friends, with them t' oppose
(If fortune favor'd) and repel the foes;
Spurr'd by my courage, by my country fir'd,
With sense of honor and revenge inspir'd.

"Pantheus, Apollo's priest, a sacred name,
Had scap'd the Grecian swords, and pass'd the flame:
With relics loaden, to my doors he fled,
And by the hand his tender grandson led.
'What hope, O Pantheus? whither can we run?
Where make a stand? and what may yet be done?'
Scarce had I said, when Pantheus, with a groan:
'Troy is no more, and Ilium was a town!
The fatal day, th' appointed hour, is come,
When wrathful Jove's irrevocable doom
Transfers the Trojan state to Grecian hands.
The fire consumes the town, the foe commands;
And armed hosts, an unexpected force,
Break from the bowels of the fatal horse.
Within the gates, proud Sinon throws about
The flames; and foes for entrance press without,
With thousand others, whom I fear to name,
More than from Argos or Mycenæ came.
To sev'ral posts their parties they divide;
Some block the narrow streets, some scour the wide:
The bold they kill, th' unwary they surprise;
Who fights finds death, and death finds him who flies.
The warders of the gate but scarce maintain
Th' unequal combat, and resist in vain.'

"I heard; and Heav'n, that well-born souls inspires,
Prompts me thro' lifted swords and rising fires
To run where clashing arms and clamor calls,
And rush undaunted to defend the walls.
Ripheus and Iph'itus by my side engage,
For valor one renown'd, and one for age.
Dymas and Hypanis by moonlight knew
My motions and my mien, and to my party drew;
With young Corœbus, who by love was led
To win renown and fair Cassandra's bed,
And lately brought his troops to Priam's aid,
Forewarn'd in vain by the prophetic maid.

Whom when I saw resolv'd in arms to fall,
And that one spirit animated all:
'Brave souls!' said I,—'but brave, alas! in vain—
Come, finish what our cruel fates ordain.
You see the desp'rate state of our affairs,
And heav'n's protecting pow'rs are deaf to pray'rs.
The passive gods behold the Greeks defile
Their temples, and abandon to the spoil
Their own abodes: we, feeble few, conspire
To save a sinking town, involv'd in fire.
Then let us fall, but fall amidst our foes:
Despair of life the means of living shows.'
So bold a speech incourag'd their desire
Of death, and added fuel to their fire.

"As hungry wolves, with raging appetite,
Scour thro' the fields, nor fear the stormy night—
Their whelps at home expect the promis'd food,
And long to temper their dry chaps in blood—
So rush'd we forth at once; resolv'd to die,
Resolv'd, in death, the last extremes to try.
We leave the narrow lanes behind, and dare
Th' unequal combat in the public square:
Night was our friend; our leader was despair.
What tongue can tell the slaughter of that night?
What eyes can weep the sorrows and affright?
An ancient and imperial city falls:
The streets are fill'd with frequent funerals;
Houses and holy temples float in blood,
And hostile nations make a common flood.
Not only Trojans fall; but, in their turn,
The vanquish'd triumph, and the victors mourn.
Ours take new courage from despair and night:
Confus'd the fortune is, confus'd the fight.
All parts resound with tumults, plaints, and fears;
And grisly Death in sundry shapes appears.
Androgeos fell among us, with his band,
Who thought us Grecians newly come to land.
'From whence,' said he, 'my friends, this long delay?
You loiter, while the spoils are borne away:
Our ships are laden with the Trojan store;

And you, like truants, come too late ashore.'
He said, but soon corrected his mistake,
Found, by the doubtful answers which we make:
Amaz'd, he would have shunn'd th' unequal fight;
But we, more num'rous, intercept his flight.
As when some peasant, in a bushy brake,
Has with unwary footing press'd a snake;
He starts aside, astonish'd, when he spies
His rising crest, blue neck, and rolling eyes;
So from our arms surpris'd Androgeos flies.
In vain; for him and his we compass'd round,
Possess'd with fear, unknowing of the ground,
And of their lives an easy conquest found.
Thus Fortune on our first endeavor smil'd.
Corœbus then, with youthful hopes beguil'd,
Swoln with success, and of a daring mind,
This new invention fatally design'd.
'My friends,' said he, 'since Fortune shows the way,
'T is fit we should th' auspicious guide obey.
For what has she these Grecian arms bestow'd,
But their destruction, and the Trojans' good?
Then change we shields, and their devices bear:
Let fraud supply the want of force in war.
They find us arms.' This said, himself he dress'd
In dead Androgeos' spoils, his upper vest,
His painted buckler, and his plumy crest.
Thus Ripheus, Dymas, all the Trojan train,
Lay down their own attire, and strip the slain.
Mix'd with the Greeks, we go with ill presage,
Flatter'd with hopes to glut our greedy rage;
Unknown, assaulting whom we blindly meet,
And strew with Grecian carcasses the street.
Thus while their straggling parties we defeat,
Some to the shore and safer ships retreat;
And some, oppress'd with more ignoble fear,
Remount the hollow horse, and pant in secret there.

"But, ah! what use of valor can be made,
When heav'n's propitious pow'rs refuse their aid!
Behold the royal prophetess, the fair
Cassandra, dragg'd by her dishevel'd hair,

Whom not Minerva's shrine, nor sacred bands,
In safety could protect from sacrilegious hands:
On heav'n she cast her eyes, she sigh'd, she cried—
'Twas all she could—her tender arms were tied.
So sad a sight Corœbus could not bear;
But, fir'd with rage, distracted with despair,
Amid the barb'rous ravishers he flew:
Our leader's rash example we pursue.
But storms of stones, from the proud temple's height,
Pour down, and on our batter'd helms alight:
We from our friends receiv'd this fatal blow,
Who thought us Grecians, as we seem'd in show.
They aim at the mistaken crests, from high;
And ours beneath the pond'rous ruin lie.
Then, mov'd with anger and disdain, to see
Their troops dispers'd, the royal virgin free,
The Grecians rally, and their pow'rs unite,
With fury charge us, and renew the fight.
The brother kings with Ajax join their force,
And the whole squadron of Thessalian horse.
"Thus, when the rival winds their quarrel try,
Contending for the kingdom of the sky,
South, east, and west, on airy coursers borne;
The whirlwind gathers, and the woods are torn:
Then Nereus strikes the deep; the billows rise,
And, mix'd with ooze and sand, pollute the skies.
The troops we squander'd first again appear
From several quarters, and enclose the rear.
They first observe, and to the rest betray,
Our diff'rent speech; our borrow'd arms survey.
Oppress'd with odds, we fall; Corœbus first,
At Pallas' altar, by Peneleus pierc'd.
Then Ripheus follow'd, in th' unequal fight;
Just of his word, observant of the right:
Heav'n thought not so. Dymas their fate attends,
With Hypanis, mistaken by their friends.
Nor, Pantheus, thee, thy miter, nor the bands
Of awful Phœbus, sav'd from impious hands.
Ye Trojan flames, your testimony bear,
What I perform'd, and what I suffer'd there;

THE SECOND BOOK OF THE ÆNEIS

No sword avoiding in the fatal strife,
Expos'd to death, and prodigal of life;
Witness, ye heavens! I live not by my fault:
I strove to have deserv'd the death I sought.
But, when I could not fight, and would have died,
Borne off to distance by the growing tide,
Old Iphitus and I were hurried thence,
With Pelias wounded, and without defense.
New clamors from th' invested palace ring:
We run to die, or disengage the king.
So hot th' assault, so high the tumult rose,
While ours defend, and while the Greeks oppose
As all the Dardan and Argolic race
Had been contracted in that narrow space;
Or as all Ilium else were void of fear,
And tumult, war, and slaughter, only there.
Their targets in a tortoise cast, the foes,
Secure advancing, to the turrets rose:
Some mount the scaling ladders; some, more bold,
Swerve upwards, and by posts and pillars hold;
Their left hand gripes their bucklers in th' ascent,
While with their right they seize the battlement.
From their demolish'd tow'rs the Trojans throw
Huge heaps of stones, that, falling, crush the foe;
And heavy beams and rafters from the sides
(Such arms their last necessity provides)
And gilded roofs, come tumbling from on high,
The marks of state and ancient royalty.
The guards below, fix'd in the pass, attend
The charge undaunted, and the gate defend.
Renew'd in courage with recover'd breath,
A second time we ran to tempt our death,
To clear the palace from the foe, succeed
The weary living, and revenge the dead.

"A postern door, yet unobserv'd and free,
Join'd by the length of a blind gallery,
To the king's closet led: a way well known
To Hector's wife, while Priam held the throne,
Thro' which she brought Astyanax, unseen,
To cheer his grandsire and his grandsire's queen.

Thro' this we pass, and mount the tow'r, from whence
With unavailing arms the Trojans make defense.
From this the trembling king had oft descried
The Grecian camp, and saw their navy ride.
Beams from its lofty height with swords we hew,
Then, wrenching with our hands, th' assault renew;
And, where the rafters on the columns meet,
We push them headlong with our arms and feet.
The lightning flies not swifter than the fall,
Nor thunder louder than the ruin'd wall:
Down goes the top at once; the Greeks beneath
Are piecemeal torn, or pounded into death.
Yet more succeed, and more to death are sent;
We cease not from above, nor they below relent.
Before the gate stood Pyrrhus, threat'ning loud,
With glitt'ring arms conspicuous in the crowd.
So shines, renew'd in youth, the crested snake,
Who slept the winter in a thorny brake,
And, casting off his slough when spring returns,
Now looks aloft, and with new glory burns;
Restor'd with pois'nous herbs, his ardent sides
Reflect the sun; and rais'd on spires he rides;
High o'er the grass, hissing he rolls along,
And brandishes by fits his forky tongue.
Proud Periphas, and fierce Automedon,
His father's charioteer, together run
To force the gate; the Scyrian infantry
Rush on in crowds, and the barr'd passage free.
Ent'ring the court, with shouts the skies they rend;
And flaming firebrands to the roofs ascend.
Himself, among the foremost, deals his blows,
And with his ax repeated strokes bestows
On the strong doors; then all their shoulders ply,
Till from the posts the brazen hinges fly.
He hews apace; the double bars at length
Yield to his ax and unresisted strength.
A mighty breach is made: the rooms conceal'd
Appear, and all the palace is reveal'd;
The halls of audience, and of public state,
And where the lonely queen in secret sate.

Arm'd soldiers now by trembling maids are seen,
With not a door, and scarce a space, between.
The house is fill'd with loud laments and cries,
And shrieks of women rend the vaulted skies;
The fearful matrons run from place to place,
And kiss the thresholds, and the posts embrace.
The fatal work inhuman Pyrrhus plies,
And all his father sparkles in his eyes;
Nor bars, nor fighting guards, his force sustain:
The bars are broken, and the guards are slain.
In rush the Greeks, and all the apartments fill;
Those few defendants whom they find, they kill.
Not with so fierce a rage the foaming flood
Roars, when he finds his rapid course withstood;
Bears down the dams with unresisted sway,
And sweeps the cattle and the cots away.
These eyes beheld him when he march'd between
The brother kings: I saw th' unhappy queen,
The hundred wives, and where old Priam stood,
To stain his hallow'd altar with his brood.
The fifty nuptial beds (such hopes had he,
So large a promise, of a progeny),
The posts, of plated gold, and hung with spoils,
Fell the reward of the proud victor's toils.
Where'er the raging fire had left a space,
The Grecians enter and possess the place.
 "Perhaps you may of Priam's fate enquire.
He, when he saw his regal town on fire,
His ruin'd palace, and his ent'ring foes,
On ev'ry side inevitable woes,
In arms, disus'd, invests his limbs, decay'd,
Like them, with age; a late and useless aid.
His feeble shoulders scarce the weight sustain;
Loaded, not arm'd, he creeps along with pain,
Despairing of success, ambitious to be slain!
Uncover'd but by heav'n, there stood in view
An altar; near the hearth a laurel grew,
Dodder'd with age, whose boughs encompass round
The household gods, and shade the holy ground.
Here Hecuba, with all her helpless train

Of dames, for shelter sought, but sought in vain.
Driv'n like a flock of doves along the sky,
Their images they hug, and to their altars fly.
The Queen, when she beheld her trembling lord,
And hanging by his side a heavy sword,
'What rage,' she cried, 'has seiz'd my husband's mind?
What arms are these, and to what use design'd?
These times want other aids! Were Hector here,
Ev'n Hector now in vain, like Priam, would appear.
With us, one common shelter thou shalt find,
Or in one common fate with us be join'd.'
She said, and with a last salute embrac'd
The poor old man, and by the laurel plac'd.
Behold! Polites, one of Priam's sons,
Pursued by Pyrrhus, there for safety runs.
Thro' swords and foes, amaz'd and hurt, he flies
Thro' empty courts and open galleries.
Him Pyrrhus, urging with his lance, pursues,
And often reaches, and his thrusts renews.
The youth, transfix'd, with lamentable cries,
Expires before his wretched parent's eyes:
Whom gasping at his feet when Priam saw,
The fear of death gave place to nature's law;
And, shaking more with anger than with age,
'The gods,' said he, 'requite thy brutal rage!
As sure they will, barbarian, sure they must,
If there be gods in heav'n, and gods be just—
Who tak'st in wrongs an insolent delight;
With a son's death t' infect a father's sight.
Not he, whom thou and lying fame conspire
To call thee his—not he, thy vaunted sire,
Thus us'd my wretched age: the gods he fear'd,
The laws of nature and of nations heard.
He cheer'd my sorrows, and, for sums of gold,
The bloodless carcass of my Hector sold;
Pitied the woes a parent underwent,
And sent me back in safety from his tent.'

"This said, his feeble hand a javelin threw,
Which, flutt'ring, seem'd to loiter as it flew:
Just, and but barely, to the mark it held,

And faintly tinkled on the brazen shield.
  "Then Pyrrhus thus: 'Go thou from me to fate,
And to my father my foul deeds relate.
Now die!' With that he dragg'd the trembling sire,
Slidd'ring thro' clotter'd blood and holy mire,
(The mingled paste his murder'd son had made,)
Haul'd from beneath the violated shade,
And on the sacred pile the royal victim laid.
His right hand held his bloody falchion bare,
His left he twisted in his hoary hair;
Then, with a speeding thrust, his heart he found:
The lukewarm blood came rushing thro' the wound,
And sanguine streams distain'd the sacred ground.
Thus Priam fell, and shar'd one common fate
With Troy in ashes, and his ruin'd state:
He, who the scepter of all Asia sway'd,
Whom monarchs like domestic slaves obey'd.
On the bleak shore now lies th' abandon'd king,
A headless carcass, and a nameless thing.
  "Then, not before, I felt my cruddled blood
Congeal with fear, my hair with horror stood:
My father's image fill'd my pious mind,
Lest equal years might equal fortune find.
Again I thought on my forsaken wife,
And trembled for my son's abandon'd life.
I look'd about, but found myself alone,
Deserted at my need! My friends were gone.
Some spent with toil, some with despair oppress'd,
Leap'd headlong from the heights; the flames consum'd
    the rest.
Thus, wand'ring in my way, without a guide,
The graceless Helen in the porch I spied
Of Vesta's temple; there she lurk'd alone;
Muffled she sate, and, what she could, unknown:
But, by the flames that cast their blaze around,
That common bane of Greece and Troy I found.
For Ilium burnt, she dreads the Trojan sword;
More dreads the vengeance of her injur'd lord;
Ev'n by those gods who refug'd her abhorr'd.
Trembling with rage, the strumpet I regard,

Resolv'd to give her guilt the due reward:
'Shall she triumphant sail before the wind,
And leave in flames unhappy Troy behind?
Shall she her kingdom and her friends review,
In state attended with a captive crew,
While unreveng'd the good old Priam falls,
And Grecian fires consume the Trojan walls?
For this the Phrygian fields and Xanthian flood
Were swell'd with bodies, and were drunk with blood?
'Tis true, a soldier can small honor gain,
And boast no conquest, from a woman slain:
Yet shall the fact not pass without applause,
Of vengeance taken in so just a cause;
The punish'd crime shall set my soul at ease,
And murm'ring manes of my friends appease.'
Thus while I rave, a gleam of pleasing light
Spread o'er the place; and, shining heav'nly bright,
My mother stood reveal'd before my sight
Never so radiant did her eyes appear;
Not her own star confess'd a light so clear:
Great in her charms, as when on gods above
She looks, and breathes herself into their love.
She held my hand, the destin'd blow to break;
Then from her rosy lips began to speak:
'My son, from whence this madness, this neglect
Of my commands, and those whom I protect?
Why this unmanly rage? Recall to mind
Whom you forsake, what pledges leave behind.
Look if your helpless father yet survive,
Or if Ascanius or Creüsa live.
Around your house the greedy Grecians err;
And these had perish'd in the nightly war,
But for my presence and protecting care.
Not Helen's face, nor Paris, was in fault;
But by the gods was this destruction brought.
Now cast your eyes around, while I dissolve
The mists and films that mortal eyes involve,
Purge from your sight the dross, and make you see
The shape of each avenging deity.
Enlighten'd thus, my just commands fulfil,

Nor fear obedience to your mother's will.
Where yon disorder'd heap of ruin lies,
Stones rent from stones; where clouds of dust arise—
Amid that smother Neptune holds his place,
Below the wall's foundation drives his mace,
And heaves the building from the solid base.
Look where, in arms, imperial Juno stands
Full in the Scæan gate, with loud commands,
Urging on shore the tardy Grecian bands.
See! Pallas, of her snaky buckler proud,
Bestrides the tow'r, refulgent thro' the cloud:
See! Jove new courage to the foe supplies,
And arms against the town the partial deities.
Haste hence, my son; this fruitless labor end:
Haste, where your trembling spouse and sire attend:
Haste; and a mother's care your passage shall befriend.'
She said, and swiftly vanish'd from my sight,
Obscure in clouds and gloomy shades of night.
I look'd, I listen'd; dreadful sounds I hear;
And the dire forms of hostile gods appear.
Troy sunk in flames I saw (nor could prevent),
And Ilium from its old foundations rent;
Rent like a mountain ash, which dar'd the winds,
And stood the sturdy strokes of lab'ring hinds.
About the roots the cruel ax resounds;
The stumps are pierc'd with oft-repeated wounds:
The war is felt on high; the nodding crown
Now threats a fall, and throws the leafy honors down.
To their united force it yields, tho' late,
And mourns with mortal groans th' approaching fate:
The roots no more their upper load sustain;
But down she falls, and spreads a ruin thro' the plain.
  "Descending thence, I scape thro' foes and fire:
Before the goddess, foes and flames retire.
Arriv'd at home, he, for whose only sake,
Or most for his, such toils I undertake,
The good Anchises, whom, by timely flight,
I purpos'd to secure on Ida's height,
Refus'd the journey, resolute to die
And add his fun'rals to the fate of Troy,

Rather than exile and old age sustain.
'Go you, whose blood runs warm in ev'ry vein.
Had Heav'n decreed that I should life enjoy,
Heav'n had decreed to save unhappy Troy.
'Tis sure, enough, if not too much, for one,
Twice to have seen our Ilium overthrown.
Make haste to save the poor remaining crew,
And give this useless corpse a long adieu.
These weak old hands suffice to stop my breath;
At least the pitying foes will aid my death,
To take my spoils, and leave my body bare:
As for my sepulcher, let Heav'n take care.
'Tis long since I, for my celestial wife
Loath'd by the gods, have dragg'd a ling'ring life;
Since ev'ry hour and moment I expire,
Blasted from heav'n by Jove's avenging fire.'
This oft repeated, he stood fix'd to die:
Myself, my wife, my son, my family,
Intreat, pray, beg, and raise a doleful cry—
'What, will he still persist, on death resolve,
And in his ruin all his house involve!'
He still persists his reasons to maintain;
Our pray'rs, our tears, our loud laments, are vain.

"Urg'd by despair, again I go to try
The fate of arms, resolv'd in fight to die:
'What hope remains, but what my death must give?
Can I, without so dear a father, live?
You term it prudence, what I baseness call:
Could such a word from such a parent fall?
If Fortune please, and so the gods ordain,
That nothing should of ruin'd Troy remain,
And you conspire with Fortune to be slain,
The way to death is wide, th' approaches near:
For soon relentless Pyrrhus will appear,
Reeking with Priam's blood—the wretch who slew
The son (inhuman) in the father's view,
And then the sire himself to the dire altar drew.
O goddess mother, give me back to Fate;
Your gift was undesir'd, and came too late!
Did you, for this, unhappy me convey

Thro' foes and fires, to see my house a prey?
Shall I my father, wife, and son behold,
Welt'ring in blood, each other's arms infold?
Haste! gird my sword, tho' spent and overcome:
'Tis the last summons to receive our doom.
I hear thee, Fate; and I obey thy call!
Not unreveng'd the foe shall see my fall.
Restore me to the yet unfinish'd fight:
My death is wanting to conclude the night.'
Arm'd once again, my glitt'ring sword I wield,
While th' other hand sustains my weighty shield,
And forth I rush to seek th' abandon'd field.
I went; but sad Creüsa stopp'd my way,
And cross the threshold in my passage lay,
Embrac'd my knees, and, when I would have gone,
Shew'd me my feeble sire and tender son:
'If death be your design, at least,' said she,
'Take us along to share your destiny.
If any farther hopes in arms remain,
This place, these pledges of your love, maintain.
To whom do you expose your father's life,
Your son's, and mine, your now forgotten wife!'
While thus she fills the house with clam'rous cries,
Our hearing is diverted by our eyes:
For, while I held my son, in the short space
Betwixt our kisses and our last embrace;
Strange to relate, from young Iülus' head
A lambent flame arose, which gently spread
Around his brows, and on his temples fed.
Amaz'd, with running water we prepare
To quench the sacred fire, and slake his hair;
But old Anchises, vers'd in omens, rear'd
His hands to heav'n, and this request preferr'd:
'If any vows, almighty Jove, can bend
Thy will; if piety can pray'rs commend,
Confirm the glad presage which thou art pleas'd to send.'
Scarce had he said, when, on our left, we hear
A peal of rattling thunder roll in air:
There shot a streaming lamp along the sky,
Which on the winged lightning seem'd to fly;

From o'er the roof the blaze began to move,
And, trailing, vanish'd in th' Idæan grove.
It swept a path in heav'n, and shone a guide,
Then in a steaming stench of sulphur died.

"The good old man with suppliant hands implor'd
The gods' protection, and their star ador'd.
'Now, now,' said he, 'my son, no more delay!
I yield, I follow where Heav'n shews the way.
Keep, O my country gods, our dwelling place,
And guard this relic of the Trojan race,
This tender child! These omens are your own,
And you can yet restore the ruin'd town.
At least accomplish what your signs foreshow:
I stand resign'd, and am prepar'd to go.'

"He said. The crackling flames appear on high,
And driving sparkles dance along the sky.
With Vulcan's rage the rising winds conspire,
And near our palace roll the flood of fire.
'Haste, my dear father, ('tis no time to wait,)
And load my shoulders with a willing freight.
Whate'er befalls, your life shall be my care;
One death, or one deliv'rance, we will share.
My hand shall lead our little son; and you,
My faithful consort, shall our steps pursue.
Next, you, my servants, heed my strict commands:
Without the walls a ruin'd temple stands,
To Ceres hallow'd once; a cypress nigh
Shoots up her venerable head on high,
By long religion kept; there bend your feet,
And in divided parties let us meet.
Our country gods, the relics, and the bands,
Hold you, my father, in your guiltless hands:
In me 'tis impious holy things to bear,
Red as I am with slaughter, new from war,
Till in some living stream I cleanse the guilt
Of dire debate, and blood in battle spilt.'
Thus, ord'ring all that prudence could provide,
I clothe my shoulders with a lion's hide
And yellow spoils; then, on my bending back,
The welcome load of my dear father take;

THE SECOND BOOK OF THE ÆNEIS

While on my better hand Ascanius hung,
And with unequal paces tripp'd along.
Creüsa kept behind; by choice we stray
Thro' ev'ry dark and ev'ry devious way.
I, who so bold and dauntless, just before,
The Grecian darts and shock of lances bore,
At ev'ry shadow now am seiz'd with fear,
Not for myself, but for the charge I bear;
Till, near the ruin'd gate arriv'd at last,
Secure, and deeming all the danger past,
A frightful noise of trampling feet we hear.
My father, looking thro' the shades, with fear,
Cried out: 'Haste, haste, my son, the foes are nigh;
Their swords and shining armor I descry.'
Some hostile god, for some unknown offense,
Had sure bereft my mind of better sense;
For, while thro' winding ways I took my flight,
And sought the shelter of the gloomy night,
Alas! I lost Creüsa: hard to tell
If by her fatal destiny she fell,
Or weary sate, or wander'd with affright;
But she was lost for ever to my sight.
I knew not, or reflected, till I meet
My friends, at Ceres' now deserted seat.
We met: not one was wanting; only she
Deceiv'd her friends, her son, and wretched me.
  "What mad expressions did my tongue refuse!
Whom did I not, of gods or men, accuse!
This was the fatal blow, that pain'd me more
Than all I felt from ruin'd Troy before.
Stung with my loss, and raving with despair,
Abandoning my now forgotten care,
Of counsel, comfort, and of hope bereft,
My sire, my son, my country gods I left.
In shining armour once again I sheathe
My limbs, not feeling wounds, nor fearing **death**.
Then headlong to the burning walls I run,
And seek the danger I was forc'd to shun.
I tread my former tracks; thro' night explore
Each passage, ev'ry street I cross'd before.

All things were full of horror and affright,
And dreadful ev'n the silence of the night.
Then to my father's house I make repair,
With some small glimpse of hope to find her there.
Instead of her, the cruel Greeks I met;
The house was fill'd with foes, with flames beset.
Driv'n on the wings of winds, whole sheets of fire,
Thro' air transported, to the roofs aspire.
From thence to Priam's palace I resort,
And search the citadel and desart court.
Then, unobserv'd, I pass by Juno's church:
A guard of Grecians had possess'd the porch;
There Phœnix and Ulysses watch the prey,
And thither all the wealth of Troy convey:
The spoils which they from ransack'd houses brought,
And golden bowls from burning altars caught,
The tables of the gods, the purple vests,
The people's treasure, and the pomp of priests.
A rank of wretched youths, with pinion'd hands,
And captive matrons, in long order stands.
Then, with ungovern'd madness, I proclaim,
Thro' all the silent street, Creüsa's name:
Creüsa still I call; at length she hears,
And sudden thro' the shades of night appears—
Appears, no more Creüsa, nor my wife,
But a pale specter, larger than the life.
Aghast, astonish'd, and struck dumb with fear,
I stood; like bristles rose my stiffen'd hair.
Then thus the ghost began to soothe my grief:
'Nor tears, nor cries, can give the dead relief.
Desist, my much-lov'd lord, t' indulge your pain;
You bear no more than what the gods ordain.
My fates permit me not from hence to fly;
Nor he, the great controller of the sky.
Long wand'ring ways for you the pow'rs decree;
On land hard labors, and a length of sea.
Then, after many painful years are past,
On Latium's happy shore you shall be cast,
Where gentle Tiber from his bed beholds
The flow'ry meadows, and the feeding folds.

There end your toils; and there your fates provide
A quiet kingdom, and a royal bride:
There fortune shall the Trojan line restore,
And you for lost Creüsa weep no more.
Fear not that I shall watch, with servile shame,
Th' imperious looks of some proud Grecian dame;
Or, stooping to the victor's lust, disgrace
My goddess mother, or my royal race.
And now, farewell! The parent of the gods
Restrains my fleeting soul in her abodes:
I trust our common issue to your care.'
She said, and gliding pass'd unseen in air.
I strove to speak: but horror tied my tongue;
And thrice about her neck my arms I flung,
And, thrice deceiv'd, on vain embraces hung.
Light as an empty dream at break of day,
Or as a blast of wind, she rush'd away.

"Thus having pass'd the night in fruitless pain,
I to my longing friends return again,
Amaz'd th' augmented number to behold,
Of men and matrons mix'd, of young and old;
A wretched exil'd crew together brought,
With arms appointed, and with treasure fraught,
Resolv'd, and willing, under my command,
To run all hazards both of sea and land.
The Morn began, from Ida, to display
Her rosy cheeks; and Phosphor led the day:
Before the gates the Grecians took their post,
And all pretense of late relief was lost.
I yield to Fate, unwillingly retire,
And, loaded, up the hill convey my sire."

THE THIRD BOOK OF THE ÆNEIS

THE ARGUMENT.—*Æneas proceeds in his relation: he gives an account of the fleet with which he sail'd, and the success of his first voyage to Thrace. From thence he directs his course to Delos, and asks the oracle what place the gods had appointed for his habitation. By a mistake of the oracle's answer, he settles in Crete; his household gods give him the true sense of the oracle, in a dream. He follows their advice, and makes the best of his way for Italy. He is cast on several shores, and meets with very surprising adventures, till at length he lands on Sicily, where his father Anchises dies. This is the place which he was sailing from, when the tempest rose, and threw him upon the Carthaginian coast.*

WHEN Heav'n had overturn'd the Trojan state
When Priam's throne, by too severe a fate;
When ruin'd Troy became the Grecians' prey,
And Ilium's lofty tow'rs in ashes lay;
Warn'd by celestial omens, we retreat,
To seek in foreign lands a happier seat.
Near old Antandros, and at Ida's foot,
The timber of the sacred groves we cut,
And build our fleet; uncertain yet to find
What place the gods for our repose assign'd.
Friends daily flock; and scarce the kindly spring
Began to clothe the ground, and birds to sing,
When old Anchises summon'd all to sea:
The crew my father and the Fates obey.
With sighs and tears I leave my native shore,
And empty fields, where Ilium stood before.
My sire, my son, our less and greater gods,
All sail at once, and cleave the briny floods.

"Against our coast appears a spacious land,
Which once the fierce Lycurgus did command,
(Thracia the name—the people bold in war;
Vast are their fields, and tillage is their care,)
A hospitable realm while Fate was kind,
With Troy in friendship and religion join'd.
I land; with luckless omens then adore

Their gods, and draw a line along the shore;
I lay the deep foundations of a wall,
And Ænos, nam'd from me, the city call.
To Dionæan Venus vows are paid,
And all the pow'rs that rising labors aid;
A bull on Jove's imperial altar laid.
Not far, a rising hillock stood in view;
Sharp myrtles on the sides, and cornels grew.
There, while I went to crop the sylvan scenes,
And shade our altar with their leafy greens,
I pull'd a plant—with horror I relate
A prodigy so strange and full of fate.
The rooted fibers rose, and from the wound
Black bloody drops distill'd upon the ground.
Mute and amaz'd, my hair with terror stood;
Fear shrunk my sinews, and congeal'd my blood.
Mann'd once again, another plant I try:
That other gush'd with the same sanguine dye.
Then, fearing guilt for some offense unknown,
With pray'rs and vows the Dryads I atone,
With all the sisters of the woods, and most
The God of Arms, who rules the Thracian coast,
That they, or he, these omens would avert,
Release our fears, and better signs impart.
Clear'd, as I thought, and fully fix'd at length
To learn the cause, I tugged with all my strength:
I bent my knees against the ground; once more
The violated myrtle ran with gore.
Scarce dare I tell the sequel: from the womb
Of wounded earth, and caverns of the tomb,
A groan, as of a troubled ghost, renew'd
My fright, and then these dreadful words ensued:
'Why dost thou thus my buried body rend?
O spare the corpse of thy unhappy friend!
Spare to pollute thy pious hands with blood:
The tears distil not from the wounded wood;
But ev'ry drop this living tree contains
Is kindred blood, and ran in Trojan veins.
O fly from this unhospitable shore,
Warn'd by my fate; for I am Polydore!

Here loads of lances, in my blood embrued,
Again shoot upward, by my blood renew'd.'
 "My falt'ring tongue and shiv'ring limbs declare
My horror, and in bristles rose my hair.
When Troy with Grecian arms was closely pent,
Old Priam, fearful of the war's event,
This hapless Polydore to Thracia sent:
Loaded with gold, he sent his darling, far
From noise and tumults, and destructive war,
Committed to the faithless tyrant's care;
Who, when he saw the pow'r of Troy decline,
Forsook the weaker, with the strong to join;
Broke ev'ry bond of nature and of truth,
And murder'd, for his wealth, the royal youth.
O sacred hunger of pernicious gold!
What bands of faith can impious lucre hold?
Now, when my soul had shaken off her fears,
I call my father and the Trojan peers;
Relate the prodigies of Heav'n, require
What he commands, and their advice desire.
All vote to leave that execrable shore,
Polluted with the blood of Polydore;
But, ere we sail, his fun'ral rites prepare,
Then, to his ghost, a tomb and altars rear.
In mournful pomp the matrons walk the round,
With baleful cypress and blue fillets crown'd,
With eyes dejected, and with hair unbound.
Then bowls of tepid milk and blood we pour,
And thrice invoke the soul of Polydore.
 "Now, when the raging storms no longer reign,
But southern gales invite us to the main,
We launch our vessels, with a prosp'rous wind,
And leave the cities and the shores behind.
 "An island in th' Ægæan main appears;
Neptune and wat'ry Doris claim it theirs.
It floated once, till Phœbus fix'd the sides
To rooted earth, and now it braves the tides.
Here, borne by friendly winds, we come ashore,
With needful ease our weary limbs restore,
And the Sun's temple and his town adore.

"Anius, the priest and king, with laurel crown'd,
His hoary locks with purple fillets bound,
Who saw my sire the Delian shore ascend,
Came forth with eager haste to meet his friend;
Invites him to his palace; and, in sign
Of ancient love, their plighted hands they join.
Then to the temple of the god I went,
And thus, before the shrine, my vows present:
'Give, O Thymbræus, give a resting place
To the sad relics of the Trojan race;
A seat secure, a region of their own,
A lasting empire, and a happier town.
Where shall we fix? where shall our labors end?
Whom shall we follow, and what fate attend?
Let not my pray'rs a doubtful answer find;
But in clear auguries unveil thy mind.'
Scarce had I said: he shook the holy ground,
The laurels, and the lofty hills around;
And from the tripos rush'd a bellowing sound.
Prostrate we fell; confess'd the present god,
Who gave this answer from his dark abode:
'Undaunted youths, go, seek that mother earth
From which your ancestors derive their birth.
The soil that sent you forth, her ancient race
In her old bosom shall again embrace.
Thro' the wide world th' Æneian house shall reign,
And children's children shall the crown sustain.'
Thus Phœbus did our future fates disclose:
A mighty tumult, mix'd with joy, arose.

"All are concern'd to know what place the god
Assign'd, and where determin'd our abode.
My father, long revolving in his mind
The race and lineage of the Trojan kind,
Thus answer'd their demands: 'Ye princes, hear
Your pleasing fortune, and dispel your fear.
The fruitful isle of Crete, well known to fame,
Sacred of old to Jove's imperial name,
In the mid ocean lies, with large command,
And on its plains a hundred cities stand.
Another Ida rises there, and we

From thence derive our Trojan ancestry.
From thence, as 'tis divulg'd by certain fame,
To the Rhœtean shores old Teucrus came;
There fix'd, and there the seat of empire chose,
Ere Ilium and the Trojan tow'rs arose.
In humble vales they built their soft abodes,
Till Cybele, the mother of the gods,
With tinkling cymbals charm'd th' Idæan woods,
She secret rites and ceremonies taught,
And to the yoke the savage lions brought.
Let us the land which Heav'n appoints, explore;
Appease the winds, and seek the Gnossian shore.
If Jove assists the passage of our fleet,
The third propitious dawn discovers Crete.'
Thus having said, the sacrifices, laid
On smoking altars, to the gods he paid:
A bull, to Neptune an oblation due,
Another bull to bright Apollo slew;
A milk-white ewe, the western winds to please,
And one coal-black, to calm the stormy seas.
Ere this, a flying rumor had been spread
That fierce Idomeneus from Crete was fled,
Expell'd and exil'd; that the coast was free
From foreign or domestic enemy.

"We leave the Delian ports, and put to sea;
By Naxos, fam'd for vintage, make our way;
Then green Donysa pass; and sail in sight
Of Paros' isle, with marble quarries white.
We pass the scatter'd isles of Cyclades,
That, scarce distinguish'd, seem to stud the seas.
The shouts of sailors double near the shores;
They stretch their canvas, and they ply their oars.
'All hands aloft! for Crete! for Crete!' they cry,
And swiftly thro' the foamy billows fly.
Full on the promis'd land at length we bore,
With joy descending on the Cretan shore.
With eager haste a rising town I frame,
Which from the Trojan Pergamus I name:
The name itself was grateful; I exhort
To found their houses, and erect a fort.

Our ships are haul'd upon the yellow strand;
The youth begin to till the labor'd land;
And I, myself, new marriages promote,
Give laws, and dwellings I divide by lot;
When rising vapors choke the wholesome air,
And blasts of noisome winds corrupt the year;
The trees devouring caterpillars burn;
Parch'd was the grass, and blighted was the corn:
Nor 'scape the beasts; for Sirius, from on high,
With pestilential heat infects the sky:
My men—some fall, the rest in fevers fry.
Again my father bids me seek the shore
Of sacred Delos, and the god implore,
To learn what end of woes we might expect,
And to what clime our weary course direct.
 " 'Twas night, when ev'ry creature, void of cares,
The common gift of balmy slumber shares:
The statues of my gods (for such they seem'd),
Those gods whom I from flaming Troy redeem'd,
Before me stood, majestically bright,
Full in the beams of Phœbe's ent'ring light.
Then thus they spoke, and eas'd my troubled mind:
'What from the Delian god thou go'st to find,
He tells thee here, and sends us to relate.
Those pow'rs are we, companions of thy fate,
Who from the burning town by thee were brought,
Thy fortune follow'd, and thy safety wrought.
Thro' seas and lands as we thy steps attend,
So shall our care thy glorious race befriend.
An ample realm for thee thy fates ordain,
A town that o'er the conquer'd world shall reign.
Thou, mighty walls for mighty nations build;
Nor let thy weary mind to labors yield:
But change thy seat; for not the Delian god,
Nor we, have giv'n thee Crete for our abode.
A land there is, Hesperia call'd of old,
(The soil is fruitful, and the natives bold—
Th' Œnotrians held it once,) by later fame
Now call'd Italia, from the leader's name.
Iasius there and Dardanus were born;

From thence we came, and thither must return.
Rise, and thy sire with these glad tidings greet.
Search Italy; for Jove denies thee Crete.'
  "Astonish'd at their voices and their sight,
(Nor were they dreams, but visions of the night;
I saw, I knew their faces, and descried,
In perfect view, their hair with fillets tied;)
I started from my couch; a clammy sweat
On all my limbs and shiv'ring body sate.
To heav'n I lift my hands with pious haste,
And sacred incense in the flames I cast.
Thus to the gods their perfect honors done,
More cheerful, to my good old sire I run,
And tell the pleasing news. In little space
He found his error of the double race;
Not, as before he deem'd, deriv'd from Crete;
No more deluded by the doubtful seat:
Then said: 'O son, turmoil'd in Trojan fate!
Such things as these Cassandra did relate.
This day revives within my mind what she
Foretold of Troy renew'd in Italy,
And Latian lands; but who could then have thought
That Phrygian gods to Latium should be brought,
Or who believ'd what mad Cassandra taught?
Now let us go where Phœbus leads the way.'
  "He said; and we with glad consent obey,
Forsake the seat, and, leaving few behind,
We spread our sails before the willing wind.
Now from the sight of land our galleys move,
With only seas around and skies above;
When o'er our heads descends a burst of rain,
And night with sable clouds involves the main;
The ruffling winds the foamy billows raise;
The scatter'd fleet is forc'd to sev'ral ways;
The face of heav'n is ravish'd from our eyes,
And in redoubled peals the roaring thunder flies.
Cast from our course, we wander in the dark.
No stars to guide, no point of land to mark.
Ev'n Palinurus no distinction found
Betwixt the night and day; such darkness reign'd around

Three starless nights the doubtful navy strays,
Without distinction, and three sunless days;
The fourth renews the light, and, from our shrouds,
We view a rising land, like distant clouds;
The mountain-tops confirm the pleasing sight,
And curling smoke ascending from their height.
The canvas falls; their oars the sailors ply;
From the rude strokes the whirling waters fly.
At length I land upon the Strophades,
Safe from the danger of the stormy seas.
Those isles are compass'd by th' Ionian main,
The dire abode where the foul Harpies reign,
Forc'd by the winged warriors to repair
To their old homes, and leave their costly fare.
Monsters more fierce offended Heav'n ne'er sent
From hell's abyss, for human punishment:
With virgin faces, but with wombs obscene,
Foul paunches, and with ordure still unclean;
With claws for hands, and looks for ever lean.
"We landed at the port, and soon beheld
Fat herds of oxen graze the flow'ry field,
And wanton goats without a keeper stray'd.
With weapons we the welcome prey invade,
Then call the gods for partners of our feast,
And Jove himself, the chief invited guest.
We spread the tables on the greensward ground;
We feed with hunger, and the bowls go round;
When from the mountain-tops, with hideous cry,
And clatt'ring wings, the hungry Harpies fly;
They snatch the meat, defiling all they find,
And, parting, leave a loathsome stench behind,
Close by a hollow rock, again we sit,
New dress the dinner, and the beds refit,
Secure from sight, beneath a pleasing shade,
Where tufted trees a native arbor made.
Again the holy fires on altars burn;
And once again the rav'nous birds return,
Or from the dark recesses where they lie,
Or from another quarter of the sky;
With filthy claws their odious meal repeat,

And mix their loathsome ordures with their meat.
I bid my friends for vengeance then prepare,
And with the hellish nation wage the war.
They, as commanded, for the fight provide,
And in the grass their glitt'ring weapons hide;
Then, when along the crooked shore we hear
Their clatt'ring wings, and saw the foes appear,
Misenus sounds a charge: we take th' alarm,
And our strong hands with swords and bucklers arm.
In this new kind of combat all employ
Their utmost force, the monsters to destroy.
In vain—the fated skin is proof to wounds;
And from their plumes the shining sword rebounds.
At length rebuff'd, they leave their mangled prey,
And their stretch'd pinions to the skies display.
Yet one remain'd—the messenger of Fate:
High on a craggy cliff Celæno sate,
And thus her dismal errand did relate:
'What! not contented with our oxen slain,
Dare you with Heav'n an impious war maintain,
And drive the Harpies from their native reign?
Heed therefore what I say; and keep in mind
What Jove decrees, what Phœbus has design'd,
And I, the Furies' queen, from both relate—
You seek th' Italian shores, foredoom'd by fate:
Th' Italian shores are granted you to find,
And a safe passage to the port assign'd.
But know, that ere your promis'd walls you build,
My curses shall severely be fulfill'd.
Fierce famine is your lot for this misdeed,
Reduc'd to grind the plates on which you feed.'
She said, and to the neighb'ring forest flew.
Our courage fails us, and our fears renew.
Hopeless to win by war, to pray'rs we fall,
And on th' offended Harpies humbly call,
And whether gods or birds obscene they were,
Our vows for pardon and for peace prefer.
But old Anchises, off'ring sacrifice,
And lifting up to heav'n his hands and eyes,
Ador'd the greater gods: 'Avert,' said he,

'These omens; render vain this prophecy,
And from th' impending curse a pious people free!'
  "Thus having said, he bids us put to sea;
We loose from shore our haulsers, and obey,
And soon with swelling sails pursue the wat'ry way.
Amidst our course, Zacynthian woods appear;
And next by rocky Neritos we steer:
We fly from Ithaca's detested shore,
And curse the land which dire Ulysses bore.
At length Leucate's cloudy top appears,
And the Sun's temple, which the sailor fears.
Resolv'd to breathe a while from labor past,
Our crooked anchors from the prow we cast,
And joyful to the little city haste.
Here, safe beyond our hopes, our vows we pay
To Jove, the guide and patron of our way.
The customs of our country we pursue,
And Trojan games on Actian shores renew.
Our youth their naked limbs besmear with oil,
And exercise the wrastlers' noble toil;
Pleas'd to have sail'd so long before the wind,
And left so many Grecian towns behind.
The sun had now fulfill'd his annual course,
And Boreas on the seas display'd his force:
I fix'd upon the temple's lofty door
The brazen shield which vanquish'd Abas bore;
The verse beneath my name and action speaks:
'These arms Æneas took from conqu'ring Greeks.'
Then I command to weigh; the seamen ply
Their sweeping oars; the smoking billows fly.
The sight of high Phæacia soon we lost,
And skimm'd along Epirus' rocky coast.
  "Then to Chaonia's port our course we bend,
And, landed, to Buthrotus' heights ascend.
Here wondrous things were loudly blaz'd by fame:
How Helenus reviv'd the Trojan name,
And reign'd in Greece; that Priam's captive son
Succeeded Pyrrhus in his bed and throne;
And fair Andromache, restor'd by fate,
Once more was happy in a Trojan mate.

I leave my galleys riding in the port,
And long to see the new Dardanian court.
By chance, the mournful queen, before the gate,
Then solemniz'd her former husband's fate.
Green altars, rais'd of turf, with gifts she crown'd,
And sacred priests in order stand around,
And thrice the name of hapless Hector sound.
The grove itself resembles Ida's wood;
And Simoïs seem'd the well-dissembled flood.
But when at nearer distance she beheld
My shining armor and my Trojan shield,
Astonish'd at the sight, the vital heat
Forsakes her limbs; her veins no longer beat:
She faints, she falls, and scarce recov'ring strength,
Thus, with a falt'ring tongue, she speaks at length:

"'Are you alive, O goddess-born?' she said,
'Or if a ghost, then where is Hector's shade?'
At this, she cast a loud and frightful cry.
With broken words I made this brief reply:
'All of me that remains appears in sight;
I live, if living be to loathe the light.
No phantom; but I drag a wretched life,
My fate resembling that of Hector's wife.
What have you suffer'd since you lost your lord?
By what strange blessing are you now restor'd?
Still are your Hector's? or is Hector fled,
And his remembrance lost in Pyrrhus' bed?'
With eyes dejected, in a lowly tone,
After a modest pause she thus begun:

"'O only happy maid of Priam's race,
Whom death deliver'd from the foes' embrace!
Commanded on Achilles' tomb to die,
Not forc'd, like us, to hard captivity,
Or in a haughty master's arms to lie.
In Grecian ships unhappy we were borne,
Endur'd the victor's lust, sustain'd the scorn:
Thus I submitted to the lawless pride
Of Pyrrhus, more a handmaid than a bride.
Cloy'd with possession, he forsook my bed,
And Helen's lovely daughter sought to wed;

Then me to Trojan Helenus resign'd,
And his two slaves in equal marriage join'd;
Till young Orestes, pierc'd with deep despair,
And longing to redeem the promis'd fair,
Before Apollo's altar slew the ravisher.
By Pyrrhus' death the kingdom we regain'd:
At least one half with Helenus remain'd.
Our part, from Chaon, he Chaonia calls,
And names from Pergamus his rising walls.
But you, what fates have landed on our coast?
What gods have sent you, or what storms have toss'd?
Does young Ascanius life and health enjoy,
Sav'd from the ruins of unhappy Troy?
O tell me how his mother's loss he bears,
What hopes are promis'd from his blooming years,
How much of Hector in his face appears?'
She spoke; and mix'd her speech with mournful cries,
And fruitless tears came trickling from her eyes.

"At length her lord descends upon the plain,
In pomp, attended with a num'rous train;
Receives his friends, and to the city leads,
And tears of joy amidst his welcome sheds.
Proceeding on, another Troy I see,
Or, in less compass, Troy's epitome.
A riv'let by the name of Xanthus ran,
And I embrace the Scæan gate again.
My friends in porticoes were entertain'd,
And feasts and pleasures thro' the city reign'd.
The tables fill'd the spacious hall around,
And golden bowls with sparkling wine were crown'd.
Two days we pass'd in mirth, till friendly gales,
Blown from the south, supplied our swelling sails.
Then to the royal seer I thus began:
'O thou, who know'st, beyond the reach of man,
The laws of heav'n, and what the stars decree;
Whom Phœbus taught unerring prophecy,
From his own tripod, and his holy tree;
Skill'd in the wing'd inhabitants of air,
What auspices their notes and flights declare:
O say—for all religious rites portend

A happy voyage, and a prosp'rous end;
And ev'ry power and omen of the sky
Direct my course for destin'd Italy;
But only dire Celæno, from the gods,
A dismal famine fatally forebodes—
O say what dangers I am first to shun,
What toils to vanquish, and what course to run.'
　"The prophet first with sacrifice adores
The greater gods; their pardon then implores;
Unbinds the fillet from his holy head;
To Phœbus, next, my trembling steps he led,
Full of religious doubts and awful dread.
Then, with his god possess'd, before the shrine,
These words proceeded from his mouth divine:
'O goddess-born, (for Heav'n's appointed will,
With greater auspices of good than ill,
Foreshows thy voyage, and thy course directs;
Thy fates conspire, and Jove himself protects,)
Of many things some few I shall explain,
Teach thee to shun the dangers of the main,
And how at length the promis'd shore to gain.
The rest the fates from Helenus conceal,
And Juno's angry pow'r forbids to tell.
First, then, that happy shore, that seems so nigh,
Will far from your deluded wishes fly;
Long tracts of seas divide your hopes from Italy:
For you must cruise along Sicilian shores,
And stem the currents with your struggling oars;
Then round th' Italian coast your navy steer;
And, after this, to Circe's island veer;
And, last, before your new foundations rise,
Must pass the Stygian lake, and view the nether skies.
Now mark the signs of future ease and rest,
And bear them safely treasur'd in thy breast.
When, in the shady shelter of a wood,
And near the margin of a gentle flood,
Thou shalt behold a sow upon the ground,
With thirty sucking young encompass'd round;
The dam and offspring white as falling snow—
These on thy city shall their name bestow,

And there shall end thy labors and thy woe.
Nor let the threaten'd famine fright thy mind,
For Phœbus will assist, and Fate the way will find.
Let not thy course to that ill coast be bent,
Which fronts from far th' Epirian continent:
Those parts are all by Grecian foes possess'd;
The salvage Locrians here the shores infest;
There fierce Idomeneus his city builds,
And guards with arms the Salentinian fields;
And on the mountain's brow Petilia stands,
Which Philoctetes with his troops commands.
Ev'n when thy fleet is landed on the shore,
And priests with holy vows the gods adore,
Then with a purple veil involve your eyes,
Lest hostile faces blast the sacrifice.
These rites and customs to the rest commend,
That to your pious race they may descend.
  "'When, parted hence, the wind, that ready waits
For Sicily, shall bear you to the straits
Where proud Pelorus opes a wider way,
Tack to the larboard, and stand off to sea:
Veer starboard sea and land. Th' Italian shore
And fair Sicilia's coast were one, before
An earthquake caus'd the flaw: the roaring tides
The passage broke that land from land divides;
And where the lands retir'd, the rushing ocean rides.
Distinguish'd by the straits, on either hand,
Now rising cities in long order stand,
And fruitful fields: so much can time invade
The mold'ring work that beauteous Nature made.
Far on the right, her dogs foul Scylla hides:
Charybdis roaring on the left presides,
And in her greedy whirlpool sucks the tides;
Then spouts them from below: with fury driv'n,
The waves mount up and wash the face of heav'n.
But Scylla from her den, with open jaws,
The sinking vessel in her eddy draws,
Then dashes on the rocks. A human face,
And virgin bosom, hides her tail's disgrace:
Her parts obscene below the waves descend,

With dogs inclos'd, and in a dolphin end.
'Tis safer, then, to bear aloof to sea,
And coast Pachynus, tho' with more delay,
Than once to view misshapen Scylla near,
And the loud yell of wat'ry wolves to hear.

"'Besides, if faith to Helenus be due,
And if prophetic Phœbus tell me true,
Do not this precept of your friend forget,
Which therefore more than once I must repeat:
Above the rest, great Juno's name adore;
Pay vows to Juno; Juno's aid implore.
Let gifts be to the mighty queen design'd,
And mollify with pray'rs her haughty mind.
Thus, at the length, your passage shall be free,
And you shall safe descend on Italy.
Arriv'd at Cumæ, when you view the flood
Of black Avernus, and the sounding wood,
The mad prophetic Sibyl you shall find,
Dark in a cave, and on a rock reclin'd.
She sings the fates, and, in her frantic fits,
The notes and names, inscrib'd, to leaves commits.
What she commits to leaves, in order laid,
Before the cavern's entrance are display'd:
Unmov'd they lie; but, if a blast of wind
Without, or vapors issue from behind,
The leaves are borne aloft in liquid air,
And she resumes no more her museful care,
Nor gathers from the rocks her scatter'd verse,
Nor sets in order what the winds disperse.
Thus, many not succeeding, most upbraid
The madness of the visionary maid,
And with loud curses leave the mystic shade.

"'Think it not loss of time a while to stay,
Tho' thy companions chide thy long delay;
Tho' summon'd to the seas, tho' pleasing gales
Invite thy course, and stretch thy swelling sails:
But beg the sacred priestess to relate
With willing words, and not to write thy fate.
The fierce Italian people she will show,
And all thy wars, and all thy future woe,

THE THIRD BOOK OF THE ÆNEIS 143

And what thou mayst avoid, and what must undergo.
She shall direct thy course, instruct thy mind,
And teach thee how the happy shores to find.
This is what Heav'n allows me to relate:
Now part in peace; pursue thy better fate,
And raise, by strength of arms, the Trojan state.'

"This when the priest with friendly voice declar'd,
He gave me license, and rich gifts prepar'd:
Bounteous of treasure, he supplied my want
With heavy gold, and polish'd elephant;
Then Dodonæan caldrons put on board,
And ev'ry ship with sums of silver stor'd.
A trusty coat of mail to me he sent,
Thrice chain'd with gold, for use and ornament;
The helm of Pyrrhus added to the rest,
That flourish'd with a plume and waving crest.
Nor was my sire forgotten, nor my friends;
And large recruits he to my navy sends:
Men, horses, captains, arms, and warlike stores;
Supplies new pilots, and new sweeping oars.
Meantime, my sire commands to hoist our sails,
Lest we should lose the first auspicious gales.

"The prophet bless'd the parting crew, and last,
With words like these, his ancient friend embrac'd:
'Old happy man, the care of gods above,
Whom heav'nly Venus honor'd with her love,
And twice preserv'd thy life, when Troy was lost,
Behold from far the wish'd Ausonian coast:
There land; but take a larger compass round,
For that before is all forbidden ground.
The shore that Phœbus has design'd for you,
At farther distance lies, conceal'd from view.
Go happy hence, and seek your new abodes,
Blest in a son, and favor'd by the gods:
For I with useless words prolong your stay,
When southern gales have summon'd you away.'

"Nor less the queen our parting thence deplor'd,
Nor was less bounteous than her Trojan lord.
A noble present to my son she brought,
A robe with flow'rs on golden tissue wrought,

A Phrygian vest; and loads with gifts beside
Of precious texture, and of Asian pride.
'Accept,' she said, 'these monuments of love,
Which in my youth with happier hands I wove:
Regard these trifles for the giver's sake;
'Tis the last present Hector's wife can make.
Thou call'st my lost Astyanax to mind;
In thee his features and his form I find:
His eyes so sparkled with a lively flame;
Such were his motions; such was all his frame;
And ah! had Heav'n so pleas'd, his years had been the same
  "With tears I took my last adieu, and said:
'Your fortune, happy pair, already made,
Leaves you no farther wish. My diff'rent state,
Avoiding one, incurs another fate.
To you a quiet seat the gods allow:
You have no shores to search, no seas to plow,
Nor fields of flying Italy to chase:
(Deluding visions, and a vain embrace!)
You see another Simoïs, and enjoy
The labor of your hands, another Troy,
With better auspice than her ancient tow'rs,
And less obnoxious to the Grecian pow'rs.
If e'er the gods, whom I with vows adore,
Conduct my steps to Tiber's happy shore;
If ever I ascend the Latian throne,
And build a city I may call my own;
As both of us our birth from Troy derive,
So let our kindred lines in concord live,
And both in acts of equal friendship strive.
Our fortunes, good or bad, shall be the same:
The double Troy shall differ but in name;
That what we now begin may never end,
But long to late posterity descend.'
  "Near the Ceraunian rocks our course we bore;
The shortest passage to th' Italian shore.
Now had the sun withdrawn his radiant light,
And hills were hid in dusky shades of night:
We land, and, on the bosom of the ground,
A safe retreat and a bare lodging found.

Close by the shore we lay; the sailors keep
Their watches, and the rest securely sleep.
The night, proceeding on with silent pace,
Stood in her noon, and view'd with equal face
Her steepy rise and her declining race.
Then wakeful Palinurus rose, to spy
The face of heav'n, and the nocturnal sky;
And listen'd ev'ry breath of air to try;
Observes the stars, and notes their sliding course,
The Pleiads, Hyads, and their wat'ry force;
And both the Bears is careful to behold,
And bright Orion, arm'd with burnish'd gold.
Then, when he saw no threat'ning tempest nigh,
But a sure promise of a settled sky,
He gave the sign to weigh; we break our sleep,
Forsake the pleasing shore, and plow the deep.

"And now the rising morn with rosy light
Adorns the skies, and puts the stars to flight;
When we from far, like bluish mists, descry
The hills, and then the plains, of Italy.
Achates first pronounc'd the joyful sound;
Then, 'Italy!' the cheerful crew rebound.
My sire Anchises crown'd a cup with wine,
And, off'ring, thus implor'd the pow'rs divine:
'Ye gods, presiding over lands and seas,
And you who raging winds and waves appease,
Breathe on our swelling sails a prosp'rous wind,
And smooth our passage to the port assign'd!'
The gentle gales their flagging force renew,
And now the happy harbor is in view.
Minerva's temple then salutes our sight,
Plac'd, as a landmark, on the mountain's height.
We furl our sails, and turn the prows to shore;
The curling waters round the galleys roar.
The land lies open to the raging east,
Then, bending like a bow, with rocks compress'd,
Shuts out the storms; the winds and waves complain,
And vent their malice on the cliffs in vain.
The port lies hid within; on either side
Two tow'ring rocks the narrow mouth divide.

The temple, which aloft we view'd before,
To distance flies, and seems to shun the shore.
Scarce landed, the first omens I beheld
Were four white steeds that cropp'd the flow'ry field.
'War, war is threaten'd from this foreign ground,'
My father cried, 'where warlike steeds are found.
Yet, since reclaim'd to chariots they submit,
And bend to stubborn yokes, and champ the bit,
Peace may succeed to war.' Our way we bend
To Pallas, and the sacred hill ascend;
There prostrate to the fierce *virago* pray,
Whose temple was the landmark of our way.
Each with a Phrygian mantle veil'd his head,
And all commands of Helenus obey'd,
And pious rites to Grecian Juno paid.
These dues perform'd, we stretch our sails, and stand
To sea, forsaking that suspected land.

"From hence Tarentum's bay appears in view,
For Hercules renown'd, if fame be true.
Just opposite, Lacinian Juno stands;
Caulonian tow'rs, and Scylacæan strands,
For shipwrecks fear'd. Mount Ætna thence we spy,
Known by the smoky flames which cloud the sky.
Far off we hear the waves with surly sound
Invade the rocks, the rocks their groans rebound.
The billows break upon the sounding strand,
And roll the rising tide, impure with sand.
Then thus Anchises, in experience old:
' 'Tis that Charybdis which the seer foretold,
And those the promis'd rocks! Bear off to sea!'
With haste the frighted mariners obey.
First Palinurus to the larboard veer'd;
Then all the fleet by his example steer'd.
To heav'n aloft on ridgy waves we ride,
Then down to hell descend, when they divide;
And thrice our galleys knock'd the stony ground,
And thrice the hollow rocks return'd the sound,
And thrice we saw the stars, that stood with dews around.
The flagging winds forsook us, with the sun;
And, wearied, on Cyclopian shores we run.

The port capacious, and secure from wind,
Is to the foot of thund'ring Ætna join'd.
By turns a pitchy cloud she rolls on high;
By turns hot embers from her entrails fly,
And flakes of mounting flames, that lick the sky.
Oft from her bowels massy rocks are thrown,
And, shiver'd by the force, come piecemeal down.
Oft liquid lakes of burning sulphur flow,
Fed from the fiery springs that boil below.
Enceladus, they say, transfix'd by Jove,
With blasted limbs came tumbling from above;
And, where he fell, th' avenging father drew
This flaming hill, and on his body threw.
As often as he turns his weary sides,
He shakes the solid isle, and smoke the heavens hides.
In shady woods we pass the tedious night,
Where bellowing sounds and groans our souls affright,
Of which no cause is offer'd to the sight;
For not one star was kindled in the sky,
Nor could the moon her borrow'd light supply;
For misty clouds involv'd the firmament,
The stars were muffled, and the moon was pent.

"Scarce had the rising sun the day reveal'd,
Scarce had his heat the pearly dews dispell'd,
When from the woods there bolts, before our sight,
Somewhat betwixt a mortal and a sprite,
So thin, so ghastly meager, and so wan,
So bare of flesh, he scarce resembled man.
This thing, all tatter'd, seem'd from far t' implore
Our pious aid, and pointed to the shore.
We look behind, then view his shaggy beard;
His clothes were tagg'd with thorns, and filth his limbs
    besmear'd;
The rest, in mien, in habit, and in face,
Appear'd a Greek, and such indeed he was.
He cast on us, from far, a frightful view,
Whom soon for Trojans and for foes he knew;
Stood still, and paus'd; then all at once began
To stretch his limbs, and trembled as he ran.
Soon as approach'd, upon his knees he falls,

And thus with tears and sighs for pity calls:
'Now, by the pow'rs above, and what we share
From Nature's common gift, this vital air,
O Trojans, take me hence! I beg no more;
But bear me far from this unhappy shore.
'Tis true, I am a Greek, and farther own,
Among your foes besieg'd th' imperial town.
For such demerits if my death be due,
No more for this abandon'd life I sue;
This only favor let my tears obtain,
To throw me headlong in the rapid main:
Since nothing more than death my crime demands,
I die content, to die by human hands.'
He said, and on his knees my knees embrac'd:
I bade him boldly tell his fortune past,
His present state, his lineage, and his name,
Th' occasion of his fears, and whence he came.
The good Anchises rais'd him with his hand;
Who, thus encourag'd, answer'd our demand:
'From Ithaca, my native soil, I came
To Troy; and Achæmenides my name.
Me my poor father with Ulysses sent;
(O had I stay'd, with poverty content!)
But, fearful for themselves, my countrymen
Left me forsaken in the Cyclops' den.
The cave, tho' large, was dark; the dismal floor
Was pav'd with mangled limbs and putrid gore.
Our monstrous host, of more than human size,
Erects his head, and stares within the skies;
Bellowing his voice, and horrid is his hue.
Ye gods, remove this plague from mortal view!
The joints of slaughter'd wretches are his food;
And for his wine he quaffs the streaming blood.
These eyes beheld, when with his spacious hand
He seiz'd two captives of our Grecian band;
Stretch'd on his back, he dash'd against the stones
Their broken bodies, and their crackling bones:
With spouting blood the purple pavement swims,
While the dire glutton grinds the trembling limbs.

" 'Not unreveng'd Ulysses bore their fate,

Nor thoughtless of his own unhappy state;
For, gorg'd with flesh, and drunk with human wine
While fast asleep the giant lay supine,
Snoring aloud, and belching from his maw
His indigested foam, and morsels raw;
We pray; we cast the lots, and then surround
The monstrous body, stretch'd along the ground:
Each, as he could approach him, lends a hand
To bore his eyeball with a flaming brand.
Beneath his frowning forehead lay his eye;
For only one did the vast frame supply—
But that a globe so large, his front it fill'd,
Like the sun's disk or like a Grecian shield.
The stroke succeeds; and down the pupil bends:
This vengeance follow'd for our slaughter'd friends.
But haste, unhappy wretches, haste to fly!
Your cables cut, and on your oars rely!
Such, and so vast as Polypheme appears,
A hundred more this hated island bears:
Like him, in caves they shut their woolly sheep;
Like him, their herds on tops of mountains keep;
Like him, with mighty strides, they stalk from steep to steep,
And now three moons their sharpen'd horns renew,
Since thus, in woods and wilds, obscure from view,
I drag my loathsome days with mortal fright,
And in deserted caverns lodge by night;
Oft from the rocks a dreadful prospect see
Of the huge Cyclops, like a walking tree:
From far I hear his thund'ring voice resound,
And trampling feet that shake the solid ground.
Cornels and salvage berries of the wood,
And roots and herbs, have been my meager food.
While all around my longing eyes I cast,
I saw your happy ships appear at last.
On those I fix'd my hopes, to these I run;
'Tis all I ask, this cruel race to shun;
What other death you please, yourselves bestow.'

"Scarce had he said, when on the mountain's brow
We saw the giant shepherd stalk before
His following flock, and leading to the shore:

A monstrous bulk, deform'd, depriv'd of sight;
His staff a trunk of pine, to guide his steps aright.
His pond'rous whistle from his neck descends;
His woolly care their pensive lord attends;
This only solace his hard fortune sends.
Soon as he reach'd the shore and touch'd the waves,
From his bor'd eye the gutt'ring blood he laves:
He gnash'd his teeth, and groan'd; thro' seas he strides,
And scarce the topmost billows touch'd his sides.
  "Seiz'd with a sudden fear, we run to sea,
The cables cut, and silent haste away;
The well-deserving stranger entertain;
Then, buckling to the work, our oars divide the main.
The giant harken'd to the dashing sound:
But, when our vessels out of reach he found,
He strided onward, and in vain essay'd
Th' Ionian deep, and durst no farther wade.
With that he roar'd aloud: the dreadful cry
Shakes earth, and air, and seas; the billows fly
Before the bellowing noise to distant Italy.
The neighb'ring Ætna trembling all around,
The winding caverns echo to the sound.
His brother Cyclops hear the yelling roar,
And, rushing down the mountains, crowd the shore.
We saw their stern distorted looks, from far,
And one-eye'd glance, that vainly threaten'd war:
A dreadful council, with their heads on high;
(The misty clouds about their foreheads fly;)
Not yielding to the tow'ring tree of Jove,
Or tallest cypress of Diana's grove.
New pangs of mortal fear our minds assail;
We tug at ev'ry oar, and hoist up ev'ry sail,
And take th' advantage of the friendly gale.
Forewarn'd by Helenus, we strive to shun
Charybdis' gulf, nor dare to Scylla run.
An equal fate on either side appears:
We, tacking to the left, are free from fears;
For, from Pelorus' point, the North arose,
And drove us back where swift Pantagias flows.
His rocky mouth we pass, and make our way

THE THIRD BOOK OF THE ÆNEIS

By Thapsus and Megara's winding bay.
This passage Achæmenides had shown,
Tracing the course which he before had run.
  "Right o'er against Plemmyrium's wat'ry strand,
There lies an isle once call'd th' Ortygian land.
Alpheüs, as old fame reports, has found
From Greece a secret passage under ground,
By love to beauteous Arethusa led;
And, mingling here, they roll in the same sacred bed.
As Helenus enjoin'd, we next adore
Diana's name, protectress of the shore.
With prosp'rous gales we pass the quiet sounds
Of still Elorus, and his fruitful bounds.
Then, doubling Cape Pachynus, we survey
The rocky shore extended to the sea.
The town of Camarine from far we see,
And fenny lake, undrain'd by fate's decree.
In sight of the Geloan fields we pass,
And the large walls, where mighty Gela was;
Then Agragas, with lofty summits crown'd,
Long for the race of warlike steeds renown'd.
We pass'd Selinus, and the palmy land,
And widely shun the Lilybæan strand,
Unsafe, for secret rocks and moving sand.
At length on shore the weary fleet arriv'd,
Which Drepanum's unhappy port receiv'd.
Here, after endless labors, often toss'd
By raging storms, and driv'n on ev'ry coast,
My dear, dear father, spent with age, I lost:
Ease of my cares, and solace of my pain,
Sav'd thro' a thousand toils, but sav'd in vain.
The prophet, who my future woes reveal'd,
Yet this, the greatest and the worst, conceal'd;
And dire Celæno, whose foreboding skill
Denounc'd all else, was silent of this ill.
This my last labor was. Some friendly god
From thence convey'd us to your blest abode."
  Thus, to the list'ning queen, the royal guest
His wand'ring course and all his toils express'd;
And here concluding, he retir'd to rest.

THE FOURTH BOOK
OF THE ÆNEIS

THE ARGUMENT.—Dido discovers to her sister her passion for Æneas, and her thoughts of marrying him. She prepares a hunting match for his entertainment. Juno, by Venus's consent, raises a storm, which separates the hunters, and drives Æneas and Dido into the same cave, where their marriage is suppos'd to be completed. Jupiter dispatches Mercury to Æneas, to warn him from Carthage. Æneas secretly prepares for his voyage. Dido finds out his design, and, to put a stop to it, makes use of her own and her sister's entreaties, and discovers all the variety of passions that are incident to a neglected lover. When nothing would prevail upon him, she contrives her own death, with which this book concludes.

BUT anxious cares already seiz'd the queen:
   She fed within her veins a flame unseen;
   The hero's valor, acts, and birth inspire
Her soul with love, and fan the secret fire.
His words, his looks, imprinted in her heart,
Improve the passion, and increase the smart.
Now, when the purple morn had chas'd away
The dewy shadows, and restor'd the day,
Her sister first with early care she sought,
And thus in mournful accents eas'd her thought:
  "My dearest Anna, what new dreams affright
My lab'ring soul! what visions of the night
Disturb my quiet, and distract my breast
With strange ideas of our Trojan guest!
His worth, his actions, and majestic air,
A man descended from the gods declare.
Fear ever argues a degenerate kind;
His birth is well asserted by his mind.
Then, what he suffer'd, when by Fate betray'd!
What brave attempts for falling Troy he made!
Such were his looks, so gracefully he spoke,
That, were I not resolv'd against the yoke
Of hapless marriage, never to be curst
With second love, so fatal was my first,
To this one error I might yield again;

THE FOURTH BOOK OF THE ÆNEIS 153

For, since Sichæus was untimely slain,
This only man is able to subvert
The fix'd foundations of my stubborn heart.
And, to confess my frailty, to my shame,
Somewhat I find within, if not the same,
Too like the sparkles of my former flame.
But first let yawning earth a passage rend,
And let me thro' the dark abyss descend;
First let avenging Jove, with flames from high,
Drive down this body to the nether sky,
Condemn'd with ghosts in endless night to lie,
Before I break the plighted faith I gave!
No! he who had my vows shall ever have;
For, whom I lov'd on earth, I worship in the grave."

  She said: the tears ran gushing from her eyes,
And stopp'd her speech. Her sister thus replies:
"O dearer than the vital air I breathe,
Will you to grief your blooming years bequeath,
Condemn'd to waste in woes your lonely life,
Without the joys of mother or of wife?
Think you these tears, this pompous train of woe,
Are known or valued by the ghosts below?
I grant that, while your sorrows yet were green,
It well became a woman, and a queen,
The vows of Tyrian princes to neglect,
To scorn Hyarbas, and his love reject,
With all the Libyan lords of mighty name;
But will you fight against a pleasing flame!
This little spot of land, which Heav'n bestows,
On ev'ry side is hemm'd with warlike foes;
Gætulian cities here are spread around,
And fierce Numidians there your frontiers bound;
Here lies a barren waste of thirsty land,
And there the Syrtes raise the moving sand;
Barcæan troops besiege the narrow shore,
And from the sea Pygmalion threatens more.
Propitious Heav'n, and gracious Juno, lead
This wand'ring navy to your needful aid:
How will your empire spread, your city rise,
From such a union, and with such allies?

Implore the favor of the pow'rs above,
And leave the conduct of the rest to love.
Continue still your hospitable way,
And still invent occasions of their stay,
Till storms and winter winds shall cease to threat,
And planks and oars repair their shatter'd fleet."

 These words, which from a friend and sister came,
With ease resolv'd the scruples of her fame,
And added fury to the kindled flame.
Inspir'd with hope, the project they pursue;
On ev'ry altar sacrifice renew:
A chosen ewe of two years old they pay
To Ceres, Bacchus, and the God of Day;
Preferring Juno's pow'r, for Juno ties
The nuptial knot and makes the marriage joys.
The beauteous queen before her altar stands,
And holds the golden goblet in her hands.
A milk-white heifer she with flow'rs adorns,
And pours the ruddy wine betwixt her horns;
And, while the priests with pray'r the gods invoke,
She feeds their altars with Sabæan smoke,
With hourly care the sacrifice renews,
And anxiously the panting entrails views.
What priestly rites, alas! what pious art,
What vows avail to cure a bleeding heart!
A gentle fire she feeds within her veins,
Where the soft god secure in silence reigns.

 Sick with desire, and seeking him she loves,
From street to street the raving Dido roves.
So when the watchful shepherd, from the blind,
Wounds with a random shaft the careless hind,
Distracted with her pain she flies the woods,
Bounds o'er the lawn, and seeks the silent floods,
With fruitless care; for still the fatal dart
Sticks in her side, and rankles in her heart.
And now she leads the Trojan chief along
The lofty walls, amidst the busy throng;
Displays her Tyrian wealth, and rising town,
Which love, without his labor, makes his own.
This pomp she shows, to tempt her wand'ring guest;

THE FOURTH BOOK OF THE ÆNEIS

Her falt'ring tongue forbids to speak the rest
When day declines, and feasts renew the night,
Still on his face she feeds her famish'd sight;
She longs again to hear the prince relate
His own adventures and the Trojan fate.
He tells it o'er and o'er; but still in vain,
For still she begs to hear it once again.
The hearer on the speaker's mouth depends,
And thus the tragic story never ends.

   Then, when they part, when Phœbe's paler light
Withdraws, and falling stars to sleep invite,
She last remains, when ev'ry guest is gone,
Sits on the bed he press'd, and sighs alone;
Absent, her absent hero sees and hears;
Or in her bosom young Ascanius bears,
And seeks the father's image in the child,
If love by likeness might be so beguil'd.

   Meantime the rising tow'rs are at a stand;
No labors exercise the youthful band,
Nor use of arts, nor toils of arms they know;
The mole is left unfinish'd to the foe;
The mounds, the works, the walls, neglected lie,
Short of their promis'd heighth, that seem'd to threat the sky.

   But when imperial Juno, from above,
Saw Dido fetter'd in the chains of love,
Hot with the venom which her veins inflam'd,
And by no sense of shame to be reclaim'd,
With soothing words to Venus she begun:
"High praises, endless honors, you have won,
And mighty trophies, with your worthy son!
Two gods a silly woman have undone!
Nor am I ignorant, you both suspect
This rising city, which my hands erect:
But shall celestial discord never cease?
'Tis better ended in a lasting peace.
You stand possess'd of all your soul desir'd:
Poor Dido with consuming love is fir'd.
Your Trojan with my Tyrian let us join;
So Dido shall be yours, Æneas mine:
One common kingdom, one united line.

Eliza shall a Dardan lord obey,
And lofty Carthage for a dow'r convey."
Then Venus, who her hidden fraud descried,
Which would the scepter of the world misguide
To Libyan shores, thus artfully replied:
"Who, but a fool, would wars with Juno choose,
And such alliance and such gifts refuse,
If Fortune with our joint desires comply?
The doubt is all from Jove and destiny;
Lest he forbid, with absolute command,
To mix the people in one common land—
Or will the Trojan and the Tyrian line
In lasting leagues and sure succession join?
But you, the partner of his bed and throne,
May move his mind; my wishes are your own."

"Mine," said imperial Juno, "be the care;
Time urges, now, to perfect this affair:
Attend my counsel, and the secret share.
When next the Sun his rising light displays,
And gilds the world below with purple rays,
The queen, Æneas, and the Tyrian court
Shall to the shady woods, for sylvan game, resort.
There, while the huntsmen pitch their toils around,
And cheerful horns from side to side resound,
A pitchy cloud shall cover all the plain
With hail, and thunder, and tempestuous rain;
The fearful train shall take their speedy flight,
Dispers'd, and all involv'd in gloomy night;
One cave a grateful shelter shall afford
To the fair princess and the Trojan lord.
I will myself the bridal bed prepare,
If you, to bless the nuptials, will be there:
So shall their loves be crown'd with due delights,
And Hymen shall be present at the rites."
The Queen of Love consents, and closely smiles
At her vain project, and discover'd wiles.

The rosy morn was risen from the main,
And horns and hounds awake the princely train:
They issue early thro' the city gate,
Where the more wakeful huntsmen ready wait,

THE FOURTH BOOK OF THE ÆNEIS

With nets, and toils, and darts, beside the force
Of Spartan dogs, and swift Massylian horse.
The Tyrian peers and officers of state
For the slow queen in antechambers wait;
Her lofty courser, in the court below,
Who his majestic rider seems to know,
Proud of his purple trappings, paws the ground,
And champs the golden bit, and spreads the foam around,
The queen at length appears; on either hand
The brawny guards in martial order stand.
A flow'r'd simar with golden fringe she wore,
And at her back a golden quiver bore;
Her flowing hair a golden caul restrains,
A golden clasp the Tyrian robe sustains.
Then young Ascanius, with a sprightly grace,
Leads on the Trojan youth to view the chase.
But far above the rest in beauty shines
The great Æneas, when the troop he joins;
Like fair Apollo, when he leaves the frost
Of wint'ry Xanthus, and the Lycian coast,
When to his native Delos he resorts,
Ordains the dances, and renews the sports;
Where painted Scythians, mix'd with Cretan bands,
Before the joyful altars join their hands:
Himself, on Cynthus walking, sees below
The merry madness of the sacred show.
Green wreaths of bays his length of hair inclose;
A golden fillet binds his awful brows;
His quiver sounds: not less the prince is seen
In manly presence, or in lofty mien.

   Now had they reach'd the hills, and storm'd the seat
Of salvage beasts, in dens, their last retreat.
The cry pursues the mountain goats: they bound
From rock to rock, and keep the craggy ground;
Quite otherwise the stags, a trembling train,
In herds unsingled, scour the dusty plain,
And a long chase in open view maintain.
The glad Ascanius, as his courser guides,
Spurs thro' the vale, and these and those outrides.
His horse's flanks and sides are forc'd to feel

The clanking lash, and goring of the steel.
Impatiently he views the feeble prey,
Wishing some nobler beast to cross his way,
And rather would the tusky boar attend,
Or see the tawny lion downward bend.

    Meantime, the gath'ring clouds obscure the skies:
From pole to pole the forky lightning flies;
The rattling thunders roll; and Juno pours
A wintry deluge down, and sounding show'rs.
The company, dispers'd, to converts ride,
And seek the homely cots, or mountain's hollow side.
The rapid rains, descending from the hills,
To rolling torrents raise the creeping rills.
The queen and prince, as love or fortune guides,
One common cavern in her bosom hides.
Then first the trembling earth the signal gave,
And flashing fires enlighten all the cave;
Hell from below, and Juno from above,
And howling nymphs, were conscious of their love
From this ill-omen'd hour in time arose
Debate and death, and all succeeding woes.

    The queen, whom sense of honor could not move,
No longer made a secret of her love,
But call'd it marriage, by that specious name
To veil the crime and sanctify the shame.

    The loud report thro' Libyan cities goes.
Fame, the great ill, from small beginnings grows:
Swift from the first; and ev'ry moment brings
New vigor to her flights, new pinions to her wings.
Soon grows the pigmy to gigantic size;
Her feet on earth, her forehead in the skies.
Inrag'd against the gods, revengeful Earth
Produc'd her last of the Titanian birth.
Swift is her walk, more swift her winged haste:
A monstrous phantom, horrible and vast.
As many plumes as raise her lofty flight,
So many piercing eyes inlarge her sight;
Millions of opening mouths to Fame belong,
And ev'ry mouth is furnish'd with a tongue,
And round with list'ning ears the flying plague is hung.

THE FOURTH BOOK OF THE ÆNEIS

She fills the peaceful universe with cries;
No slumbers ever close her wakeful eyes;
By day, from lofty tow'rs her head she shews,
And spreads thro' trembling crowds disastrous news;
With court informers haunts, and royal spies;
Things done relates, not done she feigns, and mingles truth with lies.

Talk is her business, and her chief delight
To tell of prodigies and cause affright.
She fills the people's ears with Dido's name,
Who, lost to honor and the sense of shame,
Admits into her throne and nuptial bed
A wand'ring guest, who from his country fled:
Whole days with him she passes in delights,
And wastes in luxury long winter nights,
Forgetful of her fame and royal trust,
Dissolv'd in ease, abandon'd to her lust.

The goddess widely spreads the loud report,
And flies at length to King Hyarba's court.
When first possess'd with this unwelcome news
Whom did he not of men and gods accuse?
This prince, from ravish'd Garamantis born,
A hundred temples did with spoils adorn,
In Ammon's honor, his celestial sire;
A hundred altars fed with wakeful fire;
And, thro' his vast dominions, priests ordain'd,
Whose watchful care these holy rites maintain'd.
The gates and columns were with garlands crown'd,
And blood of victim beasts enrich'd the ground.

He, when he heard a fugitive could move
The Tyrian princess, who disdain'd his love,
His breast with fury burn'd, his eyes with fire,
Mad with despair, impatient with desire;
Then on the sacred altars pouring wine,
He thus with pray'rs implor'd his sire divine:
"Great Jove! propitious to the Moorish race,
Who feast on painted beds, with off'rings grace
Thy temples, and adore thy pow'r divine
With blood of victims, and with sparkling wine,
Seest thou not this? or do we fear in vain

Thy boasted thunder, and thy thoughtless reign?
Do thy broad hands the forky lightnings lance?
Thine are the bolts, or the blind work of chance?
A wand'ring woman builds, within our state,
A little town, bought at an easy rate;
She pays me homage, and my grants allow
A narrow space of Libyan lands to plow;
Yet, scorning me, by passion blindly led,
Admits a banish'd Trojan to her bed!
And now this other Paris, with his train
Of conquer'd cowards, must in Afric reign!
(Whom, what they are, their looks and garb confess,
Their locks with oil perfum'd, their Lydian dress.)
He takes the spoil, enjoys the princely dame;
And I, rejected I, adore an empty name."

His vows, in haughty terms, he thus preferr'd,
And held his altar's horns. The mighty Thund'rer heard
Then cast his eyes on Carthage, where he found
The lustful pair in lawless pleasure drown'd,
Lost in their loves, insensible of shame,
And both forgetful of their better fame.
He calls Cyllenius, and the god attends,
By whom his menacing command he sends:
"Go, mount the western winds, and cleave the sky;
Then, with a swift descent, to Carthage fly:
There find the Trojan chief, who wastes his days
In slothful riot and inglorious ease,
Nor minds the future city, giv'n by fate.
To him this message from my mouth relate:
'Not so fair Venus hop'd, when twice she won
Thy life with pray'rs, nor promis'd such a son.
Hers was a hero, destin'd to command
A martial race, and rule the Latian land,
Who should his ancient line from Teucer draw,
And on the conquer'd world impose the law.'
If glory cannot move a mind so mean,
Nor future praise from fading pleasure wean,
Yet why should he defraud his son of fame,
And grudge the Romans their immortal name!
What are his vain designs! what hopes he more

THE FOURTH BOOK OF THE ÆNEIS

From his long ling'ring on a hostile shore,
Regardless to redeem his honor lost,
And for his race to gain th' Ausonian coast!
Bid him with speed the Tyrian court forsake;
With this command the slumb'ring warrior wake."

Hermes obeys; with golden pinions binds
His flying feet, and mounts the western winds:
And, whether o'er the seas or earth he flies,
With rapid force they bear him down the skies.
But first he grasps within his awful hand
The mark of sov'reign pow'r, his magic wand;
With this he draws the ghosts from hollow graves;
With this he drives them down the Stygian waves;
With this he seals in sleep the wakeful sight,
And eyes, tho' clos'd in death, restores to light.
Thus arm'd, the god begins his airy race,
And drives the racking clouds along the liquid space;
Now sees the tops of Atlas, as he flies,
Whose brawny back supports the starry skies;
Atlas, whose head, with piny forests crown'd,
Is beaten by the winds, with foggy vapors bound.
Snows hide his shoulders; from beneath his chin
The founts of rolling streams their race begin;
A beard of ice on his large breast depends.
Here, pois'd upon his wings, the god descends:
Then, rested thus, he from the tow'ring height
Plung'd downward, with precipitated flight,
Lights on the seas, and skims along the flood.
As waterfowl, who seek their fishy food,
Less, and yet less, to distant prospect show;
By turns they dance aloft, and dive below:
Like these, the steerage of his wings he plies,
And near the surface of the water flies,
Till, having pass'd the seas, and cross'd the sands,
He clos'd his wings, and stoop'd on Libyan lands:
Where shepherds once were hous'd in homely sheds,
Now tow'rs within the clouds advance their heads.
Arriving there, he found the Trojan prince
New ramparts raising for the town's defense.
A purple scarf, with gold embroider'd o'er,

(Queen Dido's gift,) about his waist he wore;
A sword, with glitt'ring gems diversified,
For ornament, not use, hung idly by his side.
  Then thus, with winged words, the god began,
Resuming his own shape: "Degenerate man,
Thou woman's property, what mak'st thou here,
These foreign walls and Tyrian tow'rs to rear,
Forgetful of thy own? All-pow'rful Jove,
Who sways the world below and heav'n above,
Has sent me down with this severe command:
What means thy ling'ring in the Libyan land?
If glory cannot move a mind so mean,
Nor future praise from flitting pleasure wean,
Regard the fortunes of thy rising heir:
The promis'd crown let young Ascanius wear,
To whom th' Ausonian scepter, and the state
Of Rome's imperial name is ow'd by fate."
So spoke the god; and, speaking, took his flight,
Involv'd in clouds, and vanish'd out of sight.
  The pious prince was seiz'd with sudden fear;
Mute was his tongue, and upright stood his hair.
Revolving in his mind the stern command,
He longs to fly, and loathes the charming land.
What should he say? or how should he begin?
What course, alas! remains to steer between
Th' offended lover and the pow'rful queen?
This way and that he turns his anxious mind,
And all expedients tries, and none can find.
Fix'd on the deed, but doubtful of the means,
After long thought, to this advice he leans:
Three chiefs he calls, commands them to repair
The fleet, and ship their men with silent care;
Some plausible pretense he bids them find,
To color what in secret he design'd.
Himself, meantime, the softest hours would choose,
Before the love-sick lady heard the news;
And move her tender mind, by slow degrees,
To suffer what the sov'reign pow'r decrees:
Jove will inspire him, when, and what to say.
They hear with pleasure, and with haste obey.

But soon the queen perceives the thin disguise:
(What arts can blind a jealous woman's eyes!)
She was the first to find the secret fraud,
Before the fatal news was blaz'd abroad.
Love the first motions of the lover hears,
Quick to presage, and ev'n in safety fears.
Nor impious Fame was wanting to report
The ships repair'd, the Trojans' thick resort,
And purpose to forsake the Tyrian court.
Frantic with fear, impatient of the wound,
And impotent of mind, she roves the city round.
Less wild the Bacchanalian dames appear,
When, from afar, their nightly god they hear,
And howl about the hills, and shake the wreathy spear.
At length she finds the dear perfidious man;
Prevents his form'd excuse, and thus began:
"Base and ungrateful! could you hope to fly,
And undiscover'd scape a lover's eye?
Nor could my kindness your compassion move,
Nor plighted vows, nor dearer bands of love?
Or is the death of a despairing queen
Not worth preventing, tho' too well foreseen?
Ev'n when the wintry winds command your stay,
You dare the tempests, and defy the sea.
False as you are, suppose you were not bound
To lands unknown, and foreign coasts to sound;
Were Troy restor'd, and Priam's happy reign,
Now durst you tempt, for Troy, the raging main?
See whom you fly! am I the foe you shun?
Now, by those holy vows, so late begun,
By this right hand, (since I have nothing more
To challenge, but the faith you gave before;)
I beg you by these tears too truly shed,
By the new pleasures of our nuptial bed;
If ever Dido, when you most were kind,
Were pleasing in your eyes, or touch'd your mind;
By these my pray'rs, if pray'rs may yet have place,
Pity the fortunes of a falling race.
For you I have provok'd a tyrant's hate,
Incens'd the Libyan and the Tyrian state;

For you alone I suffer in my fame,
Bereft of honor, and expos'd to shame.
Whom have I now to trust, ungrateful guest?
(That only name remains of all the rest!)
What have I left? or whither can I fly?
Must I attend Pygmalion's cruelty,
Or till Hyarba shall in triumph lead
A queen that proudly scorn'd his proffer'd bed?
Had you deferr'd, at least, your hasty flight,
And left behind some pledge of our delight,
Some babe to bless the mother's mournful sight,
Some young Æneas, to supply your place,
Whose features might express his father's face;
I should not then complain to live bereft
Of all my husband, or be wholly left."

  Here paus'd the queen. Unmov'd he holds his eyes,
By Jove's command; nor suffer'd love to rise,
Tho' heaving in his heart; and thus at length replies:
"Fair queen, you never can enough repeat
Your boundless favors, or I own my debt;
Nor can my mind forget Eliza's name,
While vital breath inspires this mortal frame.
This only let me speak in my defense:
I never hop'd a secret flight from hence,
Much less pretended to the lawful claim
Of sacred nuptials, or a husband's name.
For, if indulgent Heav'n would leave me free,
And not submit my life to fate's decree,
My choice would lead me to the Trojan shore,
Those relics to review, their dust adore,
And Priam's ruin'd palace to restore.
But now the Delphian oracle commands,
And fate invites me to the Latian lands.
That is the promis'd place to which I steer,
And all my vows are terminated there.
If you, a Tyrian, and a stranger born,
With walls and tow'rs a Libyan town adorn,
Why may not we—like you, a foreign race—
Like you, seek shelter in a foreign place?
As often as the night obscures the skies

THE FOURTH BOOK OF THE ÆNEIS 165

With humid shades, or twinkling stars arise,
Anchises' angry ghost in dreams appears,
Chides my delay, and fills my soul with fears;
And young Ascanius justly may complain
Of his defrauded fate and destin'd reign.
Ev'n now the herald of the gods appear'd:
Waking I saw him, and his message heard.
From Jove he came commission'd, heav'nly bright
With radiant beams, and manifest to sight
(The sender and the sent I both attest):
These walls he enter'd, and those words express'd.
Fair queen, oppose not what the gods command;
Forc'd by my fate, I leave your happy land."

Thus while he spoke, already she began,
With sparkling eyes, to view the guilty man;
From head to foot survey'd his person o'er,
Nor longer these outrageous threats forebore:
"False as thou art, and, more than false, forsworn!
Not sprung from noble blood, nor goddess-born,
But hewn from harden'd entrails of a rock!
And rough Hyrcanian tigers gave thee suck!
Why should I fawn? what have I worse to fear?
Did he once look, or lent a list'ning ear,
Sigh'd when I sobb'd, or shed one kindly tear?—
All symptoms of a base ungrateful mind,
So foul, that, which is worse, 'tis hard to find.
Of man's injustice why should I complain?
The gods, and Jove himself, behold in vain
Triumphant treason; yet no thunder flies,
Nor Juno views my wrongs with equal eyes;
Faithless is earth, and faithless are the skies!
Justice is fled, and Truth is now no more!
I sav'd the shipwrack'd exile on my shore;
With needful food his hungry Trojans fed;
I took the traitor to my throne and bed:
Fool that I was—'tis little to repeat
The rest—I stor'd and rigg'd his ruin'd fleet.
I rave, I rave! A god's command he pleads,
And makes Heav'n accessary to his deeds.
Now Lycian lots, and now the Delian god,

Now Hermes is employ'd from Jove's abode,
To warn him hence; as if the peaceful state
Of heav'nly pow'rs were touch'd with human fate!
But go! thy flight no longer I detain—
Go seek thy promis'd kingdom thro' the main!
Yet, if the heav'ns will hear my pious vow,
The faithless waves, not half so false as thou,
Or secret sands, shall sepulchers afford
To thy proud vessels, and their perjur'd lord.
Then shalt thou call on injur'd Dido's name:
Dido shall come in a black sulph'ry flame,
When death has once dissolv'd her mortal frame;
Shall smile to see the traitor vainly weep:
Her angry ghost, arising from the deep,
Shall haunt thee waking, and disturb thy sleep.
At least my shade thy punishment shall know,
And Fame shall spread the pleasing news below."

Abruptly here she stops; then turns away
Her loathing eyes, and shuns the sight of day.
Amaz'd he stood, revolving in his mind
What speech to frame, and what excuse to find.
Her fearful maids their fainting mistress led,
And softly laid her on her iv'ry bed.

But good Æneas, tho' he much desir'd
To give that pity which her grief requir'd;
Tho' much he mourn'd, and labor'd with his love,
Resolv'd at length, obeys the will of Jove;
Reviews his forces: they with early care
Unmoor their vessels, and for sea prepare.
The fleet is soon afloat, in all its pride,
And well-calk'd galleys in the harbor ride.
Then oaks for oars they fell'd; or, as they stood,
Of its green arms despoil'd the growing wood,
Studious of flight. The beach is cover'd o'er
With Trojan bands, that blacken all the shore:
On ev'ry side are seen, descending down,
Thick swarms of soldiers, loaden from the town.
Thus, in battalia, march embodied ants,
Fearful of winter, and of future wants,
T' invade the corn, and to their cells convey

The plunder'd forage of their yellow prey.
The sable troops, along the narrow tracks,
Scarce bear the weighty burthen on their backs:
Some set their shoulders to the pond'rous grain;
Some guard the spoil; some lash the lagging train;
All ply their sev'ral tasks, and equal toil sustain.

   What pangs the tender breast of Dido tore,
When, from the tow'r, she saw the cover'd shore,
And heard the shouts of sailors from afar,
Mix'd with the murmurs of the wat'ry war!
All-pow'rful Love! what changes canst thou cause
In human hearts, subjected to thy laws!
Once more her haughty soul the tyrant bends:
To pray'rs and mean submissions she descends.
No female arts or aids she left untried,
Nor counsels unexplor'd, before she died.
"Look, Anna! look! the Trojans crowd to sea;
They spread their canvas, and their anchors weigh.
The shouting crew their ships with garlands bind,
Invoke the sea gods, and invite the wind.
Could I have thought this threat'ning blow so near,
My tender soul had been forewarn'd to bear.
But do not you my last request deny;
With yon perfidious man your int'rest try,
And bring me news, if I must live or die.
You are his fav'rite; you alone can find
The dark recesses of his inmost mind:
In all his trusted secrets you have part,
And know the soft approaches to his heart.
Haste then, and humbly seek my haughty foe;
Tell him, I did not with the Grecians go,
Nor did my fleet against his friends employ,
Nor swore the ruin of unhappy Troy,
Nor mov'd with hands profane his father's dust:
Why should he then reject a suit so just!
Whom does he shun, and whither would he fly!
Can he this last, this only pray'r deny!
Let him at least his dang'rous flight delay,
Wait better winds, and hope a calmer sea.
The nuptials he disclaims I urge no more:

Let him pursue the promis'd Latian shore.
A short delay is all I ask him now;
A pause of grief, an interval from woe,
Till my soft soul be temper'd to sustain
Accustom'd sorrows, and inur'd to pain.
If you in pity grant this one request,
My death shall glut the hatred of his breast."
This mournful message pious Anna bears,
And seconds with her own her sister's tears:
But all her arts are still employ'd in vain;
Again she comes, and is refus'd again.
His harden'd heart nor pray'rs nor threat'nings move;
Fate, and the god, had stopp'd his ears to love.

As, when the winds their airy quarrel try,
Justling from ev'ry quarter of the sky,
This way and that the mountain oak they bend,
His boughs they shatter, and his branches rend;
With leaves and falling mast they spread the ground;
The hollow valleys echo to the sound:
Unmov'd, the royal plant their fury mocks,
Or, shaken, clings more closely to the rocks;
Far as he shoots his tow'ring head on high,
So deep in earth his fix'd foundations lie.
No less a storm the Trojan hero bears;
Thick messages and loud complaints he hears,
And bandied words, still beating on his ears.
Sighs, groans, and tears proclaim his inward pains;
But the firm purpose of his heart remains.

The wretched queen, pursued by cruel fate,
Begins at length the light of heav'n to hate,
And loathes to live. Then dire portents she sees,
To hasten on the death her soul decrees:
Strange to relate! for when, before the shrine,
She pours in sacrifice the purple wine,
The purple wine is turn'd to putrid blood,
And the white offer'd milk converts to mud.
This dire presage, to her alone reveal'd,
From all, and ev'n her sister, she conceal'd.
A marble temple stood within the grove,
Sacred to death, and to her murther'd love;

THE FOURTH BOOK OF THE ÆNEIS

That honor'd chapel she had hung around
With snowy fleeces, and with garlands crown'd:
Oft, when she visited this lonely dome,
Strange voices issued from her husband's tomb;
She thought she heard him summon her away,
Invite her to his grave, and chide her stay.
Hourly 'tis heard, when with a boding note
The solitary screech owl strains her throat,
And, on a chimney's top, or turret's height,
With songs obscene disturbs the silence of the night.
Besides, old prophecies augment her fears;
And stern Æneas in her dreams appears,
Disdainful as by day: she seems, alone,
To wander in her sleep, thro' ways unknown,
Guideless and dark; or, in a desert plain,
To seek her subjects, and to seek in vain:
Like Pentheus, when, distracted with his fear,
He saw two suns, and double Thebes, appear;
Or mad Orestes, when his mother's ghost
Full in his face infernal torches toss'd,
And shook her snaky locks: he shuns the sight,
Flies o'er the stage, surpris'd with mortal fright;
The Furies guard the door and intercept his flight.

  Now, sinking underneath a load of grief,
From death alone she seeks her last relief;
The time and means resolv'd within her breast,
She to her mournful sister thus address'd
(Dissembling hope, her cloudy front she clears,
And a false vigor in her eyes appears):
"Rejoice!" she said. "Instructed from above,
My lover I shall gain, or lose my love.
Nigh rising Atlas, next the falling sun,
Long tracts of Ethiopian climates run:
There a Massylian priestess I have found,
Honor'd for age, for magic arts renown'd:
Th' Hesperian temple was her trusted care;
'Twas she supplied the wakeful dragon's fare.
She poppy seeds in honey taught to steep,
Reclaim'd his rage, and sooth'd him into sleep.
She watch'd the golden fruit; her charms unbind

The chains of love, or fix them on the mind:
She stops the torrents, leaves the channel dry,
Repels the stars, and backward bears the sky.
The yawning earth rebellows to her call,
Pale ghosts ascend, and mountain ashes fall.
Witness, ye gods, and thou my better part,
How loth I am to try this impious art!
Within the secret court, with silent care,
Erect a lofty pile, expos'd in air:
Hang on the topmost part the Trojan vest,
Spoils, arms, and presents, of my faithless guest.
Next, under these, the bridal bed be plac'd,
Where I my ruin in his arms embrac'd:
All relics of the wretch are doom'd to fire;
For so the priestess and her charms require."

 Thus far she said, and farther speech forbears;
A mortal paleness in her face appears:
Yet the mistrustless Anna could not find
The secret fun'ral in these rites design'd;
Nor thought so dire a rage possess'd her mind.
Unknowing of a train conceal'd so well,
She fear'd no worse than when Sichæus fell;
Therefore obeys. The fatal pile they rear,
Within the secret court, expos'd in air.
The cloven holms and pines are heap'd on high,
And garlands on the hollow spaces lie.
Sad cypress, vervain, yew, compose the wreath,
And ev'ry baleful green denoting death.
The queen, determin'd to the fatal deed,
The spoils and sword he left, in order spread,
And the man's image on the nuptial bed.

 And now (the sacred altars plac'd around)
The priestess enters, with her hair unbound,
And thrice invokes the pow'rs below the ground.
Night, Erebus, and Chaos she proclaims,
And threefold Hecate, with her hundred names,
And three Dianas: next, she sprinkles round
With feign'd Avernian drops the hallow'd ground;
Culls hoary simples, found by Phœbe's light,
With brazen sickles reap'd at noon of night;

Then mixes baleful juices in the bowl,
And cuts the forehead of a newborn foal,
Robbing the mother's love. The destin'd queen
Observes, assisting at the rites obscene;
A leaven'd cake in her devoted hands
She holds, and next the highest altar stands:
One tender foot was shod, her other bare;
Girt was her gather'd gown, and loose her hair.
Thus dress'd, she summon'd, with her dying breath,
The heav'ns and planets conscious of her death,
And ev'ry pow'r, if any rules above,
Who minds, or who revenges, injur'd love.

   'Twas dead of night, when weary bodies close
Their eyes in balmy sleep and soft repose:
The winds no longer whisper thro' the woods,
Nor murm'ring tides disturb the gentle floods.
The stars in silent order mov'd around;
And Peace, with downy wings, was brooding on the ground.
The flocks and herds, and party-color'd fowl,
Which haunt the woods, or swim the weedy pool,
Stretch'd on the quiet earth, securely lay,
Forgetting the past labors of the day.
All else of nature's common gift partake:
Unhappy Dido was alone awake.
Nor sleep, nor ease, the furious queen can find;
Sleep fled her eyes, as quiet fled her mind.
Despair, and rage, and love divide her heart;
Despair and rage had some, but love the greater part.

   Then thus she said within her secret mind:
"What shall I do? what succor can I find?
Become a suppliant to Hyarba's pride,
And take my turn, to court and be denied?
Shall I with this ungrateful Trojan go,
Forsake an empire, and attend a foe?
Himself I refug'd, and his train reliev'd—
'Tis true—but am I sure to be receiv'd?
Can gratitude in Trojan souls have place!
Laomedon still lives in all his race!
Then, shall I seek alone the churlish crew,
Or with my fleet their flying sails pursue?

What force have I but those whom scarce before
I drew reluctant from their native shore?
Will they again embark at my desire,
Once more sustain the seas, and quit their second Tyre?
Rather with steel thy guilty breast invade,
And take the fortune thou thyself hast made.
Your pity, sister, first seduc'd my mind,
Or seconded too well what I design'd.
These dear-bought pleasures had I never known,
Had I continued free, and still my own;
Avoiding love, I had not found despair,
But shar'd with salvage beasts the common air.
Like them, a lonely life I might have led,
Not mourn'd the living, nor disturb'd the dead."
These thoughts she brooded in her anxious breast.
On board, the Trojan found more easy rest.
Resolv'd to sail, in sleep he pass'd the night;
And order'd all things for his early flight.

   To whom once more the winged god appears;
His former youthful mien and shape he wears,
And with this new alarm invades his ears:
"Sleep'st thou, O goddess-born! and canst thou drown
Thy needful cares, so near a hostile town,
Beset with foes; nor hear'st the western gales
Invite thy passage, and inspire thy sails?
She harbors in her heart a furious hate,
And thou shalt find the dire effects too late;
Fix'd on revenge, and obstinate to die.
Haste swiftly hence, while thou hast pow'r to fly.
The sea with ships will soon be cover'd o'er,
And blazing firebrands kindle all the shore.
Prevent her rage, while night obscures the skies,
And sail before the purple morn arise.
Who knows what hazards thy delay may bring?
Woman's a various and a changeful thing."
Thus Hermes in the dream; then took his flight
Aloft in air unseen, and mix'd with night.

   Twice warn'd by the celestial messenger,
The pious prince arose with hasty fear;
Then rous'd his drowsy train without delay:

"Haste to your banks; your crooked anchors weigh,
And spread your flying sails, and stand to sea.
A god commands: he stood before my sight,
And urg'd us once again to speedy flight.
O sacred pow'r, what pow'r soe'er thou art,
To thy blest orders I resign my heart.
Lead thou the way; protect thy Trojan bands,
And prosper the design thy will commands."
He said: and, drawing forth his flaming sword,
His thund'ring arm divides the many-twisted cord.
An emulating zeal inspires his train:
They run; they snatch; they rush into the main.
With headlong haste they leave the desert shores,
And brush the liquid seas with lab'ring oars.

Aurora now had left her saffron bed,
And beams of early light the heav'ns o'erspread,
When, from a tow'r, the queen, with wakeful eyes,
Saw day point upward from the rosy skies.
She look'd to seaward; but the sea was void,
And scarce in ken the sailing ships descried.
Stung with despite, and furious with despair,
She struck her trembling breast, and tore her hair.
"And shall th' ungrateful traitor go," she said,
"My land forsaken, and my love betray'd?
Shall we not arm? not rush from ev'ry street,
To follow, sink, and burn his perjur'd fleet?
Haste, haul my galleys out! pursue the foe!
Bring flaming brands! set sail, and swiftly row!
What have I said? where am I? Fury turns
My brain; and my distemper'd bosom burns.
Then, when I gave my person and my throne,
This hate, this rage, had been more timely shown.
See now the promis'd faith, the vaunted name,
The pious man, who, rushing thro' the flame,
Preserv'd his gods, and to the Phrygian shore
The burthen of his feeble father bore!
I should have torn him piecemeal; strow'd in floods
His scatter'd limbs, or left expos'd in woods;
Destroy'd his friends and son; and, from the fire,
Have set the reeking boy before the sire.

Events are doubtful, which on battles wait:
Yet where's the doubt, to souls secure of fate?
My Tyrians, at their injur'd queen's command,
Had toss'd their fires amid the Trojan band;
At once extinguish'd all the faithless name;
And I myself, in vengeance of my shame,
Had fall'n upon the pile, to mend the fun'ral flame.
Thou Sun, who view'st at once the world below;
Thou Juno, guardian of the nuptial vow;
Thou Hecate hearken from thy dark abodes!
Ye Furies, fiends, and violated gods,
All pow'rs invok'd with Dido's dying breath,
Attend her curses and avenge her death!
If so the Fates ordain, and Jove commands,
Th' ungrateful wretch should find the Latian lands,
Yet let a race untam'd, and haughty foes,
His peaceful entrance with dire arms oppose:
Oppress'd with numbers in th' unequal field,
His men discourag'd, and himself expell'd,
Let him for succor sue from place to place,
Torn from his subjects, and his son's embrace.
First, let him see his friends in battle slain,
And their untimely fate lament in vain;
And when, at length, the cruel war shall cease,
On hard conditions may he buy his peace:
Nor let him then enjoy supreme command;
But fall, untimely, by some hostile hand,
And lie unburied on the barren sand!
These are my pray'rs, and this my dying will;
And you, my Tyrians, ev'ry curse fulfil.
Perpetual hate and mortal wars proclaim,
Against the prince, the people, and the name.
These grateful off'rings on my grave bestow;
Nor league, nor love, the hostile nations know!
Now, and from hence, in ev'ry future age,
When rage excites your arms, and strength supplies the rage
Rise some avenger of our Libyan blood,
With fire and sword pursue the perjur'd brood;
Our arms, our seas, our shores, oppos'd to theirs;
And the same hate descend on all our heirs!"

THE FOURTH BOOK OF THE ÆNEIS

This said, within her anxious mind she weighs
The means of cutting short her odious days.
Then to Sichæus' nurse she briefly said
(For, when she left her country, hers was dead):
"Go, Barce, call my sister. Let her care
The solemn rites of sacrifice prepare;
The sheep, and all th' atoning off'rings, bring,
Sprinkling her body from the crystal spring
With living drops; then let her come, and thou
With sacred fillets bind thy hoary brow.
Thus will I pay my vows to Stygian Jove,
And end the cares of my disastrous love;
Then cast the Trojan image on the fire,
And, as that burns, my passions shall expire."

The nurse moves onward, with officious care,
And all the speed her aged limbs can bear.
But furious Dido, with dark thoughts involv'd,
Shook at the mighty mischief she resolv'd.
With livid spots distinguish'd was her face;
Red were her rolling eyes, and discompos'd her pace;
Ghastly she gaz'd, with pain she drew her breath,
And nature shiver'd at approaching death.

Then swiftly to the fatal place she pass'd,
And mounts the fun'ral pile with furious haste;
Unsheathes the sword the Trojan left behind
(Not for so dire an enterprise design'd).
But when she view'd the garments loosely spread,
Which once he wore, and saw the conscious bed,
She paus'd, and with a sigh the robes embrac'd;
Then on the couch her trembling body cast,
Repress'd the ready tears, and spoke her last:
"Dear pledges of my love, while Heav'n so pleas'd,
Receive a soul, of mortal anguish eas'd:
My fatal course is finish'd; and I go,
A glorious name, among the ghosts below.
A lofty city by my hands is rais'd,
Pygmalion punish'd, and my lord appeas'd.
What could my fortune have afforded more,
Had the false Trojan never touch'd my shore!"
Then kiss'd the couch; and, "Must I die," she said,

"And unreveng'd? 'Tis doubly to be dead!
Yet ev'n this death with pleasure I receive:
On any terms, 'tis better than to live.
These flames, from far, may the false Trojan view;
These boding omens his base flight pursue!"
   She said, and struck; deep enter'd in her side
The piercing steel, with reeking purple dyed:
Clogg'd in the wound the cruel weapon stands;
The spouting blood came streaming on her hands.
Her sad attendants saw the deadly stroke,
And with loud cries the sounding palace shook.
Distracted, from the fatal sight they fled,
And thro' the town the dismal rumor spread.
First from the frighted court the yell began;
Redoubled, thence from house to house it ran:
The groans of men, with shrieks, laments, and cries
Of mixing women, mount the vaulted skies.
Not less the clamor, than if—ancient Tyre,
Or the new Carthage, set by foes on fire—
The rolling ruin, with their lov'd abodes,
Involv'd the blazing temples of their gods.
   Her sister hears; and, furious with despair,
She beats her breast, and rends her yellow hair,
And, calling on Eliza's name aloud,
Runs breathless to the place, and breaks the crowd.
"Was all that pomp of woe for this prepar'd;
These fires, this fun'ral pile, these altars rear'd?
Was all this train of plots contriv'd," said she,
"All, only to deceive unhappy me?
Which is the worst? Didst thou in death pretend
To scorn thy sister, or delude thy friend?
Thy summon'd sister, and thy friend, had come;
One sword had serv'd us both, one common tomb:
Was I to raise the pile, the pow'rs invoke,
Not to be present at the fatal stroke?
At once thou hast destroy'd thyself and me,
Thy town, thy senate, and thy colony!
Bring water; bathe the wound; while I in death
Lay close my lips to hers, and catch the flying breath."
This said, she mounts the pile with eager haste,

And in her arms the gasping queen embrac'd;
Her temples chaf'd; and her own garments tore,
To stanch the streaming blood, and cleanse the gore.
Thrice Dido tried to raise her drooping head,
And, fainting thrice, fell grov'ling on the bed;
Thrice op'd her heavy eyes, and sought the light,
But, having found it, sicken'd at the sight,
And clos'd her lids at last in endless night.
   Then Juno, grieving that she should sustain
A death so ling'ring, and so full of pain,
Sent Iris down, to free her from the strife
Of lab'ring nature, and dissolve her life.
For since she died, not doom'd by Heav'n's decree,
Or her own crime, but human casualty,
And rage of love, that plung'd her in despair,
The Sisters had not cut the topmost hair,
Which Proserpine and they can only know;
Nor made her sacred to the shades below.
Downward the various goddess took her flight,
And drew a thousand colors from the light;
Then stood above the dying lover's head,
And said: "I thus devote thee to the dead.
This off'ring to th' infernal gods I bear."
Thus while she spoke, she cut the fatal hair:
The struggling soul was loos'd, and life dissolv'd in air.

THE FIFTH BOOK
OF THE ÆNEIS

THE ARGUMENT.—Æneas, setting sail from Afric, is driven by a storm on the coas
of Sicily, where he is hospitably receiv'd by his friend Acestes, king of part of tl
island, and born of Trojan parentage. He applies himself to celebrate the memo
of his father with divine honors, and accordingly institutes funeral games, and a
points prizes for those who should conquer in them. While the ceremonies we
performing, Juno sends Iris to persuade the Trojan women to burn the ships, wh
upon her instigation, set fire to them; which burnt four, and would have consum
the rest, had not Jupiter, by a miraculous shower, extinguish'd it. Upon this, Æne;
by the advice of one of his generals, and a vision of his father, builds a city for tl
women, old men, and others, who were either unfit for war, or weary of the voya;
and sails for Italy. Venus procures of Neptune a safe voyage for him and all l
men, excepting only his pilot Palinurus, who is unfortunately lost.

MEANTIME the Trojan cuts his wat'ry way,
Fix'd on his voyage, thro' the curling sea;
Then, casting back his eyes, with dire amaze,
Sees on the Punic shore the mounting blaze.
The cause unknown; yet his presaging mind
The fate of Dido from the fire divin'd;
He knew the stormy souls of womankind,
What secret springs their eager passions move,
How capable of death for injur'd love.
Dire auguries from hence the Trojans draw;
Till neither fires nor shining shores they saw.
Now seas and skies their prospect only bound;
An empty space above, a floating field around.
But soon the heav'ns with shadows were o'erspread;
A swelling cloud hung hov'ring o'er their head:
Livid it look'd, the threat'ning of a storm;
Then night and horror ocean's face deform.
The pilot, Palinurus, cried aloud:
"What gusts of weather from that gath'ring cloud
My thoughts presage! Ere yet the tempest roars,
Stand to your tackle, mates, and stretch your oars;
Contract your swelling sails, and luff to wind."
The frighted crew perform the task assign'd.

THE FIFTH BOOK OF THE ÆNEIS

Then, to his fearless chief: "Not Heav'n," said he,
"Tho' Jove himself should promise Italy,
Can stem the torrent of this raging sea.
Mark how the shifting winds from west arise,
And what collected night involves the skies!
Nor can our shaken vessels live at sea,
Much less against the tempest force their way.
'Tis fate diverts our course, and fate we must obey.
Not far from hence, if I observ'd aright
The southing of the stars, and polar light,
Sicilia lies, whose hospitable shores
In safety we may reach with struggling oars."
Æneas then replied: "Too sure I find
We strive in vain against the seas and wind:
Now shift your sails; what place can please me more
Than what you promise, the Sicilian shore,
Whose hallow'd earth Anchises' bones contains,
And where a prince of Trojan lineage reigns?"
The course resolv'd, before the western wind
They scud amain, and make the port assign'd.

Meantime Acestes, from a lofty stand,
Beheld the fleet descending on the land;
And, not unmindful of his ancient race,
Down from the cliff he ran with eager pace,
And held the hero in a strict embrace.
Of a rough Libyan bear the spoils he wore,
And either hand a pointed jav'lin bore.
His mother was a dame of Dardan blood;
His sire Crinisus, a Sicilian flood.
He welcomes his returning friends ashore
With plenteous country cates and homely store.

Now, when the following morn had chas'd away
The flying stars, and light restor'd the day,
Æneas call'd the Trojan troops around,
And thus bespoke them from a rising ground:
"Offspring of heav'n, divine Dardanian race!
The sun, revolving thro' th' ethereal space,
The shining circle of the year has fill'd,
Since first this isle my father's ashes held:
And now the rising day renews the year;

A day for ever sad, for ever dear.
This would I celebrate with annual games,
With gifts on altars pil'd, and holy flames,
Tho' banish'd to Gætulia's barren sands,
Caught on the Grecian seas, or hostile lands:
But since this happy storm our fleet has driv'n
(Not, as I deem, without the will of Heav'n)
Upon these friendly shores and flow'ry plains,
Which hide Anchises and his blest remains,
Let us with joy perform his honors due,
And pray for prosp'rous winds, our voyage to renew;
Pray, that in towns and temples of our own,
The name of great Anchises may be known,
And yearly games may spread the gods' renown.
Our sports Acestes, of the Trojan race,
With royal gifts ordain'd, is pleas'd to grace:
Two steers on ev'ry ship the king bestows;
His gods and ours shall share your equal vows.
Besides, if, nine days hence, the rosy morn
Shall with unclouded light the skies adorn,
That day with solemn sports I mean to grace:
Light galleys on the seas shall run a wat'ry race;
Some shall in swiftness for the goal contend,
And others try the twanging bow to bend;
The strong, with iron gauntlets arm'd, shall stand
Oppos'd in combat on the yellow sand.
Let all be present at the games prepar'd,
And joyful victors wait the just reward.
But now assist the rites, with garlands crown'd."
He said, and first his brows with myrtle bound.
Then Helymus, by his example led,
And old Acestes, each adorn'd his head;
Thus young Ascanius, with a sprightly grace,
His temples tied, and all the Trojan race.

   Æneas then advanc'd amidst the train,
By thousands follow'd thro' the flow'ry plain,
To great Anchises' tomb; which when he found,
He pour'd to Bacchus, on the hallow'd ground,
Two bowls of sparkling wine, of milk two more,
And two (from offer'd bulls) of purple gore,

THE FIFTH BOOK OF THE ÆNEIS

With roses then the sepulcher he strow'd
And thus his father's ghost bespoke aloud:
"Hail, O ye holy manes! hail again,
Paternal ashes, now review'd in vain!
The gods permitted not, that you, with me,
Should reach the promis'd shores of Italy,
Or Tiber's flood, what flood soe'er it be."
Scarce had he finish'd, when, with speckled pride,
A serpent from the tomb began to glide;
His hugy bulk on sev'n high volumes roll'd;
Blue was his breadth of back, but streak'd with scaly gold:
Thus riding on his curls, he seem'd to pass
A rolling fire along, and singe the grass.
More various colors thro' his body run,
Than Iris when her bow imbibes the sun.
Betwixt the rising altars, and around,
The sacred monster shot along the ground;
With harmless play amidst the bowls he pass'd,
And with his lolling tongue assay'd the taste:
Thus fed with holy food, the wondrous guest
Within the hollow tomb retir'd to rest.
The pious prince, surpris'd at what he view'd,
The fun'ral honors with more zeal renew'd,
Doubtful if this place's genius were,
Or guardian of his father's sepulcher.
Five sheep, according to the rites, he slew;
As many swine, and steers of sable hue;
New gen'rous wine he from the goblets pour'd.
And call'd his father's ghost, from hell restor'd.
The glad attendants in long order come,
Off'ring their gifts at great Anchises' tomb:
Some add more oxen; some divide the spoil;
Some place the chargers on the grassy soil;
Some blow the fires, and offer'd entrails broil.

Now came the day desir'd. The skies were bright
With rosy luster of the rising light:
The bord'ring people, rous'd by sounding fame
Of Trojan feasts and great Acestes' name,
The crowded shore with acclamations fill,
Part to behold, and part to prove their skill.

And first the gifts in public view they place,
Green laurel wreaths, and palm, the victors' grace:
Within the circle, arms and tripods lie,
Ingots of gold and silver, heap'd on high,
And vests embroider'd, of the Tyrian dye.
The trumpet's clangor then the feast proclaims,
And all prepare for their appointed games.
Four galleys first, which equal rowers bear,
Advancing, in the wat'ry lists appear.
The speedy Dolphin, that outstrips the wind,
Bore Mnestheus, author of the Memmian kind:
Gyas the vast Chimæra's bulk commands,
Which rising, like a tow'ring city stands;
Three Trojans tug at ev'ry lab'ring oar;
Three banks in three degrees the sailors bore;
Beneath their sturdy strokes the billows roar.
Sergesthus, who began the Sergian race,
In the great Centaur took the leading place;
Cloanthus on the sea-green Scylla stood,
From whom Cluentius draws his Trojan blood.

 Far in the sea, against the foaming shore,
There stands a rock: the raging billows roar
Above his head in storms; but, when 'tis clear,
Uncurl their ridgy backs, and at his foot appear.
In peace below the gentle waters run;
The cormorants above lie basking in the sun.
On this the hero fix'd an oak in sight,
The mark to guide the mariners aright.
To bear with this, the seamen stretch their oars;
Then round the rock they steer, and seek the former shore
The lots decide their place. Above the rest,
Each leader shining in his Tyrian vest;
The common crew with wreaths of poplar boughs
Their temples crown, and shade their sweaty brows:
Besmear'd with oil, their naked shoulders shine.
All take their seats, and wait the sounding sign:
They gripe their oars; and ev'ry panting breast
Is rais'd by turns with hope, by turns with fear depress'd.
The clangor of the trumpet gives the sign;
At once they start, advancing in a line:

THE FIFTH BOOK OF THE ÆNEIS

With shouts the sailors rend the starry skies;
Lash'd with their oars, the smoky billows rise;
Sparkles the briny main, and the vex'd ocean fries.
Exact in time, with equal strokes they row:
At once the brushing oars and brazen prow
Dash up the sandy waves, and ope the depths below.
Not fiery coursers, in a chariot race,
Invade the field with half so swift a pace;
Not the fierce driver with more fury lends
The sounding lash, and, ere the stroke descends,
Low to the wheels his pliant body bends.
The partial crowd their hopes and fears divide,
And aid with eager shouts the favor'd side.
Cries, murmurs, clamors, with a mixing sound,
From woods to woods, from hills to hills rebound.

Amidst the loud applauses of the shore,
Gyas outstripp'd the rest, and sprung before:
Cloanthus, better mann'd, pursued him fast,
But his o'er-masted galley check'd his haste.
The Centaur and the Dolphin brush the brine
With equal oars, advancing in a line;
And now the mighty Centaur seems to lead,
And now the speedy Dolphin gets ahead;
Now board to board the rival vessels row,
The billows lave the skies, and ocean groans below.
They reach'd the mark. Proud Gyas and his train
In triumph rode, the victors of the main;
But, steering round, he charg'd his pilot stand
More close to shore, and skim along the sand—
"Let others bear to sea!" Menœtes heard;
But secret shelves too cautiously he fear'd,
And, fearing, sought the deep; and still aloof he steer'd.
With louder cries the captain call'd again:
"Bear to the rocky shore, and shun the main."
He spoke, and, speaking, at his stern he saw
The bold Cloanthus near the shelvings draw.
Betwixt the mark and him the Scylla stood,
And in a closer compass plow'd the flood.
He pass'd the mark; and, wheeling, got before:
Gyas blasphem'd the gods, devoutly swore,

Cried out for anger, and his hair he tore.
Mindless of others' lives (so high was grown
His rising rage) and careless of his own,
The trembling dotard to the deck he drew;
Then hoisted up, and overboard he threw:
This done, he seiz'd the helm; his fellows cheer'd,
Turn'd short upon the shelves, and madly steer'd.
  Hardly his head the plunging pilot rears,
Clogg'd with his clothes, and cumber'd with his years:
Now dropping wet, he climbs the cliff with pain.
The crowd, that saw him fall and float again,
Shout from the distant shore; and loudly laugh'd,
To see his heaving breast disgorge the briny draught.
The following Centaur, and the Dolphin's crew,
Their vanish'd hopes of victory renew;
While Gyas lags, they kindle in the race,
To reach the mark. Sergesthus takes the place;
Mnestheus pursues; and while around they wind,
Comes up, not half his galley's length behind;
Then, on the deck, amidst his mates appear'd,
And thus their drooping courage he cheer'd:
"My friends, and Hector's followers heretofore,
Exert your vigor; tug the lab'ring oar;
Stretch to your strokes, my still unconquer'd crew,
Whom from the flaming walls of Troy I drew.
In this, our common int'rest, let me find
That strength of hand, that courage of the mind,
As when you stemm'd the strong Malean flood,
And o'er the Syrtes' broken billows row'd.
I seek not now the foremost palm to gain;
Tho' yet—but, ah! that haughty wish is vain!
Let those enjoy it whom the gods ordain.
But to be last, the lags of all the race!—
Redeem yourselves and me from that disgrace."
Now, one and all, they tug amain; they row
At the full stretch, and shake the brazen prow.
The sea beneath 'em sinks; their lab'ring sides
Are swell'd, and sweat runs gutt'ring down in tides.
Chance aids their daring with unhop'd success;
Sergesthus, eager with his beak to press

Betwixt the rival galley and the rock,
Shuts up th' unwieldly Centaur in the lock.
The vessel struck; and, with the dreadful shock,
Her oars she shiver'd, and her head she broke.
The trembling rowers from their banks arise,
And, anxious for themselves, renounce the prize.
With iron poles they heave her off the shores,
And gather from the sea their floating oars.
The crew of Mnestheus, with elated minds,
Urge their success, and call the willing winds;
Then ply their oars, and cut their liquid way
In larger compass on the roomy sea.
As, when the dove her rocky hold forsakes,
Rous'd in a fright, her sounding wings she shakes;
The cavern rings with clatt'ring; out she flies,
And leaves her callow care, and cleaves the skies:
At first she flutters; but at length she springs
To smoother flight, and shoots upon her wings:
So Mnestheus in the Dolphin cuts the sea;
And, flying with a force, that force assists his way.
Sergesthus in the Centaur soon he pass'd,
Wedg'd in the rocky shoals, and sticking fast.
In vain the victor he with cries implores,
And practices to row with shatter'd oars.
Then Mnestheus bears with Gyas, and outflies:
The ship, without a pilot, yields the prize.
Unvanquish'd Scylla now alone remains;
Her he pursues, and all his vigor strains.
Shouts from the fav'ring multitude arise;
Applauding Echo to the shouts replies;
Shouts, wishes, and applause run rattling thro' the skies.
These clamors with disdain the Scylla heard,
Much grudg'd the praise, but more the robb'd reward:
Resolv'd to hold their own, they mend their pace,
All obstinate to die, or gain the race.
Rais'd with success, the Dolphin swiftly ran;
For they can conquer, who believe they can.
Both urge their oars, and fortune both supplies,
And both perhaps had shar'd an equal prize;
When to the seas Cloanthus holds his hands,

And succor from the wat'ry pow'rs demands:
"Gods of the liquid realms, on which I row!
If, giv'n by you, the laurel bind my brow,
Assist to make me guilty of my vow!
A snow-white bull shall on your shore be slain;
His offer'd entrails cast into the main,
And ruddy wine, from golden goblets thrown,
Your grateful gift and my return shall own."
The choir of nymphs, and Phorcus, from below,
With virgin Panopea, heard his vow;
And old Portunus, with his breadth of hand,
Push'd on, and sped the galley to the land.
Swift as a shaft, or winged wind, she flies,
And, darting to the port, obtains the prize.

The herald summons all, and then proclaims
Cloanthus conqu'ror of the naval games.
The prince with laurel crowns the victor's head,
And three fat steers are to his vessel led,
The ship's reward; with gen'rous wine beside,
And sums of silver, which the crew divide.
The leaders are distinguish'd from the rest;
The victor honor'd with a nobler vest,
Where gold and purple strive in equal rows,
And needlework its happy cost bestows.
There Ganymede is wrought with living art,
Chasing thro' Ida's groves the trembling hart:
Breathless he seems, yet eager to pursue;
When from aloft descends, in open view,
The bird of Jove, and, sousing on his prey,
With crooked talons bears the boy away.
In vain, with lifted hands and gazing eyes,
His guards behold him soaring thro' the skies,
And dogs pursue his flight with imitated cries.

Mnestheus the second victor was declar'd;
And, summon'd there, the second prize he shar'd.
A coat of mail, which brave Demoleüs bore,
More brave Æneas from his shoulders tore,
In single combat on the Trojan shore:
This was ordain'd for Mnestheus to possess;
In war for his defense, for ornament in peace.

Rich was the gift, and glorious to behold,
But yet so pond'rous with its plates of gold,
That scarce two servants could the weight sustain;
Yet, loaded thus, Demoleüs o'er the plain
Pursued and lightly seiz'd the Trojan train.
The third, succeeding to the last reward,
Two goodly bowls of massy silver shar'd,
With figures prominent, and richly wrought,
And two brass caldrons from Dodona brought.

   Thus all, rewarded by the hero's hands,
Their conqu'ring temples bound with purple bands;
And now Sergesthus, clearing from the rock,
Brought back his galley shatter'd with the shock.
Forlorn she look'd, without an aiding oar,
And, houted by the vulgar, made to shore.
As when a snake, surpris'd upon the road,
Is crush'd athwart her body by the load
Of heavy wheels; or with a mortal wound
Her belly bruis'd, and trodden to the ground:
In vain, with loosen'd curls, she crawls along;
Yet, fierce above, she brandishes her tongue;
Glares with her eyes, and bristles with her scales;
But, groveling in the dust, her parts unsound she trails:
So slowly to the port the Centaur tends,
But, what she wants in oars, with sails amends.
Yet, for his galley sav'd, the grateful prince
Is pleas'd th' unhappy chief to recompense.
Pholoe, the Cretan slave, rewards his care,
Beauteous herself, with lovely twins as fair.

   From thence his way the Trojan hero bent
Into the neighb'ring plain, with mountains pent,
Whose sides were shaded with surrounding wood.
Full in the midst of this fair valley stood
A native theater, which, rising slow
By just degrees, o'erlook'd the ground below.
High on a sylvan throne the leader sate;
A num'rous train attend in solemn state.
Here those that in the rapid course delight,
Desire of honor and the prize invite.
The rival runners without order stand;

The Trojans mix'd with the Sicilian band.
First Nisus, with Euryalus, appears;
Euryalus a boy of blooming years,
With a sprightly grace and equal beauty crown'd;
Nisus, for friendship to the youth renown'd.
Diores next, of Priam's royal race,
Then Salius joined with Patron, took their place;
(But Patron in Arcadia had his birth,
And Salius his from Arcananian earth;)
Then two Sicilian youths—the names of these,
Swift Helymus, and lovely Panopes:
Both jolly huntsmen, both in forest bred,
And owning old Acestes for their head;
With sev'ral others of ignobler name,
Whom time has not deliver'd o'er to fame.

To these the hero thus his thoughts explain'd,
In words when gen'ral approbation gain'd:
"One common largess is for all design'd,
(The vanquish'd and the victor shall be join'd,)
Two darts of polish'd steel and Gnosian wood,
A silver-studded ax, alike bestow'd.
The foremost three have olive wreaths decreed:
The first of these obtains a stately steed,
Adorn'd with trappings: and the next in fame,
The quiver of an Amazonian dame,
With feather'd Thracian arrows well supplied:
A golden belt shall gird his manly side,
Which with a sparkling diamond shall be tied.
The third this Grecian helmet shall content."
He said. To their appointed base they went;
With beating hearts th' expected sign receive,
And, starting all at once, the barrier leave.
Spread out, as on the wingèd winds, they flew,
And seiz'd the distant goal with greedy view.
Shot from the crowd, swift Nisus all o'erpass'd;
Nor storms, nor thunder, equal half his haste.
The next, but tho' the next, yet far disjoin'd,
Came Salius, and Euryalus behind;
Then Helymus, whom young Diores plied,
Step after step, and almost side by side,

THE FIFTH BOOK OF THE ÆNEIS

His shoulders pressing; and, in longer space,
Had won, or left at least a dubious race.

Now, spent, the goal they almost reach at last,
When eager Nisus, hapless in his haste,
Slipp'd first, and, slipping, fell upon the plain,
Soak'd with the blood of oxen newly slain.
The careless victor had not mark'd his way;
But, treading where the treach'rous puddle lay,
His heels flew up; and on the grassy floor
He fell, besmear'd with filth and holy gore.
Not mindless then, Euryalus, of thee,
Nor of the sacred bonds of amity,
He strove th' immediate rival's hope to cross,
And caught the foot of Salius as he rose.
So Salius lay extended on the plain;
Euryalus springs out, the prize to gain,
And leaves the crowd: applauding peals attend
The victor to the goal, who vanquish'd by his friend.
Next Helymus; and then Diores came,
By two misfortunes made the third in fame.

But Salius enters, and, exclaiming loud
For justice, deafens and disturbs the crowd;
Urges his cause may in the court be heard;
And pleads the prize is wrongfully conferr'd.
But favor for Euryalus appears;
His blooming beauty, with his tender years,
Had brib'd the judges for the promis'd prize.
Besides, Diores fills the court with cries,
Who vainly reaches at the last reward,
If the first palm on Salius be conferr'd.
Then thus the prince: "Let no disputes arise:
Where fortune plac'd it, I award the prize.
But fortune's errors give me leave to mend,
At least to pity my deserving friend."
He said, and, from among the spoils, he draws
(Pond'rous with shaggy mane and golden paws)
A lion's hide: to Salius this he gives.
Nisus with envy sees the gift, and grieves.
"If such rewards to vanquish'd men are due."
He said, "and falling is to rise by you,

What prize may Nisus from your bounty claim,
Who merited the first rewards and fame?
In falling, both an equal fortune tried;
Would fortune for my fall so well provide!"
With this he pointed to his face, and show'd
His hand and all his habit smear'd with blood.
Th' indulgent father of the people smil'd,
And caus'd to be produc'd an ample shield,
Of wondrous art, by Didymaon wrought,
Long since from Neptune's bars in triumph brought.
This giv'n to Nisus, he divides the rest,
And equal justice in his gifts express'd.

The race thus ended, and rewards bestow'd,
Once more the prince bespeaks th' attentive crowd:
"If there be here whose dauntless courage dare
In gauntlet-fight, with limbs and body bare,
His opposite sustain in open view,
Stand forth the champion, and the games renew.
Two prizes I propose, and thus divide:
A bull with gilded horns, and fillets tied,
Shall be the portion of the conqu'ring chief;
A sword and helm shall cheer the loser's grief."

Then haughty Dares in the lists appears;
Stalking he strides, his head erected bears:
His nervous arms the weighty gauntlet wield,
And loud applauses echo thro' the field.
Dares alone in combat us'd to stand
The match of mighty Paris, hand to hand;
The same, at Hector's fun'rals, undertook
Gigantic Butes, of th' Amycian stock,
And, by the stroke of his resistless hand,
Stretch'd the vast bulk upon the yellow sand
Such Dares was; and such he strode along,
And drew the wonder of the gazing throng.
His brawny back and ample breast he shows,
His lifted arms around his head he throws,
And deals in whistling air his empty blows.
His match is sought; but, thro' the trembling band,
Not one dares answer to the proud demand.
Presuming of his force, with sparkling eyes

THE FIFTH BOOK OF THE ÆNEIS

Already he devours the promis'd prize.
He claims the bull with awless insolence,
And, having seiz'd his horns, accosts the prince:
"If none my matchless valor dares oppose,
How long shall Dares wait his dastard foes?
Permit me, chief, permit without delay,
To lead this uncontended gift away."
The crowd assents, and with redoubled cries
For the proud challenger demands the prize.

Acestes, fir'd with just disdain, to see
The palm usurp'd without a victory,
Reproach'd Entellus thus, who sate beside,
And heard and saw, unmov'd, the Trojan's pride:
"Once, but in vain, a champion of renown,
So tamely can you bear the ravish'd crown,
A prize in triumph borne before your sight,
And shun, for fear, the danger of the fight?
Where is our Eryx now, the boasted name,
The god who taught your thund'ring arm the game?
Where now your baffled honor? Where the spoil
That fill'd your house, and fame that fill'd our isle?"
Entellus, thus: "My soul is still the same,
Unmov'd with fear, and mov'd with martial fame;
But my chill blood is curdled in my veins,
And scarce the shadow of a man remains.
O could I turn to that fair prime again,
That prime of which this boaster is so vain,
The brave, who this decrepid age defies,
Should feel my force, without the promis'd prize."

He said; and, rising at the word, he threw
Two pond'rous gauntlets down in open view;
Gauntlets which Eryx wont in fight to wield
And sheathe his hands with in the listed field.
With fear and wonder seiz'd, the crowd beholds
The gloves of death, with sev'n distinguish'd folds
Of tough bull-hides; the space within is spread
With iron, or with loads of heavy lead.
Dares himself was daunted at the sight,
Renounc'd his challenge, and refus'd to fight.
Astonish'd at their weight, the hero stands,

And pois'd the pond'rous engines in his hands.
"What had your wonder," said Entelus, "been,
Had you the gauntlets of Alcides seen,
Or view'd the stern debate on this unhappy green!
These which I bear your brother Eryx bore,
Still mark'd with batter'd brains and mingled gore.
With these he long sustain'd th' Herculean arm;
And these I wielded while my blood was warm,
This languish'd frame while better spirits fed,
Ere age unstrung my nerves, or time o'ersnow'd my head.
But if the challenger these arms refuse,
And cannot wield their weight, or dare not use;
If great Æneas and Acestes join
In his request, these gauntlets I resign;
Let us with equal arms perform the fight,
And let him leave to fear, since I resign my right."

This said, Entellus for the strife prepares;
Stripp'd of his quilted coat, his body bares;
Compos'd of mighty bones and brawn, he stands,
A goodly tow'ring object on the sands.
Then just Æneas equal arms supplied,
Which round their shoulders to their wrists they tied.
Both on the tiptoe stand, at full extent,
Their arms aloft, their bodies inly bent;
Their heads from aiming blows they bear afar;
With clashing gauntlets then provoke the war.
One on his youth and pliant limbs relies;
One on his sinews and his giant size.
The last is stiff with age, his motion slow;
He heaves for breath, he staggers to and fro,
And clouds of issuing smoke his nostrils loudly blow.
Yet equal in success, they ward, they strike;
Their ways are diff'rent, but their art alike.
Before, behind, the blows are dealt; around
Their hollow sides the rattling thumps resound.
A storm of strokes, well meant, with fury flies,
And errs about their temples, ears, and eyes.
Nor always errs; for oft the gauntlet draws
A sweeping stroke along the crackling jaws.
Heavy with age, Entellus stands his ground,

THE FIFTH BOOK OF THE ÆNEIS

But with his warping body wards the wound.
His hand and watchful eye keep even pace;
While Dares traverses and shifts his place,
And, like a captain who beleaguers round
Some strong-built castle on a rising ground,
Views all th' approaches with observing eyes:
This and that other part in vain he tries,
And more on industry than force relies.
With hands on high, Entellus threats the foe;
But Dares watch'd the motion from below,
And slipp'd aside, and shunn'd the long descending blow.
Entellus wastes his forces on the wind,
And, thus deluded of the stroke design'd,
Headlong and heavy fell; his ample breast
And weighty limbs his ancient mother press'd.
So falls a hollow pine, that long had stood
On Ida's height, or Erymanthus' wood,
Torn from the roots. The diff'ring nations rise,
And shouts and mingled murmurs rend the skies.
Acestus runs with eager haste, to raise
The fall'n companion of his youthful days.
Dauntless he rose, and to the fight return'd;
With shame his glowing cheeks, his eyes with fury burn'd.
Disdain and conscious virtue fir'd his breast;
And with redoubled force his foe he press'd.
He lays on load with either hand, amain,
And headlong drives the Trojan o'er the plain;
Nor stops, nor stays; nor rest nor breath allows;
But storms of strokes descend about his brows,
A rattling tempest, and a hail of blows.
But now the prince, who saw the wild increase
Of wounds, commands the combatants to cease,
And bounds Entellus' wrath, and bids the peace.
First to the Trojan, spent with toil, he came,
And sooth'd his sorrow for the suffer'd shame.
"What fury seiz'd my friend? The gods," said he,
"To him propitious, and averse to thee,
Have giv'n his arm superior force to thine.
'Tis madness to contend with strength divine."
The gauntlet fight thus ended, from the shore

His faithful friends unhappy Dares bore:
His mouth and nostrils pour'd a purple flood,
And pounded teeth came rushing with his blood.
Faintly he stagger'd thro' the hissing throng,
And hung his head, and trail'd his legs along.
The sword and casque are carried by his train;
But with his foe the palm and ox remain.

The champion, then, before Æneas came,
Proud of his prize, but prouder of his fame:
"O goddess-born, and you, Dardanian host,
Mark with attention, and forgive my boast;
Learn what I was, by what remains; and know
From what impending fate you sav'd my foe."
Sternly he spoke, and then confronts the bull;
And, on his ample forehead aiming full,
The deadly stroke, descending, pierc'd the skull.
Down drops the beast, nor needs a second wound,
But sprawls in pangs of death, and spurns the ground.
Then, thus: "In Dares' stead I offer this.
Eryx, accept a nobler sacrifice;
Take the last gift my wither'd arms can yield:
Thy gauntlets I resign, and here renounce the field."

This done, Æneas orders, for the close,
The strife of archers with contending bows.
The mast Sergesthus' shatter'd galley bore
With his own hands he raises on the shore.
A flutt'ring dove upon the top they tie,
The living mark at which their arrows fly.
The rival archers in a line advance,
Their turn of shooting to receive from chance.
A helmet holds their names; the lots are drawn:
On the first scroll was read Hippocoön.
The people shout. Upon the next was found
Young Mnestheus, late with naval honors crown'd.
The third contain'd Eurytion's noble name,
Thy brother, Pandarus, and next in fame,
Whom Pallas urg'd the treaty to confound,
And send among the Greeks a feather'd wound.
Acestes in the bottom last remain'd,
Whom not his age from youthful sports restrain'd.

THE FIFTH BOOK OF THE ÆNEIS

Soon all with vigor bend their trusty bows,
And from the quiver each his arrow chose.
Hippocoön's was the first: with forceful sway
It flew, and, whizzing, cut the liquid way.
Fix'd in the mast the feather'd weapon stands:
The fearful pigeon flutters in her bands,
And the tree trembles, and the shouting cries
Of the pleas'd people rend the vaulted skies.
Then Mnestheus to the head his arrow drove,
With lifted eyes, and took his aim above,
But made a glancing shot, and miss'd the dove;
Yet miss'd so narrow, that he cut the cord
Which fasten'd by the foot the flitting bird.
The captive thus releas'd, away she flies,
And beats with clapping wings the yielding skies.
His bow already bent, Eurytion stood;
And, having first invok'd his brother god,
His winged shaft with eager haste he sped.
The fatal message reach'd her as she fled:
She leaves her life aloft; she strikes the ground,
And renders back the weapon in the wound.
Acestes, grudging at his lot, remains,
Without a prize to gratify his pains.
Yet, shooting upward, sends his shaft, to show
An archer's art, and boast his twanging bow.
The feather'd arrow gave a dire portent,
And latter augurs judge from this event.
Chaf'd by the speed, it fir'd; and, as it flew,
A trail of following flames ascending drew:
Kindling they mount, and mark the shiny way;
Across the skies as falling meteors play,
And vanish into wind, or in a blaze decay.
The Trojans and Sicilians wildly stare,
And, trembling, turn their wonder into pray'r.
The Dardan prince put on a smiling face,
And strain'd Acestes with a close embrace;
Then, hon'ring him with gifts above the rest,
Turn'd the bad omen, nor his fears confess'd.
"The gods," said he, "this miracle have wrought,
And order'd you the prize without the lot.

Accept this goblet, rough with figur'd gold,
Which Thracian Cisseus gave my sire of old:
This pledge of ancient amity receive,
Which to my second sire I justly give."
He said, and, with the trumpet's cheerful sound,
Proclaim'd him victor, and with laurel crown'd.
Nor good Eurytion envied him the prize,
Tho' he transfix'd the pigeon in the skies.
Who cut the line, with second gifts was grac'd;
The third was his whose arrow pierc'd the mast.

The chief, before the games were wholly done,
Call'd Periphantes, tutor to his son,
And whisper'd thus: "With speed Ascanius find;
And, if his childish troop be ready join'd,
On horseback let him grace his grandsire's day,
And lead his equals arm'd in just array."
He said; and, calling out, the cirque he clears.
The crowd withdrawn, an open plain appears.
And now the noble youths, of form divine,
Advance before their fathers, in a line;
The riders grace the steeds; the steeds with glory shine.

Thus marching on in military pride,
Shouts of applause resound from side to side.
Their casques adorn'd with laurel wreaths they wear,
Each brandishing aloft a cornel spear.
Some at their backs their gilded quivers bore;
Their chains of burnish'd gold hung down before.
Three graceful troops they form'd upon the green;
Three graceful leaders at their head were seen;
Twelve follow'd ev'ry chief, and left a space between.
The first young Priam led; a lovely boy,
Whose grandsire was th' unhappy king of Troy;
(His race in after times was known to fame,
New honors adding to the Latian name)—
And well the royal boy his Thracian steed became,
White were the fetlocks of his feet before,
And on his front a snowy star he bore.
Then beauteous Atys, with Iülus bred,
Of equal age, the second squadron led.
The last in order, but the first in place,

First in the lovely features of his face,
Rode fair Ascanius on a fiery steed,
Queen Dido's gift, and of the Tyrian breed.
Sure coursers for the rest the king ordains,
With golden bits adorn'd, and purple reins.

    The pleas'd spectators peals of shouts renew,
And all the parents in the children view;
Their make, their motions, and their sprightly grace,
And hopes and fears alternate in their face.

    Th' unfledg'd commanders and their martial train
First make the circuit of the sandy plain
Around their sires, and, at th' appointed sign,
Drawn up in beauteous order, form a line.
The second signal sounds: the troop divides
In three distinguish'd parts, with three distinguish'd guides.
Again they close, and once again disjoin;
In troop to troop oppos'd, and line to line.
They meet; they wheel; they throw their darts afar
With harmless rage and well-dissembled war.
Then in a round the mingled bodies run:
Flying they follow, and pursuing shun;
Broken, they break; and, rallying, they renew
In other forms the military shew.
At last, in order, undiscern'd they join,
And march together in a friendly line.
And, as the Cretan labyrinth of old,
With wand'ring ways and many a winding fold,
Involv'd the weary feet, without redress,
In a round error, which denied recess;
So fought the Trojan boys in warlike play,
Turn'd and return'd, and still a diff'rent way.
Thus dolphins in the deep each other chase
In circles, when they swim around the wat'ry race.
This game, these carousels, Ascanius taught;
And, building Alba, to the Latins brought;
Shew'd what he learn'd: the Latin sires impart
To their succeeding sons the graceful art;
From these imperial Rome receiv'd the game,
Which Troy, the youths the Trojan troop, they name.

    Thus far the sacred sports they celebrate:

But Fortune soon resum'd her ancient hate;
For, while they pay the dead his annual dues,
Those envied rites Saturnian Juno views;
And sends the goddess of the various bow,
To try new methods of revenge below;
Supplies the winds to wing her airy way,
Where in the port secure the navy lay.
Swiftly fair Iris down her arch descends,
And, undiscern'd, her fatal voyage ends.
She saw the gath'ring crowd; and, gliding thence,
The desart shore, and fleet without defense.
The Trojan matrons, on the sands alone,
With sighs and tears Anchises' death bemoan;
Then, turning to the sea their weeping eyes,
Their pity to themselves renews their cries.
"Alas!" said one, "what oceans yet remain
For us to sail! what labors to sustain!"
All take the word, and, with a gen'ral groan,
Implore the gods for peace, and places of their own.

   The goddess, great in mischief, views their pains,
And in a woman's form her heav'nly limbs restrains.
In face and shape old Beroe she became,
Doryclus' wife, a venerable dame,
Once blest with riches, and a mother's name.
Thus chang'd, amidst the crying crowd she ran,
Mix'd with the matrons, and these words began:
"O wretched we, whom not the Grecian pow'r,
Nor flames, destroy'd, in Troy's unhappy hour!
O wretched we, reserv'd by cruel Fate,
Beyond the ruins of the sinking state!
Now sev'n revolving years are wholly run,
Since this improsp'rous voyage we begun;
Since, toss'd from shores to shores, from lands to lands,
Inhospitable rocks and barren sands,
Wand'ring in exile thro' the stormy sea,
We search in vain for flying Italy.
Now cast by fortune on this kindred land,
What should our rest and rising walls withstand,
Or hinder here to fix our banish'd band?
O country lost, and gods redeem'd in vain,

THE FIFTH BOOK OF THE ÆNEIS

If still in endless exile we remain!
Shall we no more the Trojan walls renew,
Or streams of some dissembled Simoïs view?
Haste! join with me! th' unhappy fleet consume!
Cassandra bids; and I declare her doom.
In sleep I saw her; she supplied my hands
(For this I more than dreamt) with flaming brands:
'With these,' said she, 'these wand'ring ships destroy:
These are your fatal seats, and this your Troy.'
Time calls you now; the precious hour employ:
Slack not the good presage, while Heav'n inspires
Our minds to dare, and gives the ready fires.
See! Neptune's altars minister their brands:
The god is pleas'd; the god supplies our hands."
Then from the pile a flaming fire she drew,
And, toss'd in air, amidst the galleys threw.

Wrapp'd in amaze, the matrons wildly stare:
Then Pyrgo, reverenc'd for her hoary hair,
Pyrgo, the nurse of Priam's num'rous race:
"No Beroe this, tho' she belies her face!
What terrors from her frowning front arise!
Behold a goddess in her ardent eyes!
What rays around her heav'nly face are seen!
Mark her majestic voice, and more than mortal mien!
Beroe but now I left, whom, pin'd with pain,
Her age and anguish from these rites detain,"
She said. The matrons, seiz'd with new amaze,
Roll their malignant eyes, and on the navy gaze.
They fear, and hope, and neither part obey:
They hope the fated land, but fear the fatal way.
The goddess, having done her task below,
Mounts up on equal wings, and bends her painted bow.
Struck with the sight, and seiz'd with rage divine,
The matrons prosecute their mad design:
They shriek aloud; they snatch, with impious hands,
The food of altars; fires and flaming brands.
Green boughs and saplings, mingled in their haste,
And smoking torches, on the ships they cast.
The flame, unstopp'd at first, more fury gains,
And Vulcan rides at large with loosen'd reins:

Triumphant to the painted sterns he soars,
And seizes, in his way, the banks and crackling oars.
Eumelus was the first the news to bear,
While yet they crowd the rural theater.
Then, what they hear, is witness'd by their eyes:
A storm of sparkles and of flames arise.
Ascanius took th' alarm, while yet he led
His early warriors on his prancing steed,
And, spurring on, his equals soon o'erpass'd;
Nor could his frighted friends reclaim his haste.
Soon as the royal youth appear'd in view,
He sent his voice before him as he flew:
"What madness moves you, matrons, to destroy
The last remainders of unhappy Troy!
Not hostile fleets, but your own hopes, you burn,
And on your friends your fatal fury turn.
Behold your own Ascanius!" While he said,
He drew his glitt'ring helmet from his head,
In which the youths to sportful arms he led.
By this, Æneas and his train appear;
And now the women, seiz'd with shame and fear,
Dispers'd, to woods and caverns take their flight,
Abhor their actions, and avoid the light;
Their friends acknowledge, and their error find.
And shake the goddess from their alter'd mind.

Not so the raging fires their fury cease,
But, lurking in the seams, with seeming peace,
Work on their way amid the smold'ring tow,
Sure in destruction, but in motion slow.
The silent plague thro' the green timber eats,
And vomits out a tardy flame by fits.
Down to the keels, and upward to the sails,
The fire descends, or mounts, but still prevails;
Nor buckets pour'd, nor strength of human hand,
Can the victorious element withstand.

The pious hero rends his robe, and throws
To heav'n his hands, and with his hands his vows.
"O Jove," he cried, "if pray'rs can yet have place;
If thou abhorr'st not all the Dardan race;
If any spark of pity still remain;

THE FIFTH BOOK OF THE ÆNEIS

If gods are gods, and not invok'd in vain;
Yet spare the relics of the Trojan train!
Yet from the flames our burning vessels free,
Or let thy fury fall alone on me!
At this devoted head thy thunder throw,
And send the willing sacrifice below!"

Scarce had he said, when southern storms arise:
From pole to pole the forky lightning flies;
Loud rattling shakes the mountains and the plain;
Heav'n bellies downward, and descends in rain.
Whole sheets of water from the clouds are sent,
Which, hissing thro' the planks, the flames prevent,
And stop the fiery pest. Four ships alone
Burn to the waist, and for the fleet atone.

But doubtful thoughts the hero's heart divide;
If he should still in Sicily reside,
Forgetful of his fates, or tempt the main,
In hope the promis'd Italy to gain.
Then Nautes, old and wise, to whom alone
The will of Heav'n by Pallas was foreshown;
Vers'd in portents, experienc'd, and inspir'd
To tell events, and what the Fates requir'd;
Thus while he stood, to neither part inclin'd,
With cheerful words reliev'd his lab'ring mind:
"O goddess-born! resign'd in ev'ry state,
With patience bear, with prudence push your fate.
By suff'ring well, our Fortune we subdue;
Fly when she frowns, and, when she calls, pursue.
Your friend Acestes is of Trojan kind;
To him disclose the secrets of your mind:
Trust in his hands your old and useless train;
Too num'rous for the ships which yet remain:
The feeble, old, indulgent of their ease,
The dames who dread the dangers of the seas,
With all the dastard crew, who dare not stand
The shock of battle with your foes by land.
Here you may build a common town for all,
And, from Acestes' name, Acesta call."
The reasons, with his friend's experience join'd,
Encourag'd much, but more disturb'd his mind

'Twas dead of night; when to his slumb'ring eyes
His father's shade descended from the skies,
And thus he spoke: "O more than vital breath,
Lov'd while I liv'd, and dear ev'n after death;
O son, in various toils and troubles toss'd,
The King of Heav'n employs my careful ghost
On his commands: the god, who sav'd from fire
Your flaming fleet, and heard your just desire.
The wholesome counsel of your friend receive,
And here the coward train and women leave:
The chosen youth, and those who nobly dare,
Transport, to tempt the dangers of the war.
The stern Italians will their courage try;
Rough are their manners, and their minds are high.
But first to Pluto's palace you shall go,
And seek my shade among the blest below:
For not with impious ghosts my soul remains,
Nor suffers with the damn'd perpetual pains,
But breathes the living air of soft Elysian plains.
The chaste Sibylla shall your steps convey,
And blood of offer'd victims free the way.
There shall you know what realm the gods assign,
And learn the fates and fortunes of your line.
But now, farewell! I vanish with the night,
And feel the blast of heav'n's approaching light."
He said, and mix'd with shades, and took his airy flight.
"Whither so fast?" the filial duty cried;
"And why, ah why, the wish'd embrace denied?"

He said, and rose; as holy zeal inspires,
He rakes hot embers, and renews the fires;
His country gods and Vesta then adores
With cakes and incense, and their aid implores.
Next, for his friends and royal host he sent,
Reveal'd his vision, and the gods' intent,
With his own purpose. All, without delay,
The will of Jove, and his desires, obey.
They list with women, each degenerate name,
Who dares not hazard life for future fame.
These they cashier: the brave remaining few,
Oars, banks, and cables, half consum'd, renew.

The prince designs a city with the plow;
The lots their sev'ral tenements allow.
This part is nam'd from Ilium, that, from Troy,
And the new king ascends the throne with joy;
A chosen senate from the people draws;
Appoints the judges, and ordains the laws.
Then, on the top of Eryx, they begin
A rising temple to the Paphian queen.
Anchises, last, is honor'd as a god;
A priest is added, annual gifts bestow'd,
And groves are planted round his blest abode.
Nine days they pass in feasts, their temples crown'd;
And fumes of incense in the fanes abound.
Then from the south arose a gentle breeze
That curl'd the smoothness of the glassy seas;
The rising winds a ruffling gale afford,
And call the merry mariners aboard.

Now loud laments along the shores resound,
Of parting friends in close embraces bound.
The trembling women, the degenerate train,
Who shunn'd the frightful dangers of the main,
E'en those desire to sail, and take their share
Of the rough passage and the promis'd war:
Whom good Æneas cheers, and recommends
To their new master's care his fearful friends.
On Eryx' altars three fat calves he lays;
A lamb, new-fallen, to the stormy seas;
Then slips his haulsers, and his anchors weighs.
High on the deck the godlike hero stands,
With olive crown'd, a charger in his hands;
Then cast the reeking entrails in the brine,
And pour'd the sacrifice of purple wine.
Fresh gales arise; with equal strokes they vie,
And brush the buxom seas, and o'er the billows fly.

Meantime the mother goddess, full of fears,
To Neptune thus address'd, with tender tears:
"The pride of Jove's imperious queen, the rage,
The malice which no suff'rings can assuage,
Compel me to these pray'rs; since neither fate,
Nor time, nor pity, can remove her hate:

E'en Jove is thwarted by his haughty wife;
Still vanquish'd, yet she still renews the strife.
As if 't were little to consume the town
Which aw'd the world, and wore th' imperial crown,
She prosecutes the ghost of Troy with pains,
And gnaws, e'en to the bones, the last remains.
Let her the causes of her hatred tell;
But you can witness its effects too well.
You saw the storm she rais'd on Libyan floods,
That mix'd the mounting billows with the clouds;
When, bribing Æolus, she shook the main,
And mov'd rebellion in your wat'ry reign.
With fury she possess'd the Dardan dames,
To burn their fleet with execrable flames,
And forc'd Æneas, when his ships were lost,
To leave his foll'wers on a foreign coast.
For what remains, your godhead I implore,
And trust my son to your protecting pow'r.
If neither Jove's nor Fate's decree withstand,
Secure his passage to the Latian land."

Then thus the mighty Ruler of the Main:
"What may not Venus hope from Neptune's reign?
My kingdom claims your birth; my late defense
Of your indanger'd fleet may claim your confidence.
Nor less by land than sea my deeds declare
How much your lov'd Æneas is my care.
Thee, Xanthus, and thee, Simoïs, I attest.
Your Trojan troops when proud Achilles press'd,
And drove before him headlong on the plain,
And dash'd against the walls the trembling train;
When floods were fill'd with bodies of the slain;
When crimson Xanthus, doubtful of his way,
Stood up on ridges to behold the sea;
(New heaps came tumbling in, and chok'd his way;)
When your Æneas fought, but fought with odds
Of force unequal, and unequal gods;
I spread a cloud before the victor's sight,
Sustain'd the vanquish'd, and secur'd his flight;
E'en then secur'd him, when I sought with joy
The vow'd destruction of ungrateful Troy.

My will's the same: fair goddess, fear no more,
Your fleet shall safely gain the Latian shore;
Their lives are giv'n; one destin'd head alone
Shall perish, and for multitudes atone."
Thus having arm'd with hopes her anxious mind,
His finny team Saturnian Neptune join'd,
Then ads the foamy bridle to their jaws,
And to the loosen'd reins permits the laws.
High on the waves his azure car he guides;
Its axles thunder, and the sea subsides,
And the smooth ocean rolls her silent tides.
The tempests fly before their father's face,
Trains of inferior gods his triumph grace,
And monster whales before their master play,
And choirs of Tritons crowd the wat'ry way.
The marshal'd pow'rs in equal troops divide
To right and left; the gods his better side
Inclose, and on the worse the Nymphs and Nereids ride.

  Now smiling hope, with sweet vicissitude,
Within the hero's mind his joys renew'd.
He calls to raise the masts, the sheets display;
The cheerful crew with diligence obey;
They scud before the wind, and sail in open sea.
Ahead of all the master pilot steers;
And, as he leads, the following navy veers.
The steeds of Night had travel'd half the sky,
The drowsy rowers on their benches lie,
When the soft God of Sleep, with easy flight,
Descends, and draws behind a trail of light.
Thou, Palinurus, art his destin'd prey;
To thee alone he takes his fatal way.
Dire dreams to thee, and iron sleep, he bears;
And, lighting on thy prow, the form of Phorbas wears.
Then thus the traitor god began his tale:
"The winds, my friend, inspire a pleasing gale;
The ships, without thy care, securely sail.
Now steal an hour of sweet repose; and I
Will take the rudder and thy room supply."
To whom the yawning pilot, half asleep:
"Me dost thou bid to trust the treach'rous deep,

The harlot-smiles of her dissembling face,
And to her faith commit the Trojan race?
Shall I believe the Siren South again,
And, oft betray'd, not know the monster main?"
He said: his fasten'd hands the rudder keep,
And, fix'd on heav'n, his eyes repel invading sleep.
The god was wroth, and at his temples threw
A branch in Lethe dipp'd, and drunk with Stygian dew:
The pilot, vanquish'd by the pow'r divine,
Soon clos'd his swimming eyes, and lay supine.
Scarce were his limbs extended at their length,
The god, insulting with superior strength,
Fell heavy on him, plung'd him in the sea,
And, with the stern, the rudder tore away.
Headlong he fell, and, struggling in the main,
Cried out for helping hands, but cried in vain.
The victor dæmon mounts obscure in air,
While the ship sails without the pilot's care.
On Neptune's faith the floating fleet relies;
But what the man forsook, the god supplies,
And o'er the dang'rous deep secure the navy flies;
Glides by the Sirens' cliffs, a shelfy coast,
Long infamous for ships and sailors lost,
And white with bones. Th' impetuous ocean roars,
And rocks rebellow from the sounding shores.
The watchful hero felt the knocks, and found
The tossing vessel sail'd on shoaly ground.
Sure of his pilot's loss, he takes himself
The helm, and steers aloof, and shuns the shelf.
Inly he griev'd, and, groaning from the breast,
Deplor'd his death; and thus his pain express'd:
"For faith repos'd on seas, and on the flatt'ring sky,
Thy naked corpse is doom'd on shores unknown to lie."

THE SIXTH BOOK
OF THE ÆNEIS

THE ARGUMENT.—The Sibyl foretells Æneas the adventures he should meet with in Italy. She attends him to hell; describing to him the various scenes of that place, and conducting him to his father Anchises, who instructs him in those sublime mysteries of the soul of the world, and the transmigration; and shews him that glorious race of heroes which was to descend from him, and his posterity.

HE said, and wept; then spread his sails before
The winds, and reach'd at length the Cumæan shore:
Their anchors dropp'd, his crew the vessels moor.
They turn their heads to sea, their sterns to land,
And greet with greedy joy th' Italian strand.
Some strike from clashing flints their fiery seed;
Some gather sticks, the kindled flames to feed,
Or search for hollow trees, and fell the woods,
Or trace thro' valleys the discover'd floods.
Thus, while their sev'ral charges they fulfil,
The pious prince ascends the sacred hill
Where Phœbus is ador'd; and seeks the shade
Which hides from sight his venerable maid
(Deep in a cave the Sibyl makes abode);
Thence full of fate returns, and of the god.
Thro' Trivia's grove they walk; and now behold,
And enter now, the temple roof'd with gold.
When Dædalus, to fly the Cretan shore,
His heavy limbs on jointed pinions bore
(The first who sail'd in air), 'tis sung by Fame,
To the Cumæan coast at length he came,
And here alighting, built this costly frame.
Inscrib'd to Phœbus, here he hung on high
The steerage of his wings, that cut the sky:
Then, o'er the lofty gate his art emboss'd
Androgeos' death, and off'rings to his ghost;
Sev'n youths from Athens yearly sent, to meet
The fate appointed by revengeful Crete.

And next to those the dreadful urn was plac'd,
In which the destin'd names by lots were cast:
The mournful parents stand around in tears,
And rising Crete against their shore appears.
There too, in living sculpture, might be seen
The mad affection of the Cretan queen;
Then how she cheats her bellowing lover's eye;
The rushing leap, the doubtful progeny,
The lower part a beast, a man above,
The monument of their polluted love.
Not far from thence he grav'd the wondrous maze,
A thousand doors, a thousand winding ways:
Here dwells the monster, hid from human view,
Not to be found, but by the faithful clew;
Till the kind artist, mov'd with pious grief,
Lent to the loving maid this last relief,
And all those erring paths describ'd so well
That Theseus conquer'd and the monster fell.
Here hapless Icarus had found his part,
Had not the father's grief restrain'd his art.
He twice assay'd to cast his son in gold;
Twice from his hands he dropp'd the forming mold.

All this with wond'ring eyes Æneas view'd;
Each varying object his delight renew'd:
Eager to read the rest—Achates came,
And by his side the mad divining dame,
The priestess of the god, Deïphobe her name.
"Time suffers not," she said, "to feed your eyes
With empty pleasures; haste the sacrifice.
Sev'n bullocks, yet unyok'd, for Phœbus choose,
And for Diana sev'n unspotted ewes."
This said, the servants urge the sacred rites,
While to the temple she the prince invites.
A spacious cave, within its farmost part,
Was hew'd and fashion'd by laborious art
Thro' the hill's hollow sides: before the place,
A hundred doors a hundred entries grace;
As many voices issue, and the sound
Of Sybil's words as many times rebound.
Now to the mouth they come. Aloud she cries:

THE SIXTH BOOK OF THE ÆNEIS

"This is the time; enquire your destinies.
He comes; behold the god!" Thus while she said,
(And shiv'ring at the sacred entry stay'd,)
Her color chang'd; her face was not the same,
And hollow groans from her deep spirit came.
Her hair stood up; convulsive rage possess'd
Her trembling limbs, and heav'd her lab'ring breast.
Greater than human-kind she seem'd to look,
And, with an accent more than mortal, spoke.
Her staring eyes with sparkling fury roll;
When all the god came rushing on her soul.
Swiftly she turn'd, and, foaming as she spoke:
"Why this delay?" she cried—"the pow'rs invoke!
Thy pray'rs alone can open this abode;
Else vain are my demands, and dumb the god."

She said no more. The trembling Trojans hear,
O'erspread with a damp sweat and holy fear.
The prince himself, with awful dread possess'd,
His vows to great Apollo thus address'd:
"Indulgent god, propitious pow'r to Troy,
Swift to relieve, unwilling to destroy,
Directed by whose hand the Dardan dart
Pierc'd the proud Grecian's only mortal part:
Thus far, by Fate's decrees and thy commands,
Thro' ambient seas and thro' devouring sands,
Our exil'd crew has sought th' Ausonian ground;
And now, at length, the flying coast is found.
Thus far the fate of Troy, from place to place,
With fury has pursued her wand'ring race.
Here cease, ye pow'rs, and let your vengeance end:
Troy is no more, and can no more offend.
And thou, O sacred maid, inspir'd to see
Th' event of things in dark futurity;
Give me what Heav'n has promis'd to my fate,
To conquer and command the Latian state;
To fix my wand'ring gods, and find a place
For the long exiles of the Trojan race.
Then shall my grateful hands a temple rear
To the twin gods, with vows and solemn pray'r;
And annual rites, and festivals, and games,

Shall be perform'd to their auspicious names.
Nor shalt thou want thy honors in my land;
For there thy faithful oracles shall stand,
Preserv'd in shrines; and ev'ry sacred lay,
Which, by thy mouth, Apollo shall convey:
All shall be treasur'd by a chosen train
Of holy priests, and ever shall remain.
But O! commit not thy prophetic mind
To flitting leaves, the sport of ev'ry wind,
Lest they disperse in air our empty fate;
Write not, but, what the pow'rs ordain, relate."

Struggling in vain, impatient of her load,
And lab'ring underneath the pond'rous god,
The more she strove to shake him from her breast,
With more and far superior force he press'd;
Commands his entrance, and, without control,
Usurps her organs and inspires her soul.
Now, with a furious blast, the hundred doors
Ope of themselves; a rushing whirlwind roars
Within the cave, and Sibyl's voice restores:
"Escap'd the dangers of the wat'ry reign,
Yet more and greater ills by land remain.
The coast, so long desir'd (nor doubt th' event),
Thy troops shall reach, but, having reach'd, repent.
Wars, horrid wars, I view—a field of blood,
And Tiber rolling with a purple flood.
Simoïs nor Xanthus shall be wanting there:
A new Achilles shall in arms appear,
And he, too, goddess-born. Fierce Juno's hate,
Added to hostile force, shall urge thy fate.
To what strange nations shalt not thou resort,
Driv'n to solicit aid at ev'ry court!
The cause the same which Ilium once oppress'd;
A foreign mistress, and a foreign guest.
But thou, secure of soul, unbent with woes,
The more thy fortune frowns, the more oppose.
The dawnings of thy safety shall be shown
From whence thou least shalt hope, a Grecian town."

Thus, from the dark recess, the Sibyl spoke,
And the resisting air the thunder broke;

The cave rebellow'd, and the temple shook.
Th' ambiguous god, who rul'd her lab'ring breast,
In these mysterious words his mind express'd;
Some truths reveal'd, in terms involv'd the rest.
At length her fury fell, her foaming ceas'd,
And, ebbing in her soul, the god decreas'd.
Then thus the chief: "No terror to my view,
No frightful face of danger can be new.
Inur'd to suffer, and resolv'd to dare,
The Fates, without my pow'r, shall be without my care.
This let me crave, since near your grove the road
To hell lies open, and the dark abode
Which Acheron surrounds, th' innavigable flood;
Conduct me thro' the regions void of light,
And lead me longing to my father's sight.
For him, a thousand dangers I have sought,
And, rushing where the thickest Grecians fought,
Safe on my back the sacred burthen brought.
He, for my sake, the raging ocean tried,
And wrath of Heav'n, my still auspicious guide,
And bore beyond the strength decrepid age supplied.
Oft, since he breath'd his last, in dead of night
His reverend image stood before my sight;
Enjoin'd to seek, below, his holy shade;
Conducted there by your unerring aid.
But you, if pious minds by pray'rs are won,
Oblige the father, and protect the son.
Yours is the pow'r; nor Proserpine in vain
Has made you priestess of her nightly reign.
If Orpheus, arm'd with his enchanting lyre,
The ruthless king with pity could inspire,
And from the shades below redeem his wife;
If Pollux, off'ring his alternate life,
Could free his brother, and can daily go
By turns aloft, by turns descend below—
Why name I Theseus, or his greater friend,
Who trod the downward path, and upward could ascend?
Not less than theirs from Jove my lineage came;
My mother greater, my descent the same."
So pray'd the Trojan prince, and, while he pray'd,

His hand upon the holy altar laid.
   Then thus replied the prophetess divine:
"O goddess-born of great Anchises' line,
The gates of hell are open night and day;
Smooth the descent, and easy is the way:
But to return, and view the cheerful skies,
In this the task and mighty labor lies.
To few great Jupiter imparts this grace,
And those of shining worth and heav'nly race,
Betwixt those regions and our upper light,
Deep forests and impenetrable night
Possess the middle space: th' infernal bounds
Cocytus, with his sable waves, surrounds.
But if so dire a love your soul invades,
As twice below to view the trembling shades;
If you so hard a toil will undertake,
As twice to pass th' innavigable lake;
Receive my counsel. In the neighb'ring grove
There stands a tree; the queen of Stygian Jove
Claims it her own; thick woods and gloomy night
Conceal the happy plant from human sight.
One bough it bears; but (wondrous to behold!)
The ductile rind and leaves of radiant gold:
This from the vulgar branches must be torn,
And to fair Proserpine the present borne,
Ere leave be giv'n to tempt the nether skies.
The first thus rent a second will arise,
And the same metal the same room supplies.
Look round the wood, with lifted eyes, to see
The lurking gold upon the fatal tree:
Then rend it off, as holy rites command;
The willing metal will obey thy hand.
Following with ease, if favor'd by thy fate,
Thou art foredoom'd to view the Stygian state:
If not, no labor can the tree constrain;
And strength of stubborn arms and steel are vain.
Besides, you know not, while you here attend,
Th' unworthy fate of your unhappy friend:
Breathless he lies; and his unburied ghost,
Depriv'd of fun'ral rites, pollutes your host.

Pay first his pious dues; and, for the dead,
Two sable sheep around his hearse be led;
Then, living turfs upon his body lay:
This done, securely take the destin'd way,
To find the regions destitute of day."

She said, and held her peace. Æneas went
Sad from the cave, and full of discontent,
Unknowing whom the sacred Sibyl meant.
Achates, the companion of his breast,
Goes grieving by his side, with equal cares oppress'd.
Walking, they talk'd, and fruitlessly divin'd
What friend the priestess by those words design'd.
But soon they found an object to deplore:
Misenus lay extended on the shore;
Son of the God of Winds: none so renown'd
The warrior trumpet in the field to sound;
With breathing brass to kindle fierce alarms,
And rouse to dare their fate in honorable arms.
He serv'd great Hector, and was ever near,
Not with his trumpet only, but his spear.
But by Pelides' arms when Hector fell,
He chose Æneas; and he chose as well.
Swoln with applause, and aiming still at more,
He now provokes the sea gods from the shore;
With envy Triton heard the martial sound,
And the bold champion, for his challenge, drown'd;
Then cast his mangled carcass on the strand:
The gazing crowd around the body stand.
All weep; but most Æneas mourns his fate,
And hastens to perform the funeral state.
In altar-wise, a stately pile they rear;
The basis broad below, and top advanc'd in air.
An ancient wood, fit for the work design'd,
(The shady covert of the salvage kind,)
The Trojans found: the sounding ax is plied;
Firs, pines, and pitch trees, and the tow'ring pride
Of forest ashes, feel the fatal stroke,
And piercing wedges cleave the stubborn oak.
Huge trunks of trees, fell'd from the steepy crown
Of the bare mountains, roll with ruin down.

Arm'd like the rest the Trojan prince appears,
And by his pious labor urges theirs.
  Thus while he wrought, revolving in his mind
The ways to compass what his wish design'd,
He cast his eyes upon the gloomy grove,
And then with vows implor'd the Queen of Love:
"O may thy pow'r, propitious still to me,
Conduct my steps to find the fatal tree,
In this deep forest; since the Sibyl's breath
Foretold, alas! too true, Misenus' death."
Scarce had he said, when, full before his sight,
Two doves, descending from their airy flight,
Secure upon the grassy plain alight.
He knew his mother's birds; and thus he pray'd:
"Be you my guides, with your auspicious aid,
And lead my footsteps, till the branch be found,
Whose glitt'ring shadow gilds the sacred ground.
And thou, great parent, with celestial care,
In this distress be present to my pray'r!"
Thus having said, he stopp'd with watchful sight,
Observing still the motions of their flight,
What course they took, what happy signs they shew.
They fed, and, flutt'ring, by degrees withdrew
Still farther from the place, but still in view:
Hopping and flying, thus they led him on
To the slow lake, whose baleful stench to shun
They wing'd their flight aloft; then, stooping low,
Perch'd on the double tree that bears the golden bough
Thro' the green leafs the glitt'ring shadows glow;
As, on the sacred oak, the wintry mistletoe,
Where the proud mother views her precious brood,
And happier branches, which she never sow'd.
Such was the glitt'ring; such the ruddy rind,
And dancing leaves, that wanton'd in the wind.
He seiz'd the shining bough with griping hold,
And rent away, with ease, the ling'ring gold;
Then to the Sibyl's palace bore the prize.
  Meantime, the Trojan troops, with weeping eyes,
To dead Misenus pay his obsequies.
First, from the ground a lofty pile they rear,

THE SIXTH BOOK OF THE ÆNEIS

Of pitch trees, oaks, and pines, and unctuous fir:
The fabric's front with cypress twigs they strew,
And stick the sides with boughs of baleful yew.
The topmost part his glitt'ring arms adorn;
Warm waters, then, in brazen caldrons borne,
Are pour'd to wash his body, joint by joint,
And fragrant oils the stiffen'd limbs anoint.
With groans and cries Misenus they deplore:
Then on a bier, with purple cover'd o'er,
The breathless body, thus bewail'd, they lay,
And fire the pile, their faces turn'd away—
Such reverend rites their fathers us'd to pay.
Pure oil and incense on the fire they throw,
And fat of victims, which his friends bestow.
These gifts the greedy flames to dust devour;
Then, on the living coals red wine they pour;
And, last, the relics by themselves dispose,
Which in a brazen urn the priests inclose.
Old Corynæus compass'd thrice the crew,
And dipp'd an olive branch in holy dew;
Which thrice he sprinkled round, and thrice aloud
Invok'd the dead, and then dismiss'd the crowd.
But good Æneas order'd on the shore
A stately tomb, whose top a trumpet bore,
A soldier's fauchion, and a seaman's oar.
Thus was his friend interr'd; and deathless fame
Still to the lofty cape consigns his name.
These rites perform'd, the prince, without delay,
Hastes to the nether world his destin'd way.
Deep was the cave; and, downward as it went
From the wide mouth, a rocky rough descent;
And here th' access a gloomy grove defends,
And there th' unnavigable lake extends,
O'er whose unhappy waters, void of light,
No bird presumes to steer his airy flight;
Such deadly stenches from the depths arise,
And steaming sulphur, that infects the skies.
From hence the Grecian bards their legends make,
And give the name Avernus to the lake.
Four sable bullocks, in the yoke untaught,

For sacrifice the pious hero brought.
The priestess pours the wine betwixt their horns;
Then cuts the curling hair; that first oblation burns,
Invoking Hecate hither to repair:
A pow'rful name in hell and upper air.
The sacred priests with ready knives bereave
The beasts of life, and in full bowls receive
The streaming blood: a lamb to Hell and Night
(The sable wool without a streak of white)
Æneas offers; and, by Fate's decree,
A barren heifer, Proserpine, to thee,
With holocausts he Pluto's altar fills;
Sev'n brawny bulls with his own hand he kills;
Then on the broiling entrails oil he pours;
Which, ointed thus, the raging flame devours.
Late the nocturnal sacrifice begun,
Nor ended till the next returning sun.
Then earth began to bellow, trees to dance,
And howling dogs in glimm'ring light advance,
Ere Hecate came. "Far hence be souls profane!"
The Sibyl cried, "and from the grove abstain!
Now, Trojan, take the way thy fates afford;
Assume thy courage, and unsheathe thy sword."
She said, and pass'd along the gloomy space;
The prince pursued her steps with equal pace.

Ye realms, yet unreveal'd to human sight,
Ye gods who rule the regions of the night,
Ye gliding ghosts, permit me to relate
The mystic wonders of your silent state!

Obscure they went thro' dreary shades, that led
Along the waste dominions of the dead.
Thus wander travelers in woods by night,
By the moon's doubtful and malignant light,
When Jove in dusky clouds involves the skies,
And the faint crescent shoots by fits before their eyes.

Just in the gate and in the jaws of hell,
Revengeful Cares and sullen Sorrows dwell,
And pale Diseases, and repining Age,
Want, Fear, and Famine's unresisted rage;
Here Toils, and Death, and Death's half-brother, Sleep,

Forms terrible to view, their sentry keep;
With anxious Pleasures of a guilty mind,
Deep Frauds before, and open Force behind;
The Furies' iron beds; and Strife, that shakes
Her hissing tresses and unfolds her snakes.
Full in the midst of this infernal road,
An elm displays her dusky arms abroad:
The God of Sleep there hides his heavy head,
And empty dreams on ev'ry leaf are spread.
Of various forms unnumber'd specters more,
Centaurs, and double shapes, besiege the door.
Before the passage, horrid Hydra stands,
And Briareus with all his hundred hands;
Gorgons, Geryon with his triple frame;
And vain Chimæra vomits empty flame.
The chief unsheath'd his shining steel, prepar'd,
Tho' seiz'd with sudden fear, to force the guard,
Off'ring his brandish'd weapon at their face;
Had not the Sibyl stopp'd his eager pace,
And told him what those empty phantoms were:
Forms without bodies, and impassive air.
Hence to deep Acheron they take their way,
Whose troubled eddies, thick with ooze and clay,
Are whirl'd aloft, and in Cocytus lost.
There Charon stands, who rules the dreary coast—
A sordid god: down from his hoary chin
A length of beard descends, uncomb'd, unclean;
His eyes, like hollow furnaces on fire;
A girdle, foul with grease, binds his obscene attire.
He spreads his canvas; with his pole he steers;
The freights of flitting ghosts in his thin bottom bears.
He look'd in years; yet in his years were seen
A youthful vigor and autumnal green.
An airy crowd came rushing where he stood,
Which fill'd the margin of the fatal flood:
Husbands and wives, boys and unmarried maids,
And mighty heroes' more majestic shades,
And youths, intomb'd before their fathers' eyes,
With hollow groans, and shrieks, and feeble cries.
Thick as the leaves in autumn strow the woods,

Or fowls, by winter forc'd, forsake the floods,
And wing their hasty flight to happier lands;
Such, and so thick, the shiv'ring army stands,
And press for passage with extended hands.
Now these, now those, the surly boatman bore:
The rest he drove to distance from the shore.
The hero, who beheld with wond'ring eyes
The tumult mix'd with shrieks, laments, and cries,
Ask'd of his guide, what the rude concourse meant;
Why to the shore the thronging people bent;
What forms of law among the ghosts were us'd;
Why some were ferried o'er, and some refus'd.

"Son of Anchises, offspring of the gods,"
The Sibyl said, "you see the Stygian floods,
The sacred stream which heav'n's imperial state
Attests in oaths, and fears to violate.
The ghosts rejected are th' unhappy crew
Depriv'd of sepulchers and fun'ral due:
The boatman, Charon; those, the buried host,
He ferries over to the farther coast;
Nor dares his transport vessel cross the waves
With such whose bones are not compos'd in graves.
A hundred years they wander on the shore;
At length, their penance done, are wafted o'er."
The Trojan chief his forward pace repress'd,
Revolving anxious thoughts within his breast,
He saw his friends, who, whelm'd beneath the waves,
Their fun'ral honors claim'd, and ask'd their quiet graves.
The lost Leucaspis in the crowd he knew,
And the brave leader of the Lycian crew,
Whom, on the Tyrrhene seas, the tempests met;
The sailors master'd, and the ship o'erset.

Amidst the spirits, Palinurus press'd,
Yet fresh from life, a new-admitted guest,
Who, while he steering view'd the stars, and bore
His course from Afric to the Latian shore,
Fell headlong down. The Trojan fix'd his view,
And scarcely thro' the gloom the sullen shadow knew.
Then thus the prince: "What envious pow'r, O friend,
Brought your lov'd life to this disastrous end?

THE SIXTH BOOK OF THE ÆNEIS

For Phœbus, ever true in all he said,
Has in your fate alone my faith betray'd.
The god foretold you should not die, before
You reach'd, secure from seas, th' Italian shore.
Is this th' unerring pow'r?" The ghost replied;
"Nor Phœbus flatter'd, nor his answers lied;
Nor envious gods have sent me to the deep:
But, while the stars and course of heav'n I keep,
My wearied eyes were seiz'd with fatal sleep.
I fell; and, with my weight, the helm constrain'd
Was drawn along, which yet my gripe retain'd.
Now by the winds and raging waves I swear,
Your safety, more than mine, was then my care;
Lest, of the guide bereft, the rudder lost,
Your ship should run against the rocky coast.
Three blust'ring nights, borne by the southern blast,
I floated, and discover'd land at last:
High on a mounting wave my head I bore,
Forcing my strength, and gath'ring to the shore.
Panting, but past the danger, now I seiz'd
The craggy cliffs, and my tir'd members eas'd.
While, cumber'd with my dropping clothes, I lay,
The cruel nation, covetous of prey,
Stain'd with my blood th' unhospitable coast;
And now, by winds and waves, my lifeless limbs are toss'd:
Which, O, avert, by yon ethereal light,
Which I have lost for this eternal night!
Or, if by dearer ties you may be won,
By your dead sire, and by your living son,
Redeem from this reproach my wand'ring ghost;
Or with your navy seek the Velin coast,
And in a peaceful grave my corpse compose;
Or, if a nearer way your mother shows,
Without whose aid you durst not undertake
This frightful passage o'er the Stygian lake,
Lend to this wretch your hand, and waft him o'er
To the sweet banks of yon forbidden shore."
Scarce had he said, the prophetess began:
"What hopes delude thee, miserable man?
Think'st thou, thus unintomb'd, to cross the floods,

To view the Furies and infernal gods,
And visit, without leave, the dark abodes?
Attend the term of long revolving years;
Fate, and the dooming gods, are deaf to tears.
This comfort of thy dire misfortune take:
The wrath of Heav'n, inflicted for thy sake,
With vengeance shall pursue th' inhuman coast,
Till they propitiate thy offended ghost,
And raise a tomb, with vows and solemn pray'r;
And Palinurus' name the place shall bear."
This calm'd his cares; sooth'd with his future fame,
And pleas'd to hear his propagated name.

Now nearer to the Stygian lake they draw:
Whom, from the shore, the surly boatman saw;
Observ'd their passage thro' the shady wood,
And mark'd their near approaches to the flood.
Then thus he call'd aloud, inflam'd with wrath:
"Mortal, whate'er, who this forbidden path
In arms presum'st to tread, I charge thee, stand,
And tell thy name, and bus'ness in the land.
Know this, the realm of night—the Stygian shore:
My boat conveys no living bodies o'er;
Nor was I pleas'd great Theseus once to bear,
Who forc'd a passage with his pointed spear,
Nor strong Alcides—men of mighty fame,
And from th' immortal gods their lineage came.
In fetters one the barking porter tied,
And took him trembling from his sov'reign's side:
Two sought by force to seize his beauteous bride."
To whom the Sibyl thus: "Compose thy mind;
Nor frauds are here contriv'd, nor force design'd.
Still may the dog the wand'ring troops constrain
Of airy ghosts, and vex the guilty train,
And with her grisly lord his lovely queen remain.
The Trojan chief, whose lineage is from Jove,
Much fam'd for arms, and more for filial love,
Is sent to seek his sire in your Elysian grove.
If neither piety, nor Heav'n's command,
Can gain his passage to the Stygian strand,
This fatal present shall prevail at least."

Then shew'd the shining bough, conceal'd within her vest.
No more was needful: for the gloomy god
Stood mute with awe, to see the golden rod;
Admir'd the destin'd off'ring to his queen—
A venerable gift, so rarely seen.
His fury thus appeas'd, he puts to land;
The ghosts forsake their seats at his command:
He clears the deck, receives the mighty freight;
The leaky vessel groans beneath the weight.
Slowly she sails, and scarcely stems the tides;
The pressing water pours within her sides.
His passengers at length are wafted o'er,
Expos'd, in muddy weeds, upon the miry shore.

No sooner landed, in his den they found
The triple porter of the Stygian sound,
Grim Cerberus, who soon began to rear
His crested snakes, and arm'd his bristling hair.
The prudent Sibyl had before prepar'd
A sop, in honey steep'd, to charm the guard;
Which, mix'd with pow'rful drugs, she cast before
His greedy grinning jaws, just op'd to roar.
With three enormous mouths he gapes; and straight,
With hunger press'd, devours the pleasing bait.
Long draughts of sleep his monstrous limbs enslave;
He reels, and, falling, fills the spacious cave.
The keeper charm'd, the chief without delay
Pass'd on, and took th' irremeable way.
Before the gates, the cries of babes new-born,
Whom fate had from their tender mothers torn,
Assault his ears: then those whom form of laws
Condemn'd to die, when traitors judg'd their cause.
Nor want they lots, nor judges to review
The wrongful sentence, and award a new.
Minos, the strict inquisitor, appears;
And lives and crimes, with his assessors, hears.
Round in his urn the blended balls he rolls,
Absolves the just, and dooms the guilty souls.
The next, in place and punishment, are they
Who prodigally throw their souls away;
Fools, who, repining at their wretched state,

And loathing anxious life, suborn'd their fate.
With late repentance now they would retrieve
The bodies they forsook, and wish to live;
Their pains and poverty desire to bear,
To view the light of heav'n, and breathe the vital air:
But Fate forbids; the Stygian floods oppose,
And with nine circling streams the captive souls inclose.
  Not far from thence, the Mournful Fields appear
So call'd from lovers that inhabit there.
The souls whom that unhappy flame invades,
In secret solitude and myrtle shades
Make endless moans, and, pining with desire,
Lament too late their unextinguish'd fire.
Here Procris, Eriphyle here he found,
Baring her breast, yet bleeding with the wound
Made by her son. He saw Pasiphae there,
With Phædra's ghost, a foul incestuous pair.
There Laodamia, with Evadne, moves,
Unhappy both, but loyal in their loves:
Cæneus, a woman once, and once a man,
But ending in the sex she first began.
Not far from these Phœnician Dido stood,
Fresh from her wound, her bosom bath'd in blood;
Whom when the Trojan hero hardly knew,
Obscure in shades, and with a doubtful view,
(Doubtful as he who sees, thro' dusky night,
Or thinks he sees, the moon's uncertain light,)
With tears he first approach'd the sullen shade;
And, as his love inspir'd him, thus he said:
"Unhappy queen! then is the common breath
Of rumor true, in your reported death,
And I, alas! the cause? By Heav'n, I vow,
And all the pow'rs that rule the realms below,
Unwilling I forsook your friendly state,
Commanded by the gods, and forc'd by Fate—
Those gods, that Fate, whose unresisted might
Have sent me to these regions void of light,
Thro' the vast empire of eternal night.
Nor dar'd I to presume, that, press'd with grief,
My flight should urge you to this dire relief.

THE SIXTH BOOK OF THE ÆNEIS

Stay, stay your steps, and listen to my vows:
'Tis the last interview that Fate allows!"
In vain he thus attempts her mind to move
With tears, and pray'rs, and late-repenting love.
Disdainfully she look'd; then turning round,
But fix'd her eyes unmov'd upon the ground,
And what he says and swears, regards no more
Than the deaf rocks, when the loud billows roar;
But whirl'd away, to shun his hateful sight,
Hid in the forest and the shades of night;
Then sought Sichæus thro' the shady grove,
Who answer'd all her cares, and equal'd all her love.

Some pious tears the pitying hero paid,
And follow'd with his eyes the flitting shade,
Then took the forward way, by Fate ordain'd,
And, with his guide, the farther fields attain'd,
Where, sever'd from the rest, the warrior souls remain'd.
Tydeus he met, with Meleager's race,
The pride of armies, and the soldiers' grace;
And pale Adrastus with his ghastly face.
Of Trojan chiefs he view'd a num'rous train,
All much lamented, all in battle slain;
Glaucus and Medon, high above the rest,
Antenor's sons, and Ceres' sacred priest.
And proud Idæus, Priam's charioteer,
Who shakes his empty reins, and aims his airy spear.
The gladsome ghosts, in circling troops, attend
And with unwearied eyes behold their friend;
Delight to hover near, and long to know
What bus'ness brought him to the realms below.
But Argive chiefs, and Agamemnon's train,
When his refulgent arms flash'd thro' the shady plain,
Fled from his well-known face, with wonted fear,
As when his thund'ring sword and pointed spear
Drove headlong to their ships, and glean'd the routed rear.
They rais'd a feeble cry, with trembling notes;
But the weak voice deceiv'd their gasping throats.

Here Priam's son, Deïphobus, he found,
Whose face and limbs were one continued wound:
Dishonest, with lopp'd arms, the youth appears,

Spoil'd of his nose, and shorten'd of his ears.
He scarcely knew him, striving to disown
His blotted form, and blushing to be known;
And therefore first began: "O Teucer's race,
Who durst thy faultless figure thus deface?
What heart could wish, what hand inflict, this dire disgrace?
'Twas fam'd, that in our last and fatal night
Your single prowess long sustain'd the fight,
Till tir'd, not forc'd, a glorious fate you chose,
And fell upon a heap of slaughter'd foes.
But, in remembrance of so brave a deed,
A tomb and fun'ral honors I decreed;
Thrice call'd your manes on the Trojan plains:
The place your armor and your name retains.
Your body too I sought, and, had I found,
Design'd for burial in your native ground."

  The ghost replied: "Your piety has paid
All needful rites, to rest my wand'ring shade;
But cruel Fate, and my more cruel wife,
To Grecian swords betray'd my sleeping life.
These are the monuments of Helen's love:
The shame I bear below, the marks I bore above.
You know in what deluding joys we pass'd
The night that was by Heav'n decreed our last:
For, when the fatal horse, descending down,
Pregnant with arms, o'erwhelm'd th' unhappy town,
She feign'd nocturnal orgies; left my bed,
And, mix'd with Trojan dames, the dances led;
Then, waving high her torch, the signal made,
Which rous'd the Grecians from their ambuscade.
With watching overworn, with cares oppress'd,
Unhappy I had laid me down to rest,
And heavy sleep my weary limbs possess'd.
Meantime my worthy wife our arms mislaid,
And from beneath my head my sword convey'd;
The door unlatch'd, and, with repeated calls,
Invites her former lord within my walls.
Thus in her crime her confidence she plac'd,
And with new treasons would redeem the past.
What need I more? Into the room they ran,

And meanly murther'd a defenseless man.
Ulysses, basely born, first led the way.
Avenging pow'rs! with justice if I pray,
That fortune be their own another day!
But answer you; and in your turn relate,
What brought you, living, to the Stygian state:
Driv'n by the winds and errors of the sea,
Or did you Heav'n's superior doom obey?
Or tell what other chance conducts your way,
To view with mortal eyes our dark retreats,
Tumults and torments of th' infernal seats."

   While thus in talk the flying hours they pass,
The sun had finish'd more than half his race:
And they, perhaps, in words and tears had spent
The little time of stay which Heav'n had lent;
But thus the Sibyl chides their long delay:
"Night rushes down, and headlong drives the day:
'Tis here, in different paths, the way divides;
The right to Pluto's golden palace guides;
The left to that unhappy region tends,
Which to the depth of Tartarus descends;
The seat of night profound, and punish'd fiends."
Then thus Deïphobus: "O sacred maid,
Forbear to chide, and be your will obey'd!
Lo! to the secret shadows I retire,
To pay my penance till my years expire.
Proceed, auspicious prince, with glory crown'd,
And born to better fates than I have found."
He said; and, while he said, his steps he turn'd
To secret shadows, and in silence mourn'd.

   The hero, looking on the left, espied
A lofty tow'r, and strong on ev'ry side
With treble walls, which Phlegethon surrounds,
Whose fiery flood the burning empire bounds;
And, press'd betwixt the rocks, the bellowing noise **resounds.**
Wide is the fronting gate, and, rais'd on high
With adamantine columns, threats the sky.
Vain is the force of man, and Heav'n's as vain,
To crush the pillars which the pile sustain.
Sublime on these a tow'r of steel is rear'd;

And dire Tisiphone there keeps the ward,
Girt in her sanguine gown, by night and day,
Observant of the souls that pass the downward way.
From hence are heard the groans of ghosts, the pains
Of sounding lashes and of dragging chains.
The Trojan stood astonish'd at their cries,
And ask'd his guide from whence those yells arise;
And what the crimes, and what the tortures were,
And loud laments that rent the liquid air.

She thus replied; "The chaste and holy race
Are all forbidden this polluted place.
But Hecate, when she gave to rule the woods,
Then led me trembling thro' these dire abodes,
And taught the tortures of th' avenging gods.
These are the realms of unrelenting fate;
And awful Rhadamanthus rules the state.
He hears and judges each committed crime;
Enquires into the manner, place, and time.
The conscious wretch must all his acts reveal,
(Loth to confess, unable to conceal),
From the first moment of his vital breath,
To his last hour of unrepenting death.
Straight, o'er the guilty ghost, the Fury shakes
The sounding whip and brandishes her snakes,
And the pale sinner, with her sisters, takes.
Then, of itself, unfolds th' eternal door;
With dreadful sounds the brazen hinges roar.
You see, before the gate, what stalking ghost
Commands the guard, what sentries keep the post.
More formidable Hydra stands within,
Whose jaws with iron teeth severely grin.
The gaping gulf low to the center lies,
And twice as deep as earth is distant from the skies,
The rivals of the gods, the Titan race.
Here, sing'd with lightning, roll within th' unfathom'd space.
Here lie th' Alæan twins, (I saw them both,)
Enormous bodies, of gigantic growth,
Who dar'd in fight the Thund'rer to defy,
Affect his heav'n, and force him from the sky.
Salmoneus, suff'ring cruel pains, I found,

THE SIXTH BOOK OF THE ÆNEIS

For emulating Jove; the rattling sound
Of mimic thunder, and the glitt'ring blaze
Of pointed lightnings, and their forky rays.
Thro' Elis and the Grecian towns he flew;
Th' audacious wretch four fiery coursers drew:
He wav'd a torch aloft, and, madly vain,
Sought godlike worship from a servile train.
Ambitious fool! with horny hoofs to pass
O'er hollow arches of resounding brass,
To rival thunder in its rapid course,
And imitate inimitable force!
But he, the King of Heav'n, obscure on high,
Bar'd his red arm, and, launching from the sky
His writhen bolt, not shaking empty smoke,
Down to the deep abyss the flaming felon strook.
There Tityus was to see, who took his birth
From heav'n, his nursing from the foodful earth.
Here his gigantic limbs, with large embrace,
Infold nine acres of infernal space.
A rav'nous vulture, in his open'd side,
Her crooked beak and cruel talons tried;
Still for the growing liver digg'd his breast;
The growing liver still supplied the feast;
Still are his entrails fruitful to their pains:
Th' immortal hunger lasts, th' immortal food remains.
Ixion and Perithoüs I could name,
And more Thessalian chiefs of mighty fame.
High o'er their heads a mold'ring rock is plac'd,
That promises a fall, and shakes at ev'ry blast.
They lie below, on golden beds display'd;
And genial feasts with regal pomp are made.
The Queen of Furies by their sides is set,
And snatches from their mouths th' untasted meat,
Which if they touch, her hissing snakes she rears,
Tossing her torch, and thund'ring in their ears.
Then they, who brothers' better claim disown,
Expel their parents, and usurp the throne;
Defraud their clients, and, to lucre sold,
Sit brooding on unprofitable gold;
Who dare not give, and e'en refuse to lend

To their poor kindred, or a wanting friend.
Vast is the throng of these; nor less the train
Of lustful youths, for foul adult'ry slain:
Hosts of deserters, who their honor sold,
And basely broke their faith for bribes of gold.
All these within the dungeon's depth remain,
Despairing pardon, and expecting pain.
Ask not what pains; nor farther seek to know
Their process, or the forms of law below.
Some roll a weighty stone; some, laid along,
And bound with burning wires, on spokes of wheels are [hung
Unhappy Theseus, doom'd for ever there,
Is fix'd by Fate on his eternal chair;
And wretched Phlegyas warns the world with cries
(Could warning make the world more just or wise):
'Learn righteousness, and dread th' avenging deities.'
To tyrants others have their country sold,
Imposing foreign lords, for foreign gold;
Some have old laws repeal'd, new statutes made,
Not as the people pleas'd, but as they paid;
With incest some their daughters' bed profan'd:
All dar'd the worst of ills, and, what they dar'd, attain'd.
Had I a hundred mouths, a hundred tongues,
And throats of brass, inspir'd with iron lungs,
I could not half those horrid crimes repeat,
Nor half the punishments those crimes have met.
But let us haste our voyage to pursue:
The walls of Pluto's palace are in view;
The gate, and iron arch above it, stands
On anvils labor'd by the Cyclops' hands.
Before our farther way the Fates allow,
Here must we fix on high the golden bough."

She said: and thro' the gloomy shades they pass'd,
And chose the middle path. Arriv'd at last,
The prince with living water sprinkled o'er
His limbs and body; then approach'd the door.
Possess'd the porch, and on the front above
He fix'd the fatal bough requir'd by Pluto's love.
These holy rites perform'd, they took their way
Where long extended plains of pleasure lay:

The verdant fields with those of heav'n may vie,
With ether vested, and a purple sky;
The blissful seats of happy souls below.
Stars of their own, and their own suns, they know;
Their airy limbs in sports they exercise,
And on the green contend the wrestler's prize.
Some in heroic verse divinely sing;
Others in artful measures lead the ring.
The Thracian bard, surrounded by the rest,
There stands conspicuous in his flowing vest;
His flying fingers, and harmonious quill,
Strikes sev'n distinguish'd notes, and sev'n at once they fill.
Here found they Teucer's old heroic race,
Born better times and happier years to grace.
Assaracus and Ilus here enjoy
Perpetual fame, with him who founded Troy.
The chief beheld their chariots from afar,
Their shining arms, and coursers train'd to war:
Their lances fix'd in earth, their steeds around,
Free from their harness, graze the flow'ry ground.
The love of horses which they had, alive,
And care of chariots, after death survive.
Some cheerful souls were feasting on the plain;
Some did the song, and some the choir maintain,
Beneath a laurel shade, where mighty Po
Mounts up to woods above, and hides his head below.
Here patriots live, who, for their country's good,
In fighting fields, were prodigal of blood:
Priests of unblemish'd lives here make abode
And poets worthy their inspiring god;
And searching wits, of more mechanic parts,
Who grac'd their age with new-invented arts:
Those who to worth their bounty did extend,
And those who knew that bounty to commend.
The heads of these with holy fillets bound,
And all their temples were with garlands crown'd.

 To these the Sibyl thus her speech address'd,
And first to him surrounded by the rest
(Tow'ring his height, and ample was his breast):
"Say, happy souls, divine Musæus, say,

Where lives Anchises, and where lies our way
To find the hero, for whose only sake
We sought the dark abodes, and cross'd the bitter lake?"
To this the sacred poet thus replied:
"In no fix'd place the happy souls reside.
In groves we live, and lie on mossy beds,
By crystal streams, that murmur thro' the meads:
But pass yon easy hill, and thence descend;
The path conducts you to your journey's end."
This said, he led them up the mountain's brow,
And shews them all the shining fields below.
They wind the hill, and thro' the blissful meadows go.

   But old Anchises, in a flow'ry vale,
Review'd his muster'd race, and took the tale:
Those happy spirits, which, ordain'd by Fate,
For future beings and new bodies wait—
With studious thought observ'd th' illustrious throng,
In nature's order as they pass'd along:
Their names, their fates, their conduct, and their care,
In peaceful senates and successful war.
He, when Æneas on the plain appears,
Meets him with open arms, and falling tears.
"Welcome," he said, "the gods' undoubted race!
O long expected to my dear embrace!
Once more 't is giv'n me to behold your face!
The love and pious duty which you pay
Have pass'd the perils of so hard a way
'Tis true, computing times, I now believ'd
The happy day approach'd; nor are my hopes deceiv'd.
What length of lands, what oceans have you pass'd;
What storms sustain'd, and on what shores been cast.
How have I feared your fate! but fear'd it most,
When love assail'd you, on the Libyan coast."
To this, the filial duty thus replies:
"Your sacred ghost before my sleeping eyes
Appear'd, and often urg'd this painful enterprise.
After long tossing on the Tyrrhene sea,
My navy rides at anchor in the bay.
But reach your hand, O parent shade, nor shun
The dear embraces of your longing son!"

He said; and falling tears his face bedew:
Then thrice around his neck his arms he threw;
And thrice the flitting shadow slipp'd away,
Like winds, or empty dreams that fly the day.

   Now, in a secret vale, the Trojan sees
A sep'rate grove, thro' which a gentle breeze
Plays with a passing breath, and whispers thro' the trees
And, just before the confines of the wood,
The gliding Lethe leads her silent flood.
About the boughs an airy nation flew,
Thick as the humming bees, that hunt the golden dew;
In summer's heat on tops of lilies feed,
And creep within their bells, to suck the balmy seed:
The winged army roams the fields around;
The rivers and the rocks remurmur to the sound.
Æneas wond'ring stood, then ask'd the cause
Which to the stream the crowding people draws.
Then thus the sire: "The souls that throng the flood
Are those to whom, by fate, are other bodies ow'd:
In Lethe's lake they long oblivion taste,
Of future life secure, forgetful of the past.
Long has my soul desir'd this time and place,
To set before your sight your glorious race,
That this presaging joy may fire your mind
To seek the shores by destiny design'd."—
"O father, can it be, that souls sublime
Return to visit our terrestrial clime,
And that the gen'rous mind, releas'd by death,
Can covet lazy limbs and mortal breath?"

   Anchises then, in order, thus begun
To clear those wonders to his godlike son:
"Know, first, that heav'n, and earth's compacted frame,
And flowing waters, and the starry flame,
And both the radiant lights, one common soul
Inspires and feeds, and animates the whole.
This active mind, infus'd thro' all the space,
Unites and mingles with the mighty mass.
Hence men and beasts the breath of life obtain,
And birds of air, and monsters of the main.
Th' ethereal vigor is in all the same,

And every soul is fill'd with equal flame;
As much as earthy limbs, and gross allay
Of mortal members, subject to decay,
Blunt not the beams of heav'n and edge of day.
From this coarse mixture of terrestrial parts,
Desire and fear by turns possess their hearts,
And grief, and joy; nor can the groveling mind,
In the dark dungeon of the limbs confin'd,
Assert the native skies, or own its heav'nly kind:
Nor death itself can wholly wash their stains;
But long-contracted filth e'en in the soul remains.
The relics of inveterate vice they wear,
And spots of sin obscene in ev'ry face appear.
For this are various penances enjoin'd;
And some are hung to bleach upon the wind,
Some plung'd in waters, others purg'd in fires,
Till all the dregs are drain'd, and all the rust expires.
All have their manes, and those manes bear:
The few, so cleans'd, to these abodes repair,
And breathe, in ample fields, the soft Elysian air.
Then are they happy, when by length of time
The scurf is worn away of each committed crime;
No speck is left of their habitual stains,
But the pure ether of the soul remains.
But, when a thousand rolling years are past,
(So long their punishments and penance last,)
Whole droves of minds are, by the driving god,
Compell'd to drink the deep Lethæan flood,
In large forgetful draughts to steep the cares
Of their past labors, and their irksome years,
That, unrememb'ring of its former pain,
The soul may suffer mortal flesh again."

   Thus having said, the father spirit leads
The priestess and his son thro' swarms of shades,
And takes a rising ground, from thence to see
The long procession of his progeny.
"Survey," pursued the sire, "this airy throng,
As, offer'd to thy view, they pass along.
These are th' Italian names, which Fate will join
With ours, and graff upon the Trojan line.

THE SIXTH BOOK OF THE ÆNEIS

Observe the youth who first appears in sight,
And holds the nearest station to the light,
Already seems to snuff the vital air,
And leans just forward, on a shining spear:
Silvius is he, thy last-begotten race,
But first in order sent, to fill thy place;
An Alban name, but mix'd with Dardan blood,
Born in the covert of a shady wood:
Him fair Lavinia, thy surviving wife,
Shall breed in groves, to lead a solitary life.
In Alba he shall fix his royal seat,
And, born a king, a race of kings beget.
Then Procas, honor of the Trojan name,
Capys, and Numitor, of endless fame.
A second Silvius after these appears;
Silvius Æneas, for thy name he bears;
For arms and justice equally renown'd,
Who, late restor'd, in Alba shall be crown'd.
How great they look! how vig'rously they wield
Their weighty lances, and sustain the shield!
But they, who crown'd with oaken wreaths appear,
Shall Gabian walls and strong Fidena rear;
Nomentum, Bola, with Pometia, found;
And raise Collatian tow'rs on rocky ground.
All these shall then be towns of mighty fame,
Tho' now they lie obscure, and lands without a name.
See Romulus the great, born to restore
The crown that once his injur'd grandsire wore.
This prince a priestess of your blood shall bear,
And like his sire in arms he shall appear.
Two rising crests his royal head adorn;
Born from a god, himself to godhead born:
His sire already signs him for the skies,
And marks the seat amidst the deities.
Auspicious chief! thy race, in times to come,
Shall spread the conquests of imperial Rome—
Rome, whose ascending tow'rs shall heav'n invade,
Involving earth and ocean in her shade;
High as the Mother of the Gods in place,
And proud, like her, of an immortal race.

Then, when in pomp she makes the Phrygian round,
With golden turrets on her temples crown'd;
A hundred gods her sweeping train supply;
Her offspring all, and all command the sky.

"Now fix your sight, and stand intent, to see
Your Roman race, and Julian progeny.
The mighty Cæsar waits his vital hour,
Impatient for the world, and grasps his promis'd pow'r.
But next behold the youth of form divine,
Cæsar himself, exalted in his line;
Augustus, promis'd oft, and long foretold,
Sent to the realm that Saturn rul'd of old;
Born to restore a better age of gold.
Afric and India shall his pow'r obey;
He shall extend his propagated sway
Beyond the solar year, without the starry way,
Where Atlas turns the rolling heav'ns around,
And his broad shoulders with their lights are crown'd.
At his foreseen approach, already quake
The Caspian kingdoms and Mæotian lake:
Their seers behold the tempest from afar,
And threat'ning oracles denounce the war.
Nile hears him knocking at his sev'nfold gates,
And seeks his hidden spring, and fears his nephew's fates.
Nor Hercules more lands or labors knew,
Not tho' the brazen-footed hind he slew,
Freed Erymanthus from the foaming boar,
And dipp'd his arrows in Lernæan gore;
Nor Bacchus, turning from his Indian war,
By tigers drawn triumphant in his car,
From Nisus' top descending on the plains,
With curling vines around his purple reins.
And doubt we yet thro' dangers to pursue
The paths of honor, and a crown in view?
But what's the man, who from afar appears?
His head with olive crown'd, his hand a censer bears,
His hoary beard and holy vestments bring
His lost idea back: I know the Roman king.
He shall to peaceful Rome new laws ordain,
Call'd from his mean abode a scepter to sustain.

THE SIXTH BOOK OF THE ÆNEIS

Him Tullus next in dignity succeeds,
An active prince, and prone to martial deeds.
He shall his troops for fighting fields prepare,
Disus'd to toils, and triumphs of the war.
By dint of sword his crown he shall increase,
And scour his armor from the rust of peace.
Whom Ancus follows, with a fawning air,
But vain within, and proudly popular.
Next view the Tarquin kings, th' avenging sword
Of Brutus, justly drawn, and Rome restor'd.
He first renews the rods and ax severe,
And gives the consuls royal robes to wear.
His sons, who seek the tyrant to sustain,
And long for arbitrary lords again,
With ignominy scourg'd, in open sight,
He dooms to death deserv'd, asserting public right.
Unhappy man, to break the pious laws
Of nature, pleading in his children's cause!
Howe'er the doubtful fact is understood,
'Tis love of honor, and his country's good:
The consul, not the father, sheds the blood.
Behold Torquatus the same track pursue;
And, next, the two devoted Decii view:
The Drusian line, Camillus loaded home
With standards well redeem'd, and foreign foes o'ercome.
The pair you see in equal armor shine,
Now, friends below, in close embraces join;
But, when they leave the shady realms of night,
And, cloth'd in bodies, breathe your upper light,
With mortal hate each other shall pursue:
What wars, what wounds, what slaughter shall ensue!
From Alpine heights the father first descends;
His daughter's husband in the plain attends:
His daughter's husband arms his eastern friends.
Embrace again, my sons, be foes no more;
Nor stain your country with her children's gore!
And thou, the first, lay down thy lawless claim,
Thou, of my blood, who bear'st the Julian name!
Another comes, who shall in triumph ride,
And to the Capitol his chariot guide,

From conquer'd Corinth, rich with Grecian spoils.
And yet another, fam'd for warlike toils,
On Argos shall impose the Roman laws,
And on the Greeks revenge the Trojan cause;
Shall drag in chains their Achillean race;
Shall vindicate his ancestors' disgrace,
And Pallas, for her violated place.
Great Cato there, for gravity renown'd,
And conqu'ring Cossus goes with laurels crown'd.
Who can omit the Gracchi? who declare
The Scipios' worth, those thunderbolts of war,
The double bane of Carthage? Who can see
Without esteem for virtuous poverty,
Severe Fabricius, or can cease t' admire
The plowman consul in his coarse attire?
Tir'd as I am, my praise the Fabii claim;
And thou, great hero, greatest of thy name,
Ordain'd in war to save the sinking state,
And, by delays, to put a stop to fate!
Let others better mold the running mass
Of metals, and inform the breathing brass,
And soften into flesh a marble face;
Plead better at the bar; describe the skies,
And when the stars descend, and when they rise.
But, Rome, 't is thine alone, with awful sway,
To rule mankind, and make the world obey,
Disposing peace and war by thy own majestic way;
To tame the proud, the fetter'd slave to free:
These are imperial arts, and worthy thee."

  He paus'd; and, while with wond'ring eyes they view'd
The passing spirits, thus his speech renew'd:
"See great Marcellus! how, untir'd in toils,
He moves with manly grace, how rich with regal spoils!
He, when his country, threaten'd with alarms,
Requires his courage and his conqu'ring arms,
Shall more than once the Punic bands affright;
Shall kill the Gaulish king in single fight;
Then to the Capitol in triumph move,
And the third spoils shall grace Feretrian Jove."
Æneas here beheld, of form divine,

A godlike youth in glitt'ring armor shine,
With great Marcellus keeping equal pace;
But gloomy were his eyes, dejected was his face.
He saw, and, wond'ring, ask'd his airy guide,
What and of whence was he, who press'd the hero's side:
"His son, or one of his illustrious name?
How like the former, and almost the same!
Observe the crowds that compass him around;
All gaze, and all admire, and raise a shouting sound:
But hov'ring mists around his brows are spread,
And night, with sable shades, involves his head."
"Seek not to know," the ghost replied with tears,
"The sorrows of thy sons in future years.
This youth (the blissful vision of a day)
Shall just be shown on earth, and snatch'd away.
The gods too high had rais'd the Roman state,
Were but their gifts as permanent as great.
What groans of men shall fill the Martian field!
How fierce a blaze his flaming pile shall yield!
What fun'ral pomp shall floating Tiber see,
When, rising from his bed, he views the sad solemnity!
No youth shall equal hopes of glory give,
No youth afford so great a cause to grieve;
The Trojan honor, and the Roman boast,
Admir'd when living, and ador'd when lost!
Mirror of ancient faith in early youth!
Undaunted worth, inviolable truth!
No foe, unpunish'd, in the fighting field
Shall dare thee, foot to foot, with sword and shield;
Much less in arms oppose thy matchless force,
When thy sharp spurs shall urge thy foaming horse.
Ah! couldst thou break thro' Fate's severe decree,
A new Marcellus shall arise in thee!
Full canisters of fragrant lilies bring,
Mix'd with the purple roses of the spring;
Let me with fun'ral flow'rs his body strow;
This gift which parents to their children owe
This unavailing gift, at least, I may bestow!"
Thus having said, he led the hero round
The confines of the blest Elysian ground;

Which when Anchises to his son had shown,
And fir'd his mind to mount the promis'd throne,
He tells the future wars, ordain'd by Fate;
The strength and customs of the Latian state;
The prince, and people; and forearms his care
With rules, to push his fortune, or to bear.

   Two gates the silent house of Sleep adorn;
Of polish'd iv'ry this, that of transparent horn:
True visions thro' transparent horn arise;
Thro' polish'd iv'ry pass deluding lies.
Of various things discoursing as he pass'd,
Anchises hither bends his steps at last.
Then, thro' the gate of iv'ry, he dismiss'd
His valiant offspring and divining guest.
Straight to the ships Æneas took his way,
Embark'd his men, and skimm'd along the sea,
Still coasting, till he gain'd Cajeta's bay.
At length on oozy ground his galleys moor;
Their heads are turn'd to sea, their sterns to shore.

THE SEVENTH BOOK
OF THE ÆNEIS

THE ARGUMENT.—King Latinus entertains Æneas, and promises him his only
daughter, Lavinia, the heiress of his crown. Turnus, being in love with her, favor'd
by her mother, and stirr'd up by Juno and Alecto, breaks the treaty which was
made, and engages in his quarrel Mezentius, Camilla, Messapus, and many others of
the neighboring princes; whose forces, and the names of their commanders, are here
particularly related.

AND thou, O matron of immortal fame,
 Here dying, to the shore hast left thy name;
 Cajeta still the place is call'd from thee,
The nurse of great Æneas' infancy.
Here rest thy bones in rich Hesperia's plains;
Thy name ('t is all a ghost can have) remains.
 Now, when the prince her fun'ral rites had paid,
He plow'd the Tyrrhene seas with sails display'd.
From land a gentle breeze arose by night,
Serenely shone the stars, the moon was bright,
And the sea trembled with her silver light.
Now near the shelves of Circe's shores they run,
(Circe the rich, the daughter of the Sun,)
A dang'rous coast: the goddess wastes her days
In joyous songs; the rocks resound her lays:
In spinning, or the loom, she spends the night,
And cedar brands supply her father's light.
From hence were heard, rebellowing to the main,
The roars of lions that refuse the chain,
The grunts of bristled boars, and groans of bears,
And herds of howling wolves that stun the sailors' ears.
These from their caverns, at the close of night,
Fill the sad isle with horror and affright.
Darkling they mourn their fate, whom Circe's pow'r,
(That watch'd the moon and planetary hour,)
With words and wicked herbs from human-kind
Had alter'd, and in brutal shapes confin'd.

Which monsters lest the Trojans' pious host
Should bear, or touch upon th' inchanted coast,
Propitious Neptune steer'd their course by night
With rising gales that sped their happy flight.
Supplied with these, they skim the sounding shore,
And hear the swelling surges vainly roar.
Now, when the rosy morn began to rise,
And wav'd her saffron streamer thro' the skies;
When Thetis blush'd in purple not her own,
And from her face the breathing winds were blown,
A sudden silence sate upon the sea,
And sweeping oars, with struggling, urge their way.

  The Trojan, from the main, beheld a wood,
Which thick with shades and a brown horror stood:
Betwixt the trees the Tiber took his course,
With whirlpools dimpled; and with downward force,
That drove the sand along, he took his way,
And roll'd his yellow billows to the sea.
About him, and above, and round the wood,
The birds that haunt the borders of his flood,
That bath'd within, or basked upon his side,
To tuneful songs their narrow throats applied.
The captain gives command; the joyful train
Glide thro' the gloomy shade, and leave the main.

  Now, Erato, thy poet's mind inspire,
And fill his soul with thy celestial fire!
Relate what Latium was; her ancient kings;
Declare the past and present state of things,
When first the Trojan fleet Ausonia sought,
And how the rivals lov'd, and how they fought.
These are my theme, and how the war began,
And how concluded by the godlike man:
For I shall sing of battles, blood, and rage,
Which princes and their people did engage;
And haughty souls, that, mov'd with mutual hate,
In fighting fields pursued and found their fate;
That rous'd the Tyrrhene realm with loud alarms,
And peaceful Italy involv'd in arms.
A larger scene of action is display'd;
And, rising hence, a greater work is weigh'd.

THE SEVENTH BOOK OF THE ÆNEIS

Latinus, old and mild, had long possess'd
The Latin scepter, and his people blest:
His father Faunus; a Laurentian dame
His mother; fair Marica was her name.
But Faunus came from Picus: Picus drew
His birth from Saturn, if records be true.
Thus King Latinus, in the third degree,
Had Saturn author of his family.
But this old peaceful prince, as Heav'n decreed,
Was blest with no male issue to succeed:
His sons in blooming youth were snatch'd by fate;
One only daughter heir'd the royal state.
Fir'd with her love, and with ambition led,
The neighb'ring princes court her nuptial bed.
Among the crowd, but far above the rest,
Young Turnus to the beauteous maid address'd.
Turnus, for high descent and graceful mien,
Was first, and favor'd by the Latian queen;
With him she strove to join Lavinia's hand,
But dire portents the purpos'd match withstand.

Deep in the palace, of long growth, there stood
A laurel's trunk, a venerable wood;
Where rites divine were paid; whose holy hair
Was kept and cut with superstitious care.
This plant Latinus, when his town he wall'd,
Then found, and from the tree Laurentum call'd;
And last, in honor of his new abode,
He vow'd the laurel to the laurel's god.
It happen'd once (a boding prodigy!)
A swarm of bees, that cut the liquid sky,
(Unknown from whence they took their airy flight,)
Upon the topmost branch in clouds alight;
There with their clasping feet together clung,
And a long cluster from the laurel hung.
An ancient augur prophesied from hence:
"Behold on Latian shores a foreign prince!
From the same parts of heav'n his navy stands,
To the same parts on earth; his army lands;
The town he conquers, and the tow'r commands."
Yet more, when fair Lavinia fed the fire

Before the gods, and stood beside her sire,
(Strange to relate!) the flames, involv'd in smoke
Of incense, from the sacred altar broke,
Caught her dishevel'd hair and rich attire;
Her crown and jewels crackled in the fire:
From thence the fuming trail began to spread
And lambent glories danc'd about her head.
This new portent the seer with wonder views,
Then pausing, thus his prophecy renews:
"The nymph, who scatters flaming fires around,
Shall shine with honor, shall herself be crown'd;
But, caus'd by her irrevocable fate,
War shall the country waste, and change the state."

Latinus, frighted with this dire ostent,
For counsel to his father Faunus went,
And sought the shades renown'd for prophecy
Which near Albunea's sulph'rous fountain lie.
To these the Latian and the Sabine land
Fly, when distress'd, and thence relief demand.
The priest on skins of off'rings takes his ease,
And nightly visions in his slumber sees;
A swarm of thin aërial shapes appears,
And, flutt'ring round his temples, deafs his ears:
These he consults, the future fates to know,
From pow'rs above, and from the fiends below.
Here, for the gods' advice, Latinus flies,
Off'ring a hundred sheep for sacrifice:
Their woolly fleeces, as the rites requir'd,
He laid beneath him, and to rest retir'd.
No sooner were his eyes in slumber bound,
When, from above, a more than mortal sound
Invades his ears; and thus the vision spoke:
"Seek not, my seed, in Latian bands to yoke
Our fair Lavinia, nor the gods provoke.
A foreign son upon thy shore descends,
Whose martial fame from pole to pole extends.
His race, in arms and arts of peace renown'd,
Not Latium shall contain, nor Europe bound:
'T is theirs whate'er the sun surveys around."
These answers, in the silent night receiv'd,

THE SEVENTH BOOK OF THE ÆNEIS

The king himself divulg'd, the land believ'd:
The fame thro' all the neighb'ring nations flew,
When now the Trojan navy was in view.

  Beneath a shady tree, the hero spread
His table on the turf, with cakes of bread;
And, with his chiefs, on forest fruits he fed.
They sate; and, (not without the god's command,)
Their homely fare dispatch'd, the hungry band
Invade their trenchers next, and soon devour,
To mend the scanty meal, their cakes of flour.
Ascanius this observ'd, and smiling said:
"See, we devour the plates on which we fed."
The speech had omen, that the Trojan race
Should find repose, and this the time and place.
Æneas took the word, and thus replies,
Confessing fate with wonder in his eyes:
"All hail, O earth! all hail, my household gods!
Behold the destin'd place of your abodes!
For thus Anchises prophesied of old,
And this our fatal place of rest foretold:
'When, on a foreign shore, instead of meat,
By famine forc'd, your trenchers you shall eat,
Then ease your weary Trojans will attend,
And the long labors of your voyage end.
Remember on that happy coast to build,
And with a trench inclose the fruitful field.'
This was that famine, this the fatal place
Which ends the wand'ring of our exil'd race.
Then, on to-morrow's dawn, your care employ,
To search the land, and where the cities lie,
And what the men; but give this day to joy.
Now pour to Jove; and, after Jove is blest,
Call great Anchises to the genial feast:
Crown high the goblets with a cheerful draught;
Enjoy the present hour; adjourn the future thought."

  Thus having said, the hero bound his brows
With leafy branches, then perform'd his vows;
Adoring first the genius of the place,
Then Earth, the mother of the heav'nly race,
The nymphs, and native godheads yet unknown,

And Night, and all the stars that gild her sable throne,
And ancient Cybel, and Idæan Jove,
And last his sire below, and mother-queen above.
Then heav'n's high monarch thunder'd thrice aloud,
And thrice he shook aloft a golden cloud.
Soon thro' the joyful camp a rumor flew,
The time was come their city to renew.
Then ev'ry brow with cheerful green is crown'd,
The feasts are doubled, and the bowls go round.

  When next the rosy morn disclos'd the day,
The scouts to sev'ral parts divide their way,
To learn the natives' names, their towns explore,
The coasts and trendings of the crooked shore:
Here Tiber flows, and here Numicus stands;
Here warlike Latins hold the happy lands.
The pious chief, who sought by peaceful ways
To found his empire, and his town to raise,
A hundred youths from all his train selects,
And to the Latian court their course directs,
(The spacious palace where their prince resides,)
And all their heads with wreaths of olive hides.
They go commission'd to require a peace,
And carry presents to procure access.
Thus while they speed their pace, the prince designs
His new-elected seat, and draws the lines.
The Trojans round the place a rampire cast,
And palisades about the trenches plac'd.

  Meantime the train, proceeding on their way,
From far the town and lofty tow'rs survey;
At length approach the walls. Without the gate,
They see the boys and Latian youth debate
The martial prizes on the dusty plain:
Some drive the cars, and some the coursers rein;
Some bend the stubborn bow for victory,
And some with darts their active sinews try.
A posting messenger, dispatch'd from hence,
Of this fair troop, advis'd their aged prince
That foreign men of mighty stature came;
Uncouth their habit, and unknown their name.
The king ordains their entrance, and ascends

THE SEVENTH BOOK OF THE ÆNEIS

His regal seat, surrounded by his friends.
  The palace built by Picus, vast and proud,
Supported by a hundred pillars stood,
And round incompass'd with a rising wood.
The pile o'erlook'd the town, and drew the sight;
Surpris'd at once with reverence and delight.
There kings receiv'd the marks of sov'reign pow'r;
In state the monarchs march'd; the lictors bore
Their awful axes and the rods before.
Here the tribunal stood, the house of pray'r,
And here the sacred senators repair;
All at large tables, in long order set,
A ram their off'ring, and a ram their meat.
Above the portal, carv'd in cedar wood,
Plac'd in their ranks, their godlike grandsires stood;
Old Saturn, with his crooked scythe, on high;
And Italus, that led the colony;
And ancient Janus, with his double face,
And bunch of keys, the porter of the place.
There good Sabinus, planter of the vines,
On a short pruning hook his head reclines,
And studiously surveys his gen'rous wines;
Then warlike kings, who for their country fought,
And honorable wounds from battle brought.
Around the posts hung helmets, darts, and spears,
And captive chariots, axes, shields, and bars,
And broken beaks of ships, the trophies of their wars.
Above the rest, as chief of all the band,
Was Picus plac'd, a buckler in his hand;
His other wav'd a long divining wand.
Girt in his Gabin gown the hero sate,
Yet could not with his art avoid his fate:
For Circe long had lov'd the youth in vain,
Till love, refus'd, converted to disdain:
Then, mixing pow'rful herbs, with magic art,
She chang'd his form, who could not change his heart;
Constrain'd him in a bird, and made him fly,
With party-color'd plumes, a chatt'ring pie.
  In this high temple, on a chair of state,
The seat of audience, old Latinus sate;

Then gave admission to the Trojan train;
And thus with pleasing accents he began:
"Tell me, ye Trojans, for that name you own,
Nor is your course upon our coasts unknown—
Say what you seek, and whither were you bound:
Were you by stress of weather cast aground?
(Such dangers as on seas are often seen,
And oft befall to miserable men,)
Or come, your shipping in our ports to lay,
Spent and disabled in so long a way?
Say what you want: the Latians you shall find
Not forc'd to goodness, but by will inclin'd;
For, since the time of Saturn's holy reign,
His hospitable customs we retain.
I call to mind (but time the tale has worn)
Th' Aurunci told, that Dardanus, tho' born
On Latian plains, yet sought the Phrygian shore,
And Samothracia, Samos call'd before.
From Tuscan Coritum he claim'd his birth;
But after, when exempt from mortal earth,
From thence ascended to his kindred skies,
A god, and, as a god, augments their sacrifice."
 He said. Ilioneus made this reply:
"O king, of Faunus' royal family!
Nor wintry winds to Latium forc'd our way,
Nor did the stars our wand'ring course betray.
Willing we sought your shores; and, hither bound,
The port, so long desir'd, at length we found;
From our sweet homes and ancient realms expell'd;
Great as the greatest that the sun beheld.
The god began our line, who rules above;
And, as our race, our king descends from Jove:
And hither are we come, by his command,
To crave admission in your happy land.
How dire a tempest, from Mycenæ pour'd,
Our plains, our temples, and our town devour'd;
What was the waste of war, what fierce alarms
Shook Asia's crown with European arms;
E'en such have heard, if any such there be,
Whose earth is bounded by the frozen sea;

And such as, born beneath the burning sky
And sultry sun, betwixt the tropics lie.
From that dire deluge, thro' the wat'ry waste,
Such length of years, such various perils past,
At last escap'd, to Latium we repair,
To beg what you without your want may spare:
The common water, and the common air;
Sheds which ourselves will build, and mean abodes,
Fit to receive and serve our banish'd gods.
Nor our admission shall your realm disgrace,
Nor length of time our gratitude efface.
Besides, what endless honor you shall gain,
To save and shelter Troy's unhappy train!
Now, by my sov'reign, and his fate, I swear,
Renown'd for faith in peace, for force in war;
Oft our alliance other lands desir'd,
And, what we seek of you, of us requir'd.
Despite not then, that in our hands we bear
These holy boughs, and sue with words of pray'r.
Fate and the gods, by their supreme command,
Have doom'd our ships to seek the Latian land.
To these abodes our fleet Apollo sends;
Here Dardanus was born, and hither tends;
Where Tuscan Tiber rolls with rapid force,
And where Numicus opes his holy source.
Besides, our prince presents, with his request,
Some small remains of what his sire possess'd.
This golden charger, snatch'd from burning Troy,
Anchises did in sacrifice employ;
This royal robe and this tiara wore
Old Priam, and this golden scepter bore
In full assemblies, and in solemn games;
These purple vests were weav'd by Dardan dames."

 Thus while he spoke, Latinus roll'd around
His eyes, and fix'd awhile upon the ground.
Intent he seem'd, and anxious in his breast;
Not by the scepter mov'd, or kingly vest,
But pond'ring future things of wondrous weight;
Succession, empire, and his daughter's fate.
On these he mus'd within his thoughtful mind,

And then revolv'd what Faunus had divin'd.
This was the foreign prince, by fate decreed
To share his scepter, and Lavinia's bed;
This was the race that sure portents foreshew
To sway the world, and land and sea subdue.
At length he rais'd his cheerful head, and spoke:
"The pow'rs," said he, "the pow'rs we both invoke,
To you, and yours, and mine, propitious be,
And firm our purpose with their augury!
Have what you ask; your presents I receive;
Land, where and when you please, with ample leave;
Partake and use my kingdom as your own;
All shall be yours, while I command the crown:
And, if my wish'd alliance please your king,
Tell him he should not send the peace, but bring.
Then let him not a friend's embraces fear;
The peace is made when I behold him here.
Besides this answer, tell my royal guest,
I add to his commands my own request:
One only daughter heirs my crown and state,
Whom not our oracles, nor Heav'n, nor fate,
Nor frequent prodigies, permit to join
With any native of th' Ausonian line.
A foreign son-in-law shall come from far
(Such is our doom), a chief renown'd in war,
Whose race shall bear aloft the Latian name,
And thro' the conquer'd world diffuse our fame
Himself to be the man the fates require,
I firmly judge, and, what I judge, desire."

He said, and then on each bestow'd a steed.
Three hundred horses, in high stables fed,
Stood ready, shining all, and smoothly dress'd;
Of these he chose the fairest and the best,
To mount the Trojan troop. At his command
The steeds caparison'd with purple stand,
With golden trappings, glorious to behold
And champ betwixt their teeth the foaming gold.
Then to his absent guest the king decreed
A pair of coursers born of heav'nly breed,
Who from their nostrils breath'd ethereal fire;

Whom Circe stole from her celestial sire,
By substituting mares produc'd on earth,
Whose wombs conceiv'd a more than mortal birth.
These draw the chariot which Latinus sends,
And the rich present to the prince commends.
Sublime on stately steeds the Trojans borne,
To their expecting lord with peace return.

  But jealous Juno, from Pachynus' height,
As she from Argos took her airy flight,
Beheld with envious eyes this hateful sight.
She saw the Trojan and his joyful train
Descend upon the shore, desert the main,
Design a town, and, with unhop'd success,
Th' embassadors return with promis'd peace.
Then, pierc'd with pain, she shook her haughty head,
Sigh'd from her inward soul, and thus she said:
"O hated offspring of my Phrygian foes!
O fates of Troy, which Juno's fates oppose!
Could they not fall unpitied on the plain,
But slain revive, and, taken, scape again?
When execrable Troy in ashes lay,
Thro' fires and swords and seas they forc'd their way.
Then vanquish'd Juno must in vain contend,
Her rage disarm'd, her empire at an end.
Breathless and tir'd, is all my fury spent?
Or does my glutted spleen at length relent?
As if 'twere little from their town to chase,
I thro' the seas pursued their exil'd race;
Ingag'd the heav'ns, oppos'd the stormy main;
But billows roar'd, and tempests rag'd in vain.
What have my Scyllas and my Syrtes done,
When these they overpass, and those they shun?
On Tiber's shores they land, secure of fate,
Triumphant o'er the storms and Juno's hate.
Mars could in mutual blood the Centaurs bathe,
And Jove himself gave way to Cynthia's wrath,
Who sent the tusky boar to Calydon;
(What great offense had either people done?)
But I, the consort of the Thunderer,
Have wag'd a long and unsuccessful war,

With various arts and arms in vain have toil'd,
And by a mortal man at length am foil'd.
If native pow'r prevail not, shall I doubt
To seek for needful succor from without?
If Jove and Heav'n my just desires deny,
Hell shall the pow'r of Heav'n and Jove supply.
Grant that the Fates have firm'd, by their decree,
The Trojan race to reign in Italy;
At least I can defer the nuptial day,
And with protracted wars the peace delay:
With blood the dear alliance shall be bought,
And both the people near destruction brought;
So shall the son-in-law and father join,
With ruin, war, and waste of either line.
O fatal maid, thy marriage is endow'd
With Phrygian, Latian, and Rutulian blood!
Bellona leads thee to thy lover's hand;
Another queen brings forth another brand,
To burn with foreign fires another land!
A second Paris, diff'ring but in name,
Shall fire his country with a second flame."

Thus having said, she sinks beneath the ground,
With furious haste, and shoots the Stygian sound,
To rouse Alecto from th' infernal seat
Of her dire sisters, and their dark retreat.
This Fury, fit for her intent, she chose;
One who delights in wars and human woes.
Ev'n Pluto hates his own mis-shapen race;
Her sister Furies fly her hideous face;
So frightful are the forms the monster takes,
So fierce the hissings of her speckled snakes.
Her Juno finds, and thus inflames her spite:
"O virgin daughter of eternal Night,
Give me this once thy labor, to sustain
My right, and execute my just disdain.
Let not the Trojans, with a feign'd pretense
Of proffer'd peace, delude the Latian prince.
Expel from Italy that odious name,
And let not Juno suffer in her fame.
'Tis thine to ruin realms, o'erturn a state,

Betwixt the dearest friends to raise debate,
And kindle kindred blood to mutual hate.
Thy hand o'er towns the fun'ral torch displays,
And forms a thousand ills ten thousand ways.
Now shake, from out thy fruitful breast, the seeds
Of envy, discord, and of cruel deeds:
Confound the peace establish'd, and prepare
Their souls to hatred, and their hands to war."

Smear'd as she was with black Gorgonian blood,
The Fury sprang above the Stygian flood;
And on her wicker wings, sublime thro' night,
She to the Latian palace took her flight:
There sought the queen's apartment, stood before
The peaceful threshold, and besieg'd the door.
Restless Amata lay, her swelling breast
Fir'd with disdain for Turnus dispossess'd,
And the new nuptials of the Trojan guest.
From her black bloody locks the Fury shakes
Her darling plague, the fav'rite of her snakes;
With her full force she threw the pois'nous dart,
And fix'd it deep within Amata's heart,
That, thus envenom'd, she might kindle rage,
And sacrifice to strife her house and husband's age.
Unseen, unfelt, the fiery serpent skims
Betwixt her linen and her naked limbs;
His baleful breath inspiring, as he glides,
Now like a chain around her neck he rides,
Now like a fillet to her head repairs,
And with his circling volumes folds her hairs.
At first the silent venom slid with ease,
And seiz'd her cooler senses by degrees;
Then, ere th' infected mass was fir'd too far,
In plaintive accents she began the war,
And thus bespoke her husband: "Shall," she said,
"A wand'ring prince enjoy Lavinia's bed?
If nature plead not in a parent's heart,
Pity my tears, and pity her desert.
I know, my dearest lord, the time will come,
You would, in vain, reverse your cruel doom;
The faithless pirate soon will set to sea,

And bear the royal virgin far away!
A guest like him, a Trojan guest, before,
In shew of friendship sought the Spartan shore,
And ravish'd Helen from her husband bore.
Think on a king's inviolable word;
And think on Turnus, her once plighted lord:
To this false foreigner you give your throne,
And wrong a friend, a kinsman, and a son.
Resume your ancient care; and, if the god
Your sire, and you, resolve on foreign blood,
Know all are foreign, in a larger sense,
Not born your subjects, or deriv'd from hence.
Then, if the line of Turnus you retrace,
He springs from Inachus of Argive race."

But when she saw her reasons idly spent,
And could not move him from his fix'd intent,
She flew to rage; for now the snake possess'd
Her vital parts, and poison'd all her breast;
She raves, she runs with a distracted pace,
And fills with horrid howls the public place.
And, as young striplings whip the top for sport,
On the smooth pavement of an empty court;
The wooden engine flies and whirls about,
Admir'd, with clamors, of the beardless rout;
They lash aloud; each other they provoke,
And lend their little souls at ev'ry stroke:
Thus fares the queen; and thus her fury blows
Amidst the crowd, and kindles as she goes.
Nor yet content, she strains her malice more,
And adds new ills to those contriv'd before:
She flies the town, and, mixing with a throng
Of madding matrons, bears the bride along,
Wand'ring thro' woods and wilds, and devious ways,
And with these arts the Trojan match delays.
She feign'd the rites of Bacchus; cried aloud,
And to the buxom god the virgin vow'd.
"Evoe! O Bacchus!" thus began the song;
And "Evoe!" answer'd all the female throng.
"O virgin! worthy thee alone!" she cried;
"O worthy thee alone!" the crew replied.

"For thee she feeds her hair, she leads thy dance,
And with thy winding ivy wreathes her lance."
Like fury seiz'd the rest; the progress known,
All seek the mountains, and forsake the town:
All, clad in skins of beasts, the jav'lin bear,
Give to the wanton winds their flowing hair,
And shrieks and shoutings rend the suff'ring air.
The queen herself, inspir'd with rage divine,
Shook high above her head a flaming pine;
Then roll'd her haggard eyes around the throng,
And sung, in Turnus' name, the nuptial song:
"Io, ye Latian dames! if any here
Hold your unhappy queen, Amata, dear;
If there be here," she said, "who dare maintain
My right, nor think the name of mother vain;
Unbind your fillets, loose your flowing hair,
And orgies and nocturnal rites prepare."

Amata's breast the Fury thus invades,
And fires with rage, amid the sylvan shades;
Then, when she found her venom spread so far,
The royal house embroil'd in civil war,
Rais'd on her dusky wings, she cleaves the skies,
And seeks the palace where young Turnus lies.
His town, as fame reports, was built of old
By Danae, pregnant with almighty gold,
Who fled her father's rage, and, with a train
Of following Argives, thro' the stormy main,
Driv'n by the southern blasts, was fated here to reign.
'Twas Ardua once; now Ardea's name it bears;
Once a fair city, now consum'd with years.
Here, in his lofty palace, Turnus lay,
Betwixt the confines of the night and day,
Secure in sleep. The Fury laid aside
Her looks and limbs, and with new methods tried
The foulness of th' infernal form to hide.
Propp'd on a staff, she takes a trembling mien:
Her face is furrow'd, and her front obscene;
Deep-dinted wrinkles on her cheek she draws;
Sunk are her eyes, and toothless are her jaws;
Her hoary hair with holy fillets bound,

Her temples with an olive wreath are crown'd.
Old Chalybe, who kept the sacred fane
Of Juno, now she seem'd, and thus began,
(Appearing in a dream) to rouse the careless man:
"Shall Turnus then such endless toil sustain
In fighting fields, and conquer towns in vain?
Win, for a Trojan head to wear the prize,
Usurp thy crown, enjoy thy victories?
The bride and scepter which thy blood has bought,
The king transfers; and foreign heirs are sought.
Go now, deluded man, and seek again
New toils, new dangers, on the dusty plain.
Repel the Tuscan foes; their city seize;
Protect the Latians in luxurious ease.
This dream all-pow'rful Juno sends; I bear
Her mighty mandates, and her words you hear.
Haste; arm your Ardeans; issue to the plain;
With fate to friend, assault the Trojan train:
Their thoughtless chiefs, their painted ships, that lie
In Tiber's mouth, with fire and sword destroy.
The Latian king, unless he shall submit,
Own his old promise, and his new forget—
Let him, in arms, the pow'r of Turnus prove,
And learn to fear whom he disdains to love.
For such is Heav'n's command." The youthful prince
With scorn replied, and made this bold defense:
"You tell me, mother, what I knew before:
The Phrygian fleet is landed on the shore.
I neither fear nor will provoke the war;
My fate is Juno's most peculiar care.
But time has made you dote, and vainly tell
Of arms imagin'd in your lonely cell.
Go; be the temple and the gods your care;
Permit to men the thought of peace and war."

These haughty words Alecto's rage provoke,
And frighted Turnus trembled as she spoke.
Her eyes grow stiffen'd, and with sulphur burn;
Her hideous looks and hellish form return;
Her curling snakes with hissings fill the place,
And open all the furies of her face:

THE SEVENTH BOOK OF THE ÆNEIS 255

Then, darting fire from her malignant eyes,
She cast him backward as he strove to rise,
And, ling'ring, sought to frame some new replies.
High on her head she rears two twisted snakes;
Her chains she rattles, and her whip she shakes;
And, churning bloody foam, thus loudly speaks:
"Behold whom time has made to dote, and tell
Of arms imagin'd in her lonely cell!
Behold the Fates' infernal minister!
War, death, destruction, in my hand I bear."

Thus having said, her smold'ring torch, impress'd
With her full force, she plung'd into his breast.
Aghast he wak'd; and, starting from his bed,
Cold sweat, in clammy drops, his limbs o'erspread.
"Arms! arms!" he cries: "my sword and shield prepare!"
He breathes defiance, blood, and mortal war.
So, when with crackling flames a caldron fries,
The bubbling waters from the bottom rise:
Above the brims they force their fiery way;
Black vapors climb aloft, and cloud the day.

The peace polluted thus, a chosen band
He first commissions to the Latian land,
In threat'ning embassy; then rais'd the rest,
To meet in arms th' intruding Trojan guest,
To force the foes from the Lavinian shore,
And Italy's indanger'd peace restore.
Himself alone an equal match he boasts,
To fight the Phrygian and Ausonian hosts.
The gods invok'd, the Rutuli prepare
Their arms, and warn each other to the war.
His beauty these, and those his blooming age,
The rest his house and his own fame ingage.

While Turnus urges thus his enterprise,
The Stygian Fury to the Trojans flies;
New frauds invents, and takes a steepy stand,
Which overlooks the vale with wide command;
Where fair Ascanius and his youthful train,
With horns and hounds, a hunting match ordain,
And pitch their toils around the shady plain.
The Fury fires the pack; they snuff, they vent,

And feed their hungry nostrils with the scent.
'Twas of a well-grown stag, whose antlers rise
High o'er his front; his beams invade the skies.
From this light cause th' infernal maid prepares
The country churls to mischief, hate, and wars.

    The stately beast the two Tyrrhidæ bred,
Snatch'd from his dam, and the tame youngling fed.
Their father Tyrrheus did his fodder bring,
Tyrrheus, chief ranger to the Latian king:
Their sister Silvia cherish'd with her care
The little wanton, and did wreaths prepare
To hang his budding horns, with ribbons tied
His tender neck, and comb'd his silken hide,
And bath'd his body. Patient of command
In time he grew, and, growing us'd to hand,
He waited at his master's board for food;
Then sought his salvage kindred in the wood,
Where grazing all the day, at night he came
To his known lodgings, and his country dame.

    This household beast, that us'd the woodland grounds,
Was view'd at first by the young hero's hounds,
As down the stream he swam, to seek retreat
In the cool waters, and to quench his heat.
Ascanius young, and eager of his game,
Soon bent his bow, uncertain in his aim;
But the dire fiend the fatal arrow guides,
Which pierc'd his bowels thro' his panting sides.
The bleeding creature issues from the floods,
Possess'd with fear, and seeks his known abodes,
His old familiar hearth and household gods.
He falls; he fills the house with heavy groans,
Implores their pity, and his pain bemoans.
Young Silvia beats her breast, and cries aloud
For succor from the clownish neighborhood:
The churls assemble; for the fiend, who lay
In the close woody covert, urg'd their way.
One with a brand yet burning from the flame,
Arm'd with a knotty club another came:
Whate'er they catch or find, without their care,

Their fury makes an instrument of war.
Tyrrheus, the foster father of the beast,
Then clench'd a hatchet in his horny fist,
But held his hand from the descending stroke,
And left his wedge within the cloven oak,
To whet their courage and their rage provoke.
And now the goddess, exercis'd in ill,
Who watch'd an hour to work her impious will,
Ascends the roof, and to her crooked horn,
Such as was then by Latian shepherds borne,
Adds all her breath. The rocks and woods around,
And mountains, tremble at th' infernal sound.
The sacred lake of Trivia from afar,
The Veline fountains, and sulphureous Nar,
Shake at the baleful blast, the signal of the war.
Young mothers wildly stare, with fear possess'd,
And strain their helpless infants to their breast.

  The clowns, a boist'rous, rude, ungovern'd crew,
With furious haste to the loud summons flew.
The pow'rs of Troy, then issuing on the plain,
With fresh recruits their youthful chief sustain:
Not theirs a raw and unexperienc'd train,
But a firm body of embattled men.
At first, while fortune favor'd neither side,
The fight with clubs and burning brands was tried;
But now, both parties reinforc'd, the fields
Are bright with flaming swords and brazen shields.
A shining harvest either host displays,
And shoots against the sun with equal rays.
Thus, when a black-brow'd gust begins to rise,
White foam at first on the curl'd ocean fries;
Then roars the main, the billows mount the skies;
Till, by the fury of the storm full blown,
The muddy bottom o'er the clouds is thrown.
First Almon falls, old Tyrrheus' eldest care,
Pierc'd with an arrow from the distant war:
Fix'd in his throat the flying weapon stood,
And stopp'd his breath, and drank his vital blood.
Huge heaps of slain around the body rise:
Among the rest, the rich Galesus lies;

A good old man, while peace he preach'd in vain,
Amidst the madness of th' unruly train:
Five herds, five bleating flocks, his pastures fill'd;
His lands a hundred yoke of oxen till'd.

Thus, while in equal scales their fortune stood
The Fury bath'd them in each other's blood;
Then, having fix'd the fight, exulting flies,
And bears fulfill'd her promise to the skies.
To Juno thus she speaks: "Behold! 'tis done,
The blood already drawn, the war begun;
The discord is complete; nor can they cease
The dire debate, nor you command the peace.
Now, since the Latian and the Trojan brood
Have tasted vengeance and the sweets of blood;
Speak, and my pow'r shall add this office more:
The neighb'ring nations of th' Ausonian shore
Shall hear the dreadful rumor, from afar,
Of arm'd invasion, and embrace the war."
Then Juno thus: "The grateful work is done,
The seeds of discord sow'd, the war begun;
Frauds, fears, and fury have possess'd the state,
And fix'd the causes of a lasting hate.
A bloody Hymen shall th' alliance join
Betwixt the Trojan and Ausonian line:
But thou with speed to night and hell repair;
For not the gods, nor angry Jove, will bear
Thy lawless wand'ring walks in upper air.
Leave what remains to me." Saturnia said:
The sullen fiend her sounding wings display'd,
Unwilling left the light, and sought the nether shade.

In midst of Italy, well known to fame,
There lies a lake (Amsanctus is the name)
Below the lofty mounts: on either side
Thick forests the forbidden entrance hide.
Full in the center of the sacred wood
An arm arises of the Stygian flood,
Which, breaking from beneath with bellowing sound,
Whirls the black waves and rattling stones around.
Here Pluto pants for breath from out his cell,
And opens wide the grinning jaws of hell.

THE SEVENTH BOOK OF THE ÆNEIS

To this infernal lake the Fury flies;
Here hides her hated head, and frees the lab'ring skies.
   Saturnian Juno now, with double care,
Attends the fatal process of the war.
The clowns, return'd, from battle bear the slain,
Implore the gods, and to their king complain.
The corps of Almon and the rest are shown;
Shrieks, clamors, murmurs, fill the frighted town.
Ambitious Turnus in the press appears,
And, aggravating crimes, augments their fears;
Proclaims his private injuries aloud,
A solemn promise made, and disavow'd;
A foreign son is sought, and a mix'd mongrel brood.
Then they, whose mothers, frantic with their fear,
In woods and wilds the flags of Bacchus bear,
And lead his dances with dishevel'd hair,
Increase the clamor, and the war demand,
(Such was Amata's interest in the land,)
Against the public sanctions of the peace,
Against all omens of their ill success.
With fates averse, the rout in arms resort,
To force their monarch, and insult the court.
But, like a rock unmov'd, a rock that braves
The raging tempest and the rising waves—
Propp'd on himself he stands; his solid sides
Wash off the seaweeds, and the sounding tides—
So stood the pious prince, unmov'd, and long
Sustain'd the madness of the noisy throng.
But, when he found that Juno's pow'r prevail'd,
And all the methods of cool counsel fail'd,
He calls the gods to witness their offense,
Disclaims the war, asserts his innocence.
"Hurried by fate," he cries, "and borne before
A furious wind, we leave the faithful shore.
O more than madmen! you yourselves shall bear
The guilt of blood and sacrilegious war:
Thou, Turnus, shalt atone it by thy fate,
And pray to Heav'n for peace, but pray too late.
For me, my stormy voyage at an end,
I to the port of death securely tend.

"The fun'ral pomp which to your kings you pay,
Is all I want, and all you take away."
He said no more, but, in his walls confin'd,
Shut out the woes which he too well divin'd;
Nor with the rising storm would vainly strive,
But left the helm, and let the vessel drive.

A solemn custom was observ'd of old,
Which Latium held, and now the Romans hold,
Their standard when in fighting fields they rear
Against the fierce Hyrcanians, or declare
The Scythian, Indian, or Arabian war;
Or from the boasting Parthians would regain
Their eagles, lost in Carrhæ's bloody plain.
Two gates of steel (the name of Mars they bear,
And still are worship'd with religious fear)
Before his temple stand: the dire abode,
And the fear'd issues of the furious god,
Are fenc'd with brazen bolts; without the gates,
The wary guardian Janus doubly waits.
Then, when the sacred senate votes the wars,
The Roman consul their decree declares,
And in his robes the sounding gates unbars.
The youth in military shouts arise,
And the loud trumpets break the yielding skies.
These rites, of old by sov'reign princes us'd,
Were the king's office; but the king refus'd,
Deaf to their cries, nor would the gates unbar
Of sacred peace, or loose th' imprison'd war;
But hid his head, and, safe from loud alarms,
Abhorr'd the wicked ministry of arms.
Then heav'n's imperious queen shot down from high:
At her approach the brazen hinges fly;
The gates are forc'd, and ev'ry falling bar;
And, like a tempest, issues out the war.

The peaceful cities of th' Ausonian shore,
Lull'd in their ease, and undisturb'd before,
Are all on fire; and some, with studious care,
Their restiff steeds in sandy plains prepare;
Some their soft limbs in painful marches try,
And war is all their wish, and arms the gen'ral cry.

THE SEVENTH BOOK OF THE ÆNEIS

Part scour the rusty shields with seam; and part
New grind the blunted ax, and point the dart:
With joy they view the waving ensigns fly,
And hear the trumpet's clangor pierce the sky.
Five cities forge their arms: th' Atinian pow'rs,
Antemnæ, Tibur with her lofty tow'rs,
Ardea the proud, the Crustumerian town:
All these of old were places of renown.
Some hammer helmets for the fighting field;
Some twine young sallows to support the shield;
The croslet some, and some the cuishes mold,
With silver plated, and with ductile gold.
The rustic honors of the scythe and share
Give place to swords and plumes, the pride of war.
Old fauchions are new temper'd in the fires;
The sounding trumpet ev'ry soul inspires.
The word is giv'n; with eager speed they lace
The shining headpiece, and the shield embrace.
The neighing steeds are to the chariot tied;
The trusty weapon sits on ev'ry side.

And now the mighty labor is begun—
Ye Muses, open all your Helicon.
Sing you the chiefs that sway'd th' Ausonian land,
Their arms, and armies under their command;
What warriors in our ancient clime were bred;
What soldiers follow'd, and what heroes led.
For well you know, and can record alone,
What fame to future times conveys but darkly down.

Mezentius first appear'd upon the plain:
Scorn sate upon his brows, and sour disdain,
Defying earth and heav'n. Etruria lost,
He brings to Turnus' aid his baffled host.
The charming Lausus, full of youthful fire,
Rode in the rank, and next his sullen sire;
To Turnus only second in the grace
Of manly mien, and features of the face.
A skilful horseman, and a huntsman bred,
With fates averse a thousand men he led:
His sire unworthy of so brave a son;
Himself well worthy of a happier throne.

Next Aventinus drives his chariot round
The Latian plains, with palms and laurels crown'd.
Proud of his steeds, he smokes along the field;
His father's hydra fills his ample shield:
A hundred serpents hiss about the brims;
The son of Hercules he justly seems
By his broad shoulders and gigantic limbs;
Of heav'nly, part, and part of earthly blood,
A mortal woman mixing with a god.
For strong Alcides, after he had slain
The triple Geryon, drove from conquer'd Spain
His captive herds; and, thence in triumph led,
On Tuscan Tiber's flow'ry banks they fed.
Then on Mount Aventine the son of Jove
The priestess Rhea found, and forc'd to love.
For arms, his men long piles and jav'lins bore;
And poles with pointed steel their foes in battle gore.
Like Hercules himself his son appears,
In salvage pomp; a lion's hide he wears;
About his shoulders hangs the shaggy skin;
The teeth and gaping jaws severely grin.
Thus, like the god his father, homely dress'd,
He strides into the hall, a horrid guest.

Then two twin brothers from fair Tibur came,
(Which from their brother Tiburs took the name,)
Fierce Coras and Catillus, void of fear:
Arm'd Argive horse they led, and in the front appear.
Like cloud-born Centaurs, from the mountain's height
With rapid course descending to the fight;
They rush along; the rattling woods give way;
The branches bend before their sweepy sway.

Nor was Præneste's founder wanting there,
Whom fame reports the son of Mulciber:
Found in the fire, and foster'd in the plains,
A shepherd and a king at once he reigns,
And leads to Turnus' aid his country swains.
His own Præneste sends a chosen band,
With those who plow Saturnia's Gabine land;
Besides the succor which cold Anien yields,
The rocks of Hernicus, and dewy fields,

Anagnia fat, and Father Amasene—
A num'rous rout, but all of naked men:
Nor arms they wear, nor swords and bucklers wield,
Nor drive the chariot thro' the dusty field,
But whirl from leathern slings huge balls of lead,
And spoils of yellow wolves adorn their head;
The left foot naked, when they march to fight,
But in a bull's raw hide they sheathe the right.

   Messapus next, (great Neptune was his sire,)
Secure of steel, and fated from the fire,
In pomp appears, and with his ardor warms
A heartless train, unexercis'd in arms:
The just Faliscans he to battle brings,
And those who live where Lake Ciminia springs;
And where Feronia's grove and temple stands,
Who till Fescennian or Flavinian lands.
All these in order march, and, marching, sing
The warlike actions of their sea-born king;
Like a long team of snowy swans on high,
Which clap their wings, and cleave the liquid sky,
When, homeward from their wat'ry pastures borne,
They sing, and Asia's lakes their notes return.
Not one who heard their music from afar,
Would think these troops an army train'd to war,
But flocks of fowl, that, when the tempests roar,
With their hoarse gabbling seek the silent shore.

   Then Clausus came, who led a num'rous band
Of troops embodied from the Sabine land,
And, in himself alone, an army brought.
'Twas he, the noble Claudian race begot,
The Claudian race, ordain'd, in times to come,
To share the greatness of imperial Rome.
He led the Cures forth, of old renown,
Mutuscans from their olive-bearing town,
And all th' Eretian pow'rs; besides a band
That follow'd from Velinum's dewy land,
And Amiternian troops, of mighty fame,
And mountaineers, that from Severus came,
And from the craggy cliffs of Tetrica,
And those where yellow Tiber takes his way,

And where Himella's wanton waters play.
Casperia sends her arms, with those that lie
By Fabaris, and fruitful Foruli:
The warlike aids of Horta next appear,
And the cold Nursians come to close the rear,
Mix'd with the natives born of Latine blood,
Whom Allia washes with her fatal flood.
Not thicker billows beat the Libyan main,
When pale Orion sets in wintry rain;
Nor thicker harvests on rich Hermus rise,
Or Lycian fields, when Phœbus burns the skies,
Than stand these troops: their bucklers ring around;
Their trampling turns the turf, and shakes the solid ground.

High in his chariot then Halesus came,
A foe by birth to Troy's unhappy name:
From Agamemnon born—to Turnus' aid
A thousand men the youthful hero led,
Who till the Massic soil, for wine renown'd,
And fierce Auruncans from their hilly ground,
And those who live by Sidicinian shores,
And where with shoaly fords Vulturnus roars,
Cales' and Osca's old inhabitants,
And rough Saticulans, inur'd to wants:
Light demi-lances from afar they throw,
Fasten'd with leathern thongs, to gall the foe.
Short crooked swords in closer fight they wear;
And on their warding arm light bucklers bear.

Nor Œbalus, shalt thou be left unsung,
From nymph Semethis and old Telon sprung,
Who then in Teleboan Capri reign'd;
But that short isle th' ambitious youth disdain'd,
And o'er Campania stretch'd his ample sway,
Where swelling Sarnus seeks the Tyrrhene sea;
O'er Batulum, and where Abella sees,
From her high tow'rs, the harvest of her trees.
And these (as was the Teuton use of old)
Wield brazen swords, and brazen bucklers hold;
Sling weighty stones, when from afar they fight;
Their casques are cork, a covering thick and light.

Next these in rank, the warlike Ufens went,

And led the mountain troops that Nursia sent.
The rude Equicolæ his rule obey'd;
Hunting their sport, and plund'ring was their trade.
In arms they plow'd, to battle still prepar'd:
Their soil was barren, and their hearts were hard.

Umbro the priest the proud Marrubians led,
By King Archippus sent to Turnus' aid,
And peaceful olives crown'd his hoary head.
His wand and holy words, the viper's rage,
And venom'd wounds of serpents could assuage.
He, when he pleas'd with powerful juice to steep
Their temples, shut their eyes in pleasing sleep.
But vain were Marsian herbs, and magic art,
To cure the wound giv'n by the Dardan dart:
Yet his untimely fate th' Angitian woods
In sighs remurmur'd to the Fucine floods.

The son of fam'd Hippolytus was there,
Fam'd as his sire, and, as his mother, fair;
Whom in Egerian groves Aricia bore,
And nurs'd his youth along the marshy shore,
Where great Diana's peaceful altars flame,
In fruitful fields; and Virbius was his name.
Hippolytus, as old records have said,
Was by his stepdam sought to share her bed;
But, when no female arts his mind could move,
She turn'd to furious hate her impious love.
Torn by wild horses on the sandy shore,
Another's crimes th' unhappy hunter bore,
Glutting his father's eyes with guiltless gore.
But chaste Diana, who his death deplor'd,
With Æsculapian herbs his life restor'd.
Then Jove, who saw from high, with just disdain,
The dead inspir'd with vital breath again,
Struck to the center, with his flaming dart,
Th' unhappy founder of the godlike art.
But Trivia kept in secret shades alone
Her care, Hippolytus, to fate unknown;
And call'd him Virbius in th' Egerian grove,
Where then he liv'd obscure, but safe from Jove.
For this, from Trivia's temple and her wood

Are coursers driv'n, who shed their master's blood,
Affrighted by the monsters of the flood.
His son, the second Virbius, yet retain'd
His father's art, and warrior steeds he rein'd.

 Amid the troops, and like the leading god,
High o'er the rest in arms the graceful Turnus rode:
A triple pile of plumes his crest adorn'd,
On which with belching flames Chimæra burn'd:
The more the kindled combat rises high'r,
The more with fury burns the blazing fire.
Fair Io grac'd his shield; but Io now
With horns exalted stands, and seems to low—
A noble charge! Her keeper by her side,
To watch her walks, his hundred eyes applied;
And on the brims her sire, the wat'ry god,
Roll'd from a silver urn his crystal flood.
A cloud of foot succeeds, and fills the fields
With swords, and pointed spears, and clatt'ring shields;
Of Argives, and of old Sicanian bands,
And those who plow the rich Rutulian lands;
Auruncan youth, and those Sacrana yields,
And the proud Labicans, with painted shields,
And those who near Numician streams reside,
And those whom Tiber's holy forests hide,
Or Circe's hills from the main land divide;
Where Ufens glides along the lowly lands,
Or the black water of Pomptina stands.

 Last, from the Volscians fair Camilla came,
And led her warlike troops, a warrior dame;
Unbred to spinning, in the loom unskill'd,
She chose the nobler Pallas of the field.
Mix'd with the first, the fierce virago fought,
Sustain'd the toils of arms, the danger sought,
Outstripp'd the winds in speed upon the plain,
Flew o'er the fields, nor hurt the bearded grain:
She swept the seas, and, as she skimm'd along,
Her flying feet unbath'd on billows hung.
Men, boys, and women, stupid with surprise,
Where'er she passes, fix their wond'ring eyes:
Longing they look, and, gaping at the sight,

Devour her o'er and o'er with vast delight;
Her purple habit sits with such a grace
On her smooth shoulders, and so suits her face;
Her head with ringlets of her hair is crown'd,
And in a golden caul the curls are bound.
She shakes her myrtle jav'lin; and, behind,
Her Lycian quiver dances in the wind.

THE EIGHTH BOOK
OF THE ÆNEIS

THE ARGUMENT.—The war being now begun, both the generals make all possi[ble] preparations. Turnus sends to Diomedes. Æneas goes in person to beg succ[or] from Evander and the Tuscans. Evander receives him kindly, furnishes him w[ith] men, and sends his son Pallas with him. Vulcan, at the request of Venus, makes ar[ms] for her son Æneas, and draws on his shield the most memorable actions of [his] posterity.

WHEN Turnus had assembled all his pow'rs,
His standard planted on Laurentum's tow'rs;
When now the sprightly trumpet, from afar,
Had giv'n the signal of approaching war,
Had rous'd the neighing steeds to scour the fields,
While the fierce riders clatter'd on their shields;
Trembling with rage, the Latian youth prepare
To join th' allies, and headlong rush to war.
Fierce Ufens, and Messapus, led the crowd,
With bold Mezentius, who blasphem'd aloud.
These thro' the country took their wasteful course,
The fields to forage, and to gather force.
Then Venulus to Diomede they send,
To beg his aid Ausonia to defend,
Declare the common danger, and inform
The Grecian leader of the growing storm:
Æneas, landed on the Latian coast,
With banish'd gods, and with a baffled host,
Yet now aspir'd to conquest of the state,
And claim'd a title from the gods and fate;
What num'rous nations in his quarrel came,
And how they spread his formidable name.
What he design'd, what mischief might arise,
If fortune favor'd his first enterprise,
Was left for him to weigh, whose equal fears,
And common interest, was involv'd in theirs.

While Turnus and th' allies thus urge the war,

THE EIGHTH BOOK OF THE ÆNEIS

The Trojan, floating in a flood of care,
Beholds the tempest which his foes prepare.
This way and that he turns his anxious mind;
Thinks, and rejects the counsels he design'd;
Explores himself in vain, in ev'ry part,
And gives no rest to his distracted heart.
So, when the sun by day, or moon by night,
Strike on the polish'd brass their trembling light,
The glitt'ring species here and there divide,
And cast their dubious beams from side to side;
Now on the walls, now on the pavement play,
And to the ceiling flash the glaring day.

'Twas night; and weary nature lull'd asleep
The birds of air, and fishes of the deep,
And beasts, and mortal men. The Trojan chief
Was laid on Tiber's banks, oppress'd with grief,
And found in silent slumber late relief.
Then, thro' the shadows of the poplar wood,
Arose the father of the Roman flood;
An azure robe was o'er his body spread,
A wreath of shady reeds adorn'd his head:
Thus, manifest to sight, the god appear'd,
And with these pleasing words his sorrow cheer'd:
"Undoubted offspring of ethereal race,
O long expected in this promis'd place!
Who thro' the foes hast borne thy banish'd gods,
Restor'd them to their hearths, and old abodes;
This is thy happy home, the clime where fate
Ordains thee to restore the Trojan state.
Fear not! The war shall end in lasting peace,
And all the rage of haughty Juno cease.
And that this nightly vision may not seem
Th' effect of fancy, or an idle dream,
A sow beneath an oak shall lie along,
All white herself, and white her thirty young.
When thirty rolling years have run their race,
Thy son Ascanius, on this empty space,
Shall build a royal town, of lasting fame,
Which from this omen shall receive the name.
Time shall approve the truth. For what remains,

And how with sure success to crown thy pains,
With patience next attend. A banish'd band,
Driv'n with Evander from th' Arcadian land,
Have planted here, and plac'd on high their walls;
Their town the founder Pallanteum calls,
Deriv'd from Pallas, his great-grandsire's name;
But the fierce Latians old possession claim,
With war infesting the new colony.
These make thy friends, and on their aid rely.
To thy free passage I submit my streams.
Wake, son of Venus, from thy pleasing dreams;
And, when the setting stars are lost in day,
To Juno's pow'r thy just devotion pay;
With sacrifice the wrathful queen appease:
Her pride at length shall fall, her fury cease.
When thou return'st victorious from the war,
Perform thy vows to me with grateful care.
The god am I, whose yellow water flows
Around these fields, and fattens as it goes:
Tiber my name; among the rolling floods
Renown'd on earth, esteem'd among the gods.
This is my certain seat. In times to come,
My waves shall wash the walls of mighty Rome."

He said, and plung'd below. While yet he spoke,
His dream Æneas and his sleep forsook.
He rose, and looking up, beheld the skies
With purple blushing, and the day arise.
Then water in his hollow palm he took
From Tiber's flood, and thus the pow'rs bespoke:
"Laurentian nymphs, by whom the streams are fed,
And Father Tiber, in thy sacred bed
Receive Æneas, and from danger keep.
Whatever fount, whatever holy deep,
Conceals thy wat'ry stores; where'er they rise,
And, bubbling from below, salute the skies;
Thou, king of horned floods, whose plenteous urn
Suffices fatness to the fruitful corn,
For this thy kind compassion of our woes,
Shalt share my morning song, and ev'ning vows.
But, O be present to thy people's aid,

THE EIGHTH BOOK OF THE ÆNEIS

And firm the gracious promise thou hast made!"
Thus having said, two galleys from his stores,
With care he chooses, mans, and fits with oars.
Now on the shore the fatal swine is found.
Wondrous to tell!—She lay along the ground:
Her well-fed offspring at her udders hung;
She white herself, and white her thirty young.
Æneas takes the mother and her brood,
And all on Juno's altar are bestow'd.

The foll'wing night, and the succeeding day,
Propitious Tiber smooth'd his wat'ry way:
He roll'd his river back, and pois'd he stood,
A gentle swelling, and a peaceful flood.
The Trojans mount their ships; they put from shore,
Borne on the waves, and scarcely dip an oar.
Shouts from the land give omen to their course,
And the pitch'd vessels glide with easy force.
The woods and waters wonder at the gleam
Of shields, and painted ships that stem the stream.
One summer's night and one whole day they pass
Betwixt the greenwood shades, and cut the liquid glass.
The fiery sun had finish'd half his race,
Look'd back, and doubted in the middle space,
When they from far beheld the rising tow'rs,
The tops of sheds, and shepherds' lowly bow'rs,
Thin as they stood, which, then of homely clay,
Now rise in marble, from the Roman sway.
These cots (Evander's kingdom, mean and poor)
The Trojan saw, and turn'd his ships to shore.
'Twas on a solemn day: th' Arcadian states,
The king and prince, without the city gates,
Then paid their off'rings in a sacred grove
To Hercules, the warrior son of Jove.
Thick clouds of rolling smoke involve the skies,
And fat of entrails on his altar fries.

But, when they saw the ships that stemm'd the flood,
And glitter'd thro' the covert of the wood,
They rose with fear, and left th' unfinish'd feast,
Till dauntless Pallas reassur'd the rest
To pay the rites. Himself without delay

A jav'lin seiz'd, and singly took his way;
Then gain'd a rising ground, and call'd from far:
"Resolve me, strangers, whence, and what you are;
Your bus'ness here; and bring you peace or war?"
High on the stern Æneas took his stand,
And held a branch of olive in his hand,
While thus he spoke: "The Phrygians' arms you see,
Expell'd from Troy, provok'd in Italy
By Latian foes, with war unjustly made;
At first affianc'd, and at last betray'd.
This message bear: 'The Trojans and their chief
Bring holy peace, and beg the king's relief.'"
Struck with so great a name, and all on fire,
The youth replies: "Whatever you require,
Your fame exacts. Upon our shores descend,
A welcome guest, and, what you wish, a friend."
He said, and, downward hasting to the strand,
Embrac'd the stranger prince, and join'd his hand.

  Conducted to the grove, Æneas broke
The silence first, and thus the king bespoke:
"Best of the Greeks, to whom, by Fate's command,
I bear these peaceful branches in my hand,
Undaunted I approach you, tho' I know
Your birth is Grecian, and your land my foe;
From Atreus tho' your ancient lineage came,
And both the brother kings your kindred claim;
Yet, my self-conscious worth, your high renown,
Your virtue, thro' the neighb'ring nations blown,
Our fathers' mingled blood, Apollo's voice,
Have led me hither, less by need than choice.
Our founder Dardanus, as fame has sung,
And Greeks acknowledge, from Electra sprung:
Electra from the loins of Atlas came;
Atlas, whose head sustains the starry frame.
Your sire is Mercury, whom long before
On cold Cyllene's top fair Maia bore.
Maia the fair, on fame if we rely,
Was Atlas' daughter, who sustains the sky.
Thus from one common source our streams divide;
Ours is the Trojan, yours th' Arcadian side.

Rais'd by these hopes, I sent no news before,
Nor ask'd your leave, nor did your faith implore;
But come, without a pledge, my own ambassador.
The same Rutulians, who with arms pursue
The Trojan race, are equal foes to you.
Our host expell'd, what farther force can stay
The victor troops from universal sway?
Then will they stretch their pow'r athwart the land,
And either sea from side to side command.
Receive our offer'd faith, and give us thine;
Ours is a gen'rous and experienc'd line:
We want not hearts nor bodies for the war;
In council cautious, and in fields we dare."

He said; and, while he spoke, with piercing eyes
Evander view'd the man with vast surprise,
Pleas'd with his action, ravish'd with his face:
Then answer'd briefly, with a royal grace:
"O valiant leader of the Trojan line,
In whom the features of thy father shine,
How I recall Anchises! how I see
His motions, mien, and all my friend, in thee!
Long tho' it be, 'tis fresh within my mind,
When Priam to his sister's court design'd
A welcome visit, with a friendly stay,
And thro' th' Arcadian kingdom took his way.
Then, past a boy, the callow down began
To shade my chin, and call me first a man.
I saw the shining train with vast delight,
And Priam's goodly person pleas'd my sight:
But great Anchises, far above the rest,
With awful wonder fir'd my youthful breast.
I long'd to join in friendship's holy bands
Our mutual hearts, and plight our mutual hands.
I first accosted him: I sued, I sought,
And, with a loving force, to Pheneus brought.
He gave me, when at length constrain'd to go,
A Lycian quiver and a Gnossian bow,
A vest embroider'd, glorious to behold,
And two rich bridles, with their bits of gold,
Which my son's coursers in obedience hold.

The league you ask, I offer, as your right;
And, when to-morrow's sun reveals the light,
With swift supplies you shall be sent away.
Now celebrate with us this solemn day,
Whose holy rites admit no long delay.
Honor our annual feast; and take your seat,
With friendly welcome, at a homely treat."
Thus having said, the bowls (remov'd for fear)
The youths replac'd, and soon restor'd the cheer.
On sods of turf he set the soldiers round:
A maple throne, rais'd higher from the ground,
Receiv'd the Trojan chief; and, o'er the bed,
A lion's shaggy hide for ornament they spread.
The loaves were serv'd in canisters; the wine
In bowls; the priest renew'd the rites divine:
Broil'd entrails are their food, and beef's continued chine

But when the rage of hunger was repress'd,
Thus spoke Evander to his royal guest:
"These rites, these altars, and this feast, O king,
From no vain fears or superstition spring,
Or blind devotion, or from blinder chance,
Or heady zeal, or brutal ignorance;
But, sav'd from danger, with a grateful sense,
The labors of a god we recompense.
See, from afar, yon rock that mates the sky,
About whose feet such heaps of rubbish lie;
Such indigested ruin; bleak and bare,
How desart now it stands, expos'd in air!
'Twas once a robber's den, inclos'd around
With living stone, and deep beneath the ground.
The monster Cacus, more than half a beast,
This hold, impervious to the sun, possess'd.
The pavement ever foul with human gore;
Heads, and their mangled members, hung the door.
Vulcan this plague begot; and, like his sire,
Black clouds he belch'd, and flakes of livid fire.
Time, long expected, eas'd us of our load,
And brought the needful presence of a god.
Th' avenging force of Hercules, from Spain,
Arriv'd in triumph, from Geryon slain:

Thrice liv'd the giant, and thrice liv'd in vain.
His prize, the lowing herds, Alcides drove
Near Tiber's bank, to graze the shady grove.
Allur'd with hope of plunder, and intent
By force to rob, by fraud to circumvent,
The brutal Cacus, as by chance they stray'd,
Four oxen thence, and four fair kine, convey'd;
And, lest the printed footsteps might be seen,
He dragg'd 'em backwards to his rocky den.
The tracks averse a lying notice gave,
And led the searcher backward from the cave.

"Meantime the herdsman hero shifts his place,
To find fresh pasture and untrodden grass.
The beasts, who miss'd their mates, fill'd all around
With bellowings, and the rocks restor'd the sound.
One heifer, who had heard her love complain,
Roar'd from the cave, and made the project vain.
Alcides found the fraud; with rage he shook,
And toss'd about his head his knotted oak.
Swift as the winds, or Scythian arrows' flight,
He clomb, with eager haste, th' aërial height.
Then first we saw the monster mend his pace;
Fear in his eyes, and paleness in his face,
Confess'd the god's approach. Trembling he springs,
As terror had increas'd his feet with wings;
Nor stay'd for stairs; but down the depth he threw
His body, on his back the door he drew
(The door, a rib of living rock; with pains
His father hew'd it out, and bound with iron chains):
He broke the heavy links, the mountain clos'd,
And bars and levers to his foe oppos'd.
The wretch had hardly made his dungeon fast;
The fierce avenger came with bounding haste;
Survey'd the mouth of the forbidden hold,
And here and there his raging eyes he roll'd.
He gnash'd his teeth; and thrice he compass'd round
With winged speed the circuit of the ground.
Thrice at the cavern's mouth he pull'd in vain,
And, panting, thrice desisted from his pain.
A pointed flinty rock, all bare and black,

Grew gibbous from behind the mountain's back;
Owls, ravens, all ill omens of the night,
Here built their nests, and hither wing'd their flight.
The leaning head hung threat'ning o'er the flood,
And nodded to the left. The hero stood
Adverse, with planted feet, and, from the right,
Tugg'd at the solid stone with all his might.
Thus heav'd, the fix'd foundations of the rock
Gave way; heav'n echo'd at the rattling shock.
Tumbling, it chok'd the flood: on either side
The banks leap backward, and the streams divide;
The sky shrunk upward with unusual dread,
And trembling Tiber div'd beneath his bed.
The court of Cacus stands reveal'd to sight;
The cavern glares with new-admitted light.
So the pent vapors, with a rumbling sound,
Heave from below, and rend the hollow ground;
A sounding flaw succeeds; and, from on high,
The gods with hate beheld the nether sky:
The ghosts repine at violated night,
And curse th' invading sun, and sicken at the sight.
The graceless monster, caught in open day,
Inclos'd, and in despair to fly away,
Howls horrible from underneath, and fills
His hollow palace with unmanly yells.
The hero stands above, and from afar
Plies him with darts, and stones, and distant war.
He, from his nostrils and huge mouth, expires
Black clouds of smoke, amidst his father's fires,
Gath'ring, with each repeated blast, the night,
To make uncertain aim, and erring sight.
The wrathful god then plunges from above,
And, where in thickest waves the sparkles drove,
There lights; and wades thro' fumes, and gropes his way
Half sing'd, half stifled, till he grasps his prey.
The monster, spewing fruitless flames, he found;
He squeez'd his throat; he writh'd his neck around,
And in a knot his crippled members bound;
Then from their sockets tore his burning eyes:
Roll'd on a heap, the breathless robber lies.

The doors, unbarr'd, receive the rushing day,
And thoro' lights disclose the ravish'd prey.
The bulls, redeem'd, breathe open air again.
Next, by the feet, they drag him from his den.
The wond'ring neighborhood, with glad surprise,
Behold his shagged breast, his giant size,
His mouth that flames no more, and his extinguish'd eyes.
From that auspicious day, with rites divine,
We worship at the hero's holy shrine.
Potitius first ordain'd these annual vows:
As priests, were added the Pinarian house,
Who rais'd this altar in the sacred shade,
Where honors, ever due, for ever shall be paid.
For these deserts, and this high virtue shown,
Ye warlike youths, your heads with garlands crown:
Fill high the goblets with a sparkling flood,
And with deep draughts invoke our common god."

 This said, a double wreath Evander twin'd,
And poplars black and white his temples bind.
Then brims his ample bowl. With like design
The rest invoke the gods, with sprinkled wine.
Meantime the sun descended from the skies,
And the bright evening star began to rise.
And now the priests, Potitius at their head,
In skins of beasts involv'd, the long procession led;
Held high the flaming tapers in their hands,
As custom had prescrib'd their holy bands;
Then with a second course the tables load,
And with full chargers offer to the god.
The Salii sing, and cense his altars round
With Saban smoke, their heads with poplar bound—
One choir of old, another of the young,
To dance, and bear the burthen of the song.
The lay records the labors, and the praise,
And all th' immortal acts of Hercules:
First, how the mighty babe, when swath'd in bands,
The serpents strangled with his infant hands;
Then, as in years and matchless force he grew,
Th' Œchalian walls, and Trojan, overthrew.
Besides, a thousand hazards they relate,

Procur'd by Juno's and Eurystheus' hate:
"Thy hands, unconquer'd hero, could subdue
The cloud-born Centaurs, and the monster crew
Nor thy resistless arm the bull withstood,
Nor he, the roaring terror of the wood.
The triple porter of the Stygian seat,
With lolling tongue, lay fawning at thy feet,
And, seiz'd with fear, forgot his mangled meat.
Th' infernal waters trembled at thy sight;
Thee, god, no face of danger could affright;
Not huge Typhœus, nor th' unnumber'd snake,
Increas'd with hissing heads, in Lerna's lake.
Hail, Jove's undoubted son! an added grace
To heav'n and the great author of thy race!
Receive the grateful off'rings which we pay,
And smile propitious on thy solemn day!"
In numbers thus they sung; above the rest,
The den and death of Cacus crown the feast.
The woods to hollow vales convey the sound,
The vales to hills, and hills the notes rebound.
The rites perform'd, the cheerful train retire.

Betwixt young Pallas and his aged sire,
The Trojan pass'd, the city to survey,
And pleasing talk beguil'd the tedious way.
The stranger cast around his curious eyes,
New objects viewing still, with new surprise;
With greedy joy enquires of various things,
And acts and monuments of ancient kings.
Then thus the founder of the Roman tow'rs:
"These woods were first the seat of sylvan pow'rs,
Of Nymphs and Fauns, and salvage men, who took
Their birth from trunks of trees and stubborn oak.
Nor laws they knew, nor manners, nor the care
Of lab'ring oxen, or the shining share,
Nor arts of gain, nor what they gain'd to spare.
Their exercise the chase; the running flood
Supplied their thirst, the trees supplied their food.
Then Saturn came, who fled the pow'r of Jove,
Robb'd of his realms, and banish'd from above.
The men, dispers'd on hills, to towns he brought,

THE EIGHTH BOOK OF THE ÆNEIS

And laws ordain'd, and civil customs taught,
And Latium call'd the land where safe he lay
From his unduteous son, and his usurping sway.
With his mild empire, peace and plenty came;
And hence the golden times deriv'd their name.
A more degenerate and discolor'd age
Succeeded this, with avarice and rage.
Th' Ausonians then, and bold Sicanians came;
And Saturn's empire often chang'd the name.
Then kings, gigantic Tybris, and the rest,
With arbitrary sway the land oppress'd:
For Tiber's flood was Albula before,
Till, from the tyrant's fate, his name it bore.
I last arriv'd, driv'n from my native home
By fortune's pow'r, and fate's resistless doom.
Long toss'd on seas, I sought this happy land,
Warn'd by my mother nymph, and call'd by Heav'n's
    command."

  Thus, walking on, he spoke, and shew'd the gate,
Since call'd Carmental by the Roman state;
Where stood an altar, sacred to the name
Of old Carmenta, the prophetic dame,
Who to her son foretold th' Ænean race,
Sublime in fame, and Rome's imperial place:
Then shews the forest, which, in after times,
Fierce Romulus for perpetrated crimes
A sacred refuge made; with this, the shrine
Where Pan below the rock had rites divine:
Then tells of Argus' death, his murder'd guest,
Whose grave and tomb his innocence attest.
Thence, to the steep Tarpeian rock he leads;
Now roof'd with gold, then thatch'd with homely reeds.
A reverent fear (such superstition reigns
Among the rude) ev'n then possess'd the swains.
Some god, they knew—what god, they could not tell—
Did there amidst the sacred horror dwell.
Th' Arcadians thought him Jove; and said they saw
The mighty Thund'rer with majestic awe,
Who took his shield, and dealt his bolts around,
And scatter'd tempests on the teeming ground.

Then saw two heaps of ruins, (once they stood
Two stately towns, on either side the flood,)
Saturnia's and Janicula's remains;
And either place the founder's name retains.
Discoursing thus together, they resort
Where poor Evander kept his country court.
They view'd the ground of Rome's litigious hall;
(Once oxen low'd, where now the lawyers bawl;)
Then, stooping, thro' the narrow gate they press'd,
When thus the king bespoke his Trojan guest:
"Mean as it is, this palace, and this door,
Receiv'd Alcides, then a conqueror.
Dare to be poor; accept our homely food,
Which feasted him, and emulate a god."
Then underneath a lowly roof he led
The weary prince, and laid him on a bed;
The stuffing leaves, with hides of bears o'erspread.
Now Night had shed her silver dews around,
And with her sable wings embrac'd the ground,
When love's fair goddess, anxious for her son,
(New tumults rising, and new wars begun,)
Couch'd with her husband in his golden bed,
With these alluring words invokes his aid;
And, that her pleasing speech his mind may move,
Inspires each accent with the charms of love:
"While cruel fate conspir'd with Grecian pow'rs,
To level with the ground the Trojan tow'rs,
I ask'd not aid th' unhappy to restore,
Nor did the succor of thy skill implore;
Nor urg'd the labors of my lord in vain,
A sinking empire longer to sustain,
Tho' much I ow'd to Priam's house, and more
The dangers of Æneas did deplore.
But now, by Jove's command, and fate's decree,
His race is doom'd to reign in Italy:
With humble suit I beg thy needful art,
O still propitious pow'r, that rules my heart!
A mother kneels a suppliant for her son.
By Thetis and Aurora thou wert won
To forge impenetrable shields, and grace

THE EIGHTH BOOK OF THE ÆNEIS

With fated arms a less illustrious race.
Behold, what haughty nations are combin'd
Against the relics of the Phrygian kind,
With fire and sword my people to destroy,
And conquer Venus twice, in conqu'ring Troy."
She said; and straight her arms, of snowy hue,
About her unresolving husband threw.
Her soft embraces soon infuse desire;
His bones and marrow sudden warmth inspire;
And all the godhead feels the wonted fire.
Not half so swift the rattling thunder flies,
Or forky lightnings flash along the skies.
The goddess, proud of her successful wiles,
And conscious of her form, in secret smiles.

Then thus the pow'r, obnoxious to her charms,
Panting, and half dissolving in her arms:
"Why seek you reasons for a cause so just,
Or your own beauties or my love distrust?
Long since, had you requir'd my helpful hand,
Th' artificer and art you might command,
To labor arms for Troy: nor Jove, nor Fate,
Confin'd their empire to so short a date.
And, if you now desire new wars to wage,
My skill I promise, and my pains engage.
Whatever melting metals can conspire,
Or breathing bellows, or the forming fire,
Is freely yours: your anxious fears remove,
And think no task is difficult to love."
Trembling he spoke; and, eager of her charms,
He snatch'd the willing goddess to his arms;
Till, in her lap infus'd, he lay possess'd
Of full desire, and sunk to pleasing rest.
Now when the Night her middle race had rode,
And his first slumber had refresh'd the god—
The time when early housewives leave the bed;
When living embers on the hearth they spread,
Supply the lamp, and call the maids to rise—
With yawning mouths, and with half-open'd eyes,
They ply the distaff by the winking light,
And to their daily labor add the night:

Thus frugally they earn their children's bread,
And uncorrupted keep the nuptial bed—
Not less concern'd, nor at a later hour,
Rose from his downy couch the forging pow'r.

Sacred to Vulcan's name, an isle there lay,
Betwixt Sicilia's coasts and Lipare,
Rais'd high on smoking rocks; and, deep below,
In hollow caves the fires of Ætna glow.
The Cyclops here their heavy hammers deal;
Loud strokes, and hissings of tormented steel,
Are heard around; the boiling waters roar,
And smoky flames thro' fuming tunnels soar.
Hether the Father of the Fire, by night,
Thro' the brown air precipitates his flight.
On their eternal anvils here he found
The brethren beating, and the blows go round.
A load of pointless thunder now there lies
Before their hands, to ripen for the skies:
These darts, for angry Jove, they daily cast;
Consum'd on mortals with prodigious waste.
Three rays of writhen rain, of fire three more,
Of winged southern winds and cloudy store
As many parts, the dreadful mixture frame;
And fears are added, and avenging flame.
Inferior ministers, for Mars, repair
His broken axletrees and blunted war,
And send him forth again with furbish'd arms,
To wake the lazy war with trumpets' loud alarms.
The rest refresh the scaly snakes that fold
The shield of Pallas, and renew their gold.
Full on the crest the Gorgon's head they place,
With eyes that roll in death, and with distorted face.

"My sons," said Vulcan, "set your tasks aside;
Your strength and master-skill must now be tried.
Arms for a hero forge; arms that require
Your force, your speed, and all your forming fire."
He said. They set their former work aside,
And their new toils with eager haste divide.
A flood of molten silver, brass, and gold,
And deadly steel, in the large furnace roll'd;

THE EIGHTH BOOK OF THE ÆNEIS

Of this, their artful hands a shield prepare,
Alone sufficient to sustain the war.
Sev'n orbs within a spacious round they close:
One stirs the fire, and one the bellows blows.
The hissing steel is in the smithy drown'd;
The grot with beaten anvils groans around.
By turns their arms advance, in equal time;
By turns their hands descend, and hammers chime.
They turn the glowing mass with crooked tongs;
The fiery work proceeds, with rustic songs.

    While, at the Lemnian god's command, they urge
Their labors thus, and ply th' Æolian forge,
The cheerful morn salutes Evander's eyes,
And songs of chirping birds invite to rise.
He leaves his lowly bed: his buskins meet
Above his ankles; sandals sheathe his feet:
He sets his trusty sword upon his side,
And o'er his shoulder throws a panther's hide.
Two menial dogs before their master press'd.
Thus clad, and guarded thus, he seeks his kingly guest.
Mindful of promis'd aid, he mends his pace,
But meets Æneas in the middle space.
Young Pallas did his father's steps attend,
And true Achates waited on his friend.
They join their hands; a secret seat they choose;
Th' Arcadian first their former talk renews:
"Undaunted prince, I never can believe
The Trojan empire lost, while you survive.
Command th' assistance of a faithful friend;
But feeble are the succors I can send.
Our narrow kingdom here the Tiber bounds;
That other side the Latian state surrounds,
Insults our walls, and wastes our fruitful grounds.
But mighty nations I prepare, to join
Their arms with yours, and aid your just design.
You come, as by your better genius sent,
And fortune seems to favor your intent.
Not far from hence there stands a hilly town,
Of ancient building, and of high renown,
Torn from the Tuscans by the Lydian race,

Who gave the name of Cære to the place,
Once Agyllina call'd. It flourish'd long,
In pride of wealth and warlike people strong,
Till curs'd Mezentius, in a fatal hour,
Assum'd the crown, with arbitrary pow'r.
What words can paint those execrable times,
The subjects' suff'rings, and the tyrant's crimes!
That blood, those murthers, O ye gods, replace
On his own head, and on his impious race!
The living and the dead at his command
Were coupled, face to face, and hand to hand,
Till, chok'd with stench, in loath'd embraces tied,
The ling'ring wretches pin'd away and died.
Thus plung'd in ills, and meditating more—
The people's patience, tir'd, no longer bore
The raging monster; but with arms beset
His house, and vengeance and destruction threat.
They fire his palace: while the flame ascends,
They force his guards, and execute his friends.
He cleaves the crowd, and, favor'd by the night,
To Turnus' friendly court directs his flight.
By just revenge the Tuscans set on fire,
With arms, their king to punishment require:
Their num'rous troops, now muster'd on the strand,
My counsel shall submit to your command.
Their navy swarms upon the coasts; they cry
To hoist their anchors, but the gods deny.
An ancient augur, skill'd in future fate,
With these foreboding words restrains their hate:
'Ye brave in arms, ye Lydian blood, the flow'r
Of Tuscan youth, and choice of all their pow'r,
Whom just revenge against Mezentius arms,
To seek your tyrant's death by lawful arms;
Know this: no native of our land may lead
This pow'rful people; seek a foreign head.'
Aw'd with these words, in camps they still abide,
And wait with longing looks their promis'd guide.
Tarchon, the Tuscan chief, to me has sent
Their crown, and ev'ry regal ornament:
The people join their own with his desire;

And all my conduct, as their king, require.
But the chill blood that creeps within my veins,
And age, and listless limbs unfit for pains,
And a soul conscious of its own decay,
Have forc'd me to refuse imperial sway.
My Pallas were more fit to mount the throne,
And should, but he's a Sabine mother's son,
And half a native; but, in you, combine
A manly vigor, and a foreign line.
Where Fate and smiling Fortune shew the way,
Pursue the ready path to sov'reign sway.
The staff of my declining days, my son,
Shall make your good or ill success his own;
In fighting fields from you shall learn to dare,
And serve the hard apprenticeship of war;
Your matchless courage and your conduct view,
And early shall begin t' admire and copy you.
Besides, two hundred horse he shall command;
Tho' few, a warlike and well-chosen band.
These in my name are listed; and my son
As many more has added in his own."

  Scarce had he said; Achates and his guest,
With downcast eyes, their silent grief express'd;
Who, short of succors, and in deep despair,
Shook at the dismal prospect of the war.
But his bright mother, from a breaking cloud,
To cheer her issue, thunder'd thrice aloud;
Thrice forky lightning flash'd along the sky,
And Tyrrhene trumpets thrice were heard on high.
Then, gazing up, repeated peals they hear;
And, in a heav'n serene, refulgent arms appear:
Redd'ning the skies, and glitt'ring all around,
The temper'd metals clash, and yield a silver sound.
The rest stood trembling, struck with awe divine;
Æneas only, conscious to the sign,
Presag'd th' event, and joyful view'd, above,
Th' accomplish'd promise of the Queen of Love.
Then, to th' Arcadian king: "This prodigy
(Dismiss your fear) belongs alone to me.
Heav'n calls me to the war: th' expected sign

Is giv'n of promis'd aid, and arms divine.
My goddess mother, whose indulgent care
Foresaw the dangers of the growing war,
This omen gave, when bright Vulcanian arms,
Fated from force of steel by Stygian charms,
Suspended, shone on high: she then foreshow'd
Approaching fights, and fields to float in blood.
Turnus shall dearly pay for faith forsworn;
And corps, and swords, and shields, on Tiber borne,
Shall choke his flood: now sound the loud alarms;
And, Latian troops, prepare your perjur'd arms."

He said, and, rising from his homely throne,
The solemn rites of Hercules begun,
And on his altars wak'd the sleeping fires;
Then cheerful to his household gods retires;
There offers chosen sheep. Th' Arcadian king
And Trojan youth the same oblations bring.
Next, of his men and ships he makes review;
Draws out the best and ablest of the crew.
Down with the falling stream the refuse run,
To raise with joyful news his drooping son.
Steeds are prepar'd to mount the Trojan band,
Who wait their leader to the Tyrrhene land.
A sprightly courser, fairer than the rest,
The king himself presents his royal guest:
A lion's hide his back and limbs infold,
Precious with studded work, and paws of gold.
Fame thro' the little city spreads aloud
Th' intended march, amid the fearful crowd:
The matrons beat their breasts, dissolve in tears,
And double their devotion in their fears.
The war at hand appears with more affright,
And rises ev'ry moment to the sight.

Then old Evander, with a close embrace,
Strain'd his departing friend; and tears o'erflow his face.
"Would Heav'n," said he, "my strength and youth recall,
Such as I was beneath Præneste's wall;
Then when I made the foremost foes retire,
And set whole heaps of conquer'd shields on fire;
When Herilus in single fight I slew,

Whom with three lives Feronia did endue;
And thrice I sent him to the Stygian shore,
Till the last ebbing soul return'd no more—
Such if I stood renew'd, not these alarms,
Nor death, should rend me from my Pallas' arms;
Nor proud Mezentius, thus unpunish'd, boast
His rapes and murthers on the Tuscan coast.
Ye gods, and mighty Jove, in pity bring
Relief, and hear a father and a king!
If fate and you reserve these eyes, to see
My son return with peace and victory;
If the lov'd boy shall bless his father's sight;
If we shall meet again with more delight;
Then draw my life in length; let me sustain,
In hopes of his embrace, the worst of pain.
But if your hard decrees—which, O! I dread—
Have doom'd to death his undeserving head;
This, O this very moment, let me die!
While hopes and fears in equal balance lie;
While, yet possess'd of all his youthful charms,
I strain him close within these aged arms;
Before that fatal news my soul shall wound!"
He said, and, swooning, sunk upon the ground.
His servants bore him off, and softly laid
His languish'd limbs upon his homely bed.

The horsemen march; the gates are open'd wide;
Æneas at their head, Achates by his side.
Next these, the Trojan leaders rode along;
Last follows in the rear th' Arcadian throng.
Young Pallas shone conspicuous o'er the rest;
Gilded his arms, embroider'd was his vest.
So, from the seas, exerts his radiant head
The star by whom the lights of heav'n are led;
Shakes from his rosy locks the pearly dews,
Dispels the darkness, and the day renews.
The trembling wives the walls and turrets crowd,
And follow, with their eyes, the dusty cloud,
Which winds disperse by fits, and shew from far
The blaze of arms, and shields, and shining war.
The troops, drawn up in beautiful array,

O'er heathy plains pursue the ready way.
Repeated peals of shouts are heard around;
The neighing coursers answer to the sound,
And shake with horny hoofs the solid ground.

A greenwood shade, for long religion known,
Stands by the streams that wash the Tuscan town
Incompass'd round with gloomy hills above,
Which add a holy horror to the grove.
The first inhabitants of Grecian blood,
That sacred forest to Silvanus vow'd,
The guardian of their flocks and fields; and pay
Their due devotions on his annual day.
Not far from hence, along the river's side,
In tents secure, the Tuscan troops abide,
By Tarchon led. Now, from a rising ground,
Æneas cast his wond'ring eyes around,
And all the Tyrrhene army had in sight,
Stretch'd on the spacious plain from left to right.
Thether his warlike train the Trojan led,
Refresh'd his men, and wearied horses fed.

Meantime the mother-goddess, crown'd with charms,
Breaks thro' the clouds, and brings the fated arms.
Within a winding vale she finds her son,
On the cool river's banks, retir'd alone.
She shews her heav'nly form without disguise,
And gives herself to his desiring eyes.
"Behold," she said, "perform'd in ev'ry part,
My promise made, and Vulcan's labor'd art.
Now seek, secure, the Latian enemy,
And haughty Turnus to the field defy."
She said; and, having first her son embrac'd,
The radiant arms beneath an oak she plac'd,
Proud of the gift, he roll'd his greedy sight
Around the work, and gaz'd with vast delight.
He lifts, he turns, he poises, and admires
The crested helm, that vomits radiant fires:
His hands the fatal sword and corslet hold,
One keen with temper'd steel, one stiff with gold:
Both ample, flaming both, and beamy bright;
So shines a cloud, when edg'd with adverse light.

He shakes the pointed spear, and longs to try
The plated cuishes on his manly thigh;
But most admires the shield's mysterious mold,
And Roman triumphs rising on the gold:
For these, emboss'd, the heav'nly smith had wrought
(Not in the rolls of future fate untaught)
The wars in order, and the race divine
Of warriors issuing from the Julian line.
The cave of Mars was dress'd with mossy greens:
There, by the wolf, were laid the martial twins.
Intrepid on her swelling dugs they hung;
The foster dam loll'd out her fawning tongue:
They suck'd secure, while, bending back her head,
She lick'd their tender limbs, and form'd them as they fed.
Not far from thence new Rome appears, with games
Projected for the rape of Sabine dames.
The pit resounds with shrieks; a war succeeds,
For breach of public faith, and unexampled deeds.
Here for revenge the Sabine troops contend;
The Romans there with arms the prey defend.
Wearied with tedious war, at length they cease;
And both the kings and kingdoms plight the peace.
The friendly chiefs before Jove's altar stand,
Both arm'd, with each a charger in his hand:
A fatted sow for sacrifice is led,
With imprecations on the perjur'd head.
Near this, the traitor Metius, stretch'd between
Four fiery steeds, is dragg'd along the green,
By Tullus' doom: the brambles drink his blood,
And his torn limbs are left the vulture's food.
There, Porsena to Rome proud Tarquin brings,
And would by force restore the banish'd kings.
One tyrant for his fellow-tyrant fights;
The Roman youth assert their native rights.
Before the town the Tuscan army lies,
To win by famine, or by fraud surprise.
Their king, half-threat'ning, half-disdaining stood,
While Cocles broke the bridge, and stemm'd the flood.
The captive maids there tempt the raging tide,
Scap'd from their chains, with Clœlia for their guide.

High on a rock heroic Manlius stood,
To guard the temple, and the temple's god.
Then Rome was poor; and there you might behold
The palace thatch'd with straw, now roof'd with gold.
The silver goose before the shining gate
There flew, and, by her cackle, sav'd the state.
She told the Gauls' approach; th' approaching Gauls,
Obscure in night, ascend, and seize the walls.
The gold dissembled well their yellow hair,
And golden chains on their white necks they wear.
Gold are their vests; long Alpine spears they wield,
And their left arm sustains a length of shield.
Hard by, the leaping Salian priests advance;
And naked thro' the streets the mad Luperci dance,
In caps of wool; the targets dropp'd from heav'n.
Here modest matrons, in soft litters driv'n,
To pay their vows in solemn pomp appear,
And odorous gums in their chaste hands they bear.
Far hence remov'd, the Stygian seats are seen;
Pains of the damn'd, and punish'd Catiline
Hung on a rock—the traitor; and, around,
The Furies hissing from the nether ground.
Apart from these, the happy souls he draws,
And Cato's holy ghost dispensing laws.

Betwixt the quarters flows a golden sea;
But foaming surges there in silver play.
The dancing dolphins with their tails divide
The glitt'ring waves, and cut the precious tide.
Amid the main, two mighty fleets engage
Their brazen beaks, oppos'd with equal rage.
Actium surveys the well-disputed prize;
Leucate's wat'ry plain with foamy billows fries.
Young Cæsar, on the stern, in armor bright,
Here leads the Romans and their gods to fight:
His beamy temples shoot their flames afar,
And o'er his head is hung the Julian star.
Agrippa seconds him, with prosp'rous gales,
And, with propitious gods, his foes assails:
A naval crown, that binds his manly brows,
The happy fortune of the fight foreshows.

Rang'd on the line oppos'd, Antonius brings
Barbarian aids, and troops of Eastern kings;
Th' Arabians near, and Bactrians from afar,
Of tongues discordant, and a mingled war:
And, rich in gaudy robes, amidst the strife,
His ill fate follows him—th' Egyptian wife.
Moving they fight; with oars and forky prows
The froth is gather'd, and the water glows.
It seems, as if the Cyclades again
Were rooted up, and justled in the main;
Or floating mountains floating mountains meet;
Such is the fierce encounter of the fleet.
Fireballs are thrown, and pointed jav'lins fly;
The fields of Neptune take a purple dye.
The queen herself, amidst the loud alarms,
With cymbals toss'd her fainting soldiers warms—
Fool as she was! who had not yet divin'd
Her cruel fate, nor saw the snakes behind.
Her country gods, the monsters of the sky,
Great Neptune, Pallas, and Love's Queen defy:
The dog Anubis barks, but barks in vain,
Nor longer dares oppose th' ethereal train.
Mars in the middle of the shining shield
Is grav'd, and strides along the liquid field.
The Diræ souse from heav'n with swift descent;
And Discord, dyed in blood, with garments rent,
Divides the prease: her steps Bellona treads,
And shakes her iron rod above their heads.
This seen, Apollo, from his Actian height,
Pours down his arrows; at whose winged flight
The trembling Indians and Egyptians yield,
And soft Sabæans quit the wat'ry field.
The fatal mistress hoists her silken sails,
And, shrinking from the fight, invokes the gales.
Aghast she looks, and heaves her breast for breath,
Panting, and pale with fear of future death.
The god had figur'd her as driv'n along
By winds and waves, and scudding thro' the throng.
Just opposite, sad Nilus opens wide
His arms and ample bosom to the tide,

And spreads his mantle o'er the winding coast,
In which he wraps his queen, and hides the flying host.
The victor to the gods his thanks express'd,
And Rome, triumphant, with his presence bless'd.
Three hundred temples in the town he plac'd;
With spoils and altars ev'ry temple grac'd.
Three shining nights, and three succeeding days,
The fields resound with shouts, the streets with praise,
The domes with songs, the theaters with plays.
All altars flame: before each altar lies,
Drench'd in his gore, the destin'd sacrifice.
Great Cæsar sits sublime upon his throne,
Before Apollo's porch of Parian stone;
Accepts the presents vow'd for victory,
And hangs the monumental crowns on high.
Vast crowds of vanquish'd nations march along,
Various in arms, in habit, and in tongue.
Here, Mulciber assigns the proper place
For Carians, and th' ungirt Numidian race;
Then ranks the Thracians in the second row,
With Scythians, expert in the dart and bow.
And here the tam'd Euphrates humbly glides,
And there the Rhine submits her swelling tides,
And proud Araxes, whom no bridge could bind;
The Danes' unconquer'd offspring march behind,
And Morini, the last of human-kind.

   These figures, on the shield divinely wrought,
By Vulcan labor'd, and by Venus brought,
With joy and wonder fill the hero's thought.
Unknown the names, he yet admires the grace,
And bears aloft the fame and fortune of his race.

THE NINTH BOOK
OF THE ÆNEIS

THE ARGUMENT.—Turnus takes advantage of Æneas's absence, fires some of his ips (which are transformed into sea nymphs), and assaults his camp. The Trojans, luc'd to the last extremities, send Nisus and Euryalus to recall Æneas; which fur- shes the poet with that admirable episode of their friendship, generosity, and the nclusion of their adventures.

WHILE these affairs in distant places pass'd,
The various Iris Juno sends with haste,
To find bold Turnus, who, with anxious thought,
The secret shade of his great grandsire sought.
Retir'd alone she found the daring man,
And op'd her rosy lips, and thus began:
"What none of all the gods could grant thy vows,
That, Turnus, this auspicious day bestows.
Æneas, gone to seek th' Arcadian prince,
Has left the Trojan camp without defense;
And, short of succors there, employs his pains
In parts remote to raise the Tuscan swains.
Now snatch an hour that favors thy designs;
Unite thy forces, and attack their lines."
This said, on equal wings she pois'd her weight,
And form'd a radiant rainbow in her flight.

The Daunian hero lifts his hands and eyes,
And thus invokes the goddess as she flies:
"Iris, the grace of heav'n, what pow'r divine
Has sent thee down, thro' dusky clouds to shine?
See, they divide; immortal day appears,
And glitt'ring planets dancing in their spheres!
With joy, these happy omens I obey,
And follow to the war the god that leads the way."
Thus having said, as by the brook he stood,
He scoop'd the water from the crystal flood;
Then with his hands the drops to heav'n he throws,
And loads the pow'rs above with offer'd vows.

Now march the bold confed'rates thro' the plain,
Well hors'd, well clad; a rich and shining train.
Messapus leads the van; and, in the rear,
The sons of Tyrrheus in bright arms appear.
In the main battle, with his flaming crest,
The mighty Turnus tow'rs above the rest.
Silent they move, majestically slow,
Like ebbing Nile, or Ganges in his flow.
The Trojans view the dusty cloud from far,
And the dark menace of the distant war.
Caïcus from the rampire saw it rise,
Black'ning the fields, and thick'ning thro' the skies.
Then to his fellows thus aloud he calls:
"What rolling clouds, my friends, approach the walls?
Arm! arm! and man the works! prepare your spears
And pointed darts! the Latian host appears."

Thus warn'd, they shut their gates; with shouts ascend
The bulwarks, and, secure, their foes attend:
For their wise gen'ral, with foreseeing care,
Had charg'd them not to tempt the doubtful war,
Nor, tho' provok'd, in open fields advance,
But close within their lines attend their chance.
Unwilling, yet they keep the strict command,
And sourly wait in arms the hostile band.
The fiery Turnus flew before the rest:
A piebald steed of Thracian strain he press'd;
His helm of massy gold, and crimson was his crest.
With twenty horse to second his designs,
An unexpected foe, he fac'd the lines.
"Is there," he said, "in arms, who bravely dare
His leader's honor and his danger share?"
Then spurring on, his brandish'd dart he threw,
In sign of war: applauding shouts ensue.

Amaz'd to find a dastard race, that run
Behind the rampires and the battle shun,
He rides around the camp, with rolling eyes,
And stops at ev'ry post, and ev'ry passage tries.
So roams the nightly wolf about the fold:
Wet with descending show'rs, and stiff with cold,
He howls for hunger, and he grins for pain,

(His gnashing teeth are exercis'd in vain,)
And, impotent of anger, finds no way
In his distended paws to grasp the prey.
The mothers listen; but the bleating lambs
Securely swig the dug, beneath the dams.
Thus ranges eager Turnus o'er the plain.
Sharp with desire, and furious with disdain;
Surveys each passage with a piercing sight,
To force his foes in equal field to fight.
Thus while he gazes round, at length he spies,
Where, fenc'd with strong redoubts, their navy lies,
Close underneath the walls; the washing tide
Secures from all approach this weaker side.
He takes the wish'd occasion, fills his hand
With ready fires, and shakes a flaming brand.
Urg'd by his presence, ev'ry soul is warm'd,
And ev'ry hand with kindled firs is arm'd.
From the fir'd pines the scatt'ring sparkles fly;
Fat vapors, mix'd with flames, involve the sky.
What pow'r, O Muses, could avert the flame
Which threaten'd, in the fleet, the Trojan name?
Tell: for the fact, thro' length of time obscure,
Is hard to faith; yet shall the fame endure.

'Tis said that, when the chief prepar'd his flight,
And fell'd his timber from Mount Ida's height,
The grandam goddess then approach'd her son,
And with a mother's majesty begun:
"Grant me," she said, "the sole request I bring,
Since conquer'd heav'n has own'd you for its king.
On Ida's brows, for ages past, there stood,
With firs and maples fill'd, a shady wood;
And on the summit rose a sacred grove,
Where I was worship'd with religious love.
Those woods, that holy grove, my long delight,
I gave the Trojan prince, to speed his flight.
Now, fill'd with fear, on their behalf I come;
Let neither winds o'erset, nor waves intomb
The floating forests of the sacred pine;
But let it be their safety to be mine."
Then thus replied her awful son, who rolls

The radiant stars, and heav'n and earth controls:
"How dare you, mother, endless date demand
For vessels molded by a mortal hand?
What then is fate? Shall bold Æneas ride,
Of safety certain, on th' uncertain tide?
Yet, what I can, I grant; when, wafted o'er,
The chief is landed on the Latian shore,
Whatever ships escape the raging storms,
At my command shall change their fading forms
To nymphs divine, and plow the wat'ry way,
Like Dotis and the daughters of the sea."
To seal his sacred vow, by Styx he swore,
The lake of liquid pitch, the dreary shore,
And Phlegethon's innavigable flood,
And the black regions of his brother god.
He said; and shook the skies with his imperial nod.

And now at length the number'd hours were come,
Prefix'd by fate's irrevocable doom,
When the great Mother of the Gods was free
To save her ships, and finish Jove's decree.
First, from the quarter of the morn, there sprung
A light that sign'd the heav'ns, and shot along;
Then from a cloud, fring'd round with golden fires,
Were timbrels heard, and Berecynthian choirs;
And, last, a voice, with more than mortal sounds,
Both hosts, in arms oppos'd, with equal horror wounds:
"O Trojan race, your needless aid forbear,
And know, my ships are my peculiar care.
With greater ease the bold Rutulian may,
With hissing brands, attempt to burn the sea,
Than singe my sacred pines. But you, my charge,
Loos'd from your crooked anchors, launch at large,
Exalted each a nymph: forsake the sand,
And swim the seas, at Cybele's command."
No sooner had the goddess ceas'd to speak,
When, lo! th' obedient ships their haulsers break;
And, strange to tell, like dolphins, in the main
They plunge their prows, and dive, and spring again:
As many beauteous maids the billows sweep,
As rode before tall vessels on the deep.

THE NINTH BOOK OF THE ÆNEIS

The foes, surpris'd with wonder, stood aghast;
Messapus curb'd his fiery courser's haste;
Old Tiber roar'd, and, raising up his head,
Call'd back his waters to their oozy bed.
Turnus alone, undaunted, bore the shock,
And with these words his trembling troops bespoke:
"These monsters for the Trojans' fate are meant,
And are by Jove for black presages sent.
He takes the cowards' last relief away;
For fly they cannot, and, constrain'd to stay,
Must yield unfought, a base inglorious prey.
The liquid half of all the globe is lost;
Heav'n shuts the seas, and we secure the coast.
Theirs is no more than that small spot of ground
Which myriads of our martial men surround.
Their fates I fear not, or vain oracles.
'Twas giv'n to Venus they should cross the seas,
And land secure upon the Latian plains:
Their promis'd hour is pass'd, and mine remains.
'Tis in the fate of Turnus to destroy,
With sword and fire, the faithless race of Troy.
Shall such affronts as these alone inflame
The Grecian brothers, and the Grecian name?
My cause and theirs is one; a fatal strife,
And final ruin, for a ravish'd wife.
Was 't not enough, that, punish'd for the crime,
They fell; but will they fall a second time?
One would have thought they paid enough before,
To curse the costly sex, and durst offend no more.
Can they securely trust their feeble wall,
A slight partition, a thin interval,
Betwixt their fate and them; when Troy, tho' built
By hands divine, yet perish'd by their guilt?
Lend me, for once, my friends, your valiant hands,
To force from out their lines these dastard bands.
Less than a thousand ships will end this war,
Nor Vulcan needs his fated arms prepare.
Let all the Tuscans, all th' Arcadians, join!
Nor these, nor those, shall frustrate my design.
Let them not fear the treasons of the night,

The robb'd Palladium, the pretended flight:
Our onset shall be made in open light.
No wooden engine shall their town betray;
Fires they shall have around, but fires by day.
No Grecian babes before their camp appear,
Whom Hector's arms detain'd to the tenth tardy year.
Now, since the sun is rolling to the west,
Give we the silent night to needful rest:
Refresh your bodies, and your arms prepare;
The morn shall end the small remains of war."

The post of honor to Messapus falls,
To keep the nightly guard, to watch the walls,
To pitch the fires at distances around,
And close the Trojans in their scanty ground.
Twice seven Rutulian captains ready stand,
And twice seven hundred horse these chiefs command;
All clad in shining arms the works invest,
Each with a radiant helm and waving crest.
Stretch'd at their length, they press the grassy ground;
They laugh, they sing, (the jolly bowls go round,)
With lights and cheerful fires renew the day,
And pass the wakeful night in feasts and play.

The Trojans, from above, their foes beheld,
And with arm'd legions all the rampires fill'd.
Seiz'd with affright, their gates they first explore;
Join works to works with bridges, tow'r to tow'r:
Thus all things needful for defense abound.
Mnestheus and brave Seresthus walk the round,
Commission'd by their absent prince to share
The common danger, and divide the care.
The soldiers draw their lots, and, as they fall,
By turns relieve each other on the wall.

Nigh where the foes their utmost guards advance,
To watch the gate was warlike Nisus' chance.
His father Hyrtacus of noble blood;
His mother was a huntress of the wood,
And sent him to the wars. Well could he bear
His lance in fight, and dart the flying spear,
But better skill'd unerring shafts to send.
Beside him stood Euryalus, his friend:

Euryalus, than whom the Trojan host
No fairer face, or sweeter air, could boast—
Scarce had the down to shade his cheeks begun.
One was their care, and their delight was one:
One common hazard in the war they shar'd,
And now were both by choice upon the guard.

Then Nisus thus: "Or do the gods inspire
This warmth, or make we gods of our desire?
A gen'rous ardor boils within my breast,
Eager of action, enemy to rest:
This urges me to fight, and fires my mind
To leave a memorable name behind.
Thou see'st the foe secure; how faintly shine
Their scatter'd fires! the most, in sleep supine
Along the ground, an easy conquest lie:
The wakeful few the fuming flagon ply;
All hush'd around. Now hear what I revolve—
A thought unripe—and scarcely yet resolve.
Our absent prince both camp and council mourn;
By message both would hasten his return:
If they confer what I demand on thee,
(For fame is recompense enough for me,)
Methinks, beneath yon hill, I have espied
A way that safely will my passage guide."

Euryalus stood list'ning while he spoke,
With love of praise and noble envy struck;
Then to his ardent friend expos'd his mind:
"All this, alone, and leaving me behind!
Am I unworthy, Nisus, to be join'd?
Think'st thou I can my share of glory yield,
Or send thee unassisted to the field?
Not so my father taught my childhood arms;
Born in a siege, and bred among alarms!
Nor is my youth unworthy of my friend,
Nor of the heav'n-born hero I attend.
The thing call'd life, with ease I can disclaim,
And think it over-sold to purchase fame."

Then Nisus thus: "Alas! thy tender years
Would minister new matter to my fears.
So may the gods, who view this friendly strife,

Restore me to thy lov'd embrace with life,
Condemn'd to pay my vows, (as sure I trust,)
This thy request is cruel and unjust.
But if some chance—as many chances are,
And doubtful hazards, in the deeds of war—
If one should reach my head, there let it fall,
And spare thy life; I would not perish all.
Thy bloomy youth deserves a longer date:
Live thou to mourn thy love's unhappy fate;
To bear my mangled body from the foe,
Or buy it back, and fun'ral rites bestow.
Or, if hard fortune shall those dues deny,
Thou canst at least an empty tomb supply.
O let not me the widow's tears renew!
Nor let a mother's curse my name pursue:
Thy pious parent, who, for love of thee,
Forsook the coasts of friendly Sicily,
Her age committing to the seas and wind,
When ev'ry weary matron stay'd behind."
To this, Euryalus: "You plead in vain,
And but protract the cause you cannot gain.
No more delays, but haste!" With that, he wakes
The nodding watch; each to his office takes.
The guard reliev'd, the gen'rous couple went
To find the council at the royal tent.

All creatures else forgot their daily care,
And sleep, the common gift of nature, share;
Except the Trojan peers, who wakeful sate
In nightly council for th' indanger'd state.
They vote a message to their absent chief,
Shew their distress, and beg a swift relief.
Amid the camp a silent seat they chose,
Remote from clamor, and secure from foes.
On their left arms their ample shields they bear,
The right reclin'd upon the bending spear.
Now Nisus and his friend approach the guard,
And beg admission, eager to be heard:
Th' affair important, not to be deferr'd.
Ascanius bids 'em be conducted in,
Ord'ring the more experienc'd to begin.

THE NINTH BOOK OF THE ÆNEIS

Then Nisus thus: "Ye fathers, lend your ears;
Nor judge our bold attempt beyond our years.
The foe, securely drench'd in sleep and wine,
Neglect their watch; the fires but thinly shine;
And where the smoke in cloudy vapors flies,
Cov'ring the plain, and curling to the skies,
Betwixt two paths, which at the gate divide,
Close by the sea, a passage we have spied,
Which will our way to great Æneas guide.
Expect each hour to see him safe again,
Loaded with spoils of foes in battle slain.
Snatch we the lucky minute while we may;
Nor can we be mistaken in the way;
For, hunting in the vale, we both have seen
The rising turrets, and the stream between,
And know the winding course, with ev'ry ford."

He ceas'd; and old Alethes took the word:
"Our country gods, in whom our trust we place,
Will yet from ruin save the Trojan race,
While we behold such dauntless worth appear
In dawning youth, and souls so void of fear."
Then into tears of joy the father broke;
Each in his longing arms by turns he took;
Panted and paus'd; and thus again he spoke:
"Ye brave young men, what equal gifts can we,
In recompense of such desert, decree?
The greatest, sure, and best you can receive,
The gods and your own conscious worth will give.
The rest our grateful gen'ral will bestow,
And young Ascanius till his manhood owe."

"And I, whose welfare in my father lies,"
Ascanius adds, "by the great deities,
By my dear country, by my household gods,
By hoary Vesta's rites and dark abodes,
Adjure you both, (on you my fortune stands;
That and my faith I plight into your hands,)
Make me but happy in his safe return,
Whose wanted presence I can only mourn;
Your common gift shall two large goblets be
Of silver, wrought with curious imagery,

And high emboss'd, which, when old Priam reign'd,
My conqu'ring sire at sack'd Arisba gain'd;
And more, two tripods cast in antic mold,
With two great talents of the finest gold;
Beside a costly bowl, ingrav'd with art,
Which Dido gave, when first she gave her heart.
But, if in conquer'd Italy we reign,
When spoils by lot the victor shall obtain—
Thou saw'st the courser by proud Turnus press'd:
That, Nisus, and his arms, and nodding crest,
And shield, from chance exempt, shall be thy share:
Twelve lab'ring slaves, twelve handmaids young and fair,
All clad in rich attire, and train'd with care;
And, last, a Latian field with fruitful plains,
And a large portion of the king's domains.
But thou, whose years are more to mine allied—
No fate my vow'd affection shall divide
From thee, heroic youth! Be wholly mine;
Take full possession; all my soul is thine.
One faith, one fame, one fate, shall both attend;
My life's companion, and my bosom friend:
My peace shall be committed to thy care,
And to thy conduct my concerns in war."

Then thus the young Euryalus replied:
"Whatever fortune, good or bad, betide,
The same shall be my age, as now my youth;
No time shall find me wanting to my truth.
This only from your goodness let me gain
(And, this ungranted, all rewards are vain):
Of Priam's royal race my mother came—
And sure the best that ever bore the name—
Whom neither Troy nor Sicily could hold
From me departing, but, o'erspent and old,
My fate she follow'd. Ignorant of this
(Whatever) danger, neither parting kiss,
Nor pious blessing taken, her I leave,
And in this only act of all my life deceive.
By this right hand and conscious Night I swear,
My soul so sad a farewell could not bear.
Be you her comfort; fill my vacant place

THE NINTH BOOK OF THE ÆNEIS

(Permit me to presume so great a grace);
Support her age, forsaken and distress'd.
That hope alone will fortify my breast
Against the worst of fortunes, and of fears."
He said. The mov'd assistants melt in tears.

Then thus Ascanius, wonderstruck to see
That image of his filial piety:
"So great beginnings, in so green an age,
Exact the faith which I again ingage.
Thy mother all the dues shall justly claim,
Creüsa had, and only want the name.
Whate'er event thy bold attempt shall have,
'Tis merit to have borne a son so brave.
Now by my head, a sacred oath, I swear,
(My father us'd it,) what, returning here
Crown'd with success, I for thyself prepare,
That, if thou fail, shall thy lov'd mother share."

He said, and weeping, while he spoke the word,
From his broad belt he drew a shining sword,
Magnificent with gold. Lycaon made,
And in an iv'ry scabbard sheath'd the blade.
This was his gift. Great Mnestheus gave his friend
A lion's hide, his body to defend;
And good Alethes furnish'd him, beside,
With his own trusty helm, of temper tried.

Thus arm'd they went. The noble Trojans wait
Their issuing forth, and follow to the gate
With prayers and vows. Above the rest appears
Ascanius, manly far beyond his years,
And messages committed to their care,
Which all in winds were lost, and flitting air.

The trenches first they pass'd; then took their way
Where their proud foes in pitch'd pavilions lay;
To many fatal, ere themselves were slain.
They found the careless host dispers'd upon the plain,
Who, gorg'd, and drunk with wine, supinely snore.
Unharnass'd chariots stand along the shore:
Amidst the wheels and reins, the goblet by,
A medley of debauch and war, they lie.
Observing Nisus shew'd his friend the sight:

"Behold a conquest gain'd without a fight.
Occasion offers, and I stand prepar'd;
There lies our way; be thou upon the guard,
And look around, while I securely go,
And hew a passage thro' the sleeping foe."
Softly he spoke; then striding took his way,
With his drawn sword, where haughty Rhamnes lay;
His head rais'd high on tapestry beneath,
And heaving from his breast, he drew his breath;
A king and prophet, by King Turnus lov'd:
But fate by prescience cannot be remov'd.
Him and his sleeping slaves he slew; then spies
Where Remus, with his rich retinue, lies.
His armor-bearer first, and next he kills
His charioteer, intrench'd betwixt the wheels
And his lov'd horses; last invades their lord;
Full on his neck he drives the fatal sword:
The gasping head flies off; a purple flood
Flows from the trunk, that welters in the blood,
Which, by the spurning heels dispers'd around,
The bed besprinkles and bedews the ground.
Lamus the bold, and Lamyrus the strong,
He slew, and then Serranus fair and young.
From dice and wine the youth retir'd to rest,
And puff'd the fumy god from out his breast:
Ev'n then he dreamt of drink and lucky play—
More lucky, had it lasted till the day.
The famish'd lion thus, with hunger bold,
O'erleaps the fences of the nightly fold,
And tears the peaceful flocks: with silent awe
Trembling they lie, and pant beneath his paw.

  Nor with less rage Euryalus employs
The wrathful sword, or fewer foes destroys;
But on th' ignoble crowd his fury flew;
He Fadus, Hebesus, and Rhœtus slew.
Oppress'd with heavy sleep the former fall,
But Rhœtus wakeful, and observing all:
Behind a spacious jar he slink'd for fear;
The fatal iron found and reach'd him there;
For, as he rose, it pierc'd his naked side,

THE NINTH BOOK OF THE ÆNEIS

And, reeking, thence return'd in crimson dyed.
The wound pours out a stream of wine and blood;
The purple soul comes floating in the flood.
  Now, where Messapus quarter'd, they arrive.
The fires were fainting there, and just alive;
The warrior-horses, tied in order, fed.
Nisus observ'd the discipline, and said:
"Our eager thirst of blood may both betray;
And see the scatter'd streaks of dawning day,
Foe to nocturnal thefts. No more, my friend;
Here let our glutted execution end.
A lane thro' slaughter'd bodies we have made."
The bold Euryalus, tho' loth, obey'd.
Of arms, and arras, and of plate, they find
A precious load; but these they leave behind.
Yet, fond of gaudy spoils, the boy would stay
To make the rich caparison his prey,
Which on the steed of conquer'd Rhamnes lay.
Nor did his eyes less longingly behold
The girdle-belt, with nails of burnish'd gold.
This present Cædicus the rich bestow'd
On Remulus, when friendship first they vow'd,
And, absent, join'd in hospitable ties:
He, dying, to his heir bequeath'd the prize;
Till, by the conqu'ring Ardean troops oppress'd,
He fell; and they the glorious gift possess'd.
These glitt'ring spoils (now made the victor's gain)
He to his body suits, but suits in vain:
Messapus' helm he finds among the rest,
And laces on, and wears the waving crest.
Proud of their conquest, prouder of their prey,
They leave the camp, and take the ready way.
  But far they had not pass'd, before they spied
Three hundred horse, with Volscens for their guide.
The queen a legion to King Turnus sent;
But the swift horse the slower foot prevent,
And now, advancing, sought the leader's tent.
They saw the pair; for, thro' the doubtful shade,
His shining helm Euryalus betray'd,
On which the moon with full reflection play'd.

" 'Tis not for naught," cried Volscens from the crowd,
"These men go there;" then rais'd his voice aloud:
"Stand! stand! why thus in arms? And whither bent?
From whence, to whom, and on what errand sent?"
Silent they scud away, and haste their flight
To neighb'ring woods, and trust themselves to night.
The speedy horse all passages belay,
And spur their smoking steeds to cross their way,
And watch each entrance of the winding wood.
Black was the forest: thick with beech it stood,
Horrid with fern, and intricate with thorn;
Few paths of human feet, or tracks of beasts, were worn.
The darkness of the shades, his heavy prey,
And fear, misled the younger from his way.
But Nisus hit the turns with happier haste,
And, thoughtless of his friend, the forest pass'd,
And Alban plains, from Alba's name so call'd,
Where King Latinus then his oxen stall'd;
Till, turning at the length, he stood his ground,
And miss'd his friend, and cast his eyes around:
"Ah wretch!" he cried, "where have I left behind
Th' unhappy youth? where shall I hope to find?
Or what way take?" Again he ventures back,
And treads the mazes of his former track.
He winds the wood, and, list'ning, hears the noise
Of tramping coursers, and the riders' voice.
The sound approach'd; and suddenly he view'd
The foes inclosing, and his friend pursued,
Forelaid and taken, while he strove in vain
The shelter of the friendly shades to gain.
What should he next attempt? what arms employ,
What fruitless force, to free the captive boy?
Or desperate should he rush and lose his life,
With odds oppress'd, in such unequal strife?

 Resolv'd at length, his pointed spear he shook;
And, casting on the moon a mournful look:
"Guardian of groves, and goddess of the night,
Fair queen," he said, "direct my dart aright.
If e'er my pious father, for my sake,
Did grateful off'rings on thy altars make,

Or I increas'd them with my sylvan toils,
And hung thy holy roofs with savage spoils,
Give me to scatter these." Then from his ear
He pois'd, and aim'd, and launch'd the trembling spear.
The deadly weapon, hissing from the grove,
Impetuous on the back of Sulmo drove;
Pierc'd his thin armor, drank his vital blood,
And in his body left the broken wood.
He staggers round; his eyeballs roll in death,
And with short sobs he gasps away his breath.
All stand amaz'd—a second jav'lin flies
With equal strength, and quivers thro' the skies.
This thro' thy temples, Tagus, forc'd the way,
And in the brainpan warmly buried lay.
Fierce Volscens foams with rage, and, gazing round,
Descried not him who gave the fatal wound,
Nor knew to fix revenge: "But thou," he cries,
"Shalt pay for both," and at the pris'ner flies
With his drawn sword. Then, struck with deep despair,
That cruel sight the lover could not bear;
But from his covert rush'd in open view,
And sent his voice before him as he flew:
"Me! me!" he cried—"turn all your swords alone
On me—the fact confess'd, the fault my own.
He neither could nor durst, the guiltless youth:
Ye moon and stars, bear witness to the truth!
His only crime (if friendship can offend)
Is too much love to his unhappy friend."
Too late he speaks: the sword, which fury guides,
Driv'n with full force, had pierc'd his tender sides.
Down fell the beauteous youth: the yawning wound
Gush'd out a purple stream, and stain'd the ground.
His snowy neck reclines upon his breast,
Like a fair flow'r by the keen share oppress'd;
Like a white poppy sinking on the plain,
Whose heavy head is overcharg'd with rain.
Despair, and rage, and vengeance justly vow'd,
Drove Nisus headlong on the hostile crowd.
Volscens he seeks; on him alone he bends:
Borne back and bor'd by his surrounding friends,

Onward he press'd, and kept him still in sight;
Then whirl'd aloft his sword with all his might:
Th' unerring steel descended while he spoke,
Pierc'd his wide mouth, and thro' his weazon broke.
Dying, he slew; and, stagg'ring on the plain,
With swimming eyes he sought his lover slain;
Then quiet on his bleeding bosom fell,
Content, in death, to be reveng'd so well.

O happy friends! for, if my verse can give
Immortal life, your fame shall ever live,
Fix'd as the Capitol's foundation lies,
And spread, where'er the Roman eagle flies!

The conqu'ring party first divide the prey,
Then their slain leader to the camp convey.
With wonder, as they went, the troops were fill'd,
To see such numbers whom so few had kill'd.
Serranus, Rhamnes, and the rest, they found:
Vast crowds the dying and the dead surround;
And the yet reeking blood o'erflows the ground.
All knew the helmet which Messapus lost,
But mourn'd a purchase that so dear had cost.
Now rose the ruddy morn from Tithon's bed,
And with the dawn of day the skies o'erspread;
Nor long the sun his daily course withheld,
But added colors to the world reveal'd:
When early Turnus, wak'ning with the light,
All clad in armor, calls his troops to fight.
His martial men with fierce harangue he fir'd,
And his own ardor in their souls inspir'd.
This done—to give new terror to his foes,
The heads of Nisus and his friend he shows,
Rais'd high on pointed spears—a ghastly sight:
Loud peals of shouts ensue, and barbarous delight.

Meantime the Trojans run, where danger calls;
They line their trenches, and they man their walls.
In front extended to the left they stood;
Safe was the right, surrounded by the flood.
But, casting from their tow'rs a frightful view,
They saw the faces, which too well they knew,
Tho' then disguis'd in death, and smear'd all o'er

With filth obscene, and dropping putrid gore.
Soon hasty fame thro' the sad city bears
The mournful message to the mother's ears.
An icy cold benumbs her limbs; she shakes;
Her cheeks the blood, her hand the web forsakes.
She runs the rampires round amidst the war,
Nor fears the flying darts; she rends her hair,
And fills with loud laments the liquid air.
"Thus, then, my lov'd Euryalus appears!
Thus looks the prop of my declining years!
Was't on this face my famish'd eyes I fed?
Ah! how unlike the living is the dead!
And could'st thou leave me, cruel, thus alone?
Not one kind kiss from a departing son!
No look, no last adieu before he went,
In an ill-boding hour to slaughter sent!
Cold on the ground, and pressing foreign clay,
To Latian dogs and fowls he lies a prey!
Nor was I near to close his dying eyes,
To wash his wounds, to weep his obsequies,
To call about his corpse his crying friends,
Or spread the mantle (made for other ends)
On his dear body, which I wove with care,
Nor did my daily pains or nightly labor spare.
Where shall I find his corpse? what earth sustains
His trunk dismember'd, and his cold remains?
For this, alas! I left my needful ease,
Expos'd my life to winds and winter seas!
If any pity touch Rutulian hearts,
Here empty all your quivers, all your darts;
Or, if they fail, thou, Jove, conclude my woe,
And send me thunderstruck to shades below!"
Her shrieks and clamors pierce the Trojans' ears,
Unman their courage, and augment their fears;
Nor young Ascanius could the sight sustain,
Nor old Ilioneus his tears restrain,
But Actor and Idæus jointly sent,
To bear the madding mother to her tent.

And now the trumpets terribly, from far,
With rattling clangor, rouse the sleepy war.

The soldiers' shouts succeed the brazen sounds;
And heav'n, from pole to pole, the noise rebounds.
The Volscians bear their shields upon their head,
And, rushing forward, form a moving shed.
These fill the ditch; those pull the bulwarks down:
Some raise the ladders; others scale the town.
But, where void spaces on the walls appear,
Or thin defense, they pour their forces there.
With poles and missive weapons, from afar,
The Trojans keep aloof the rising war.
Taught, by their ten years' siege, defensive fight,
They roll down ribs of rocks, an unresisted weight,
To break the penthouse with the pond'rous blow,
Which yet the patient Volscians undergo:
But could not bear th' unequal combat long;
For, where the Trojans find the thickest throng,
The ruin falls: their shatter'd shields give way,
And their crush'd heads become an easy prey.
They shrink for fear, abated of their rage,
Nor longer dare in a blind fight engage;
Contented now to gall them from below
With darts and slings, and with the distant bow.

Elsewhere Mezentius, terrible to view,
A blazing pine within the trenches threw.
But brave Messapus, Neptune's warlike son,
Broke down the palisades, the trenches won,
And loud for ladders calls, to scale the town.

Calliope, begin! Ye sacred Nine,
Inspire your poet in his high design,
To sing what slaughter manly Turnus made,
What souls he sent below the Stygian shade,
What fame the soldiers with their captain share,
And the vast circuit of the fatal war;
For you in singing martial facts excel;
You best remember, and alone can tell.

There stood a tow'r, amazing to the sight,
Built up of beams, and of stupendous height:
Art, and the nature of the place, conspir'd
To furnish all the strength that war requir'd.
To level this, the bold Italians join;

The wary Trojans obviate their design;
With weighty stones o'erwhelm their troops below,
Shoot thro' the loopholes, and sharp jav'lins throw.
Turnus, the chief, toss'd from his thund'ring hand
Against the wooden walls, a flaming brand:
It stuck, the fiery plague; the winds were high;
The planks were season'd, and the timber dry.
Contagion caught the posts; it spread along,
Scorch'd, and to distance drove the scatter'd throng.
The Trojans fled; the fire pursued amain,
Still gath'ring fast upon the trembling train;
Till, crowding to the corners of the wall,
Down the defense and the defenders fall.
The mighty flaw makes heav'n itself resound:
The dead and dying Trojans strew the ground.
The tow'r, that follow'd on the fallen crew,
Whelm'd o'er their heads, and buried whom it slew:
Some stuck upon the darts themselves had sent;
All the same equal ruin underwent.

Young Lycus and Helenor only scape;
Sav'd—how, they know not—from the steepy leap.
Helenor, elder of the two: by birth,
On one side royal, one a son of earth,
Whom to the Lydian king Licymnia bare,
And sent her boasted bastard to the war
(A privilege which none but freemen share).
Slight were his arms, a sword and silver shield:
No marks of honor charg'd its empty field.
Light as he fell, so light the youth arose,
And rising, found himself amidst his foes;
Nor flight was left, nor hopes to force his way.
Embolden'd by despair, he stood at bay;
And—like a stag, whom all the troop surrounds
Of eager huntsmen and invading hounds—
Resolv'd on death, he dissipates his fears,
And bounds aloft against the pointed spears:
So dares the youth, secure of death; and throws
His dying body on his thickest foes.

But Lycus, swifter of his feet by far,
Runs, doubles, winds and turns, amidst the war;

Springs to the walls, and leaves his foes behind,
And snatches at the beam he first can find;
Looks up, and leaps aloft at all the stretch,
In hopes the helping hand of some kind friend to reach
But Turnus follow'd hard his hunted prey
(His spear had almost reach'd him in the way,
Short of his reins, and scarce a span behind):
"Fool!" said the chief, "tho' fleeter than the wind,
Couldst thou presume to scape, when I pursue?"
He said, and downward by the feet he drew
The trembling dastard; at the tug he falls;
Vast ruins come along, rent from the smoking walls.
Thus on some silver swan, or tim'rous hare,
Jove's bird comes sousing down from upper air;
Her crooked talons truss the fearful prey:
Then out of sight she soars, and wings her way.
So seizes the grim wolf the tender lamb,
In vain lamented by the bleating dam.

    Then rushing onward with a barb'rous cry,
The troops of Turnus to the combat fly.
The ditch with fagots fill'd, the daring foe
Toss'd firebrands to the steepy turrets throw.

    Ilioneus, as bold Lucetius came
To force the gate, and feed the kindling flame,
Roll'd down the fragment of a rock so right,
It crush'd him double underneath the weight.
Two more young Liger and Asylas slew:
To bend the bow young Liger better knew;
Asylas best the pointed jav'lin threw.
Brave Cæneus laid Ortygius on the plain;
The victor Cæneus was by Turnus slain.
By the same hand, Clonius and Itys fall,
Sagar, and Ida, standing on the wall.
From Capys' arms his fate Privernus found:
Hurt by Themilla first—but slight the wound—
His shield thrown by, to mitigate the smart,
He clapp'd his hand upon the wounded part:
The second shaft came swift and unespied,
And pierc'd his hand, and nail'd it to his side,
Transfix'd his breathing lungs and beating heart:

THE NINTH BOOK OF THE ÆNEIS

The soul came issuing out, and hiss'd against the dart.
  The son of Arcens shone amid the rest,
In glitt'ring armor and a purple vest,
(Fair was his face, his eyes inspiring love,)
Bred by his father in the Martian grove,
Where the fat altars of Palicus flame,
And sent in arms to purchase early fame.
Him when he spied from far, the Tuscan king
Laid by the lance, and took him to the sling,
Thrice whirl'd the thong around his head, and threw:
The heated lead half melted as it flew;
It pierc'd his hollow temples and his brain;
The youth came tumbling down, and spurn'd the plain.
  Then young Ascanius, who, before this day,
Was wont in woods to shoot the savage prey,
First bent in martial strife the twanging bow,
And exercis'd against a human foe—
With this bereft Numanus of his life,
Who Turnus' younger sister took to wife.
Proud of his realm, and of his royal bride,
Vaunting before his troops, and lengthen'd with a stride,
In these insulting terms the Trojans he defied:
"Twice-conquer'd cowards, now your shame is shown—
Coop'd up a second time within your town!
Who dare not issue forth in open field,
But hold your walls before you for a shield.
Thus threat you war? thus our alliance force?
What gods, what madness, hether steer'd your course?
You shall not find the sons of Atreus here,
Nor need the frauds of sly Ulysses fear.
Strong from the cradle, of a sturdy brood,
We bear our newborn infants to the flood;
There bath'd amid the stream, our boys we hold,
With winter harden'd, and inur'd to cold.
They wake before the day to range the wood,
Kill ere they eat, nor taste unconquer'd food.
No sports, but what belong to war, they know:
To break the stubborn colt, to bend the bow.
Our youth, of labor patient, earn their bread;
Hardly they work, with frugal diet fed.

From plows and harrows sent to seek renown,
They fight in fields, and storm the shaken town.
No part of life from toils of war is free,
No change in age, or diff'rence in degree.
We plow and till in arms; our oxen feel,
Instead of goads, the spur and pointed steel;
Th' inverted lance makes furrows in the plain.
Ev'n time, that changes all, yet changes us in vain:
The body, not the mind; nor can control
Th' immortal vigor, or abate the soul.
Our helms defend the young, disguise the gray:
We live by plunder, and delight in prey.
Your vests embroider'd with rich purple shine;
In sloth you glory, and in dances join.
Your vests have sweeping sleeves; with female pride
Your turbants underneath your chins are tied.
Go, Phrygians, to your Dindymus again!
Go, less than women, in the shapes of men!
Go, mix'd with eunuchs, in the Mother's rites,
Where with unequal sound the flute invites;
Sing, dance, and howl, by turns, in Ida's shade:
Resign the war to men, who know the martial trade!"

This foul reproach Ascanius could not hear
With patience, or a vow'd revenge forbear.
At the full stretch of both his hands he drew,
And almost join'd the horns of the tough yew.
But, first, before the throne of Jove he stood,
And thus with lifted hands invok'd the god:
"My first attempt, great Jupiter, succeed!
An annual off'ring in thy grove shall bleed;
A snow-white steer, before thy altar led,
Who, like his mother, bears aloft his head,
Butts with his threat'ning brows, and bellowing stands,
And dares the fight, and spurns the yellow sands."

Jove bow'd the heav'ns, and lent a gracious ear,
And thunder'd on the left, amidst the clear.
Sounded at once the bow; and swiftly flies
The feather'd death, and hisses thro' the skies.
The steel thro' both his temples forc'd the way:
Extended on the ground, Numanus lay.

THE NINTH BOOK OF THE ÆNEIS

"Go now, vain boaster, and true valor scorn!
The Phrygians, twice subdued, yet make this third
 return."
Ascanius said no more. The Trojans shake
The heav'ns with shouting, and new vigor take.
 Apollo then bestrode a golden cloud,
To view the feats of arms, and fighting crowd;
And thus the beardless victor he bespoke aloud:
"Advance, illustrious youth, increase in fame,
And wide from east to west extend thy name;
Offspring of gods thyself; and Rome shall owe
To thee a race of demigods below.
This is the way to heav'n: the pow'rs divine
From this beginning date the Julian line.
To thee, to them, and their victorious heirs,
The conquer'd war is due, and the vast world is theirs.
Troy is too narrow for thy name." He said,
And plunging downward shot his radiant head;
Dispell'd the breathing air, that broke his flight:
Shorn of his beams, a man to mortal sight.
Old Butes' form he took, Anchises' squire,
Now left, to rule Ascanius, by his sire:
His wrinkled visage, and his hoary hairs,
His mien, his habit, and his arms, he wears,
And thus salutes the boy, too forward for his years:
"Suffice it thee, thy father's worthy son,
The warlike prize thou hast already won.
The god of archers gives thy youth a part
Of his own praise, nor envies equal art.
Now tempt the war no more." He said, and flew
Obscure in air, and vanish'd from their view.
The Trojans, by his arms, their patron know,
And hear the twanging of his heav'nly bow.
Then duteous force they use, and Phœbus' name,
To keep from fight the youth too fond of fame.
Undaunted, they themselves no danger shun;
From wall to wall the shouts and clamors run.
They bend their bows; they whirl their slings around;
Heaps of spent arrows fall, and strew the ground;
And helms, and shields, and rattling arms resound.

The combat thickens, like the storm that flies
From westward, when the show'ry Kids arise;
Or patt'ring hail comes pouring on the main,
When Jupiter descends in harden'd rain,
Or bellowing clouds burst with a stormy sound,
And with an armed winter strew the ground.

 Pand'rus and Bitias, thunderbolts of war,
Whom Hiera to bold Alcanor bare
On Ida's top, two youths of height and size
Like firs that on their mother-mountain rise,
Presuming on their force, the gates unbar,
And of their own accord invite the war.
With fates averse, against their king's command,
Arm'd, on the right and on the left they stand,
And flank the passage: shining steel they wear,
And waving crests above their heads appear.
Thus two tall oaks, that Padus' banks adorn,
Lift up to heav'n their leafy heads unshorn,
And, overpress'd with nature's heavy load,
Dance to the whistling winds, and at each other nod.
In flows a tide of Latians, when they see
The gate set open, and the passage free;
Bold Quercens, with rash Tmarus, rushing on,
Equicolus, that in bright armor shone,
And Hæmon first; but soon repuls'd they fly,
Or in the well-defended pass they die.
These with success are fir'd, and those with rage,
And each on equal terms at length ingage.
Drawn from their lines, and issuing on the plain,
The Trojans hand to hand the fight maintain.

 Fierce Turnus in another quarter fought,
When suddenly th' unhop'd-for news was brought,
The foes had left the fastness of their place,
Prevail'd in fight, and had his men in chase.
He quits th' attack, and, to prevent their fate,
Runs where the giant brothers guard the gate.
The first he met, Antiphates the brave,
But base-begotten on a Theban slave,
Sarpedon's son, he slew: the deadly dart
Found passage thro' his breast, and pierc'd his heart.

Fix'd in the wound th' Italian cornel stood,
Warm'd in his lungs, and in his vital blood.
Aphidnus next, and Erymanthus dies,
And Meropes, and the gigantic size
Of Bitias, threat'ning with his ardent eyes.
Not by the feeble dart he fell oppress'd
(A dart were lost within that roomy breast),
But from a knotted lance, large, heavy, strong,
Which roar'd like thunder as it whirl'd along:
Not two bull-hides th' impetuous force withhold,
Nor coat of double mail, with scales of gold.
Down sunk the monster bulk and press'd the ground;
His arms and clatt'ring shield on the vast body sound,
Not with less ruin than the Bajan mole,
Rais'd on the seas, the surges to control—
At once comes tumbling down the rocky wall;
Prone to the deep, the stones disjointed fall
Of the vast pile; the scatter'd ocean flies;
Black sands, discolor'd froth, and mingled mud arise:
The frighted billows roll, and seek the shores;
Then trembles Prochyta, then Ischia roars:
Typhœus, thrown beneath, by Jove's command,
Astonish'd at the flaw that shakes the land,
Soon shifts his weary side, and, scarce awake,
With wonder feels the weight press lighter on his back.

The warrior god the Latian troops inspir'd,
New strung their sinews, and their courage fir'd,
But chills the Trojan hearts with cold affright:
Then black despair precipitates their flight.

When Pandarus beheld his brother kill'd,
The town with fear and wild confusion fill'd,
He turns the hinges of the heavy gate
With both his hands, and adds his shoulders to the weight;
Some happier friends within the walls inclos'd;
The rest shut out, to certain death expos'd:
Fool as he was, and frantic in his care,
T' admit young Turnus, and include the war!
He thrust amid the crowd, securely bold,
Like a fierce tiger pent amid the fold.

Too late his blazing buckler they descry,
And sparkling fires that shot from either eye,
His mighty members, and his ample breast,
His rattling armor, and his crimson crest.

  Far from that hated face the Trojans fly,
All but the fool who sought his destiny.
Mad Pandarus steps forth, with vengeance vow'd
For Bitias' death, and threatens thus aloud:
"These are not Ardea's walls, nor this the town
Amata proffers with Lavinia's crown:
'Tis hostile earth you tread. Of hope bereft,
No means of safe return by flight are left."
To whom, with count'nance calm, and soul sedate,
Thus Turnus: "Then begin, and try thy fate:
My message to the ghost of Priam bear;
Tell him a new Achilles sent thee there."

  A lance of tough ground ash the Trojan threw,
Rough in the rind, and knotted as it grew:
With his full force he whirl'd it first around;
But the soft yielding air receiv'd the wound:
Imperial Juno turn'd the course before,
And fix'd the wand'ring weapon in the door.

  "But hope not thou," said Turnus, "when I strike,
To shun thy fate: our force is not alike,
Nor thy steel temper'd by the Lemnian god."
Then rising, on his utmost stretch he stood,
And aim'd from high: the full descending blow
Cleaves the broad front and beardless cheeks in two.
Down sinks the giant with a thund'ring sound:
His pond'rous limbs oppress the trembling ground;
Blood, brains, and foam gush from the gaping wound:
Scalp, face, and shoulders the keen steel divides,
And the shar'd visage hangs on equal sides.
The Trojans fly from their approaching fate;
And, had the victor then secur'd the gate,
And to his troops without unclos'd the bars,
One lucky day had ended all his wars.
But boiling youth, and blind desire of blood,
Push'd on his fury, to pursue the crowd.
Hamstring'd behind, unhappy Gyges died;

Then Phalaris is added to his side.
The pointed jav'lins from the dead he drew,
And their friends' arms against their fellows threw.
Strong Halys stands in vain; weak Phlegys flies;
Saturnia, still at hand, new force and fire supplies.
Then Halius, Prytanis, Alcander fall—
Ingag'd against the foes who scal'd the wall:
But, whom they fear'd without, they found within.
At last, tho' late, by Lynceus he was seen.
He calls new succors, and assaults the prince:
But weak his force, and vain is their defense.
Turn'd to the right, his sword the hero drew,
And at one blow the bold aggressor slew.
He joints the neck; and, with a stroke so strong,
The helm flies off, and bears the head along.
Next him, the huntsman Amycus he kill'd,
In darts invenom'd and in poison skill'd.
Then Clytius fell beneath his fatal spear,
And Creteus, whom the Muses held so dear:
He fought with courage, and he sung the fight;
Arms were his bus'ness, verses his delight.

 The Trojan chiefs behold, with rage and grief,
Their slaughter'd friends, and hasten their relief.
Bold Mnestheus rallies first the broken train,
Whom brave Seresthus and his troop sustain.
To save the living, and revenge the dead,
Against one warrior's arms all Troy they led.
"O, void of sense and courage!" Mnestheus cried,
"Where can you hope your coward heads to hide?
Ah! where beyond these rampires can you run?
One man, and in your camp inclos'd, you shun!
Shall then a single sword such slaughter boast,
And pass unpunish'd from a num'rous host?
Forsaking honor, and renouncing fame,
Your gods, your country, and your king you shame!"
This just reproach their virtue does excite:
They stand, they join, they thicken to the fight.

 Now Turnus doubts, and yet disdains to yield,
But with slow paces measures back the field,
And inches to the walls, where Tiber's tide,

Washing the camp, defends the weaker side.
The more he loses, they advance the more,
And tread in ev'ry step he trod before.
They shout: they bear him back; and, whom by might
They cannot conquer, they oppress with weight.

As, compass'd with a wood of spears around,
The lordly lion still maintains his ground;
Grins horrible, retires, and turns again;
Threats his distended paws, and shakes his mane;
He loses while in vain he presses on,
Nor will his courage let him dare to run:
So Turnus fares, and, unresolved of flight,
Moves tardy back, and just recedes from fight.
Yet twice, inrag'd, the combat he renews,
Twice breaks, and twice his broken foes pursues.
But now they swarm, and, with fresh troops supplied,
Come rolling on, and rush from ev'ry side:
Nor Juno, who sustain'd his arms before,
Dares with new strength suffice th' exhausted store;
For Jove, with sour commands, sent Iris down,
To force th' invader from the frighted town.

With labor spent, no longer can he wield
The heavy fanchion, or sustain the shield,
O'erwhelm'd with darts, which from afar they fling:
The weapons round his hollow temples ring;
His golden helm gives way, with stony blows
Batter'd, and flat, and beaten to his brows.
His crest is rash'd away; his ample shield
Is falsified, and round with jav'lins fill'd.

The foe, now faint, the Trojans overwhelm;
And Mnestheus lays hard load upon his helm.
Sick sweat succeeds; he drops at ev'ry pore;
With driving dust his cheeks are pasted o'er;
Shorter and shorter ev'ry gasp he takes;
And vain efforts and hurtless blows he makes.
Plung'd in the flood, and made the waters fly.
The yellow god the welcome burthen bore,
And wip'd the sweat, and wash'd away the gore;
Then gently wafts him to the farther coast,
And sends him safe to cheer his anxious host.

THE TENTH BOOK OF THE ÆNEIS

THE ARGUMENT.—Jupiter, calling a council of the gods, forbids them to engage in ther party. At Æneas's return there is a bloody battle: Turnus killing Pallas; Æneas, ausus and Mezentius. Mezentius is described as an atheist: Lausus as a pious and rtuous youth. The different actions and death of these two are the subject of a noble isode.

THE gates of heav'n unfold: Jove summons all
The gods to council in the common hall.
Sublimely seated, he surveys from far
The fields, the camp, the fortune of the war,
And all th' inferior world. From first to last,
The sov'reign senate in degrees are plac'd.
  Then thus th' almighty sire began: "Ye gods,
Natives or denizens of blest abodes,
From whence these murmurs, and this change of mind,
This backward fate from what was first design'd?
Why this protracted war, when my commands
Pronounc'd a peace, and gave the Latian lands?
What fear or hope on either part divides
Our heav'ns, and arms our powers on diff'rent sides?
A lawful time of war at length will come,
(Nor need your haste anticipate the doom),
When Carthage shall contend the world with Rome,
Shall force the rigid rocks and Alpine chains,
And, like a flood, come pouring on the plains.
Then is your time for faction and debate,
For partial favor, and permitted hate.
Let now your immature dissension cease;
Sit quiet, and compose your souls to peace."
  Thus Jupiter in few unfolds the charge;
But lovely Venus thus replies at large:
"O pow'r immense, eternal energy,
(For to what else protection can we fly?)
Seest thou the proud Rutulians, how they dare

In fields, unpunish'd, and insult my care?
How lofty Turnus vaunts amidst his train,
In shining arms, triumphant on the plain?
Ev'n in their lines and trenches they contend,
And scarce their walls the Trojan troops defend:
The town is fill'd with slaughter, and o'erfloats,
With a red deluge, their increasing moats.
Æneas, ignorant, and far from thence,
Has left a camp expos'd, without defense.
This endless outrage shall they still sustain?
Shall Troy renew'd be forc'd and fir'd again?
A second siege my banish'd issue fears,
And a new Diomede in arms appears.
One more audacious mortal will be found;
And I, thy daughter, wait another wound.
Yet, if with fates averse, without thy leave,
The Latian lands my progeny receive,
Bear they the pains of violated law,
And thy protection from their aid withdraw.
But, if the gods their sure success foretell;
If those of heav'n consent with those of hell,
To promise Italy; who dare debate
The pow'r of Jove, or fix another fate?
What should I tell of tempests on the main,
Of Æolus usurping Neptune's reign?
Of Iris sent, with Bacchanalian heat
T" inspire the matrons, and destroy the fleet?
Now Juno to the Stygian sky descends,
Solicits hell for aid, and arms the fiends.
That new example wanted yet above:
An act that well became the wife of Jove!
Alecto, rais'd by her, with rage inflames
The peaceful bosoms of the Latian dames.
Imperial sway no more exalts my mind;
(Such hopes I had indeed, while Heav'n was kind;)
Now let my happier foes possess my place,
Whom Jove prefers before the Trojan race;
And conquer they, whom you with conquest grace.
Since you can spare, from all your wide command,
No spot of earth, no hospitable land,

Which may my wand'ring fugitives receive;
(Since haughty Juno will not give you leave;)
Then, father, (if I still may use that name,)
By ruin'd Troy, yet smoking from the flame,
I beg you, let Ascanius, by my care,
Be freed from danger, and dismiss'd the war:
Inglorious let him live, without a crown.
The father may be cast on coasts unknown,
Struggling with fate; but let me save the son.
Mine is Cythera, mine the Cyprian tow'rs:
In those recesses, and those sacred bow'rs,
Obscurely let him rest; his right resign
To promis'd empire, and his Julian line.
Then Carthage may th' Ausonian towns destroy,
Nor fear the race of a rejected boy.
What profits it my son to scape the fire,
Arm'd with his gods, and loaded with his sire;
To pass the perils of the seas and wind;
Evade the Greeks, and leave the war behind;
To reach th' Italian shores; if, after all,
Our second Pergamus is doom'd to fall?
Much better had he curb'd his high desires,
And hover'd o'er his ill-extinguish'd fires.
To Simoïs' banks the fugitives restore,
And give them back to war, and all the woes before."

Deep indignation swell'd Saturnia's heart:
"And must I own," she said, "my secret smart—
What with more decence were in silence kept,
And, but for this unjust reproach, had slept?
Did god or man your fav'rite son advise,
With war unhop'd the Latians to surprise?
By fate, you boast, and by the gods' decree,
He left his native land for Italy!
Confess the truth; by mad Cassandra, more
Than Heav'n inspir'd, he sought a foreign shore!
Did I persuade to trust his second Troy
To the raw conduct of a beardless boy,
With walls unfinish'd, which himself forsakes,
And thro' the waves a wand'ring voyage takes?
When have I urg'd him meanly to demand

The Tuscan aid, and arm a quiet land?
Did I or Iris give this mad advice,
Or made the fool himself the fatal choice?
You think it hard, the Latians should destroy
With swords your Trojans, and with fires your Troy!
Hard and unjust indeed, for men to draw
Their native air, nor take a foreign law!
That Turnus is permitted still to live,
To whom his birth a god and goddess give!
But yet 'tis just and lawful for your line
To drive their fields, and force with fraud to join;
Realms, not your own, among your clans divide,
And from the bridegroom tear the promis'd bride;
Petition, while you public arms prepare;
Pretend a peace, and yet provoke a war!
'Twas giv'n to you, your darling son to shroud.
To draw the dastard from the fighting crowd,
And, for a man, obtend an empty cloud.
From flaming fleets you turn'd the fire away,
And chang'd the ships to daughters of the sea.
But 'tis my crime—the Queen of Heav'n offends.
If she presume to save her suff'ring friends!
Your son, not knowing what his foes decree,
You say, is absent: absent let him be.
Yours is Cythera yours the Cyprian tow'rs
The soft recesses, and the sacred bow'rs.
Why do you then these needless arms prepare,
And thus provoke a people prone to war?
Did I with fire the Trojan town deface,
Or hinder from return your exil'd race?
Was I the cause of mischief, or the man
Whose lawless lust the fatal war began?
Think on whose faith th' adult'rous youth relied;
Who promis'd, who procur'd, the Spartan bride?
When all th' united states of Greece combin'd,
To purge the world of the perfidious kind,
Then was your time to fear the Trojan fate:
Your quarrels and complaints are now too late."

Thus Juno. Murmurs rise, with mix'd applause,
Just as they favor or dislike the cause.

So winds, when yet unfledg'd in woods they lie,
In whispers first their tender voices try,
Then issue on the main with bellowing rage,
And storms to trembling mariners presage.

  Then thus to both replied th' imperial god,
Who shakes heav'n's axles with his awful nod.
(When he begins, the silent senate stand
With rev'rence, list'ning to the dread command:
The clouds dispel; the winds their breath restrain;
And the hush'd waves lie flatted on the main.)
"Celestials, your attentive ears incline!
Since," said the god, "the Trojans must not join
In wish'd alliance with the Latian line;
Since endless jarrings and immortal hate
Tend but to discompose our happy state;
The war henceforward be resign'd to fate:
Each to his proper fortune stand or fall;
Equal and unconcern'd I look on all.
Rutulians, Trojans, are the same to me;
And both shall draw the lots their fates decree.
Let these assault, if Fortune be their friend;
And, if she favors those, let those defend:
The Fates will find their way." The Thund'rer said,
And shook the sacred honors of his head,
Attesting Styx, th' inviolable flood,
And the black regions of his brother god.
Trembled the poles of heav'n, and earth confess'd the nod.
This end the sessions had: the senate rise,
And to his palace wait their sov'reign thro' the skies.

  Meantime, intent upon their siege, the foes
Within their walls the Trojan host inclose:
They wound, they kill, they watch at ev'ry gate;
Renew the fires, and urge their happy fate.

  Th' Æneans wish in vain their wanted chief,
Hopeless of flight, more hopeless of relief.
Thin on the tow'rs they stand; and ev'n those few
A feeble, fainting, and dejected crew.
Yet in the face of danger some there stood:
The two bold brothers of Sarpedon's blood,
Asius and Acmon; both th' Assaraci;

Young Hæmon, and tho' young, resolv'd to die.
With these were Clarus and Thymœtes join'd;
Tibris and Castor, both of Lycian kind.
From Acmon's hands a rolling stone there came,
So large, it half deserv'd a mountain's name:
Strong-sinew'd was the youth, and big of bone;
His brother Mnestheus could not more have done,
Or the great father of th' intrepid son.
Some firebrands throw, some flights of arrows send;
And some with darts, and some with stones defend.

Amid the press appears the beauteous boy,
The care of Venus, and the hope of Troy.
His lovely face unarm'd, his head was bare;
In ringlets o'er his shoulders hung his hair.
His forehead circled with a diadem;
Distinguish'd from the crowd, he shines a gem,
Enchas'd in gold, or polish'd iv'ry set,
Amidst the meaner foil of sable jet.

Nor Ismarus was wanting to the war,
Directing pointed arrows from afar,
And death with poison arm'd—in Lydia born,
Where plenteous harvests the fat fields adorn;
Where proud Pactolus floats the fruitful lands,
And leaves a rich manure of golden sands.
There Capys, author of the Capuan name,
And there was Mnestheus too, increas'd in fame,
Since Turnus from the camp he cast with shame.

Thus mortal war was wag'd on either side.
Meantime the hero cuts the nightly tide:
For, anxious, from Evander when he went,
He sought the Tyrrhene camp, and Tarchon's tent;
Expos'd the cause of coming to the chief;
His name and country told, and ask'd relief;
Propos'd the terms; his own small strength declar'd;
What vengeance proud Mezentius had prepar'd:
What Turnus, bold and violent, design'd;
Then shew'd the slipp'ry state of humankind,
And fickle fortune; warn'd him to beware,
And to his wholesome counsel added pray'r.
Tarchon, without delay, the treaty signs,

THE TENTH BOOK OF THE ÆNEIS

And to the Trojan troops the Tuscan joins.
    They soon set sail; nor now the Fates withstand;
Their forces trusted with a foreign hand.
Æneas leads; upon his stern appear
Two lions carv'd, which rising Ida bear—
Ida, to wand'ring Trojans ever dear.
Under their grateful shade Æneas sate,
Revolving war's events, and various fate.
His left young Pallas kept, fix'd to his side,
And oft of winds enquir'd, and of the tide;
Oft of the stars, and of their wat'ry way;
And what he suffer'd both by land and sea.
    Now, sacred sisters, open all your spring!
The Tuscan leaders, and their army sing,
Which follow'd great Æneas to the war:
Their arms, their numbers, and their names declare.
    A thousand youths brave Massicus obey,
Borne in the Tiger thro' the foaming sea;
From Asium brought, and Cosa, by his care:
For arms, light quivers, bows and shafts, they bear.
Fierce Abas next: his men bright armor wore;
His stern Apollo's golden statue bore.
Six hundred Populonia sent along,
All skill'd in martial exercise, and strong.
Three hundred more for battle Ilva joins,
An isle renown'd for steel, and unexhausted mines.
Asylas on his prow the third appears,
Who heav'n interprets, and the wand'ring stars;
From offer'd entrails prodigies expounds,
And peals of thunder, with presaging sounds.
A thousand spears in warlike order stand,
Sent by the Pisans under his command.
    Fair Astur follows in the wat'ry field,
Proud of his manag'd horse and painted shield.
Gravisca, noisome from the neighb'ring fen,
And his own Cære, sent three hundred men;
With those which Minio's fields and Pyrgi gave,
All bred in arms, unanimous, and brave.
    Thou, Muse, the name of Cinyras renew,
And brave Cupavo follow'd but by few;

Whose helm confess'd the lineage of the man,
And bore, with wings display'd, a silver swan.
Love was the fault of his fam'd ancestry,
Whose forms and fortunes in his ensigns fly.
For Cycnus lov'd unhappy Phaeton,
And sung his loss in poplar groves, alone,
Beneath the sister shades, to soothe his grief.
Heav'n heard his song, and hasten'd his relief,
And chang'd to snowy plumes his hoary hair,
And wing'd his flight, to chant aloft in air.
His son Cupavo brush'd the briny flood:
Upon his stern a brawny Centaur stood,
Who heav'd a rock, and, threat'ning still to throw,
With lifted hands alarm'd the seas below:
They seem'd to fear the formidable sight,
And roll'd their billows on, to speed his flight.

Ocnus was next, who led his native train
Of hardy warriors thro' the wat'ry plain:
The son of Manto by the Tuscan stream,
From whence the Mantuan town derives the name—
An ancient city, but of mix'd descent:
Three sev'ral tribes compose the government;
Four towns are under each; but all obey
The Mantuan laws, and own the Tuscan sway.

Hate to Mezentius arm'd five hundred more,
Whom Mincius from his sire Benacus bore:
Mincius, with wreaths of reeds his forehead cover'd o'er.
These grave Auletes leads: a hundred sweep
With stretching oars at once the glassy deep.
Him and his martial train the Triton bears;
High on his poop the sea-green god appears:
Frowning he seems his crooked shell to sound,
And at the blast the billows dance around.
A hairy man above the waist he shows;
A porpoise tail beneath his belly grows;
And ends a fish: his breast the waves divides,
And froth and foam augment the murm'ring tides.

Full thirty ships transport the chosen train
For Troy's relief, and scour the briny main.

Now was the world forsaken by the sun,

And Phœbe half her nightly race had run.
The careful chief, who never clos'd his eyes,
Himself the rudder holds, the sails supplies.
A choir of Nereids meet him on the flood,
Once his own galleys, hewn from Ida's wood;
But now, as many nymphs, the sea they sweep,
As rode, before, tall vessels on the deep.
They know him from afar; and in a ring
Inclose the ship that bore the Trojan king.
Cymodoce, whose voice excell'd the rest,
Above the waves advanc'd her snowy breast;
Her right hand stops the stern; her left divides
The curling ocean, and corrects the tides.
She spoke for all the choir, and thus began
With pleasing words to warn th' unknowing man:
"Sleeps our lov'd lord? O goddess-born, awake!
Spread ev'ry sail, pursue your wat'ry track,
And haste your course. Your navy once were we,
From Ida's height descending to the sea;
Till Turnus, as at anchor fix'd we stood,
Presum'd to violate our holy wood.
Then, loos'd from shore, we fled his fires profane
(Unwillingly we broke our master's chain),
And since have sought you thro' the Tuscan main.
The mighty Mother chang'd our forms to these,
And gave us life immortal in the seas.
But young Ascanius, in his camp distress'd,
By your insulting foes is hardly press'd.
Th' Arcadian horsemen, and Etrurian host,
Advance in order on the Latian coast:
To cut their way the Daunian chief designs,
Before their troops can reach the Trojan lines.
Thou, when the rosy morn restores the light,
First arm thy soldiers for th' ensuing fight:
Thyself the fated sword of Vulcan wield,
And bear aloft th' impenetrable shield.
To-morrow's sun, unless my skill be vain,
Shall see huge heaps of foes in battle slain."
Parting, she spoke; and with immortal force
Push'd on the vessel in her wat'ry course;

For well she knew the way. Impell'd behind,
The ship flew forward, and outstripp'd the wind.
The rest make up. Unknowing of the cause,
The chief admires their speed, and happy omens draws.

Then thus he pray'd, and fix'd on heav'n his eyes:
"Hear thou, great Mother of the deities.
With turrets crown'd! (on Ida's holy hill
Fierce tigers, rein'd and curb'd, obey thy will.)
Firm thy own omens; lead us on to fight;
And let thy Phrygians conquer in thy right."

He said no more. And now renewing day
Had chas'd the shadows of the night away.
He charg'd the soldiers, with preventing care,
Their flags to follow, and their arms prepare;
Warn'd of th' ensuing fight, and bade 'em hope the wa
Now, from his lofty poop, he view'd below
His camp incompass'd, and th' inclosing foe.
His blazing shield, imbrac'd, he held on high;
The camp receive the sign, and with loud shouts reply.
Hope arms their courage: from their tow'rs they throw
Their darts with double force, and drive the foe.
Thus, at the signal giv'n, the cranes arise
Before the stormy south, and blacken all the skies.

King Turnus wonder'd at the fight renew'd,
Till, looking back, the Trojan fleet he view'd,
The seas with swelling canvas cover'd o'er,
And the swift ships descending on the shore.
The Latians saw from far, with dazzled eyes,
The radiant crest that seem'd in flames to rise,
And dart diffusive fires around the field,
And the keen glitt'ring of the golden shield.
Thus threat'ning comets, when by night they rise,
Shoot sanguine streams, and sadden all the skies:
So Sirius, flashing forth sinister lights,
Pale human-kind with plagues and with dry famine frights.

Yet Turnus with undaunted mind is bent
To man the shores, and hinder their descent,
And thus awakes the courage of his friends:
"What you so long have wish'd, kind Fortune sends;
In ardent arms to meet th' invading foe:

THE TENTH BOOK OF THE ÆNEIS

You find, and find him at advantage now.
Yours is the day: you need but only dare;
Your swords will make you masters of the war.
Your sires, your sons, your houses, and your lands,
And dearest wifes, are all within your hands.
Be mindful of the race from whence you came,
And emulate in arms your fathers' fame.
Now take the time, while stagg'ring yet they stand
With feet unfirm, and prepossess the strand:
Fortune befriends the bold." Nor more he said,
But balanc'd whom to leave, and whom to lead;
Then these elects, the landing to prevent;
And those he leaves, to keep the city pent.

  Meantime the Trojan sends his troops ashore:
Some are by boats expos'd, by bridges more.
With lab'ring oars they bear along the strand,
Where the tide languishes, and leap aland.
Tarchon observes the coast with careful eyes,
And, where no ford he finds, no water fries,
Nor billows with unequal murmurs roar,
But smoothly slide along, and swell the shore,
That course he steer'd, and thus he gave command:
"Here ply your oars, and at all hazard land:
Force on the vessel, that her keel may wound
This hated soil, and furrow hostile ground.
Let me securely land—I ask no more;
Then sink my ships, or shatter on the shore."

  This fiery speech inflames his fearful friends:
They tug at ev'ry oar, and ev'ry stretcher bends;
They run their ships aground; the vessels knock,
(Thus forc'd ashore,) and tremble with the shock.
Tarchon's alone was lost, that stranded stood,
Stuck on a bank, and beaten by the flood:
She breaks her back; the loosen'd sides give way,
And plunge the Tuscan soldiers in the sea.
Their broken oars and floating planks withstand
Their passage, while they labor to the land,
And ebbing tides bear back upon th' uncertain sand.

  Now Turnus leads his troops without delay,
Advancing to the margin of the sea.
The trumpets sound: Æneas first assail'd

The clowns new-rais'd and raw, and soon prevail'd.
Great Theron fell, an omen of the fight;
Great Theron, large of limbs, of giant height.
He first in open field defied the prince:
But armor scal'd with gold was no defense
Against the fated sword, which open'd wide
His plated shield, and pierc'd his naked side.
Next, Lichas fell, who, not like others born,
Was from his wretched mother ripp'd and torn;
Sacred, O Phœbus, from his birth to thee;
For his beginning life from biting steel was free.
Not far from him was Gyas laid along,
Of monstrous bulk; with Cisseus fierce and strong:
Vain bulk and strength! for, when the chief assail'd,
Nor valor nor Herculean arms avail'd,
Nor their fam'd father, wont in war to go
With great Alcides, while he toil'd below.
The noisy Pharos next receiv'd his death:
Æneas writh'd his dart, and stopp'd his bawling breath.
Then wretched Cydon had receiv'd his doom,
Who courted Clytius in his beardless bloom,
And sought with lust obscene polluted joys:
The Trojan sword had cur'd his love of boys,
Had not his sev'n bold brethren stopp'd the course
Of the fierce champions, with united force.
Sev'n darts were thrown at once; and some rebound
From his bright shield, some on his helmet sound:
The rest had reach'd him; but his mother's care
Prevented those, and turn'd aside in air.

The prince then call'd Achates, to supply
The spears that knew the way to victory—
"Those fatal weapons, which, inur'd to blood,
In Grecian bodies under Ilium stood:
Not one of those my hand shall toss in vain
Against our foes, on this contended plain."
He said; then seiz'd a mighty spear, and threw;
Which, wing'd with fate, thro' Mæon's buckler flew,
Pierc'd all the brazen plates, and reach'd his heart:
He stagger'd with intolerable smart.
Alcanor saw; and reach'd, but reach'd in vain,

THE TENTH BOOK OF THE ÆNEIS

His helping hand, his brother to sustain.
A second spear, which kept the former course,
From the same hand, and sent with equal force,
His right arm pierc'd, and holding on, bereft
His use of both, and pinion'd down his left.
Then Numitor from his dead brother drew
Th' ill-omen'd spear, and at the Trojan threw:
Preventing fate directs the lance awry,
Which, glancing, only mark'd Achates' thigh.

In pride of youth the Sabine Clausus came,
And, from afar, at Dryops took his aim.
The spear flew hissing thro' the middle space,
And pierc'd his throat, directed at his face;
It stopp'd at once the passage of his wind,
And the free soul to flitting air resign'd:
His forehead was the first that struck the ground;
Lifeblood and life rush'd mingled thro' the wound.
He slew three brothers of the Borean race,
And three, whom Ismarus, their native place,
Had sent to war, but all the sons of Thrace.
Halesus, next, the bold Aurunci leads:
The son of Neptune to his aid succeeds,
Conspicuous on his horse. On either hand,
These fight to keep, and those to win, the land.
With mutual blood th' Ausonian soil is dyed,
While on its borders each their claim decide.
As wintry winds, contending in the sky,
With equal force of lungs their titles try:
They rage, they roar; the doubtful rack of heav'n
Stands without motion, and the tide undriv'n:
Each bent to conquer, neither side to yield,
They long suspend the fortune of the field.
Both armies thus perform what courage can;
Foot set to foot, and mingled man to man.

But, in another part, th' Arcadian horse
With ill success ingage the Latin force:
For, where th' impetuous torrent, rushing down,
Huge craggy stones and rooted trees had thrown,
They left their coursers, and, unus'd to fight
On foot, were scatter'd in a shameful flight.

Pallas, who with disdain and grief had view'd
His foes pursuing, and his friends pursued,
Us'd threat'nings mix'd with pray'rs, his last resource,
With these to move their minds, with those to fire their force.
"Which way, companions? whether would you run?
By you yourselves, and mighty battles won,
By my great sire, by his establish'd name,
And early promise of my future fame;
By my youth, emulous of equal right
To share his honors—shun ignoble flight!
Trust not your feet: your hands must hew your way
Thro' yon black body, and that thick array:
'Tis thro' that forward path that we must come;
There lies our way, and that our passage home.
Nor pow'rs above, nor destinies below
Oppress our arms: with equal strength we go,
With mortal hands to meet a mortal foe.
See on what foot we stand: a scanty shore,
The sea behind, our enemies before;
No passage left, unless we swim the main;
Or, forcing these, the Trojan trenches gain."
This said, he strode with eager haste along,
And bore amidst the thickest of the throng.
Lagus, the first he met, with fate to foe,
Had heav'd a stone of mighty weight, to throw:
Stooping, the spear descended on his chine,
Just where the bone distinguished either loin:
It stuck so fast, so deeply buried lay,
That scarce the victor forc'd the steel away.
Hisbo came on: but, while he mov'd too slow
To wish'd revenge, the prince prevents his blow;
For, warding his at once, at once he press'd,
And plung'd the fatal weapon in his breast.
Then lewd Anchemolus he laid in dust,
Who stain'd his stepdame's bed with impious lust.
And, after him, the Daucian twins were slain,
Laris and Thymbrus, on the Latian plain;
So wondrous like in feature, shape, and size,
As caus'd an error in their parents' eyes—
Grateful mistake! but soon the sword decides

THE TENTH BOOK OF THE ÆNEIS 335

The nice distinction, and their fate divides:
For Thymbrus' head was lopp'd; and Laris' hand,
Dismember'd, sought its owner on the strand:
The trembling fingers yet the fauchion strain,
And threaten still th' intended stroke in vain.

Now, to renew the charge, th' Arcadians came:
Sight of such acts, and sense of honest shame,
And grief, with anger mix'd, their minds inflame.
Then, with a casual blow was Rhœteus slain,
Who chanc'd, as Pallas threw, to cross the plain:
The flying spear was after Ilus sent;
But Rhœteus happen'd on a death unmeant:
From Teuthras and from Tyres while he fled,
The lance, athwart his body, laid him dead:
Roll'd from his chariot with a mortal wound,
And intercepted fate, he spurn'd the ground.
As when, in summer, welcome winds arise,
The watchful shepherd to the forest flies,
And fires the midmost plants; contagion spreads,
And catching flames infect the neighb'ring heads;
Around the forest flies the furious blast,
And all the leafy nation sinks at last,
And Vulcan rides in triumph o'er the waste;
The pastor, pleas'd with his dire victory,
Beholds the satiate flames in sheets ascend the sky:
So Pallas' troops their scatter'd strength unite,
And, pouring on their foes, their prince delight.

Halesus came, fierce with desire of blood;
But first collected in his arms he stood:
Advancing then, he plied the spear so well,
Ladon, Demodocus, and Pheres fell.
Around his head he toss'd his glitt'ring brand,
And from Strymonius hew'd his better hand,
Held up to guard his throat; then hurl'd a stone
At Thoas' ample front, and pierc'd the bone:
It struck beneath the space of either eye;
And blood, and mingled brains, together fly.
Deep skill'd in future fates, Halesus' sire
Did with the youth to lonely groves retire:
But, when the father's mortal race was run,

Dire destiny laid hold upon the son,
And haul'd him to the war, to find, beneath
Th' Evandrian spear, a memorable death.
Pallas th' encounter seeks, but, ere he throws,
To Tuscan Tiber thus address'd his vows:
"O sacred stream, direct my flying dart,
And give to pass the proud Halesus' heart!
His arms and spoils thy holy oak shall bear."
Pleas'd with the bribe, the god receiv'd his pray'r:
For, while his shield protects a friend distress'd,
The dart came driving on, and pierc'd his breast.

But Lausus, no small portion of the war,
Permits not panic fear to reign too far,
Caus'd by the death of so renown'd a knight;
But by his own example cheers the fight.
Fierce Abas first he slew; Abas, the stay
Of Trojan hopes, and hind'rance of the day.
The Phrygian troops escap'd the Greeks in vain:
They, and their mix'd allies, now load the plain.
To the rude shock of war both armies came;
Their leaders equal, and their strength the same.
The rear so press'd the front, they could not wield
Their angry weapons, to dispute the field.
Here Pallas urges on, and Lausus there:
Of equal youth and beauty both appear,
But both by fate forbid to breathe their native air.
Their congress in the field great Jove withstands:
Both doom'd to fall, but fall by greater hands.

Meantime Juturna warns the Daunian chief
Of Lausus' danger, urging swift relief.
With his driv'n chariot he divides the crowd,
And, making to his friends, thus calls aloud:
"Let none presume his needless aid to join;
Retire, and clear the field; the fight is mine:
To this right hand is Pallas only due;
O were his father here, my just revenge to view!"
From the forbidden space his men retir'd.
Pallas their awe, and his stern words, admir'd;
Survey'd him o'er and o'er with wond'ring sight,
Struck with his haughty mien, and tow'ring height.

THE TENTH BOOK OF THE ÆNEIS

Then to the king: "Your empty vaunts forbear;
Success I hope, and fate I cannot fear;
Alive or dead, I shall deserve a name;
Jove is impartial, and to both the same."
He said, and to the void advanc'd his pace:
Pale horror sate on each Arcadian face.
Then Turnus, from his chariot leaping light,
Address'd himself on foot to single fight.
And, as a lion—when he spies from far
A bull that seems to meditate the war,
Bending his neck, and spurning back the sand—
Runs roaring downward from his hilly stand:
Imagine eager Turnus not more slow,
To rush from high on his unequal foe.

Young Pallas, when he saw the chief advance
Within due distance of his flying lance,
Prepares to charge him first, resolv'd to try
If fortune would his want of force supply;
And thus to Heav'n and Hercules address'd:
"Alcides, once on earth Evander's guest,
His son adjures you by those holy rites,
That hospitable board, those genial nights;
Assist my great attempt to gain this prize,
And let proud Turnus view, with dying eyes,
His ravish'd spoils." 'Twas heard, the vain request;
Alcides mourn'd, and stifled sighs within his breast.
Then Jove, to soothe his sorrow, thus began:
"Short bounds of life are set to mortal man.
'Tis virtue's work alone to stretch the narrow span.
So many sons of gods, in bloody fight,
Around the walls of Troy, have lost the light:
My own Sarpedon fell beneath his foe;
Nor I, his mighty sire, could ward the blow,
Ev'n Turnus shortly shall resign his breath,
And stands already on the verge of death."
This said, the god permits the fatal fight,
But from the Latian fields averts his sight.

Now with full force his spear young Pallas threw,
And, having thrown, his shining fauchion drew
The steel just graz'd along the shoulder joint,

And mark'd it slightly with the glancing point,
Fierce Turnus first to nearer distance drew,
And pois'd his pointed spear, before he threw:
Then, as the winged weapon whizz'd along,
"See now," said he, "whose arm is better strung."
The spear kept on the fatal course, unstay'd
By plates of ir'n, which o'er the shield were laid:
Thro' folded brass and tough bull hides it pass'd,
His corslet pierc'd, and reach'd his heart at last.
In vain the youth tugs at the broken wood;
The soul comes issuing with the vital blood:
He falls; his arms upon his body sound;
And with his bloody teeth he bites the ground.

Turnus bestrode the corpse: "Arcadians, hear,"
Said he; "my message to your master bear:
Such as the sire deserv'd, the son I send;
It costs him dear to be the Phrygians' friend.
The lifeless body, tell him, I bestow,
Unask'd, to rest his wand'ring ghost below."
He said, and trampled down with all the force
Of his left foot, and spurn'd the wretched corse;
Then snatch'd the shining belt, with gold inlaid;
The belt Eurytion's artful hands had made,
Where fifty fatal brides, express'd to sight,
All in the compass of one mournful night,
Depriv'd their bridegrooms of returning light.

In an ill hour insulting Turnus tore
Those golden spoils, and in a worse he wore.
O mortals, blind in fate, who never know
To bear high fortune, or endure the low!
The time shall come, when Turnus, but in vain,
Shall wish untouch'd the trophies of the slain;
Shall wish the fatal belt were far away,
And curse the dire remembrance of the day.

The sad Arcadians, from th' unhappy field,
Bear back the breathless body on a shield.
O grace and grief of war! at once restor'd,
With praises, to thy sire, at once deplor'd!
One day first sent thee to the fighting field,
Beheld whole heaps of foes in battle kill'd;

THE TENTH BOOK OF THE ÆNEIS

One day beheld thee dead, and borne upon thy shield.
This dismal news, not from uncertain fame,
But sad spectators, to the hero came:
His friends upon the brink of ruin stand,
Unless reliev'd by his victorious hand.
He whirls his sword around, without delay,
And hews thro' adverse foes an ample way,
To find fierce Turnus, of his conquest proud:
Evander, Pallas, all that friendship ow'd
To large deserts, are present to his eyes;
His plighted hand, and hospitable ties.

Four sons of Sulmo, four whom Ufens bred,
He took in fight, and living victims led,
To please the ghost of Pallas, and expire,
In sacrifice, before his fun'ral fire.
At Magus next he threw: he stoop'd below
The flying spear, and shunn'd the promis'd blow;
Then, creeping, clasp'd the hero's knees, and pray'd:
"By young Iülus, by thy father's shade,
O spare my life, and send me back to see
My longing sire, and tender progeny!
A lofty house I have, and wealth untold,
In silver ingots, and in bars of gold:
All these, and sums besides, which see no day,
The ransom of this one poor life shall pay.
If I survive, will Troy the less prevail?
A single soul's too light to turn the scale."
He said. The hero sternly thus replied:
"Thy bars and ingots, and the sums beside,
Leave for thy children's lot. Thy Turnus broke
All rules of war by one relentless stroke,
When Pallas fell: so deems, nor deems alone
My father's shadow, but my living son."
Thus having said, of kind remorse bereft,
He seiz'd his helm, and dragg'd him with his left;
Then with his right hand, while his neck he wreath'd,
Up to the hilts his shining fauchion sheath'd.

Apollo's priest, Emonides, was near;
His holy fillets on his front appear;
Glitt'ring in arms, he shone amidst the crowd;

Much of his god, more of his purple, proud.
Him the fierce Trojan follow'd thro' the field:
The holy coward fell; and, forc'd to yield,
The prince stood o'er the priest, and, at one blow,
Sent him an off'ring to the shades below.
His arms Seresthus on his shoulders bears,
Design'd a trophy to the God of Wars.

Vulcanian Cæculus renews the fight,
And Umbro, born upon the mountains' height.
The champion cheers his troops t' encounter those,
And seeks revenge himself on other foes.
At Anxur's shield he drove; and, at the blow,
Both shield and arm to ground together go.
Anxur had boasted much of magic charms,
And thought he wore impenetrable arms,
So made by mutter'd spells; and, from the spheres,
Had life secur'd, in vain, for length of years.
Then Tarquitus the field in triumph trod;
A nymph his mother, and his sire a god.
Exulting in bright arms, he braves the prince:
With his protended lance he makes defense;
Bears back his feeble foe; then, pressing on,
Arrests his better hand, and drags him down;
Stands o'er the prostrate wretch, and, as he lay,
Vain tales inventing, and prepar'd to pray,
Mows off his head: the trunk a moment stood,
Then sunk, and roll'd along the sand in blood.
The vengeful victor thus upbraids the slain:
"Lie there, proud man, unpitied, on the plain;
Lie there, inglorious, and without a tomb,
Far from thy mother and thy native home,
Expos'd to savage beasts, and birds of prey,
Or thrown for food to monsters of the sea."

On Lycas and Antæus next he ran,
Two chiefs of Turnus, and who led his van.
They fled for fear; with these, he chas'd along
Camers the yellow-lock'd, and Numa strong;
Both great in arms, and both were fair and young.
Camers was son to Volscens lately slain,
In wealth surpassing all the Latian train,

THE TENTH BOOK OF THE ÆNEIS 341

And in Amycla fix'd his silent easy reign.
And, as Ægæon, when with heav'n he strove,
Stood opposite in arms to mighty Jove;
Mov'd all his hundred hands, provok'd the war,
Defied the forky lightning from afar;
At fifty mouths his flaming breath expires,
And flash for flash returns, and fires for fires;
In his right hand as many swords he wields,
And takes the thunder on as many shields:
With strength like his, the Trojan hero stood;
And soon the fields with falling corps were strow'd,
When once his fauchion found the taste of blood.
With fury scarce to be conceiv'd, he flew
Against Niphæus, whom four coursers drew.
They, when they see the fiery chief advance,
And pushing at their chests his pointed lance,
Wheel'd with so swift a motion, mad with fear,
They threw their master headlong from the chair.
They stare, they start, nor stop their course, before
They bear the bounding chariot to the shore.

Now Lucagus and Liger scour the plains,
With two white steeds; but Liger holds the reins,
And Lucagus the lofty seat maintains:
Bold brethren both. The former wav'd in air
His flaming sword: Æneas couch'd his spear,
Unus'd to threats, and more unus'd to fear.
Then Liger thus: "Thy confidence is vain
To scape from hence, as from the Trojan plain:
Nor these the steeds which Diomede bestrode,
Nor this the chariot where Achilles rode;
Nor Venus' veil is here, near Neptune's shield;
Thy fatal hour is come, and this the field."
Thus Liger vainly vaunts: the Trojan peer
Return'd his answer with his flying spear.
As Lucagus, to lash his horses, bends,
Prone to the wheels, and his left foot protends,
Prepar'd for fight; the fatal dart arrives,
And thro' the borders of his buckler drives;
Pass'd thro' and pierc'd his groin: the deadly wound,
Cast from his chariot, roll'd him on the ground.

Whom thus the chief upbraids with scornful spite:
"Blame not the slowness of your steeds in flight;
Vain shadows did not force their swift retreat;
But you yourself forsake your empty seat."
He said, and seiz'd at once the loosen'd rein;
For Liger lay already on the plain,
By the same shock: then, stretching out his hands,
The recreant thus his wretched life demands:
"Now, by thyself, O more than mortal man!
By her and him from whom thy breath began,
Who form'd thee thus divine, I beg thee, spare
This forfeit life, and hear thy suppliant's pray'r."
Thus much he spoke, and more he would have said;
But the stern hero turn'd aside his head,
And cut him short: "I hear another man;
You talk'd not thus before the fight began.
Now take your turn; and, as a brother should,
Attend your brother to the Stygian flood."
Then thro' his breast his fatal sword he sent,
And the soul issued at the gaping vent.

  As storms the skies, and torrents tear the ground,
Thus rag'd the prince, and scatter'd deaths around.
At length Ascanius and the Trojan train
Broke from the camp, so long besieg'd in vain.

  Meantime the King of Gods and Mortal Man
Held conference with his queen, and thus began:
"My sister goddess, and well-pleasing wife,
Still think you Venus' aid supports the strife—
Sustains her Trojans—or themselves, alone,
With inborn valor force their fortune on?
How fierce in fight, with courage undecay'd!
Judge if such warriors want immortal aid."
To whom the goddess with the charming eyes,
Soft in her tone, submissively replies:
"Why, O my sov'reign lord, whose frown I fear,
And cannot, unconcern'd, your anger bear;
Why urge you thus my grief? when, if I still
(As once I was) were mistress of your will,
From your almighty pow'r your pleasing wife
Might gain the grace of length'ning Turnus' life,

Securely snatch him from the fatal fight,
And give him to his aged father's sight.
Now let him perish, since you hold it good,
And glut the Trojans with his pious blood.
Yet from our lineage he derives his name,
And, in the fourth degree, from god Pilumnus came;
Yet he devoutly pays you rites divine,
And offers daily incense at your shrine."

Then shortly thus the sov'reign god replied:
"Since in my pow'r and goodness you confide,
If for a little space, a lengthen'd span,
You beg reprieve for this expiring man,
I grant you leave to take your Turnus hence
From instant fate, and can so far dispense.
But, if some secret meaning lies beneath,
To save the short-liv'd youth from destin'd death,
Or if a farther thought you entertain,
To change the fates; you feed your hopes in vain."
To whom the goddess thus, with weeping eyes:
"And what if that request, your tongue denies,
Your heart should grant; and not a short reprieve,
But length of certain life, to Turnus give?
Now speedy death attends the guiltless youth,
If my presaging soul divines with truth;
Which, O! I wish, might err thro' causeless fears,
And you (for you have pow'r) prolong his years!"

Thus having said, involv'd in clouds, she flies,
And drives a storm before her thro' the skies.
Swift she descends, alighting on the plain,
Where the fierce foes a dubious fight maintain.
Of air condens'd a specter soon she made;
And, what Æneas was, such seem'd the shade.
Adorn'd with Dardan arms, the phantom bore
His head aloft; a plumy crest he wore;
This hand appear'd a shining sword to wield,
And that sustain'd an imitated shield.
With manly mien he stalk'd along the ground,
Nor wanted voice belied, nor vaunting sound.
(Thus haunting ghosts appear to waking sight,
Or dreadful visions in our dreams by night.)

The specter seems the Daunian chief to dare,
And flourishes his empty sword in air.
At this, advancing, Turnus hurl'd his spear:
The phantom wheel'd, and seem'd to fly for fear.
Deluded Turnus thought the Trojan fled,
And with vain hopes his haughty fancy fed.
"Whither, O coward?" (thus he calls aloud,
Nor found he spoke to wind, and chas'd a cloud,)
"Why thus forsake your bride! Receive from me
The fated land you sought so long by sea."
He said, and, brandishing at once his blade,
With eager pace pursued the flying shade.
By chance a ship was fasten'd to the shore,
Which from old Clusium King Osinius bore:
The plank was ready laid for safe ascent;
For shelter there the trembling shadow bent,
And skipp't and skulk'd, and under hatches went.
Exulting Turnus, with regardless haste,
Ascends the plank, and to the galley pass'd.
Scarce had he reach'd the prow: Saturnia's hand
The haulsers cuts, and shoots the ship from land.
With wind in poop, the vessel plows the sea,
And measures back with speed her former way.
Meantime Æneas seeks his absent foe,
And sends his slaughter'd troops to shades below.

  The guileful phantom now forsook the shroud,
And flew sublime, and vanish'd in a cloud.
Too late young Turnus the delusion found,
Far on the sea, still making from the ground.
Then, thankless for a life redeem'd by shame,
With sense of honor stung, and forfeit fame,
Fearful besides of what in fight had pass'd,
His hands and haggard eyes to heav'n he cast;
"O Jove!" he cried, "for what offense have I
Deserv'd to bear this endless infamy?
Whence am I forc'd, and whether am I borne?
How, and with what reproach, shall I return?
Shall ever I behold the Latian plain,
Or see Laurentum's lofty tow'rs again?
What will they say of their deserting chief?

The war was mine: I fly from their relief;
I led to slaughter, and in slaughter leave;
And ev'n from hence their dying groans receive.
Here, overmatch'd in fight, in heaps they lie;
There, scatter'd o'er the fields, ignobly fly.
Gape wide, O earth, and draw me down alive!
Or, O ye pitying winds, a wretch relieve!
On sands or shelves the splitting vessel drive;
Or set me shipwrack'd on some desart shore,
Where no Rutulian eyes may see me more,
Unknown to friends, or foes, or conscious Fame,
Lest she should follow, and my flight proclaim."

Thus Turnus rav'd, and various fates revolv'd:
The choice was doubtful, but the death resolv'd.
And now the sword, and now the sea took place,
That to revenge, and this to purge disgrace.
Sometimes he thought to swim the stormy main,
By stretch of arms the distant shore to gain.
Thrice he the sword assay'd, and thrice the flood;
But Juno, mov'd with pity, both withstood.
And thrice repress'd his rage; strong gales supplied,
And push'd the vessel o'er the swelling tide.
At length she lands him on his native shores,
And to his father's longing arms restores.

Meantime, by Jove's impulse, Mezentius arm'd,
Succeeding Turnus, with his ardor warm'd
His fainting friends, reproach'd their shameful flight,
Repell'd the victors, and renew'd the fight.
Against their king the Tuscan troops conspire;
Such is their hate, and such their fierce desire
Of wish'd revenge: on him, and him alone,
All hands employ'd, and all their darts are thrown.
He, like a solid rock by seas inclos'd,
To raging winds and roaring waves oppos'd,
From his proud summit looking down, disdains
Their empty menace, and unmov'd remains.

Beneath his feet fell haughty Hebrus dead,
Then Latagus, and Palmus as he fled.
At Latagus a weighty stone he flung:
His face was flatted, and his helmet rung.

But Palmus from behind receives his wound;
Hamstring'd he falls, and grovels on the ground:
His crest and armor, from his body torn,
Thy shoulders, Lausus, and thy head adorn.
Evas and Mimas, both of Troy, he slew.
Mimas his birth from fair Theano drew,
Born on that fatal night, when, big with fire,
The queen produc'd young Paris to his sire:
But Paris in the Phrygian fields was slain,
Unthinking Mimas on the Latian plain.

And, as a savage boar, on mountains bred,
With forest mast and fatt'ning marshes fed,
When once he sees himself in toils inclos'd,
By huntsmen and their eager hounds oppos'd—
He whets his tusks, and turns, and dares the war;
Th' invaders dart their jav'lins from afar:
All keep aloof, and safely shout around;
But none presumes to give a nearer wound:
He frets and froths, erects his bristled hide,
And shakes a grove of lances from his side:
Not otherwise the troops, with hate inspir'd,
And just revenge against the tyrant fir'd,
Their darts with clamor at a distance drive,
And only keep the languish'd war alive.

From Coritus came Acron to the fight,
Who left his spouse betroth'd, and unconsummate night.
Mezentius sees him thro' the squadrons ride,
Proud of the purple favors of his bride.
Then, as a hungry lion, who beholds
A gamesome goat, who frisks about the folds,
Or beamy stag, that grazes on the plain—
He runs, he roars, he shakes his rising mane,
He grins, and opens wide his greedy jaws;
The prey lies panting underneath his paws:
He fills his famish'd maw; his mouth runs o'er
With unchew'd morsels, while he churns the gore:
So proud Mezentius rushes on his foes,
And first unhappy Acron overthrows:
Stretch'd at his length, he spurns the swarthy ground;
The lance, besmear'd with blood, lies broken in the woun

THE TENTH BOOK OF THE ÆNEIS

Then with disdain the haughty victor view'd
Orodes flying, nor the wretch pursued,
Nor thought the dastard's back deserv'd a wound,
But, running, gain'd th' advantage of the ground:
Then turning short, he met him face to face,
To give his victory the better grace.
Orodes falls, in equal fight oppress'd:
Mezentius fix'd his foot upon his breast,
And rested lance; and thus aloud he cries:
"Lo! here the champion of my rebels lies!"
The fields around with *Io Pæan!* ring;
And peals of shouts applaud the conqu'ring king.
At this the vanquish'd, with his dying breath,
Thus faintly spoke, and prophesied in death:
"Nor thou, proud man, unpunish'd shalt remain:
Like death attends thee on this fatal plain."
Then, sourly smiling, thus the king replied:
"For what belongs to me, let Jove provide;
But die thou first, whatever chance ensue."
He said, and from the wound the weapon drew.
A hov'ring mist came swimming o'er his sight,
And seal'd his eyes in everlasting night.

By Cædicus, Alcathoüs was slain;
Sacrator laid Hydaspes on the plain;
Orses the strong to greater strength must yield;
He, with Parthenius, were by Rapo kill'd.
Then brave Messapus Ericetes slew,
Who from Lycaon's blood his lineage drew.
But from his headstrong horse his fate he found,
Who threw his master, as he made a bound:
The chief, alighting, stuck him to the ground;
Then Clonius, hand to hand, on foot assails:
The Trojan sinks, and Neptune's son prevails.
Agis the Lycian, stepping forth with pride,
To single fight the boldest foe defied;
Whom Tuscan Valerus by force o'ercame,
And not belied his mighty father's fame.
Salius to death the great Antronius sent:
But the same fate the victor underwent,
Slain by Nealces' hand, well-skill'd to throw

The flying dart, and draw the far-deceiving bow.
  Thus equal deaths are dealt with equal chance;
By turns they quit their ground, by turns advance:
Victors and vanquish'd, in the various field,
Nor wholly overcome, nor wholly yield.
The gods from heav'n survey the fatal strife,
And mourn the miseries of human life.
Above the rest, two goddesses appear
Concern'd for each: here Venus, Juno there.
Amidst the crowd, infernal Ate shakes
Her scourge aloft, and crest of hissing snakes.
  Once more the proud Mezentius, with disdain,
Brandish'd his spear, and rush'd into the plain,
Where tow'ring in the midmost rank she stood,
Like tall Orion stalking o'er the flood.
(When with his brawny breast he cuts the waves,
His shoulders scarce the topmost billow laves),
Or like a mountain ash, whose roots are spread,
Deep fix'd in earth; in clouds he hides his head.
  The Trojan prince beheld him from afar,
And dauntless undertook the doubtful war.
Collected in his strength, and like a rock,
Pois'd on his base, Mezentius stood the shock.
He stood, and, measuring first with careful eyes
The space his spear could reach, aloud he cries:
"My strong right hand, and sword, assist my stroke!
(Those only gods Mezentius will invoke.)
His armor, from the Trojan pirate torn,
By my triumphant Lausus shall be worn."
He said; and with his utmost force he threw
The massy spear, which, hissing as it flew,
Reach'd the celestial shield, that stopp'd the course;
But, glancing thence, the yet unbroken force
Took a new bent obliquely, and betwixt
The side and bowels fam'd Anthores fix'd.
Anthores had from Argos travel'd far,
Alcides' friend, and brother of the war;
Till, tir'd with toils, fair Italy he chose,
And in Evander's palace sought repose.
Now, falling by another's wound, his eyes

He cast to heav'n, on Argos thinks, and dies.
  The pious Trojan then his jav'lin sent;
The shield gave way; thro' treble plates it went
Of solid brass, of linen trebly roll'd,
And three bull-hides which round the buckler fold.
All these it pass'd, resistless in the course,
Transpierc'd his thigh, and spent its dying force.
The gaping wound gush'd out a crimson flood.
The Trojan, glad with sight of hostile blood,
His faunchion drew, to closer fight address'd,
And with new force his fainting foe oppress'd.
  His father's peril Lausus view'd with grief;
He sigh'd, he wept, he ran to his relief.
And here, heroic youth, 'tis here I must
To thy immortal memory be just,
And sing an act so noble and so new,
Posterity will scarce believe 'tis true.
Pain'd with his wound, and useless for the fight,
The father sought to save himself by flight:
Incumber'd, slow he dragg'd the spear along,
Which pierc'd his thigh, and in his buckler hung.
The pious youth, resolv'd on death, below
The lifted sword springs forth to face the foe;
Protects his parent, and prevents the blow.
Shouts of applause ran ringing thro' the field,
To see the son the vanquish'd father shield.
All, fir'd with gen'rous indignation, strive,
And with a storm of darts to distance drive
The Trojan chief, who, held at bay from far,
On his Vulcanian orb sustain'd the war.
  As, when thick hail comes rattling in the wind,
The plowman, passenger, and lab'ring hind
For shelter to the neighb'ring covert fly,
Or hous'd, or safe in hollow caverns lie;
But, that o'erblown, when heav'n above 'em smiles,
Return to travel, and renew their toils:
Æneas thus, o'erwhelmed on ev'ry side,
The storms of darts, undaunted, did abide;
And thus to Lausus loud with friendly threat'ning cried:
"Why wilt thou rush to certain death, and rage

In rash attempts, beyond thy tender age,
Betray'd by pious love?" Nor, thus forborne,
The youth desists, but with insulting scorn
Provokes the ling'ring prince, whose patience, tir'd,
Gave place; and all his breast with fury fir'd.
For now the Fates prepar'd their sharpen'd shears;
And lifted high the flaming sword appears,
Which, full descending with a frightful sway,
Thro' shield and corslet forc'd th' impetuous way,
And buried deep in his fair bosom lay.
The purple streams thro' the thin armor strove,
And drench'd th' imbroider'd coat his mother wove;
And life at length forsook his heaving heart,
Loth from so sweet a mansion to depart.

But when, with blood and paleness all o'erspread,
The pious prince beheld young Lausus dead,
He griev'd; he wept; the sight an image brought
Of his own filial love, a sadly pleasing thought:
Then stretch'd his hand to hold him up, and said:
"Poor hapless youth! what praises can be paid
To love so great, to such transcendent store
Of early worth, any sure presage of more?
Accept whate'er Æneas can afford;
Untouch'd thy arms, untaken be thy sword;
And all that pleas'd thee living, still remain
Inviolate, and sacred to the slain.
Thy body on thy parents I bestow,
To rest thy soul, at least, if shadows know,
Or have a sense of human things below.
There to thy fellow ghosts with glory tell:
' 'Twas by the great Æneas' hand I fell.'"
With this, his distant friends he beckons near,
Provokes their duty, and prevents their fear:
Himself assists to lift him from the ground,
With clotted locks, and blood that well'd from out the wound.

Meantime, his father, now no father, stood,
And wash'd his wounds by Tiber's yellow flood:
Oppress'd with anguish, panting, and o'erspent,
His fainting limbs against an oak he leant.

A bough his brazen helmet did sustain;
His heavier arms lay scatter'd on the plain:
A chosen train of youth around him stand;
His drooping head was rested on his hand:
His grisly beard his pensive bosom sought;
And all on Lausus ran his restless thought.
Careful, concern'd his danger to prevent,
He much enquir'd, and many a message sent
To warn him from the field—alas! in vain!
Behold, his mournful followers bear him slain!
O'er his broad shield still gush'd the yawning wound,
And drew a bloody trail along the ground.
Far off he heard their cries, far off divin'd
The dire event, with a foreboding mind.
With dust he sprinkled first his hoary head;
Then both his lifted hands to heav'n he spread;
Last, the dear corpse embracing, thus he said:
"What joys, alas! could this frail being give,
That I have been so covetous to live?
To see my son, and such a son, resign
His life, a ransom for preserving mine!
And am I then preserv'd, and art thou lost?
How much too dear has that redemption cost!
'Tis now my bitter banishment I feel:
This is a wound too deep for time to heal.
My guilt thy growing virtues did defame;
My blackness blotted thy unblemish'd name.
Chas'd from a throne, abandon'd, and exil'd
For foul misdeeds, were punishments too mild:
I ow'd my people these, and, from their hate,
With less resentment could have borne my fate.
And yet I live, and yet sustain the sight
Of hated men, and of more hated light:
But will not long." With that he rais'd from ground
His fainting limbs, that stagger'd with his wound;
Yet, with a mind resolv'd, and unappall'd
With pains or perils, for his courser call'd;
Well-mouth'd, well-manag'd, whom himself did dress
With daily care, and mounted with success;
His aid in arms, his ornament in peace.

Soothing his courage with a gentle stroke,
The steed seem'd sensible, while thus he spoke:
"O Rhœbus, we have liv'd too long for me—
If life and long were terms that could agree!
This day thou either shalt bring back the head
And bloody trophies of the Trojan dead;
This day thou either shalt revenge my woe,
For murther'd Lausus, on his cruel foe;
Or, if inexorable Fate deny
Our conquest, with thy conquer'd master die:
For, after such a lord, I rest secure,
Thou wilt no foreign reins, or Trojan load endure."
He said; and straight th' officious courser kneels,
To take his wonted weight. His hands he fills
With pointed jav'lins; on his head he lac'd
His glitt'ring helm, which terribly was grac'd
With waving horsehair, nodding from afar;
Then spurr'd his thund'ring steed amidst the war.
Love, anguish, wrath, and grief, to madness wrought,
Despair, and secret shame, and conscious thought
Of inborn worth, his lab'ring soul oppress'd,
Roll'd in his eyes, and rag'd within his breast.
Then loud he call'd Æneas thrice by name:
The loud repeated voice to glad Æneas came.
"Great Jove," he said, "and the far-shooting god,
Inspire thy mind to make thy challenge good!"
He spoke no more; but hasten'd, void of fear,
And threaten'd with his long protended spear.

To whom Mezentius thus: "Thy vaunts are vain.
My Lausus lies extended on the plain:
He's lost! thy conquest is already won;
The wretched sire is murther'd in the son.
Nor fate I fear, but all the gods defy.
Forbear thy threats: my bus'ness is to die;
But first receive this parting legacy."
He said; and straight a whirling dart he sent;
Another after, and another went.
Round in a spacious ring he rides the field,
And vainly plies th' impenetrable shield.
Thrice rode he round; and thrice Æneas wheel'd,

Turn'd as he turn'd: the golden orb withstood
The strokes, and bore about an iron wood.
Impatient of delay, and weary grown,
Still to defend, and to defend alone,
To wrench the darts which in his buckler light,
Urg'd and o'er-labor'd in unequal fight;
At length resolv'd, he throws with all his force
Full at the temples of the warrior horse.
Just where the stroke was aim'd, th' unerring spear
Made way, and stood transfix'd thro' either ear.
Seiz'd with unwonted pain, surpris'd with fright,
The wounded steed curvets, and, rais'd upright,
Lights on his feet before; his hoofs behind
Spring up in air aloft, and lash the wind.
Down comes the rider headlong from his height:
His horse came after with unwieldy weight,
And, flound'ring forward, pitching on his head,
His lord's incumber'd shoulder overlaid.

From either host, the mingled shouts and cries
Of Trojans and Rutulians rend the skies.
Æneas, hast'ning, wav'd his fatal sword
High o'er his head, with this reproachful word:
"Now; where are now thy vaunts, the fierce disdain
Of proud Mezentius, and the lofty strain?"

Struggling, and wildly staring on the skies,
With scarce recover'd sight he thus replies:
"Why these insulting words, this waste of breath,
To souls undaunted, and secure of death?
'Tis no dishonor for the brave to die,
Nor came I here with hope of victory;
Nor ask I life, nor fought with that design:
As I had us'd my fortune, use thou thine.
My dying son contracted no such band;
The gift is hateful from his murd'rer's hand.
For this, this only favor let me sue,
If pity can to conquer'd foes be due:
Refuse it not; but let my body have
The last retreat of human-kind, a grave.
Too well I know th' insulting people's hate;
Protect me from their vengeance after fate:

This refuge for my poor remains provide,
And lay my much-lov'd Lausus by my side."
He said, and to the sword his throat applied.
The crimson stream distain'd his arms around,
And the disdainful soul came rushing thro' the wound.

THE ELEVENTH BOOK OF THE ÆNEIS

THE ARGUMENT.—Æneas erects a trophy of the spoils of Mezentius, grants a truce
 burying the dead, and sends home the body of Pallas with great solemnity. Latinus
s a council, to propose offers of peace to Æneas; which occasions great animosity
wixt Turnus and Drances. In the meantime there is a sharp engagement of the
se; wherein Camilla signalizes herself; is kill'd; and the Latine troops are entirely
eated.

SCARCE had the rosy Morning rais'd her head
  Above the waves, and left her wat'ry bed;
  The pious chief, whom double cares attend
For his unburied soldiers and his friend,
Yet first to Heav'n perform'd a victor's vows:
He bar'd an ancient oak of all her boughs;
Then on a rising ground the trunk he plac'd,
Which with the spoils of his dead foe he grac'd.
The coat of arms by proud Mezentius worn,
Now on a naked snag in triumph borne,
Was hung on high, and glitter'd from afar,
A trophy sacred to the God of War.
Above his arms, fix'd on the leafless wood,
Appear'd his plumy crest, besmear'd with blood:
His brazen buckler on the left was seen;
Truncheons of shiver'd lances hung between;
And on the right was placed his corslet, bor'd;
And to the neck was tied his unavailing sword.
A crowd of chiefs inclose the godlike man,
Who thus, conspicuous in the midst, began:
"Our toils, my friends, are crown'd with sure success;
The greater part perform'd, achieve the less.
Now follow cheerful to the trembling town;
Press but an entrance, and presume it won.
Fear is no more, for fierce Mezentius lies,
As the first fruits of war, a sacrifice.
Turnus shall fall extended on the plain,

And, in this omen, is already slain.
Prepar'd in arms, pursue your happy chance;
That none unwarn'd may plead his ignorance,
And I, at Heav'n's appointed hour, may find
Your warlike ensigns waving in the wind.
Meantime the rites and fun'ral pomps prepare,
Due to your dead companions of the war:
The last respect the living can bestow,
To shield their shadows from contempt below.
That conquer'd earth be theirs, for which they fought,
And which for us with their own blood they bought;
But first the corpse of our unhappy friend
To the sad city of Evander send,
Who, not inglorious, in his age's bloom,
Was hurried hence by too severe a doom."

Thus, weeping while he spoke, he took his way,
Where, new in death, lamented Pallas lay.
Accetes watch'd the corpse; whose youth deserv'd
The father's trust; and now the son he serv'd
With equal faith, but less auspicious care.
Th' attendants of the slain his sorrow share.
A troop of Trojans mix'd with these appear,
And mourning matrons with dishevel'd hair.
Soon as the prince appears, they raise a cry;
All beat their breasts, and echoes rend the sky.
They rear his drooping forehead from the ground;
But, when Æneas view'd the grisly wound
Which Pallas in his manly bosom bore,
And the fair flesh distain'd with purple gore;
First, melting into tears, the pious man
Deplor'd so sad a sight, then thus began:
"Unhappy youth! when Fortune gave the rest
Of my full wishes, she refus'd the best!
She came; but brought not thee along, to bless
My longing eyes, and share in my success:
She grudg'd thy safe return, the triumphs due
To prosp'rous valor, in the public view.
Not thus I promis'd, when thy father lent
Thy needless succor with a sad consent;
Embrac'd me, parting for th' Etrurian land,

THE ELEVENTH BOOK OF THE ÆNEIS

And sent me to possess a large command.
He warn'd, and from his own experience told,
Our foes were warlike, disciplin'd, and bold.
And now perhaps, in hopes of thy return,
Rich odors on his loaded altars burn,
While we, with vain officious pomp, prepare
To send him back his portion of the war,
A bloody breathless body, which can owe
No farther debt, but to the pow'rs below.
The wretched father, ere his race is run,
Shall view the fun'ral honors of his son.
These are my triumphs of the Latian war,
Fruits of my plighted faith and boasted care!
And yet, unhappy sire, thou shalt not see
A son whose death disgrac'd his ancestry;
Thou shalt not blush, old man, however griev'd:
Thy Pallas no dishonest wound receiv'd.
He died no death to make thee wish, too late,
Thou hadst not liv'd to see his shameful fate:
But what a champion has th' Ausonian coast,
And what a friend hast thou, Ascanius, lost!"

Thus having mourn'd, he gave the word around,
To raise the breathless body from the ground;
And chose a thousand horse, the flow'r of all
His warlike troops, to wait the funeral,
To bear him back and share Evander's grief:
A well-becoming, but a weak relief.
Of oaken twigs they twist an easy bier,
Then on their shoulders the sad burden rear.
The body on this rural hearse is borne:
Strew'd leaves and funeral greens the bier adorn.
All pale he lies, and looks a lovely flow'r,
New cropp'd by virgin hands, to dress the bow'r:
Unfaded yet, but yet unfed below,
No more to mother earth or the green stem shall owe.
Then two fair vests, of wondrous work and cost,
Of purple woven, and with gold emboss'd,
For ornament the Trojan hero brought,
Which with her hands Sidonian Dido wrought.
One vest array'd the corpse; and one they spread

O'er his clos'd eyes, and wrapp'd around his head,
That, when the yellow hair in flame should fall,
The catching fire might burn the golden caul.
Besides, the spoils of foes in battle slain,
When he descended on the Latian plain;
Arms, trappings, horses, by the hearse are led
In long array—th' achievements of the dead.
Then, pinion'd with their hands behind, appear
Th' unhappy captives, marching in the rear,
Appointed off'rings in the victor's name,
To sprinkle with their blood the fun'ral flame.
Inferior trophies by the chiefs are borne;
Gauntlets and helms their loaded hands adorn;
And fair inscriptions fix'd, and titles read
Of Latian leaders conquer'd by the dead.

   Accœtes on his pupil's corpse attends,
With feeble steps, supported by his friends.
Pausing at ev'ry pace, in sorrow drown'd,
Betwixt their arms he sinks upon the ground;
Where grov'ling while he lies in deep despair,
He beats his breast, and rends his hoary hair.
The champion's chariot next is seen to roll,
Besmear'd with hostile blood, and honorably foul.
To close the pomp, Æthon, the steed of state,
Is led, the fun'rals of his lord to wait.
Stripp'd of his trappings, with a sullen pace
He walks; and the big tears run rolling down his face.
The lance of Pallas, and the crimson crest,
Are borne behind: the victor seiz'd the rest.
The march begins: the trumpets hoarsely sound;
The pikes and lances trail along the ground.
Thus while the Trojan and Arcadian horse
To Pallantean tow'rs direct their course,
In long procession rank'd, the pious chief
Stopp'd in the rear, and gave a vent to grief:
"The public care," he said, "which war attends,
Diverts our present woes, at least suspends.
Peace with the manes of great Pallas dwell!
Hail, holy relics! and a last farewell!"
He said no more, but, inly tho' he mourn'd,

THE ELEVENTH BOOK OF THE ÆNEIS 359

Restrain'd his tears, and to the camp return'd.
  Now suppliants, from Laurentum sent, demand
A truce, with olive branches in their hand;
Obtest his clemency, and from the plain
Beg leave to draw the bodies of their slain.
They plead, that none those common rites deny
To conquer'd foes that in fair battle die.
All cause of hate was ended in their death;
Nor could he war with bodies void of breath.
A king, they hop'd, would hear a king's request,
Whose son he once was call'd, and once his guest.
  Their suit, which was too just to be denied,
The hero grants, and farther thus replied:
"O Latian princes, how severe a fate
In causeless quarrels has involv'd your state,
And arm'd against an unoffending man,
Who sought your friendship ere the war began!
You beg a truce, which I would gladly give,
Not only for the slain, but those who live.
I came not hither but by Heav'n's command,
And sent by fate to share the Latian land.
Nor wage I wars unjust: your king denied
My proffer'd friendship, and my promis'd bride;
Left me for Turnus. Turnus then should try
His cause in arms, to conquer or to die.
My right and his are in dispute: the slain
Fell without fault, our quarrel to maintain.
In equal arms let us alone contend;
And let him vanquish, whom his fates befriend.
This is the way (so tell him) to possess
The royal virgin, and restore the peace.
Bear this message back, with ample leave,
That your slain friends may fun'ral rites receive."
  Thus having said—th' embassadors, amaz'd,
Stood mute a while, and on each other gaz'd.
Drances, their chief, who harbor'd in his breast
Long hate to Turnus, as his foe profess'd,
Broke silence first, and to the godlike man,
With graceful action bowing, thus began:
"Auspicious prince, in arms a mighty name,

But yet whose actions far transcend your fame;
Would I your justice or your force express,
Thought can but equal; and all words are less.
Your answer we shall thankfully relate,
And favors granted to the Latian state.
If wish'd success our labor shall attend,
Think peace concluded, and the king your friend:
Let Turnus leave the realm to your command,
And seek alliance in some other land:
Build you the city which your fates assign;
We shall be proud in the great work to join."

Thus Drances; and his words so well persuade
The rest impower'd, that soon a truce is made.
Twelve days the term allow'd: and, during those,
Latians and Trojans, now no longer foes,
Mix'd in the woods, for fun'ral piles prepare
To fell the timber, and forget the war.
Loud axes thro' the groaning groves resound;
Oak, mountain ash, and poplar spread the ground;
First fall from high; and some the trunks receive
In loaden wains; with wedges some they cleave.

And now the fatal news by Fame is blown
Thro' the short circuit of th' Arcadian town,
Of Pallas slain—by Fame, which just before
His triumphs on distended pinions bore.
Rushing from out the gate, the people stand,
Each with a fun'ral flambeau in his hand.
Wildly they stare, distracted with amaze:
The fields are lighten'd with a fiery blaze,
That cast a sullen splendor on their friends,
The marching troop which their dead prince attends.
Both parties meet: they raise a doleful cry;
The matrons from the walls with shrieks reply,
And their mix'd mourning rends the vaulted sky.
The town is fill'd with tumult and with tears,
Till the loud clamors reach Evander's ears:
Forgetful of his state, he runs along,
With a disorder'd pace, and cleaves the throng;
Falls on the corpse; and groaning there he lies,
With silent grief, that speaks but at his eyes.

THE ELEVENTH BOOK OF THE ÆNEIS 361

Short sighs and sobs succeed; till sorrow breaks
A passage, and at once he weeps and speaks:
 "O Pallas! thou hast fail'd thy plighted word,
To fight with caution, not to tempt the sword!
I warn'd thee, but in vain; for well I knew
What perils youthful ardor would pursue,
That boiling blood would carry thee too far,
Young as thou wert in dangers, raw to war!
O curst essay of arms, disastrous doom,
Prelude of bloody fields, and fights to come!
Hard elements of unauspicious war,
Vain vows to Heav'n, and unavailing care!
Thrice happy thou, dear partner of my bed,
Whose holy soul the stroke of Fortune fled,
Præscious of ills, and leaving me behind,
To drink the dregs of life by Fate assign'd!
Beyond the goal of nature I have gone:
My Pallas late set out, but reach'd too soon.
If, for my league against th' Ausonian state,
Amidst their weapons I had found my fate,
(Deserv'd from them,) then I had been return'd
A breathless victor, and my son had mourn'd.
Yet will I not my Trojan friend upbraid,
Nor grudge th' alliance I so gladly made.
'Twas not his fault, my Pallas fell so young,
But my own crime, for having liv'd too long.
Yet, since the gods had destin'd him to die,
At least he led the way to victory:
First for his friends he won the fatal shore,
And sent whole herds of slaughter'd foes before;
A death too great, too glorious to deplore.
Nor will I add new honors to thy grave,
Content with those the Trojan hero gave:
That funeral pomp thy Phrygian friends design'd,
In which the Tuscan chiefs and army join'd.
Great spoils and trophies, gain'd by thee, they bear:
Then let thy own achievements be thy share.
Even thou, O Turnus, hadst a trophy stood,
Whose mighty trunk had better grac'd the wood,
If Pallas had arriv'd, with equal length

Of years, to match thy bulk with equal strength.
But why, unhappy man, dost thou detain
These troops, to view the tears thou shedd'st in vain?
Go, friends, this message to your lord relate:
Tell him, that, if I bear my bitter fate,
And, after Pallas' death, live ling'ring on,
'Tis to behold his vengeance for my son.
I stay for Turnus, whose devoted head
Is owing to the living and the dead.
My son and I expect it from his hand;
'Tis all that he can give, or we demand.
Joy is no more; but I would gladly go,
To greet my Pallas with such news below."

    The morn had now dispell'd the shades of night,
Restoring toils, when she restor'd the light.
The Trojan king and Tuscan chief command
To raise the piles along the winding strand.
Their friends convey the dead to fun'ral fires;
Black smold'ring smoke from the green wood expires;
The light of heav'n is chok'd, and the new day retires.
Then thrice around the kindled piles they go
(For ancient custom had ordain'd it so);
Thrice horse and foot about the fires are led;
And thrice, with loud laments, they hail the dead.
Tears, trickling down their breasts, bedew the ground,
And drums and trumpets mix their mournful sound.
Amid the blaze, their pious brethren throw
The spoils, in battle taken from the foe:
Helms, bits emboss'd, and swords of shining steel;
One casts a target, one a chariot wheel;
Some to their fellows their own arms restore:
The fauchions which in luckless fight they bore,
Their bucklers pierc'd, their darts bestow'd in vain,
And shiver'd lances gather'd from the plain.
Whole herds of offer'd bulls, about the fire,
And bristled boars, and woolly sheep expire.
Around the piles a careful troop attends,
To watch the wasting flames, and weep their burning friend
Ling'ring along the shore, till dewy night
New decks the face of heav'n with starry light.

THE ELEVENTH BOOK OF THE ÆNEIS

The conquer'd Latians, with like pious care,
Piles without number for their dead prepare.
Part in the places where they fell are laid;
And part are to the neighb'ring fields convey'd.
The corps of kings, and captains of renown,
Borne off in state, are buried in the town;
The rest, unhonor'd, and without a name,
Are cast a common heap to feed the flame.
Trojans and Latians vie with like desires
To make the field of battle shine with fires,
And the promiscuous blaze to heav'n aspires.

  Now had the morning thrice renew'd the light,
And thrice dispell'd the shadows of the night,
When those who round the wasted fires remain,
Perform the last sad office to the slain.
They rake the yet warm ashes from below;
These, and the bones unburn'd, in earth bestow;
These relics with their country rites they grace,
And raise a mount of turf to mark the place.

  But, in the palace of the king, appears
A scene more solemn, and a pomp of tears.
Maids, matrons, widows, mix their common moans;
Orphans their sires, and sires lament their sons.
All in that universal sorrow share,
And curse the cause of this unhappy war:
A broken league, a bride unjustly sought,
A crown usurp'd, which with their blood is bought!
These are the crimes with which they load the name
Of Turnus, and on him alone exclaim:
"Let him who lords it o'er the Ausonian land
Engage the Trojan hero hand to hand:
His is the gain; our lot is but to serve;
'Tis just, the sway he seeks, he should deserve."
This Drances aggravates; and adds, with spite:
"His foe expects, and dares him to the fight."
Nor Turnus wants a party, to support
His cause and credit in the Latian court.
His former acts secure his present fame,
And the queen shades him with her mighty name.

  While thus their factious minds with fury burn,

The legates from th' Ætolian prince return:
Sad news they bring, that, after all the cost
And care employ'd, their embassy is lost;
That Diomedes refus'd his aid in war,
Unmov'd with presents, and as deaf to pray'r.
Some new alliance must elsewhere be sought,
Or peace with Troy on hard conditions bought.

　Latinus, sunk in sorrow, finds too late,
A foreign son is pointed out by fate;
And, till Æneas shall Lavinia wed,
The wrath of Heav'n is hov'ring o'er his head.
The gods, he saw, espous'd the juster side,
When late their titles in the field were tried:
Witness the fresh laments, and fun'ral tears undried.
Thus, full of anxious thought, he summons all
The Latian senate to the council hall.
The princes come, commanded by their head,
And crowd the paths that to the palace lead.
Supreme in pow'r, and reverenc'd for his years,
He takes the throne, and in the midst appears.
Majestically sad, he sits in state,
And bids his envoys their success relate.

　When Venulus began, the murmuring sound
Was hush'd, and sacred silence reign'd around.
"We have," said he, "perform'd your high command,
And pass'd with peril a long tract of land:
We reach'd the place desir'd; with wonder fill'd,
The Grecian tents and rising tow'rs beheld.
Great Diomede has compass'd round with walls
The city, which Argyripa he calls,
From his own Argos nam'd. We touch'd, with joy,
The royal hand that raz'd unhappy Troy.
When introduc'd, our presents first we bring,
Then crave an instant audience from the king.
His leave obtain'd, our native soil we name,
And tell th' important cause for which we came.
Attentively he heard us, while we spoke;
Then, with soft accents, and a pleasing look,
Made this return: 'Ausonian race, of old
Renown'd for peace, and for an age of gold,

What madness has your alter'd minds possess'd,
To change for war hereditary rest,
Solicit arms unknown, and tempt the sword,
A needless ill your ancestors abhorr'd?
We—for myself I speak, and all the name
Of Grecians, who to Troy's destruction came,
Omitting those who were in battle slain,
Or borne by rolling Simoïs to the main—
Not one but suffer'd, and too dearly bought
The prize of honor which in arms he sought;
Some doom'd to death, and some in exile driv'n,
Outcasts, abandon'd by the care of Heav'n;
So worn, so wretched, so despis'd a crew,
As ev'n old Priam might with pity view.
Witness the vessels by Minerva toss'd
In storms; the vengeful Capharean coast;
Th' Eubœan rocks! the prince, whose brother led
Our armies to revenge his injur'd bed,
In Egypt lost! Ulysses with his men
Have seen Charybdis and the Cyclops' den.
Why should I name Idomeneus, in vain
Restor'd to scepters, and expell'd again?
Or young Achilles, by his rival slain?
Ev'n he, the King of Men, the foremost name
Of all the Greeks, and most renown'd by fame,
The proud revenger of another's wife,
Yet by his own adult'ress lost his life;
Fell at his threshold; and the spoils of Troy
The foul polluters of his bed enjoy.
The gods have envied me the sweets of life,
My much lov'd country, and my more lov'd wife:
Banish'd from both, I mourn; while in the sky,
Transform'd to birds, my lost companions fly:
Hov'ring about the coasts, they make their moan,
And cuff the cliffs with pinions not their own.
What squalid specters, in the dead of night,
Break my short sleep, and skim before my sight!
I might have promis'd to myself those harms,
Mad as I was, when I, with mortal arms,
Presum'd against immortal pow'rs to move,

And violate with wounds the Queen of Love.
Such arms this hand shall never more employ;
No hate remains with me to ruin'd Troy.
I war not with its dust; nor am I glad
To think of past events, or good or bad.
Your presents I return: whate'er you bring
To buy my friendship, send the Trojan king.
We met in fight; I know him, to my cost:
With what a whirling force his lance he toss'd!
Heav'ns! what a spring was in his arm, to throw!
How high he held his shield, and rose at ev'ry blow!
Had Troy produc'd two more his match in might,
They would have chang'd the fortune of the fight:
Th' invasion of the Greeks had been return'd,
Our empire wasted, and our cities burn'd.
The long defense the Trojan people made,
The war protracted, and the siege delay'd,
Were due to Hector's and this hero's hand:
Both brave alike, and equal in command;
Æneas, not inferior in the field,
In pious reverence to the gods excell'd.
Make peace, ye Latians, and avoid with care
Th' impending dangers of a fatal war.'
He said no more; but, with this cold excuse,
Refus'd th' alliance, and advis'd a truce."

Thus Venulus concluded his report.
A jarring murmur fill'd the factious court:
As, when a torrent rolls with rapid force,
And dashes o'er the stones that stop the course,
The flood, constrain'd within a scanty space,
Roars horrible along th' uneasy race;
White foam in gath'ring eddies floats around;
The rocky shores rebellow to the sound.

The murmur ceas'd: then from his lofty throne
The king invok'd the gods, and thus begun:
"I wish, ye Latins, what we now debate
Had been resolv'd before it was too late.
Much better had it been for you and me,
Unforc'd by this our last necessity,
To have been earlier wise, than now to call

A council, when the foe surrounds the wall.
O citizens, we wage unequal war,
With men not only Heav'n's peculiar care,
But Heav'n's own race; unconquer'd in the field,
Or, conquer'd, yet unknowing how to yield.
What hopes you had in Diomedes, lay down:
Our hopes must center on ourselves alone.
Yet those how feeble, and, indeed, how vain,
You see too well; nor need my words explain.
Vanquish'd without resource; laid flat by Fate;
Factions within, a foe without the gate!
Not but I grant that all perform'd their parts
With manly force, and with undaunted hearts:
With our united strength the war we wag'd;
With equal numbers, equal arms, engag'd.
You see th' event.—Now hear what I propose,
To save our friends, and satisfy our foes.
A tract of land the Latins have possess'd
Along the Tiber, stretching to the west,
Which now Rutulians and Auruncans till,
And their mix'd cattle graze the fruitful hill.
Those mountains fill'd with firs, that lower land,
If you consent, the Trojan shall command,
Call'd into part of what is ours; and there,
On terms agreed, the common country share.
There let 'em build and settle, if they please;
Unless they choose once more to cross the seas,
In search of seats remote from Italy,
And from unwelcome inmates set us free.
Then twice ten galleys let us build with speed,
Or twice as many more, if more they need.
Materials are at hand; a well-grown wood
Runs equal with the margin of the flood:
Let them the number and the form assign;
The care and cost of all the stores be mine.
To treat the peace, a hundred senators
Shall be commission'd hence with ample pow'rs,
With olive crown'd: the presents they shall bear,
A purple robe, a royal iv'ry chair,
And all the marks of sway that Latian monarchs wear,

And sums of gold. Among yourselves debate
This great affair, and save the sinking state."
　　Then Drances took the word, who grudg'd, long since
The rising glories of the Daunian prince.
Factious and rich, bold at the council board,
But cautious in the field, he shunn'd the sword;
A close caballer, and tongue-valiant lord.
Noble his mother was, and near the throne;
But, what his father's parentage, unknown.
He rose, and took th' advantage of the times,
To load young Turnus with invidious crimes.
"Such truths, O king," said he, "your words contain,
As strike the sense, and all replies are vain;
Nor are your loyal subjects now to seek
What common needs require, but fear to speak.
Let him give leave of speech, that haughty man,
Whose pride this unauspicious war began;
For whose ambition (let me dare to say,
Fear set apart, tho' death is in my way)
The plains of Latium run with blood around.
So many valiant heroes bite the ground;
Dejected grief in ev'ry face appears;
A town in mourning, and a land in tears;
While he, th' undoubted author of our harms,
The man who menaces the gods with arms,
Yet, after all his boasts, forsook the fight,
And sought his safety in ignoble flight.
Now, best of kings, since you propose to send
Such bounteous presents to your Trojan friend;
Add yet a greater at our joint request,
One which he values more than all the rest:
Give him the fair Lavinia for his bride;
With that alliance let the league be tied,
And for the bleeding land a lasting peace provide.
Let insolence no longer awe the throne;
But, with a father's right, bestow your own.
For this maligner of the general good,
If still we fear his force, he must be woo'd;
His haughty godhead we with pray'rs implore,
Your scepter to release, and our just rights restore.

O cursed cause of all our ills, must we
Wage wars unjust, and fall in fight, for thee!
What right hast thou to rule the Latian state,
And send us out to meet our certain fate?
'Tis a destructive war: from Turnus' hand
Our peace and public safety we demand.
Let the fair bride to the brave chief remain;
If not, the peace, without the pledge, is vain.
Turnus, I know you think me not your friend,
Nor will I much with your belief contend:
I beg your greatness not to give the law
In others' realms, but, beaten, to withdraw.
Pity your own, or pity our estate;
Not twist our fortunes with your sinking fate.
Your interest is, the war should never cease;
But we have felt enough to wish the peace:
A land exhausted to the last remains,
Depopulated towns, and driven plains.
Yet, if desire of fame, and thirst of pow'r,
A beauteous princess, with a crown in dow'r,
So fire your mind, in arms assert your right,
And meet your foe, who dares you to the fight.
Mankind, it seems, is made for you alone;
We, but the slaves who mount you to the throne:
A base ignoble crowd, without a name,
Unwept, unworthy, of the fun'ral flame,
By duty bound to forfeit each his life,
That Turnus may possess a royal wife.
Permit not, mighty man, so mean a crew
Should share such triumphs, and detain from you
The post of honor, your undoubted due.
Rather alone your matchless force employ,
To merit what alone you must enjoy."

  These words, so full of malice mix'd with art,
Inflam'd with rage the youthful hero's heart.
Then, groaning from the bottom of his breast,
He heav'd for wind, and thus his wrath express'd:
"You, Drances, never want a stream of words,
Then, when the public need requires our swords.
First in the council hall to steer the state,

And ever foremost in a tongue-debate,
While our strong walls secure us from the foe,
Ere yet with blood our ditches overflow:
But let the potent orator declaim,
And with the brand of coward blot my name;
Free leave is giv'n him, when his fatal hand
Has cover'd with more corps the sanguine strand,
And high as mine his tow'ring trophies stand.
If any doubt remains, who dares the most,
Let us decide it at the Trojan's cost,
And issue both abreast, where honor calls—
Foes are not far to seek without the walls—
Unless his noisy tongue can only fight,
And feet were giv'n him but to speed his flight.
I beaten from the field? I forc'd away?
Who, but so known a dastard, dares to say?
Had he but ev'n beheld the fight, his eyes
Had witness'd for me what his tongue denies:
What heaps of Trojans by this hand were slain,
And how the bloody Tiber swell'd the main.
All saw, but he, th' Arcadian troops retire
In scatter'd squadrons, and their prince expire.
The giant brothers, in their camp, have found,
I was not forc'd with ease to quit my ground.
Not such the Trojans tried me, when, inclos'd,
I singly their united arms oppos'd:
First forc'd an entrance thro' their thick array;
Then, glutted with their slaughter, freed my way.
'Tis a destructive war? So let it be,
But to the Phrygian pirate, and to thee!
Meantime proceed to fill the people's ears
With false reports, their minds with panic fears;
Extol the strength of a twice-conquer'd race;
Our foes encourage, and our friends debase.
Believe thy fables, and the Trojan town
Triumphant stands; the Grecians are o'erthrown;
Suppliant at Hector's feet Achilles lies,
And Diomede from fierce Æneas flies.
Say rapid Aufidus with awful dread
Runs backward from the sea, and hides his head,

When the great Trojan on his bank appears;
For that's as true as thy dissembled fears
Of my revenge. Dismiss that vanity:
Thou, Drances, art below a death from me.
Let that vile soul in that vile body rest;
The lodging is well worthy of the guest.

"Now, royal father, to the present state
Of our affairs, and of this high debate:
If in your arms thus early you diffide,
And think your fortune is already tried;
If one defeat has brought us down so low,
As never more in fields to meet the foe;
Then I conclude for peace: 'tis time to treat,
And lie like vassals at the victor's feet.
But, O! if any ancient blood remains,
One drop of all our fathers', in our veins,
That man would I prefer before the rest,
Who dar'd his death with an undaunted breast;
Who comely fell, by no dishonest wound,
To shun that sight, and, dying, gnaw'd the ground.
But, if we still have fresh recruits in store,
If our confederates can afford us more;
If the contended field we bravely fought,
And not a bloodless victory was bought;
Their losses equal'd ours; and, for their slain,
With equal fires they fill'd the shining plain;
Why thus, unforc'd, should we so tamely yield,
And, ere the trumpet sounds, resign the field?
Good unexpected, evils unforeseen,
Appear by turns, as fortune shifts the scene:
Some, rais'd aloft, come tumbling down amain;
Then fall so hard, they bound and rise again.
If Diomede refuse his aid to lend,
The great Messapus yet remains our friend:
Tolumnius, who foretells events, is ours;
Th' Italian chiefs and princes join their pow'rs:
Nor least in number, nor in name the last,
Your own brave subjects have your cause embrac'd.
Above the rest, the Volscian Amazon
Contains an army in herself alone,

And heads a squadron, terrible to sight,
With glitt'ring shields, in brazen armor bright.
Yet, if the foe a single fight demand,
And I alone the public peace withstand;
If you consent, he shall not be refus'd,
Nor find a hand to victory unus'd.
This new Achilles, let him take the field,
With fated armor, and Vulcanian shield!
For you, my royal father, and my fame,
I, Turnus, not the least of all my name,
Devote my soul. He calls me hand to hand,
And I alone will answer his demand.
Drances shall rest secure, and neither share
The danger, nor divide the prize of war."

While they debate, nor these nor those will yield,
Æneas draws his forces to the field,
And moves his camp. The scouts with flying speed
Return, and thro' the frighted city spread
Th' unpleasing news, the Trojans are descried,
In battle marching by the river side,
And bending to the town. They take th' alarm:
Some tremble, some are bold; all in confusion arm.
Th' impetuous youth press forward to the field;
They clash the sword, and clatter on the shield:
The fearful matrons raise a screaming cry;
Old feeble men with fainter groans reply;
A jarring sound results, and mingles in the sky,
Like that of swans remurm'ring to the floods,
Or birds of diff'ring kinds in hollow woods.

Turnus th' occasion takes, and cries aloud:
"Talk on, ye quaint haranguers of the crowd:
Declaim in praise of peace, when danger calls,
And the fierce foes in arms approach the walls."
He said, and turning short, with speedy pace,
Casts back a scornful glance, and quits the place:
"Thou, Volusus, the Volscian troops command
To mount; and lead thyself our Ardean band.
Messapus and Catillus, post your force
Along the fields, to charge the Trojan horse.
Some guard the passes, others man the wall;
Drawn up in arms, the rest attend my call."

THE ELEVENTH BOOK OF THE ÆNEIS

They swarm from ev'ry quarter of the town,
And with disorder'd haste the rampires crown.
Good old Latinus, when he saw, too late,
The gath'ring storm just breaking on the state,
Dismiss'd the council till a fitter time,
And own'd his easy temper as his crime,
Who, forc'd against his reason, had complied
To break the treaty for the promis'd bride.

Some help to sink new trenches; others aid
To ram the stones, or raise the palisade.
Hoarse trumpets sound th' alarm; around the walls
Runs a distracted crew, whom their last labor calls.
A sad procession in the streets is seen,
Of matrons, that attend the mother queen:
High in her chair she sits, and, at her side,
With downcast eyes, appears the fatal bride.
They mount the cliff, where Pallas' temple stands;
Pray'rs in their mouths, and presents in their hands,
With censers first they fume the sacred shrine,
Then in this common supplication join:
"O patroness of arms, unspotted maid,
Propitious hear, and lend thy Latins aid!
Break short the pirate's lance; pronounce his fate,
And lay the Phrygian low before the gate."

Now Turnus arms for fight. His back and breast
Well-temper'd steel and scaly brass invest:
The cuishes which his brawny thighs infold
Are mingled metal damask'd o'er with gold.
His faithful fauchion sits upon his side;
Nor casque, nor crest, his manly features hide:
But, bare to view, amid surrounding friends,
With godlike grace, he from the tow'r descends.
Exulting in his strength, he seems to dare
His absent rival, and to promise war.
Freed from his keepers, thus, with broken reins,
The wanton courser prances o'er the plains,
Or in the pride of youth o'erleaps the mounds,
And snuffs the females in forbidden grounds,
Or seeks his wat'ring in the well-known flood,
To quench his thirst, and cool his fiery blood:
He swims luxuriant in the liquid plain,

And o'er his shoulder flows his waving mane:
He neighs, he snorts, he bears his head on high;
Before his ample chest the frothy waters fly.

   Soon as the prince appears without the gate,
The Volscians, with their virgin leader, wait
His last commands. Then, with a graceful mien,
Lights from her lofty steed the warrior queen:
Her squadron imitates, and each descends;
Whose common suit Camilla thus commends:
"If sense of honor, if a soul secure
Of inborn worth, that can all tests endure,
Can promise aught, or on itself rely
Greatly to dare, to conquer or to die;
Then, I alone, sustain'd by these, will meet
The Tyrrhene troops, and promise their defeat.
Ours be the danger, ours the sole renown:
You, gen'ral, stay behind, and guard the town:"

   Turnus a while stood mute, with glad surprise,
And on the fierce virago fix'd his eyes;
Then thus return'd: "O grace of Italy,
With what becoming thanks can I reply?
Not only words lie lab'ring in my breast,
But thought itself is by thy praise oppress'd.
Yet rob me not of all; but let me join
My toils, my hazard, and my fame, with thine.
The Trojan, not in stratagem unskill'd,
Sends his light horse before to scour the field:
Himself, thro' steep ascents and thorny brakes,
A larger compass to the city takes.
This news my scouts confirm, and I prepare
To foil his cunning, and his force to dare;
With chosen foot his passage to forelay,
And place an ambush in the winding way.
Thou, with thy Volscians, face the Tuscan horse;
The brave Messapus shall thy troops inforce
With those of Tibur, and the Latian band,
Subjected all to thy supreme command."
This said, he warns Messapus to the war,
Then ev'ry chief exhorts with equal care.
All thus encourag'd, his own troops he joins,
And hastes to prosecute his deep designs.

THE ELEVENTH BOOK OF THE ÆNEIS

Inclos'd with hills, a winding valley lies,
By nature form'd for fraud, and fitted for surprise.
A narrow track, by human steps untrode,
Leads, thro' perplexing thorns, to this obscure abode.
High o'er the vale a steepy mountain stands,
Whence the surveying sight the nether ground commands.
The top is level, an offensive seat
Of war; and from the war a safe retreat:
For, on the right and left, is room to press
The foes at hand, or from afar distress;
To drive 'em headlong downward, and to pour
On their descending backs a stony show'r.
Thither young Turnus took the well-known way,
Possess'd the pass, and in blind ambush lay.

Meantime Latonian Phœbe, from the skies,
Beheld th' approaching war with hateful eyes,
And call'd the light-foot Opis to her aid,
Her most belov'd and ever-trusty maid;
Then with a sigh began: "Camilla goes
To meet her death amidst her fatal foes:
The nymphs I lov'd of all my mortal train,
Invested with Diana's arms, in vain.
Nor is my kindness for the virgin new:
'Twas born with her; and with her years it grew.
Her father Metabus, when forc'd away
From old Privernum, for tyrannic sway,
Snatch'd up, and sav'd from his prevailing foes,
This tender babe, companion of his woes.
Casmilla was her mother; but he drown'd
One hissing letter in a softer sound,
And call'd Camilla. Thro' the woods he flies;
Wrapp'd in his robe the royal infant lies.
His foes in sight, he mends his weary pace;
With shouts and clamors they pursue the chase.
The banks of Amasene at length he gains:

The raging flood his farther flight restrains,
Rais'd o'er the borders with unusual rains.
Prepar'd to plunge into the stream, he fears,
Not for himself, but for the charge he bears.
Anxious, he stops a while, and thinks in haste;

Then, desp'rate in distress, resolves at last.
A knotty lance of well-boil'd oak he bore;
The middle part with cork he cover'd o'er:
He clos'd the child within the hollow space;
With twigs of bending osier bound the case;
Then pois'd the spear, heavy with human weight,
And thus invok'd my favor for the freight:
'Accept, great goddess of the woods,' he said,
'Sent by her sire, this dedicated maid!
Thro' air she flies a suppliant to thy shrine;
And the first weapons that she knows, are thine.'
He said; and with full force the spear he threw:
Above the sounding waves Camilla flew.
Then, press'd by foes, he stemm'd the stormy tide,
And gain'd, by stress of arms, the farther side.
His fasten'd spear he pull'd from out the ground,
And, victor of his vows, his infant nymph unbound;
Nor, after that, in towns which walls inclose,
Would trust his hunted life amidst his foes;
But, rough, in open air he chose to lie;
Earth was his couch, his cov'ring was the sky.
On hills unshorn, or in a desart den,
He shunn'd the dire society of men.
A shepherd's solitary life he led;
His daughter with the milk of mares he fed.
The dugs of bears, and ev'ry salvage beast,
He drew, and thro' her lips the liquor press'd.
The little Amazon could scarcely go:
He loads her with a quiver and a bow;
And, that she might her stagg'ring steps command,
He with a slender jav'lin fills her hand.
Her flowing hair no golden fillet bound;
Nor swept her trailing robe the dusty ground.
Instead of these, a tiger's hide o'erspread
Her back and shoulders, fasten'd to her head.
The flying dart she first attempts to fling,
And round her tender temples toss'd the sling;
Then, as her strength with years increas'd, began
To pierce aloft in air the soaring swan,
And from the clouds to fetch the heron and the crane.

THE ELEVENTH BOOK OF THE ÆNEIS

The Tuscan matrons with each other vied,
To bless their rival sons with such a bride;
But she disdains their love, to share with me
The sylvan shades and vow'd virginity.
And, O! I wish, contented with my cares
Of salvage spoils, she had not sought the wars!
Then had she been of my celestial train,
And shunn'd the fate that dooms her to be slain.
But since, opposing Heav'n's decree, she goes
To find her death among forbidden foes,
Haste with these arms, and take thy steepy flight,
Where, with the gods, averse, the Latins fight.
This bow to thee, this quiver I bequeath,
This chosen arrow, to revenge her death:
By whate'er hand Camilla shall be slain,
Or of the Trojan or Italian train,
Let him not pass unpunish'd from the plain.
Then, in a hollow cloud, myself will aid
To bear the breathless body of my maid:
Unspoil'd shall be her arms, and unprofan'd
Her holy limbs with any human hand,
And in a marble tomb laid in her native land."

She said. The faithful nymph descends from high
With rapid flight, and cuts the sounding sky:
Black clouds and stormy winds around her body fly.

By this, the Trojan and the Tuscan horse,
Drawn up in squadrons, with united force,
Approach the walls: the sprightly coursers bound,
Press forward on their bits, and shift their ground.
Shields, arms, and spears flash horribly from far;
And the fields glitter with a waving war.
Oppos'd to these, come on with furious force
Messapus, Coras, and the Latian horse;
These in the body plac'd, on either hand
Sustain'd and clos'd by fair Camilla's band.
Advancing in a line, they couch their spears;
And less and less the middle space appears.
Thick smoke obscures the field; and scarce are seen
The neighing coursers, and the shouting men.
In distance of their darts they stop their course;

Then man to man they rush, and horse to horse.
The face of heav'n their flying jav'lins hide,
And deaths unseen are dealt on either side.
Tyrrhenus, and Aconteus, void of fear,
By mettled coursers borne in full career,
Meet first oppos'd; and, with a mighty shock,
Their horses' heads against each other knock.
Far from his steed is fierce Aconteus cast,
As with an engine's force, or lightning's blast:
He rolls along in blood, and breathes his last.
The Latin squadrons take a sudden fright,
And sling their shields behind, to save their backs in flight.
Spurring at speed to their own walls they drew;
Close in the rear the Tuscan troops pursue,
And urge their flight: Asylas leads the chase;
Till, seiz'd, with shame, they wheel about and face,
Receive their foes, and raise a threat'ning cry.
The Tuscans take their turn to fear and fly.
So swelling surges, with a thund'ring roar,
Driv'n on each other's backs, insult the shore,
Bound o'er the rocks, incroach upon the land,
And far upon the beach eject the sand;
Then backward, with a swing, they take their way,
Repuls'd from upper ground, and seek their mother sea;
With equal hurry quit th' invaded shore,
And swallow back the sand and stones they spew'd before.

Twice were the Tuscans masters of the field,
Twice by the Latins, in their turn, repell'd.
Asham'd at length, to the third charge they ran;
Both hosts resolv'd, and mingled man to man.
Now dying groans are heard; the fields are strow'd
With falling bodies, and are drunk with blood.
Arms, horses, men, on heaps together lie:
Confus'd the fight, and more confus'd the cry.
Orsilochus, who durst not press too near
Strong Remulus, at distance drove his spear,
And stuck the steel beneath his horse's ear.
The fiery steed, impatient of the wound,
Curvets, and, springing upward with a bound,
His helpless lord cast backward on the ground.

THE ELEVENTH BOOK OF THE ÆNEIS

Catillus pierc'd Iolas first; then drew
His reeking lance, and at Herminius threw,
The mighty champion of the Tuscan crew.
His neck and throat unarm'd, his head was bare,
But shaded with a length of yellow hair:
Secure, he fought, expos'd on ev'ry part,
A spacious mark for swords, and for the flying dart.
Across the shoulders came the feather'd wound;
Transfix'd he fell, and doubled to the ground.
The sands with streaming blood are sanguine dyed,
And death with honor sought on either side.

  Resistless thro' the war Camilla rode,
In danger unappall'd, and pleas'd with blood.
One side was bare for her exerted breast;
One shoulder with her painted quiver press'd.
Now from afar her fatal jav'lins play;
Now with her ax's edge she hews her way:
Diana's arms upon her shoulder sound;
And when, too closely press'd, she quits the ground,
From her bent bow she sends a backward wound.
Her maids, in martial pomp, on either side,
Larina, Tulla, fierce Tarpeia, ride:
Italians all; in peace, their queen's delight;
In war, the bold companions of the fight.
So march'd the Tracian Amazons of old,
When Thermodon with bloody billows roll'd:
Such troops as these in shining arms were seen,
When Theseus met in fight their maiden queen:
Such to the field Penthisilea led,
From the fierce virgin when the Grecians fled;
With such, return'd triumphant from the war,
Her maids with cries attend the lofty car;
They clash with manly force their moony shields;
With female shouts resound the Phrygian fields.

  Who foremost, and who last, heroic maid,
On the cold earth were by thy courage laid?
Thy spear, of mountain ash, Eumenius first,
With fury driv'n, from side to side transpierc'd:
A purple stream came spouting from the wound;
Bath'd in his blood he lies, and bites the ground.

Liris and Pagasus at once she slew:
The former, as the slacken'd reins he drew
Of his faint steed; the latter, as he stretch'd
His arm to prop his friend, the jav'lin reach'd.
By the same weapon, sent from the same hand,
Both fall together, and both spurn the sand.
Amastrus next is added to the slain:
The rest in rout she follows o'er the plain:
Tereus, Harpalycus, Demophoön,
And Chromis, at full speed her fury shun.
Of all her deadly darts, not one she lost;
Each was attended with a Trojan ghost.
Young Ornithus bestrode a hunter steed,
Swift for the chase, and of Apulian breed.
Him from afar she spied, in arms unknown:
O'er his broad back an ox's hide was thrown;
His helm a wolf, whose gaping jaws were spread
A cov'ring for his cheeks, and grinn'd around his head,
He clench'd within his hand an iron prong,
And tower'd above the rest, conspicuous in the throng.
Him soon she singled from the flying train,
And slew with ease; then thus insults the slain:
"Vain hunter, didst thou think thro' woods to chase
The savage herd, a vile and trembling race?
Here cease thy vaunts, and own my victory:
A woman warrior was too strong for thee.
Yet, if the ghosts demand the conqu'ror's name.
Confessing great Camilla, save thy shame."
Then Butes and Orsilochus she slew,
The bulkiest bodies of the Trojan crew;
But Butes breast to breast: the spear descends
Above the gorget, where his helmet ends,
And o'er the shield which his left side defends.
Orsilochus and she their courses ply:
He seems to follow, and she seems to fly;
But in a narrower ring she makes the race;
And then he flies, and she pursues the chase.
Gath'ring at length on her deluded foe,
She swings her ax, and rises to the blow;
Full on the helm behind, with such a sway

THE ELEVENTH BOOK OF THE ÆNEIS

The weapon falls, the riven steel gives way:
He groans, he roars, he sues in vain for grace;
Brains, mingled with his blood, besmear his face.

Astonish'd Aunus just arrives by chance,
To see his fall; nor farther dares advance;
But, fixing on the horrid maid his eye,
He stares, and shakes, and finds it vain to fly;
Yet, like a true Ligurian, born to cheat,
(At least while fortune favor'd his deceit,)
Cries out aloud: "What courage have you shown,
Who trust your courser's strength, and not your own?
Forego the vantage of your horse, alight,
And then on equal terms begin the fight:
It shall be seen, weak woman, what you can,
When, foot to foot, you combat with a man."
He said. She glows with anger and disdain,
Dismounts with speed to dare him on the plain,
And leaves her horse at large among her train;
With her drawn sword defies him to the field,
And, marching, lifts aloft her maiden shield.
The youth, who thought his cunning did succeed,
Reins round his horse, and urges all his speed;
Adds the remembrance of the spur, and hides
The goring rowels in his bleeding sides.
"Vain fool, and coward!" cries the lofty maid,
"Caught in the train which thou thyself hast laid!
On others practice thy Ligurian arts;
Thin stratagems and tricks of little hearts
Are lost on me: nor shalt thou safe retire,
With vaunting lies, to thy fallacious sire."
At this, so fast her flying feet she sped,
That soon she strain'd beyond his horse's head:
Then turning short, at once she seiz'd the rein,
And laid the boaster grov'ling on the plain.
Not with more ease the falcon, from above,
Trusses in middle air the trembling dove,
Then plumes the prey, in her strong pounces bound:
The feathers, foul with blood, come tumbling to the ground.

Now mighty Jove, from his superior height,
With his broad eye surveys th' unequal fight.

He fires the breast of Tarchon with disdain,
And sends him to redeem th' abandon'd plain.
Betwixt the broken ranks the Tuscan rides,
And these encourages, and those he chides;
Recalls each leader, by his name, from flight;
Renews their ardor, and restores the fight.
"What panic fear has seiz'd your souls? O shame,
O brand perpetual of th' Etrurian name!
Cowards incurable, a woman's hand
Drives, breaks, and scatters your ignoble band!
Now cast away the sword, and quit the shield!
What use of weapons which you dare not wield?
Not thus you fly your female foes by night,
Nor shun the feast, when the full bowls invite;
When to fat off'rings the glad augur calls,
And the shrill hornpipe sounds to bacchanals.
These are your studied cares, your lewd delight:
Swift to debauch, but slow to manly fight."
Thus having said, he spurs amid the foes,
Not managing the life he meant to lose.
The first he found he seiz'd with headlong haste,
In his strong gripe, and clasp'd around the waist;
'Twas Venulus, whom from his horse he tore,
And, laid athwart his own, in triumph bore.
Loud shouts ensue; the Latins turn their eyes,
And view th' unusual sight with vast surprise.
The fiery Tarchon, flying o'er the plains,
Press'd in his arms the pond'rous prey sustains;
Then, with his shorten'd spear, explores around
His jointed arms, to fix a deadly wound.
Nor less the captive struggles for his life:
He writhes his body to prolong the strife,
And, fencing for his naked throat, exerts
His utmost vigor, and the point averts.
So stoops the yellow eagle from on high,
And bears a speckled serpent thro' the sky,
Fast'ning his crooked talons on the prey:
The pris'ner hisses thro' the liquid way;
Resists the royal hawk; and, tho' oppress'd,
She fights in volumes, and erects her crest:

Turn'd to her foe, she stiffens ev'ry scale,
And shoots her forky tongue, and whisks her threat'ning tail.
Against the victor, all defense is weak:
Th' imperial bird still plies her with his beak;
He tears her bowels, and her breast he gores;
Then claps his pinions, and securely soars.
Thus, thro' the midst of circling enemies,
Strong Tarchon snatch'd and bore away his prize.
The Tyrrhene troops, that shrunk before, now press
The Latins, and presume the like success.

    Then Aruns, doom'd to death, his arts assay'd,
To murther, unespied, the Volscian maid:
This way and that his winding course he bends,
And, whereso'er she turns, her steps attends.
When she retires victorious from the chase,
He wheels about with care, and shifts his place;
When, rushing on, she seeks her foes in flight,
He keeps aloof, but keeps her still in sight:
He threats, and trembles, trying ev'ry way,
Unseen to kill, and safely to betray.
Chloreus, the priest of Cybele, from far,
Glitt'ring in Phrygian arms amidst the war,
Was by the virgin view'd. The steed he press'd
Was proud with trappings, and his brawny chest
With scales of gilded brass was cover'd o'er;
A robe of Tyrian dye the rider wore.
With deadly wounds he gall'd the distant foe;
Gnossian his shafts, and Lycian was his bow:
A golden helm his front and head surrounds;
A gilded quiver from his shoulder sounds.
Gold, weav'd with linen, on his thighs he wore,
With flowers of needlework distinguish'd o'er,
With golden buckles bound, and gather'd up before.
Him the fierce maid beheld with ardent eyes,
Fond and ambitious of so rich a prize,
Or that the temple might his trophies hold,
Or else to shine herself in Trojan gold.
Blind in her haste, she chases him alone.
And seeks his life, regardless of her own.

    This lucky moment the sly traitor chose:

Then, starting from his ambush, up he rose,
And threw, but first to Heav'n address'd his vows:
"O patron of Socrate's high abodes,
Phœbus, the ruling pow'r among the gods,
Whom first we serve, whole woods of unctuous pine
Are fell'd for thee, and to thy glory shine;
By thee protected with our naked soles,
Thro' flames unsing'd we march, and tread the kindled coals
Give me, propitious pow'r, to wash away
The stains of this dishonorable day:
Nor spoils, nor triumph, from the fact I claim,
But with my future actions trust my fame.
Let me, by stealth, this female plague o'ercome,
And from the field return inglorious home."
Apollo heard, and, granting half his pray'r,
Shuffled in winds the rest, and toss'd in empty air.
He gives the death desir'd; his safe return
By southern tempests to the seas is borne.

Now, when the jav'lin whizz'd along the skies,
Both armies on Camilla turn'd their eyes,
Directed by the sound. Of either host,
Th' unhappy virgin, tho' concern'd the most,
Was only deaf; so greedy was she bent
On golden spoils, and on her prey intent;
Till in her pap the winged weapon stood
Infix'd, and deeply drunk the purple blood.
Her sad attendants hasten to sustain
Their dying lady, drooping on the plain.
Far from their sight the trembling Aruns flies,
With beating heart, and fear confus'd with joys;
Nor dares he farther to pursue his blow,
Or ev'n to bear the sight of his expiring foe.
As, when the wolf has torn a bullock's hide
At unawares, or ranch'd a shepherd's side,
Conscious of his audacious deed, he flies,
And claps his quiv'ring tail between his thighs:
So, speeding once, the wretch no more attends,
But, spurring forward, herds among his friends.

She wrench'd the jav'lin with her dying hands,
But wedg'd within her breast the weapon stands;

THE ELEVENTH BOOK OF THE ÆNEIS

The wood she draws, the steely point remains;
She staggers in her seat with agonizing pains:
(A gath'ring mist o'erclouds her cheerful eyes,
And from her cheeks the rosy color flies:)
Then turns to her, whom of her female train
She trusted most, and thus she speaks with pain:
"Acca, 'tis past! he swims before my sight,
Inexorable Death; and claims his right.
Bear my last words to Turnus; fly with speed,
And bid him timely to my charge succeed,
Repel the Trojans, and the town relieve:
Farewell! and in this kiss my parting breath receive."
She said, and, sliding, sunk upon the plain:
Dying, her open'd hand forsakes the rein;
Short, and more short, she pants; by slow degrees
Her mind the passage from her body frees.
She drops her sword; she nods her plumy crest,
Her drooping head declining on her breast:
In the last sigh her struggling soul expires,
And, murm'ring with disdain, to Stygian sounds retires.

A shout, that struck the golden stars, ensued;
Despair and rage the languish'd fight renew'd.
The Trojan troops and Tuscans, in a line,
Advance to charge; the mix'd Arcadians join.

But Cynthia's maid, high seated, from afar
Surveys the field, and fortune of the war,
Unmov'd a while, till, prostrate on the plain,
Welt'ring in blood, she sees Camilla slain,
And, round her corpse, of friends and foes a fighting train.
Then, from the bottom of her breast, she drew
A mournful sigh, and these sad words ensue:
"Too dear a fine, ah much lamented maid,
For warring with the Trojans, thou hast paid!
Nor aught avail'd, in this unhappy strife,
Diana's sacred arms, to save thy life.
Yet unreveng'd thy goodness will not leave
Her vot'ry's death, nor with vain sorrow grieve.
Branded the wretch, and be his name abhorr'd;
But after ages shall thy praise record.
Th' inglorious coward soon shall press the plain:

Thus vows thy queen, and thus the Fates ordain."

 High o'er the field there stood a hilly mound,
Sacred the place, and spread with oaks around,
Where, in a marble tomb, Dercennus lay,
A king that once in Latium bore the sway.
The beauteous Opis thither bent her flight,
To mark the traitor Aruns from the height.
Him in refulgent arms she soon espied,
Swoln with success; and loudly thus she cried:
"Thy backward steps, vain boaster, are too late;
Turn like a man, at length, and meet thy fate.
Charg'd with my message, to Camilla go,
And say I sent thee to the shades below,
An honor undeserv'd from Cynthia's bow."

 She said, and from her quiver chose with speed
The winged shaft, predestin'd for the deed;
Then to the stubborn yew her strength applied,
Till the far distant horns approach'd on either side.
The bowstring touch'd her breast, so strong she drew;
Whizzing in air the fatal arrow flew.
At once the twanging bow and sounding dart
The traitor heard, and felt the point within his heart.
Him, beating with his heels in pangs of death,
His flying friends to foreign fields bequeath.
The conqu'ring damsel, with expanded wings,
The welcome message to her mistress brings.

 Their leader lost, the Volscians quit the field,
And, unsustain'd, the chiefs of Turnus yield.
The frighted soldiers, when their captains fly,
More on their speed than on their strength rely.
Confus'd in flight, they bear each other down,
And spur their horses headlong to the town.
Driv'n by their foes, and to their fears resign'd,
Not once they turn, but take their wounds behind.
These drop the shield, and those the lance forego,
Or on their shoulders bear the slacken'd bow.
The hoofs of horses, with a rattling sound,
Beat short and thick, and shake the rotten ground.
Black clouds of dust come rolling in the sky,
And o'er the darken'd walls and rampires fly.

The trembling matrons, from their lofty stands,
Rend heav'n with female shrieks, and wring their hands.
All pressing on, pursuers and pursued,
Are crush'd in crowds, a mingled multitude.
Some happy few escape: the throng too late
Rush on for entrance, till they choke the gate.
Ev'n in the sight of home, the wretched sire
Looks on, and sees his helpless son expire.
Then, in a fright, the folding gates they close,
But leave their friends excluded with their foes.
The vanquish'd cry; the victors loudly shout;
'Tis terror all within, and slaughter all without.
Blind in their fear, they bounce against the wall,
Or, to the moats pursued, precipitate their fall.

  The Latian virgins, valiant with despair,
Arm'd on the tow'rs, the common danger share:
So much of zeal their country's cause inspir'd;
So much Camilla's great example fir'd.
Poles, sharpen'd in the flames, from high they throw,
With imitated darts, to gall the foe.
Their lives for godlike freedom they bequeath,
And crowd each other to be first in death.
Meantime to Turnus, ambush'd in the shade,
With heavy tidings came th' unhappy maid:
"The Volscians overthrown, Camilla kill'd;
The foes, entirely masters of the field,
Like a resistless flood, come rolling on:
The cry goes off the plain, and thickens to the town."

  Inflam'd with rage, (for so the Furies fire
The Daunian's breast, and so the Fates require,)
He leaves the hilly pass, the woods in vain
Possess'd, and downward issues on the plain.
Scarce was he gone, when to the straits, now freed
From secret foes, the Trojan troops succeed.
Thro' the black forest and the ferny brake,
Unknowingly secure, their way they take;
From the rough mountains to the plain descend,
And there, in order drawn, their line extend.
Both armies now in open fields are seen;
Nor far the distance of the space between.

Both to the city bend. Æneas sees,
Thro' smoking fields, his hast'ning enemies;
And Turnus views the Trojans in array,
And hears th' approaching horses proudly neigh.
Soon had their hosts in bloody battle join'd;
But westward to the sea the sun declin'd.
Intrench'd before the town both armies lie,
While Night with sable wings involves the sky.

THE TWELFTH BOOK
OF THE ÆNEIS

THE ARGUMENT.—Turnus challenges Æneas to a single combat: articles are agreed but broken by the Rutili, who wound Æneas. He is miraculously cur'd by Venus, [forc]es Turnus to a duel, and concludes the poem with his death.

WHEN Turnus saw the Latins leave the field,
    Their armies broken, and their courage quell'd,
    Himself become the mark of public spite,
His honor question'd for the promis'd fight;
The more he was with vulgar hate oppress'd,
The more his fury boil'd within his breast:
He rous'd his vigor for the last debate,
And rais'd his haughty soul to meet his fate.

As, when the swains the Libyan lion chase,
He makes a sour retreat, nor mends his pace;
But, if the pointed jav'lin pierce his side,
The lordly beast returns with double pride:
He wrenches out the steel, he roars for pain;
His sides he lashes, and erects his mane:
So Turnus fares; his eyeballs flash with fire,
Thro' his wide nostrils clouds of smoke expire.

Trembling with rage, around the court he ran.
At length approach'd the king, and thus began:
"No more excuses or delays: I stand
In arms prepar'd to combat, hand to hand,
This base deserter of his native land.
The Trojan, by his word, is bound to take
The same conditions which himself did make.
Renew the truce; the solemn rites prepare,
And to my single virtue trust the war.
The Latians unconcern'd shall see the fight;
This arm unaided shall assert your right:
Then, if my prostrate body press the plain,
To him the crown and beauteous bride remain."

389

To whom the king sedately thus replied:
"Brave youth, the more your valor has been tried,
The more becomes it us, with due respect,
To weigh the chance of war, which you neglect.
You want not wealth, or a successive throne,
Or cities which your arms have made your own:
My towns and treasures are at your command,
And stor'd with blooming beauties is my land;
Laurentum more than one Lavinia sees,
Unmarried, fair, of noble families.
Now let me speak, and you with patience hear,
Things which perhaps may grate a lover's ear,
But sound advice, proceeding from a heart
Sincerely yours, and free from fraudful art.
The gods, by signs, have manifestly shown,
No prince Italian born should heir my throne:
Oft have our augurs, in prediction skill'd,
And oft our priests, a foreign son reveal'd.
Yet, won by worth that cannot be withstood,
Brib'd by my kindness to my kindred blood,
Urg'd by my wife, who would not be denied,
I promis'd my Lavinia for your bride:
Her from her plighted lord by force I took;
All ties of treaties, and of honor, broke:
On your account I wag'd an impious war—
With what success, 'tis needless to declare;
I and my subjects feel, and you have had your share
Twice vanquish'd while in bloody fields we strive,
Scarce in our walls we keep our hopes alive:
The rolling flood runs warm with human gore;
The bones of Latians blanch the neighb'ring shore.
Why put I not an end to this debate,
Still unresolv'd, and still a slave to fate?
If Turnus' death a lasting peace can give,
Why should I not procure it whilst you live?
Should I to doubtful arms your youth betray,
What would my kinsmen the Rutulians say?
And, should you fall in fight, (which Heav'n defend!)
How curse the cause which hasten'd to his end
The daughter's lover and the father's friend?

Weigh in your mind the various chance of war;
Pity your parent's age, and ease his care."

Such balmy words he pour'd, but all in vain:
The proffer'd med'cine but provok'd the pain.
The wrathful youth, disdaining the relief,
With intermitting sobs thus vents his grief:
"The care, O best of fathers, which you take
For my concerns, at my desire forsake.
Permit me not to languish out my days,
But make the best exchange of life for praise.
This arm, this lance, can well dispute the prize;
And the blood follows, where the weapon flies.
His goddess mother is not near, to shroud
The flying coward with an empty cloud."

But now the queen, who fear'd for Turnus' life,
And loath'd the hard conditions of the strife,
Held him by force; and, dying in his death,
In these sad accents gave her sorrow breath:
"O Turnus, I adjure thee by these tears,
And whate'er price Amata's honor bears
Within thy breast, since thou art all my hope,
My sickly mind's repose, my sinking age's prop;
Since on the safety of thy life alone
Depends Latinus, and the Latian throne:
Refuse me not this one, this only pray'r,
To waive the combat, and pursue the war.
Whatever chance attends this fatal strife,
Think it includes, in thine, Amata's life.
I cannot live a slave, or see my throne
Usurp'd by strangers or a Trojan son."

At this, a flood of tears Lavinia shed;
A crimson blush her beauteous face o'erspread,
Varying her cheeks by turns with white and red.
The driving colors, never at a stay,
Run here and there, and flush, and fade away.
Delightful change! Thus Indian iv'ry shows,
Which with the bord'ring paint of purple glows;
Or lilies damask'd by the neighb'ring rose.

The lover gaz'd, and, burning with desire,
The more he look'd, the more he fed the fire:

Revenge, and jealous rage, and secret spite,
Roll in his breast, and rouse him to the fight.
Then fixing on the queen his ardent eyes,
Firm to his first intent, he thus replies:
"O mother, do not by your tears prepare
Such boding omens, and prejudge the war.
Resolv'd on fight, I am no longer free
To shun my death, if Heav'n my death decree."
Then turning to the herald, thus pursues:
"Go, greet the Trojan with ungrateful news;
Denounce from me, that, when to-morrow's light
Shall gild the heav'ns, he need not urge the fight;
The Trojan and Rutulian troops no more
Shall dye, with mutual blood, the Latian shore:
Our single swords the quarrel shall decide,
And to the victor be the beauteous bride."

He said, and striding on, with speedy pace,
He sought his coursers of the Thracian race.
At his approach they toss their heads on high,
And, proudly neighing, promise victory.
The sires of these Orythia sent from far,
To grace Pilumnus, when he went to war.
The drifts of Thracian snows were scarce so white,
Nor northern winds in fleetness match'd their flight.
Officious grooms stand ready by his side;
And some with combs their flowing manes divide,
And others stroke their chests and gently soothe their pr

He sheath'd his limbs in arms; a temper'd mass
Of golden metal those, and mountain brass.
Then to his head his glitt'ring helm he tied,
And girt his faithful fauchion to his side.
In his Ætnæan forge, the God of Fire
That fauchion labor'd for the hero's sire;
Immortal keenness on the blade bestow'd,
And plung'd it hissing in the Stygian flood.
Propp'd on a pillar, which the ceiling bore,
Was plac'd the lance Auruncan Actor wore;
Which with such force he brandish'd in his hand,
The tough ash trembled like an osier wand:
Then cried: "O pond'rous spoil of Actor slain,

THE TWELFTH BOOK OF THE ÆNEIS 393

And never yet by Turnus toss'd in vain,
Fail not this day thy wonted force; but go,
Sent by this hand, to pierce the Trojan foe!
Give me to tear his corslet from his breast,
And from that eunuch head to rend the crest;
Dragg'd in the dust, his frizzled hair to soil,
Hot from the vexing ir'n, and smear'd with fragrant oil!"

 Thus while he raves, from his wide nostrils flies
A fiery steam, and sparkles from his eyes.
So fares the bull in his lov'd female's sight:
Proudly he bellows, and preludes the fight;
He tries his goring horns against a tree,
And meditates his absent enemy;
He pushes at the winds; he digs the strand
With his black hoofs, and spurns the yellow sand.

 Nor less the Trojan, in his Lemnian arms,
To future fight his manly courage warms:
He whets his fury, and with joy prepares
To terminate at once the ling'ring wars;
To cheer his chiefs and tender son, relates
What Heav'n had promis'd, and expounds the **Fates**.
Then to the Latian king he sends, to cease
The rage of arms, and ratify the peace.

 The morn ensuing, from the mountain's height,
Had scarcely spread the skies with rosy light;
Th' ethereal coursers, bounding from the sea,
From out their flaming nostrils breath'd the day;
When now the Trojan and Rutulian guard,
In friendly labor join'd, the list prepar'd.
Beneath the walls they measure out the space;
Then sacred altars rear, on sods of grass,
Where, with religious rites, their common gods they place.
In purest white the priests their heads attire;
And living waters bear, and holy fire;
And, o'er their linen hoods and shaded hair,
Long twisted wreaths of sacred vervain wear,

 In order issuing from the town appears
The Latin legion, arm'd with pointed spears;
And from the fields, advancing on a line,
The Trojan and the Tuscan forces join:

Their various arms afford a pleasing sight;
A peaceful train they seem, in peace prepar'd for fight.
Betwixt the ranks the proud commanders ride,
Glitt'ring with gold, and vests in purple dyed;
Here Mnestheus, author of the Memmian line,
And there Messapus, born of seed divine.
The sign is giv'n; and, round the listed space,
Each man in order fills his proper place.
Reclining on their ample shields, they stand,
And fix their pointed lances in the sand.
Now, studious of the sight, a num'rous throng
Of either sex promiscuous, old and young,
Swarm from the town: by those who rest behind,
The gates and walls and houses' tops are lin'd.
Meantime the Queen of Heav'n beheld the sight,
With eyes unpleas'd, from Mount Albano's height
(Since call'd Albano by succeeding fame,
But then an empty hill, without a name).
She thence survey'd the field, the Trojan pow'rs,
The Latian squadrons, and Laurentine tow'rs.
Then thus the goddess of the skies bespake,
With sighs and tears, the goddess of the lake,
King Turnus' sister, once a lovely maid,
Ere to the lust of lawless Jove betray'd:
Compress'd by force, but, by the grateful god,
Now made the Naïs of the neighb'ring flood.
"O nymph, the pride of living lakes," said she,
"O most renown'd, and most belov'd by me,
Long hast thou known, nor need I to record,
The wanton sallies of my wand'ring lord.
Of ev'ry Latian fair whom Jove misled
To mount by stealth my violated bed,
To thee alone I grudg'd not his embrace,
But gave a part of heav'n, and an unenvied place.
Now learn from me thy near approaching grief,
Nor think my wishes want to thy relief.
While fortune favor'd, nor Heav'n's King denied
To lend my succor to the Latian side,
I sav'd thy brother, and the sinking state:
But now he struggles with unequal fate,

THE TWELFTH BOOK OF THE ÆNEIS 395

And goes, with gods averse, o'ermatch'd in might,
To meet inevitable death in fight;
Nor must I break the truce, nor can sustain the sight.
Thou, if thou dar'st, thy present aid supply;
It well becomes a sister's care to try."

At this the lovely nymph, with grief oppress'd,
Thrice tore her hair, and beat her comely breast.
To whom Saturnia thus: "Thy tears are late:
Haste, snatch him, if he can be snatch'd from Fate:
New tumults kindle; violate the truce:
Who knows what changeful fortune may produce?
'Tis not a crime t' attempt what I decree;
Or, if it were, discharge the crime on me."
She said, and, sailing on the winged wind,
Left the sad nymph suspended in her mind.

And now in pomp the peaceful kings appear:
Four steeds the chariot of Latinus bear;
Twelve golden beams around his temples play,
To mark his lineage from the God of Day.
Two snowy coursers Turnus' chariot yoke,
And in his hand two massy spears he shook:
Then issued from the camp, in arms divine,
Æneas, author of the Roman line;
And by his side Ascanius took his place,
The second hope of Rome's immortal race.
Adorn'd in white, a rev'rend priest appears,
And off'rings to the flaming altars bears;
A porket, and a lamb that never suffer'd shears.
Then to the rising sun he turns his eyes,
And strews the beasts, design'd for sacrifice,
With salt and meal: with like officious care
He marks their foreheads, and he clips their hair.
Betwixt their horns the purple wine he sheds;
With the same gen'rous juice the flame he feeds.

Æneas then unsheath'd his shining sword,
And thus with pious pray'rs the gods ador'd:
"All-seeing sun, and thou, Ausonian soil,
For which I have sustain'd so long a toil,
Thou, King of Heav'n, and thou, the Queen of Air,
Propitious now, and reconcil'd by pray'r;

Thou, God of War, whose unresisted sway
The labors and events of arms obey;
Ye living fountains, and ye running floods,
All pow'rs of ocean, all ethereal gods,
Hear, and bear record: if I fall in field,
Or, recreant in the fight, to Turnus yield,
My Trojans shall encrease Evander's town;
Ascanius shall renounce th' Ausonian crown:
All claims, all questions of debate, shall cease;
Nor he, nor they, with force infringe the peace.
But, if my juster arms prevail in fight,
(As sure they shall, if I divine aright,)
My Trojans shall not o'er th' Italians reign:
Both equal, both unconquer'd shall remain,
Join'd in their laws, their lands, and their abodes;
I ask but altars for my weary gods.
The care of those religious rites be mine;
The crown to King Latinus I resign:
His be the sov'reign sway. Nor will I share
His pow'r in peace, or his command in war.
For me, my friends another town shall frame,
And bless the rising tow'rs with fair Lavinia's name."

Thus he. Then, with erected eyes and hands,
The Latian king before his altar stands.
"By the same heav'n," said he, "and earth, and main,
And all the pow'rs that all the three contain;
By hell below, and by that upper god
Whose thunder signs the peace, who seals it with his nod
So let Latona's double offspring hear,
And double-fronted Janus, what I swear:
I touch the sacred altars, touch the flames,
And all those pow'rs attest, and all their names;
Whatever chance befall on either side,
No term of time this union shall divide:
No force, no fortune, shall my vows unbind,
Or shake the steadfast tenor of my mind;
Not tho' the circling seas should break their bound,
O'erflow the shores, or sap the solid ground;
Not tho' the lamps of heav'n their spheres forsake,
Hurl'd down, and hissing in the nether lake:

THE TWELFTH BOOK OF THE ÆNEIS

E'en as this royal scepter" (for he bore
A scepter in his hand) "shall never more
Shoot out in branches, or renew the birth:
An orphan now, cut from the mother earth
By the keen ax, dishonor'd of its hair,
And cas'd in brass, for Latian kings to bear."

When thus in public view the peace was tied
With solemn vows, and sworn on either side,
All dues perform'd which holy rites require;
The victim beasts are slain before the fire,
The trembling entrails from their bodies torn,
And to the fatten'd flames in chargers borne.

Already the Rutulians deem their man
O'ermatch'd in arms, before the fight began.
First rising fears are whisper'd thro' the crowd;
Then, gath'ring sound, they murmur more aloud.
Now, side to side, they measure with their eyes
The champions' bulk, their sinews, and their size;
The nearer they approach, the more is known
Th' apparent disadvantage of their own.
Turnus himself appears in public sight
Conscious of fate, desponding of the fight.
Slowly he moves, and at his altar stands
With eyes dejected, and with trembling hands;
And, while he mutters undistinguish'd pray'rs,
A livid deadness in his cheeks appears.

With anxious pleasure when Juturna view'd
Th' increasing fright of the mad multitude,
When their short sighs and thick'ning sobs she heard,
And found their ready minds for change prepar'd;
Dissembling her immortal form, she took
Camertus' mien, his habit, and his look;
A chief of ancient blood; in arms well known
Was his great sire, and he his greater son.
His shape assum'd, amid the ranks she ran,
And humoring their first motions, thus began:
"For shame, Rutulians, can you bear the sight
Of one expos'd for all, in single fight?
Can we, before the face of heav'n, confess
Our courage colder, or our numbers less?

View all the Trojan host, th' Arcadian band,
And Tuscan army; count 'em as they stand:
Undaunted to the battle if we go,
Scarce ev'ry second man will share a foe.
Turnus, 'tis true, in this unequal strife,
Shall lose, with honor, his devoted life,
Or change it rather for immortal fame,
Succeeding to the gods, from whence he came:
But you, a servile and inglorious band,
For foreign lords shall sow your native land,
Those fruitful fields your fighting fathers gain'd,
Which have so long their lazy sons sustain'd."
With words like these, she carried her design:
A rising murmur runs along the line.
Then ev'n the city troops, and Latians, tir'd
With tedious war, seem with new souls inspir'd:
Their champion's fate with pity they lament,
And of the league, so lately sworn, repent.

   Nor fails the goddess to foment the rage
With lying wonders, and a false presage;
But adds a sign, which, present to their eyes,
Inspires new courage, and a glad surprise.
For, sudden, in the fiery tracts above,
Appears in pomp th' imperial bird of Jove:
A plump of fowl he spies, that swim the lakes,
And o'er their heads his sounding pinions shakes;
Then, stooping on the fairest of the train,
In his strong talons truss'd a silver swan.
Th' Italians wonder at th' unusual sight;
But, while he lags, and labors in his flight,
Behold, the dastard fowl return anew,
And with united force the foe pursue:
Clam'rous around the royal hawk they fly,
And, thick'ning in a cloud, o'ershade the sky.
They cuff, they scratch, they cross his airy course;
Nor can th' incumber'd bird sustain their force;
But vex'd, not vanquish'd, drops the pond'rous prey,
And, lighten'd of his burthen, wings his way.

   Th' Ausonian bands with shouts salute the sight,
Eager of action, and demand the fight.

Then King Tolumnius vers'd in augurs' arts,
Cries out, and thus his boasted skill imparts:
"At length 'tis granted, what I long desir'd!
This, this is what my frequent vows requir'd.
Ye gods, I take your omen, and obey.
Advance, my friends, and charge! I lead the way.
These are the foreign foes, whose impious band,
Like that rapacious bird, infest our land:
But soon, like him, they shall be forc'd to sea
By strength united, and forego the prey.
Your timely succor to your country bring,
Haste to the rescue, and redeem your king."

  He said; and, pressing onward thro' the crew,
Pois'd in his lifted arm, his lance he threw.
The winged weapon, whistling in the wind,
Came driving on, nor miss'd the mark design'd.
At once the cornel rattled in the skies;
At once tumultuous shouts and clamors rise.
Nine brothers in a goodly band there stood,
Born of Arcadian mix'd with Tuscan blood,
Gylippus' sons: the fatal jav'lin flew,
Aim'd at the midmost of the friendly crew.
A passage thro' the jointed arms it found,
Just where the belt was to the body bound,
And struck the gentle youth extended on the ground.
Then, fir'd with pious rage, the gen'rous train
Run madly forward to revenge the slain.
And some with eager haste their jav'lins throw;
And some with sword in hand assault the foe.

  The wish'd insult the Latine troops embrace,
And meet their ardor in the middle space.
The Trojans, Tuscans, and Arcadian line,
With equal courage obviate their design.
Peace leaves the violated fields, and hate
Both armies urges to their mutual fate.
With impious haste their altars are o'erturn'd,
The sacrifice half-broil'd, and half-unburn'd.
Thick storms of steel from either army fly,
And clouds of clashing darts obscure the sky;
Brands from the fire are missive weapons made,

With chargers, bowls, and all the priestly trade.
Latinus, frighted, hastens from the fray,
And bears his unregarded gods away.
These on their horses vault; those yoke the car;
The rest, with swords on high, run headlong to the war.

   Messapus, eager to confound the peace,
Spurr'd his hot courser thro' the fighting prease,
At King Aulestes, by his purple known
A Tuscan prince, and by his regal crown;
And, with a shock encount'ring, bore him down.
Backward he fell; and, as his fate design'd,
The ruins of an altar were behind:
There, pitching on his shoulders and his head,
Amid the scatt'ring fires he lay supinely spread.
The beamy spear, descending from above,
His cuirass pierc'd, and thro' his body drove.
Then, with a scornful smile, the victor cries:
"The gods have found a fitter sacrifice."
Greedy of spoils, th' Italians strip the dead
Of his rich armor, and uncrown his head.

   Priest Corynæus, arm'd his better hand,
From his own altar, with a blazing brand;
And, as Ebusus with a thund'ring pace
Advanc'd to battle, dash'd it on his face:
His bristly beard shines out with sudden fires;
The crackling crop a noisome scent expires.
Following the blow, he seiz'd his curling crown
With his left hand; his other cast him down.
The prostrate body with his knees he press'd,
And plung'd his holy poniard in his breast.

   While Podalirius, with his sword, pursued
The shepherd Alsus thro' the flying crowd,
Swiftly he turns, and aims a deadly blow
Full on the front of his unwary foe.
The broad ax enters with a crashing sound,
And cleaves the chin with one continued wound;
Warm blood, and mingled brains, besmear his arms arou
An iron sleep his stupid eyes oppress'd,
And seal'd their heavy lids in endless rest.

   But good Æneas rush'd amid the bands;

Bare was his head, and naked were his hands,
In sign of truce: then thus he cries aloud:
"What sudden rage, what new desire of blood,
Inflames your alter'd minds? O Trojans, cease
From impious arms, nor violate the peace!
By human sanctions, and by laws divine,
The terms are all agreed; the war is mine.
Dismiss your fears, and let the fight ensue;
This hand alone shall right the gods and you:
Our injur'd altars, and their broken vow,
To this avenging sword the faithless Turnus owe."

Thus while he spoke, unmindful of defense,
A winged arrow struck the pious prince.
But, whether from some human hand it came,
Or hostile god, is left unknown by fame:
No human hand or hostile god was found,
To boast the triumph of so base a wound.

When Turnus saw the Trojan quit the plain,
His chiefs dismay'd, his troops a fainting train,
Th' unhop'd event his heighten'd soul inspires:
At once his arms and coursers he requires;
Then, with a leap, his lofty chariot gains,
And with a ready hand assumes the reins.
He drives impetuous, and, where'er he goes,
He leaves behind a lane of slaughter'd foes.
These his lance reaches; over those he rolls
His rapid car, and crushes out their souls:
In vain the vanquish'd fly; the victor sends
The dead men's weapons at their living friends.
Thus, on the banks of Hebrus' freezing flood,
The God of Battles, in his angry mood,
Clashing his sword against his brazen shield,
Let loose the reins, and scours along the field:
Before the wind his fiery coursers fly;
Groans the sad earth, resounds the rattling sky.
Wrath, Terror, Treason, Tumult, and Despair
(Dire faces, and deform'd) surround the car;
Friends of the god, and followers of the war.
With fury not unlike, nor less disdain,
Exulting Turnus flies along the plain:

His smoking horses, at their utmost speed,
He lashes on, and urges o'er the dead.
Their fetlocks run with blood; and, when they bound,
The gore and gath'ring dust are dash'd around.
Thamyris and Pholus, masters of the war,
He kill'd at hand, but Sthenelus afar:
From far the sons of Imbracus he slew,
Glaucus and Lades, of the Lycian crew;
Both taught to fight on foot, in battle join'd,
Or mount the courser that outstrips the wind.

  Meantime Eumedes, vaunting in the field,
New fir'd the Trojans, and their foes repell'd.
This son of Dolon bore his grandsire's name,
But emulated more his father's fame;
His guileful father, sent a nightly spy,
The Grecian camp and order to descry:
Hard enterprise! and well he might require
Achilles' car and horses, for his hire:
But, met upon the scout, th' Ætolian prince
In death bestow'd a juster recompense.
Fierce Turnus view'd the Trojan from afar,
And launch'd his jav'lin from his lofty car;
Then lightly leaping down, pursued the blow,
And, pressing with his foot his prostrate foe,
Wrench'd from his feeble hold the shining sword,
And plung'd it in the bosom of its lord.
"Possess," said he, "the fruit of all thy pains,
And measure, at thy length, our Latian plains.
Thus are my foes rewarded by my hand;
Thus may they build their town, and thus enjoy the land"

  Then Dares, Butes, Sybaris he slew,
Whom o'er his neck his flound'ring courser threw.
As when loud Boreas, with his blust'ring train,
Stoops from above, incumbent on the main;
Where'er he flies, he drives the rack before,
And rolls the billows on th' Ægæan shore:
So, where resistless Turnus takes his course,
The scatter'd squadrons bend before his force;
His crest of horses' hair is blown behind
By adverse air, and rustles in the wind.

This haughty Phegeus saw with high disdain,
And, as the chariot roll'd along the plain,
Light from the ground he leapt, and seiz'd the rein.
Thus hung in air, he still retain'd his hold,
The coursers frighted, and their course controll'd.
The lance of Turnus reach'd him as he hung,
And pierc'd his plated arms, but pass'd along,
And only raz'd the skin. He turn'd, and held
Against his threat'ning foe his ample shield;
Then call'd for aid: but, while he cried in vain,
The chariot bore him backward on the plain.
He lies revers'd; the victor king descends,
And strikes so justly where his helmet ends,
He lops the head. The Latian fields are drunk
With streams that issue from the bleeding trunk.

While he triumphs, and while the Trojans yield,
The wounded prince is forc'd to leave the field:
Strong Mnestheus, and Achates often tried,
And young Ascanius, weeping by his side,
Conduct him to his tent. Scarce can he rear
His limbs from earth, supported on his spear.
Resolv'd in mind, regardless of the smart,
He tugs with both his hands, and breaks the dart.
The steel remains. No readier way he found
To draw the weapon, than t' inlarge the wound.
Eager of fight, impatient of delay,
He begs; and his unwilling friends obey.

Iapis was at hand to prove his art,
Whose blooming youth so fir'd Apollo's heart,
That, for his love, he proffer'd to bestow
His tuneful harp and his unerring bow.
The pious youth, more studious how to save
His aged sire, now sinking to the grave,
Preferr'd the pow'r of plants, and silent praise
Of healing arts, before Phœbean bays.

Propp'd on his lance the pensive hero stood,
And heard and saw, unmov'd, the mourning crowd.
The fam'd physician tucks his robes around
With ready hands, and hastens to the wound.
With gentle touches he performs his part,

This way and that, soliciting the dart,
And exercises all his heav'nly art.
All soft'ning simples, known of sov'reign use,
He presses out, and pours their noble juice.
These first infus'd, to lenify the pain,
He tugs with pincers, but he tugs in vain.
Then to the patron of his art he pray'd:
The patron of his art refus'd his aid.

    Meantime the war approaches to the tents;
Th' alarm grows hotter, and the noise augments:
The driving dust proclaims the danger near;
And first their friends, and then their foes appear:
Their friends retreat; their foes pursue the rear.
The camp is fill'd with terror and affright:
The hissing shafts within the trench alight;
An undistinguish'd noise ascends the sky,
The shouts of those who kill, and groans of those who di

    But now the goddess mother, mov'd with grief,
And pierc'd with pity, hastens her relief.
A branch of healing dittany she brought,
Which in the Cretan fields with care she sought:
Rough is the stem, which woolly leaves surround;
The leaves with flow'rs, the flow'rs with purple crown'd,
Well known to wounded goats; a sure relief
To draw the pointed steel, and ease the grief.
This Venus brings, in clouds involv'd, and brews
Th' extracted liquor with ambrosian dews,
And od'rous *panacee*. Unseen she stands,
Temp'ring the mixture with her heav'nly hands,
And pours it in a bowl, already crown'd
With juice of med'c'nal herbs prepar'd to bathe the woun
The leech, unknowing of superior art
Which aids the cure, with this foments the part;
And in a moment ceas'd the raging smart.
Stanch'd is the blood, and in the bottom stands:
The steel, but scarcely touch'd with tender hands,
Moves up, and follows of its own accord,
And health and vigor are at once restor'd.
Iapis first perceiv'd the closing wound,
And first the footsteps of a god he found.

THE TWELFTH BOOK OF THE ÆNEIS 405

"Arms! arms!" he cries; "the sword and shield prepare,
And send the willing chief, renew'd, to war.
This is no mortal work, no cure of mine,
Nor art's effect, but done by hands divine.
Some god our general to the battle sends;
Some god preserves his life for greater ends."

The hero arms in haste; his hands infold
His thighs with cuishes of refulgent gold:
Inflam'd to fight, and rushing to the field,
That hand sustaining the celestial shield,
This gripes the lance, and with such vigor shakes,
That to the rest the beamy weapon quakes.
Then with a close embrace he strain'd his son,
And, kissing thro' his helmet, thus begun:
"My son, from my example learn the war,
In camps to suffer, and in fields to dare;
But happier chance than mine attend thy care!
This day my hand thy tender age shall shield,
And crown with honors of the conquer'd field:
Thou, when thy riper years shall send thee forth
To toils of war, be mindful of my worth;
Assert thy birthright, and in arms be known,
For Hector's nephew, and Æneas' son."
He said; and, striding, issued on the plain.
Anteus and Mnestheus, and a num'rous train,
Attend his steps; the rest their weapons take,
And, crowding to the field, the camp forsake.
A cloud of blinding dust is rais'd around,
Labors beneath their feet the trembling ground.

Now Turnus, posted on a hill, from far
Beheld the progress of the moving war:
With him the Latins view'd the cover'd plains,
And the chill blood ran backward in their veins.
Juturna saw th' advancing troops appear,
And heard the hostile sound, and fled for fear.
Æneas leads; and draws a sweeping train,
Clos'd in their ranks, and pouring on the plain.
As when a whirlwind, rushing to the shore
From the mid ocean, drives the waves before;
The painful hind with heavy heart foresees

The flatted fields, and slaughter of the trees;
With like impetuous rage the prince appears
Before his doubled front, nor less destruction bears.
And now both armies shock in open field;
Osiris is by strong Thymbræus kill'd.
Archetius, Ufens, Epulon, are slain
(All fam'd in arms, and of the Latin train)
By Gyas', Mnestheus', and Achates' hand.
The fatal augur falls, by whose command
The truce was broken, and whose lance, embrued
With Trojan blood, th' unhappy fight renew'd.
Loud shouts and clamors rend the liquid sky,
And o'er the field the frighted Latins fly.
The prince disdains the dastards to pursue,
Nor moves to meet in arms the fighting few;
Turnus alone, amid the dusky plain,
He seeks, and to the combat calls in vain.
Juturna heard, and, seiz'd with mortal fear,
Forc'd from the beam her brother's charioteer;
Assumes his shape, his armor, and his mien,
And, like Metiscus, in his seat is seen.

As the black swallow near the palace plies;
O'er empty courts, and under arches, flies;
Now hawks aloft, now skims along the flood,
To furnish her loquacious nest with food:
So drives the rapid goddess o'er the plains;
The smoking horses run with loosen'd reins.
She steers a various course among the foes;
Now here, now there, her conqu'ring brother shows;
Now with a straight, now with a wheeling flight,
She turns, and bends, but shuns the single fight.
Æneas, fir'd with fury, breaks the crowd,
And seeks his foe, and calls by name aloud:
He runs within a narrower ring, and tries
To stop the chariot; but the chariot flies.
If he but gain a glimpse, Juturna fears,
And far away the Daunian hero bears.

What should he do! Nor arts nor arms avail;
And various cares in vain his mind assail.
The great Messapus, thund'ring thro' the field,

In his left hand two pointed jav'lins held:
Encount'ring on the prince, one dart he drew,
And with unerring aim and utmost vigor threw.
Æneas saw it come, and, stooping low
Beneath his buckler, shunn'd the threat'ning blow.
The weapon hiss'd above his head, and tore
The waving plume which on his helm he wore.
Forced by this hostile act, and fir'd with spite,
That flying Turnus still declin'd the fight,
The Prince, whose piety had long repell'd
His inborn ardor, now invades the field;
Invokes the pow'rs of violated peace,
Their rites and injur'd altars to redress;
Then, to his rage abandoning the rein,
With blood and slaughter'd bodies fills the plain.

What god can tell, what numbers can display,
The various labors of that fatal day;
What chiefs and champions fell on either side,
In combat slain, or by what deaths they died;
Whom Turnus, whom the Trojan hero kill'd;
Who shar'd the fame and fortune of the field!
Jove, could'st thou view, and not avert thy sight,
Two jarring nations join'd in cruel fight,
Whom leagues of lasting love so shortly shall unite!

Æneas first Rutulian Sucro found,
Whose valor made the Trojans quit their ground;
Betwixt his ribs the jav'lin drove so just,
It reach'd his heart, nor needs a second thrust.
Now Turnus, at two blows, two brethren slew;
First from his horse fierce Amycus he threw:
Then, leaping on the ground, on foot assail'd
Diores, and in equal fight prevail'd.
Their lifeless trunks he leaves upon the place;
Their heads, distilling gore, his chariot grace.

Three cold on earth the Trojan hero threw,
Whom without respite at one charge he slew:
Cethegus, Tanaïs, Tagus, fell oppress'd,
And sad Onythes, added to the rest,
Of Theban blood, whom Peridia bore.

Turnus two brothers from the Lycian shore,

And from Apollo's fane to battle sent,
O'erthrew; nor Phœbus could their fate prevent.
Peaceful Menœtes after these he kill'd,
Who long had shunn'd the dangers of the field:
On Lerna's lake a silent life he led,
And with his nets and angle earn'd his bread;
Nor pompous cares, nor palaces, he knew,
But wisely from th' infectious world withdrew:
Poor was his house; his father's painful hand
Discharg'd his rent, and plow'd another's land.

 As flames among the lofty woods are thrown
On diff'rent sides, and both by winds are blown;
The laurels crackle in the sputt'ring fire;
The frighted sylvans from their shades retire:
Or as two neighb'ring torrents fall from high;
Rapid they run; the foamy waters fry;
They roll to sea with unresisted force,
And down the rocks precipitate their course:
Not with less rage the rival heroes take
Their diff'rent ways, nor less destruction make.
With spears afar, with swords at hand, they strike;
And zeal of slaughter fires their souls alike.
Like them, their dauntless men maintain the field;
And hearts are pierc'd, unknowing how to yield:
They blow for blow return, and wound for wound;
And heaps of bodies raise the level ground.

 Murranus, boasting of his blood, that springs
From a long royal race of Latian kings,
Is by the Trojan from his chariot thrown,
Crush'd with the weight of an unwieldy stone:
Betwixt the wheels he fell; the wheels, that bore
His living load, his dying body tore.
His starting steeds, to shun the glitt'ring sword,
Paw down his trampled limbs, forgetful of their lord.

 Fierce Hyllus threaten'd high, and, face to face,
Affronted Turnus in the middle space:
The prince encounter'd him in full career,
And at his temples aim'd the deadly spear;
So fatally the flying weapon sped,
That thro' his brazen helm it pierc'd his head.

THE TWELFTH BOOK OF THE ÆNEIS

Nor, Cisseus, couldst thou scape from Turnus' hand,
In vain the strongest of th' Arcadian band:
Nor to Cupentus could his gods afford
Availing aid against th' Ænean sword,
Which to his naked heart pursued the course;
Nor could his plated shield sustain the force.

Iolas fell, whom not the Grecian pow'rs,
Nor great subverter of the Trojan tow'rs,
Were doom'd to kill, while Heav'n prolong'd his date;
But who can pass the bounds prefix'd by fate?
In high Lyrnessus, and in Troy, he held
Two palaces, and was from each expell'd:
Of all the mighty man, the last remains
A little spot of foreign earth contains.

And now both hosts their broken troops unite
In equal ranks, and mix in mortal fight.
Seresthus and undaunted Mnestheus join
The Trojan, Tuscan, and Arcadian line:
Sea-born Messapus, with Atinas, heads
The Latin squadrons, and to battle leads.
They strike, they push, they throng the scanty space,
Resolv'd on death, impatient of disgrace;
And, where one falls, another fills his place.

The Cyprian goddess now inspires her son
To leave th' unfinish'd fight, and storm the town:
For, while he rolls his eyes around the plain
In quest of Turnus, whom he seeks in vain,
He views th' unguarded city from afar,
In careless quiet, and secure of war.
Occasion offers, and excites his mind
To dare beyond the task he first design'd.
Resolv'd, he calls his chiefs; they leave the fight:
Attended thus, he takes a neighb'ring height;
The crowding troops about their gen'ral stand,
All under arms, and wait his high command.
Then thus the lofty prince: "Hear and obey,
Ye Trojan bands, without the least delay
Jove is with us; and what I have decreed
Requires our utmost vigor, and our speed.
Your instant arms against the town prepare,

The source of mischief, and the seat of war.
This day the Latian tow'rs, that mate the sky,
Shall level with the plain in ashes lie:
The people shall be slaves, unless in time
They kneel for pardon, and repent their crime.
Twice have our foes been vanquish'd on the plain:
Then shall I wait till Turnus will be slain?
Your force against the perjur'd city bend.
There it began, and there the war shall end.
The peace profan'd our rightful arms requires;
Cleanse the polluted place with purging fires."

He finish'd; and, one soul inspiring all,
Form'd in a wedge, the foot approach the wall.
Without the town, an unprovided train
Of gaping, gazing citizens are slain.
Some firebrands, others scaling ladders bear,
And those they toss aloft, and these they rear:
The flames now launch'd, the feather'd arrows fly,
And clouds of missive arms obscure the sky.
Advancing to the front, the hero stands,
And, stretching out to heav'n his pious hands,
Attests the gods, asserts his innocence,
Upbraids with breach of faith th' Ausonian prince;
Declares the royal honor doubly stain'd,
And twice the rites of holy peace profan'd.

Dissenting clamors in the town arise;
Each will be heard, and all at once advise.
One part for peace, and one for war contends;
Some would exclude their foes, and some admit their frien
The helpless king is hurried in the throng,
And, whate'er tide prevails, is borne along.
Thus, when the swain, within a hollow rock,
Invades the bees with suffocating smoke,
They run around, or labor on their wings,
Disus'd to flight, and shoot their sleepy stings;
To shun the bitter fumes in vain they try;
Black vapors, issuing from the vent, involve the sky.

But fate and envious fortune now prepare
To plunge the Latins in the last despair.
The queen, who saw the foes invade the town,

And brands on tops of burning houses thrown,
Cast round her eyes, distracted with her fear—
No troops of Turnus in the field appear.
Once more she stares abroad, but still in vain,
And then concludes the royal youth is slain.
Mad with her anguish, impotent to bear
The mighty grief, she loathes the vital air.
She calls herself the cause of all this ill,
And owns the dire effects of her ungovern'd will;
She raves against the gods; she beats her breast;
She tears with both her hands her purple vest:
Then round a beam a running noose she tied,
And, fasten'd by the neck, obscenely died.

Soon as the fatal news by Fame was blown,
And to her dames and to her daughter known,
The sad Lavinia rends her yellow hair
And rosy cheeks; the rest her sorrow share:
With shrieks the palace rings, and madness of despair.
The spreading rumor fills the public place:
Confusion, fear, distraction, and disgrace,
And silent shame, are seen in ev'ry face.
Latinus tears his garments as he goes,
Both for his public and his private woes;
With filth his venerable beard besmears,
And sordid dust deforms his silver hairs.
And much he blames the softness of his mind,
Obnoxious to the charms of womankind,
And soon seduc'd to change what he so well design'd;
To break the solemn league so long desir'd,
Nor finish what his fates, and those of Troy, requir'd.

Now Turnus rolls aloof o'er empty plains,
And here and there some straggling foes he gleans.
His flying coursers please him less and less,
Asham'd of easy fight and cheap success.
Thus half-contented, anxious in his mind,
The distant cries come driving in the wind,
Shouts from the walls, but shouts in murmurs drown'd;
A jarring mixture, and a boding sound.
"Alas!" said he, "what mean these dismal cries?
What doleful clamors from the town arise?"

Confus'd, he stops, and backward pulls the reins.
She who the driver's office now sustains,
Replies: "Neglect, my lord, these new alarms;
Here fight, and urge the fortune of your arms:
There want not others to defend the wall.
If by your rival's hand th' Italians fall,
So shall your fatal sword his friends oppress,
In honor equal, equal in success."

To this, the prince: "O sister—for I knew
The peace infring'd proceeded first from you;
I knew you, when you mingled first in fight;
And now in vain you would deceive my sight—
Why, goddess, this unprofitable care?
Who sent you down from heav'n, involv'd in air,
Your share of mortal sorrows to sustain,
And see your brother bleeding on the plain?
For to what pow'r can Turnus have recourse,
Or how resist his fate's prevailing force?
These eyes beheld Murranus bite the ground:
Mighty the man, and mighty was the wound.
I heard my dearest friend, with dying breath,
My name invoking to revenge his death.
Brave Ufens fell with honor on the place,
To shun the shameful sight of my disgrace.
On earth supine, a manly corpse he lies;
His vest and armor are the victor's prize.
Then, shall I see Laurentum in a flame,
Which only wanted, to complete my shame?
How will the Latins hoot their champion's flight!
How Drances will insult and point them to the sight!
Is death so hard to bear? Ye gods below,
(Since those above so small compassion show,)
Receive a soul unsullied yet with shame,
Which not belies my great forefather's name!"

He said; and while he spoke, with flying speed
Came Sages urging on his foamy steed:
Fix'd on his wounded face a shaft he bore,
And, seeking Turnus, sent his voice before:
"Turnus, on you, on you alone, depends
Our last relief: compassionate your friends!

THE TWELFTH BOOK OF THE ÆNEIS 413

Like lightning, fierce Æneas, rolling on,
With arms invests, with flames invades the town:
The brands are toss'd on high; the winds conspire
To drive along the deluge of the fire.
All eyes are fix'd on you: your foes rejoice;
Ev'n the king staggers, and suspends his choice;
Doubts to deliver or defend the town,
Whom to reject, or whom to call his son.
The queen, on whom your utmost hopes were plac'd,
Herself suborning death, has breath'd her last.
'Tis true, Messapus, fearless of his fate,
With fierce Atinas' aid, defends the gate:
On ev'ry side surrounded by the foe,
The more they kill, the greater numbers grow;
An iron harvest mounts, and still remains to mow.
You, far aloof from your forsaken bands,
Your rolling chariot drive o'er empty sands."
  Stupid he sate, his eyes on earth declin'd,
And various cares revolving in his mind:
Rage, boiling from the bottom of his breast,
And sorrow mix'd with shame, his soul oppress'd;
And conscious worth lay lab'ring in his thought,
And love by jealousy to madness wrought.
By slow degrees his reason drove away
The mists of passion, and resum'd her sway.
Then, rising on his car, he turn'd his look,
And saw the town involv'd in fire and smoke.
A wooden tow'r with flames already blaz'd,
Which his own hands on beams and rafters rais'd;
And bridges laid above to join the space,
And wheels below to roll from place to place.
"Sister, the Fates have vanquish'd: let us go
The way which Heav'n and my hard fortune show.
The fight is fix'd; nor shall the branded name
Of a base coward blot your brother's fame.
Death is my choice; but suffer me to try
My force, and vent my rage before I die."
He said; and, leaping down without delay,
Thro' crowds of scatter'd foes he freed his way.
Striding he pass'd, impetuous as the wind,

And left the grieving goddess far behind.
As when a fragment, from a mountain torn
By raging tempests, or by torrents borne,
Or sapp'd by time, or loosen'd from the roots—
Prone thro' the void the rocky ruin shoots,
Rolling from crag to crag, from steep to steep;
Down sink, at once, the shepherds and their sheep:
Involv'd alike, they rush to nether ground;
Stunn'd with the shock they fall, and stunn'd from earth
    rebound:
So Turnus, hasting headlong to the town,
Should'ring and shoving, bore the squadrons down.
Still pressing onward, to the walls he drew,
Where shafts, and spears, and darts promiscuous flew,
And sanguine streams the slipp'ry ground embrue.
First stretching out his arm, in sign of peace,
He cries aloud, to make the combat cease:
"Rutulians, hold; and Latin troops, retire!
The fight is mine; and me the gods require.
'Tis just that I should vindicate alone
The broken truce, or for the breach atone.
This day shall free from wars th' Ausonian state,
Or finish my misfortunes in my fate."

  Both armies from their bloody work desist,
And, bearing backward, form a spacious list.
The Trojan hero, who receiv'd from fame
The welcome sound, and heard the champion's name,
Soon leaves the taken works and mounted walls,
Greedy of war where greater glory calls.
He springs to fight, exulting in his force;
His jointed armor rattles in the course.
Like Eryx, or like Athos, great he shows,
Or Father Apennine, when, white with snows,
His head divine obscure in clouds he hides,
And shakes the sounding forest on his sides.
The nations, overaw'd, surcease the fight;
Immovable their bodies, fix'd their sight.
Ev'n death stands still; nor from above they throw
Their darts, nor drive their batt'ring-rams below.
In silent order either army stands,

THE TWELFTH BOOK OF THE ÆNEIS

And drop their swords, unknowing, from their hands.
Th' Ausonian king beholds, with wond'ring sight,
Two mighty champions match'd in single fight,
Born under climes remote, and brought by fate,
With swords to try their titles to the state.

Now, in clos'd field, each other from afar
They view; and, rushing on, begin the war.
They launch their spears; then hand to hand they meet;
The trembling soil resounds beneath their feet:
Their bucklers clash; thick blows descend from high,
And flakes of fire from their hard helmets fly.
Courage conspires with chance, and both ingage
With equal fortune yet, and mutual rage.
As when two bulls for their fair female fight
In Sila's shades, or on Taburnus' height;
With horns adverse they meet; the keeper flies;
Mute stands the herd; the heifers roll their eyes,
And wait th' event; which victor they shall bear,
And who shall be the lord, to rule the lusty year:
With rage of love the jealous rivals burn,
And push for push, and wound for wound return;
Their dewlaps gor'd, their sides are lav'd in blood;
Loud cries and roaring sounds rebellow thro' the wood:
Such was the combat in the listed ground;
So clash their swords, and so their shields resound.

Jove sets the beam; in either scale he lays
The champions' fate, and each exactly weighs.
On this side, life and lucky chance ascends;
Loaded with death, that other scale descends.
Rais'd on the stretch, young Turnus aims a blow
Full on the helm of his unguarded foe:
Shrill shouts and clamors ring on either side,
As hopes and fears their panting hearts divide.
But all in pieces flies the traitor sword,
And, in the middle stroke, deserts his lord.
Now 'tis but death, or flight; disarm'd he flies,
When in his hand an unknown hilt he spies.
Fame says that Turnus, when his steeds he join'd,
Hurrying to war, disorder'd in his mind,
Snatch'd the first weapon which his haste could find.

What farther hopes are left thee to pursue?
Divine Æneas, (and thou know'st it too,)
Foredoom'd, to these celestial seats are due.
What more attempts for Turnus can be made,
That thus thou ling'rest in this lonely shade?
Is it becoming of the due respect
And awful honor of a god elect,
A wound unworthy of our state to feel,
Patient of human hands and earthly steel?
Or seems it just, the sister should restore
A second sword, when one was lost before,
And arm a conquer'd wretch against his conqueror?
For what, without thy knowledge and avow,
Nay more, thy dictate, durst Juturna do?
At last, in deference to my love, forbear
To lodge within thy soul this anxious care;
Reclin'd upon my breast, thy grief unload:
Who should relieve the goddess, but the god?
Now all things to their utmost issue tend,
Push'd by the Fates to their appointed end.
While leave was giv'n thee, and a lawful hour
For vengeance, wrath, and unresisted pow'r,
Toss'd on the seas, thou couldst thy foes distress,
And, driv'n ashore, with hostile arms oppress;
Deform the royal house; and, from the side
Of the just bridegroom, tear the plighted bride:
Now cease at my command." The Thund'rer said;
And, with dejected eyes, this answer Juno made:
"Because your dread decree too well I knew,
From Turnus and from earth unwilling I withdrew.
Else should you not behold me here, alone,
Involv'd in empty clouds, my friends bemoan,
But, girt with vengeful flames, in open sight
Engag'd against my foes in mortal fight.
'Tis true, Juturna mingled in the strife
By my command, to save her brother's life—
At least to try; but, by the Stygian lake,
(The most religious oath the gods can take,)
With this restriction, not to bend the bow,
Or toss the spear, or trembling dart to throw.

And now, resign'd to your superior might,
And tir'd with fruitless toils, I loathe the fight.
This let me beg (and this no fates withstand)
Both for myself and for your father's land,
That, when the nuptial bed shall bind the peace,
(Which I, since you ordain, consent to bless,)
The laws of either nation be the same;
But let the Latins still retain their name,
Speak the same language which they spoke before,
Wear the same habits which their grandsires wore.
Call them not Trojans: perish the renown
And name of Troy, with that detested town.
Latium be Latium still; let Alba reign
And Rome's immortal majesty remain."

Then thus the founder of mankind replies
(Unruffled was his front, serene his eyes):
"Can Saturn's issue, and heav'n's other heir,
Such endless anger in her bosom bear?
Be mistress, and your full desires obtain;
But quench the choler you foment in vain.
From ancient blood th' Ausonian people sprung,
Shall keep their name, their habit, and their tongue.
The Trojans to their customs shall be tied:
I will, myself, their common rites provide;
The natives shall command, the foreigners subside.
All shall be Latium; Troy without a name;
And her lost sons forget from whence they came.
From blood so mix'd, a pious race shall flow,
Equal to gods, excelling all below.
No nation more respect to you shall pay,
Or greater off'rings on your altars lay."
Juno consents, well pleas'd that her desires
Had found success, and from the cloud retires.

The peace thus made, the Thund'rer next prepares
To force the wat'ry goddess from the wars.
Deep in the dismal regions void of light,
Three daughters at a birth were born to Night:
These their brown mother, brooding on her care,
Indued with windy wings to flit in air,
With serpents girt alike, and crown'd with hissing hair.

And shiv'ring cold congeals his vital blood.
The stone drops from his arms, and, falling short
For want of vigor, mocks his vain effort.
And as, when heavy sleep has clos'd the sight,
The sickly fancy labors in the night;
We seem to run; and, destitute of force,
Our sinking limbs forsake us in the course:
In vain we heave for breath; in vain we cry;
The nerves, unbrac'd, their usual strength deny;
And on the tongue the falt'ring accents die:
So Turnus far'd; whatever means he tried,
All force of arms and points of art employ'd,
The Fury flew athwart, and made th' endeavor void.

A thousand various thoughts his soul confound;
He star'd about, nor aid nor issue found;
His own men stop the pass, and his own walls surround.
Once more he pauses, and looks out again,
And seeks the goddess charioteer in vain.
Trembling he views the thund'ring chief advance,
And brandishing aloft the deadly lance:
Amaz'd he cow'rs beneath his conqu'ring foe,
Forgets to ward, and waits the coming blow.
Astonish'd while he stands, and fix'd with fear,
Aim'd at his shield he sees th' impending spear.

The hero measur'd first, with narrow view,
The destin'd mark; and, rising as he threw,
With its full swing the fatal weapon flew.
Not with less rage the rattling thunder falls,
Or stones from batt'ring-engines break the walls:
Swift as a whirlwind, from an arm so strong,
The lance drove on, and bore the death along.
Naught could his sev'nfold shield the prince avail,
Nor aught, beneath his arms, the coat of mail:
It pierc'd thro' all, and with a grisly wound
Transfix'd his thigh, and doubled him to ground.
With groans the Latins rend the vaulted sky:
Woods, hills, and valleys, to the voice reply.

Now low on earth the lofty chief is laid,
With eyes cast upward, and with arms display'd,
And, recreant, thus to the proud victor pray'd:

THE TWELFTH BOOK OF THE ÆNEIS

"I know my death deserv'd, nor hope to live:
Use what the gods and thy good fortune give.
Yet think, O think, if mercy may be shown—
Thou hadst a father once, and hast a son—
Pity my sire, now sinking to the grave;
And for Anchises' sake old Daunus save!
Or, if thy vow'd revenge pursue my death,
Give to my friends my body void of breath!
The Latian chiefs have seen me beg my life;
Thine is the conquest, thine the royal wife:
Against a yielded man, 'tis mean ignoble strife."

In deep suspense the Trojan seem'd to stand,
And, just prepar'd to strike, repress'd his hand.
He roll'd his eyes, and ev'ry moment felt
His manly soul with more compassion melt;
When, casting down a casual glance, he spied
The golden belt that glitter'd on his side,
The fatal spoils which haughty Turnus tore
From dying Pallas, and in triumph wore.
Then, rous'd anew to wrath, he loudly cries
(Flames, while he spoke, came flashing from his eyes):
"Traitor, dost thou, dost thou to grace pretend,
Clad, as thou art, in trophies of my friend?
To his sad soul a grateful off'ring go!
'Tis Pallas, Pallas gives this deadly blow."
He rais'd his arm aloft, and, at the word,
Deep in his bosom drove the shining sword.
The streaming blood distain'd his arms around,
And the disdainful soul came rushing thro' the wound.

when he enjoin'd a fresh labor? I could not but invoke the assistan[ce] of a Muse, for this last office:

> Extremum hunc, Arethusa—
> —Negat quis carmina Gallo?

Neither am I to forget the noble present which was made me [by] Gilbert Dolben, Esq., the worthy son of the late Archbishop of Yor[k,] who, when I began this work, enrich'd me with all the sever[al] editions of Virgil, and all the commentaries of those editions [in] Latine; amongst which I could not but prefer the Dolphin's, as t[he] last, the shortest, and the most judicious. Fabrini I had also se[nt] me from Italy; but either he understands Virgil very imperfect[ly,] or I have no knowledge of my author.

Being invited by that worthy gentleman, Sir William Bowyer, [to] Denham Court, I translated the *First Georgic* at his house, and t[he] greatest part of the last *Æneid*. A more friendly entertainment [no] man ever found. No wonder, therefore, if both those versions s[ur]pass the rest, and own the satisfaction I receiv'd in his conver[se,] with whom I had the honor to be bred in Cambridge, and in t[he] same college. The *Seventh Æneid* was made English at Burleig[h,] the magnificent abode of the Earl of Exeter. In a village belongi[ng] to his family I was born; and under his roof I endeavor'd to ma[ke] that *Æneid* appear in English with as much luster as I could; th[o'] my author has not given the finishing strokes either to it, or to t[he] *Eleventh,* as I perhaps could prove in both, if I durst presume [to] criticise my master.

By a letter from Will. Walsh, of Abberley, Esq., (who has so lo[ng] honor'd me with his friendship, and who, without flattery, is the b[est] critic of our nation,) I have been inform'd that his Grace the Du[ke] of Shrewsbury has procur'd a printed copy of the *Pastorals, Georgi[cs,]* and six first *Æneids,* from my bookseller, and has read them in t[he] country, together with my friend. This noble person having be[en] pleas'd to give them a commendation, which I presume not to inse[rt,] has made me vain enough to boast of so great a favor, and to thi[nk] I have succeeded beyond my hopes; the character of his excelle[nt] judgment, the acuteness of his wit, and his general knowledge [of] good letters, being known as well to all the world, as the sweetn[ess] of his disposition, his humanity, his easiness of access, and desire of obliging those who stand in need of his protection, are known to all who have approach'd him, and to me in particular, who have formerly had the honor of his conversation. Whoever has given the world the translation of part of the *Third Georgic,* which he calls *The Power of Love,* has put me to sufficient pains to make my own not inferior to his; as my Lord Roscommon's *Silenus* had formerly given me the same trouble. The most ingenious Mr. Addison of Oxford has also been as troublesome to me as the other two, and on the same account. After his *Bees,* my latter swarm is scarcely worth the living. Mr. Cowley's *Praise of a Country Life* is excellent, but is rather an imitation of Virgil than a version. That I have recover'd, in some measure, the health which I had lost by too much application to this work, is owing, next to God's mercy, to the skill and care of Dr. Gibbons and Dr. Hobbs, the two ornaments of their profession, whom I can only pay by this acknowledgment. The whole faculty has always been ready to oblige me, and the only one of them who endeavor'd to defame me had it not in his power. I desire pardon from my readers for saying so much in relation to myself, which concerns not them; and, with my acknowledgments to all my subscribers, have only to add, that the few *Notes* which follow are *par manière d'acquit,* because I had oblig'd myself by articles to do somewhat of that kind. These scattering observations are rather guesses at my author's meaning in some passages than proofs that so he meant. The unlearn'd may have recourse to any poetical dictionary in English, for the names of persons, places, or fables, which the learned need not; but that little which I say is either new or necessary. And the first of these qualifications never fails to invite a reader, if not to please him.